GLOBAL CITIZENSHIP EDUCATION

Global Citizenship Education

Challenges and Successes

EDITED BY EVA ABOAGYE
AND S. NOMBUSO DLAMINI

UNIVERSITY OF TORONTO PRESS
Toronto Buffalo London

Toronto Buffalo London
utorontopress.com

ISBN 978-1-4875-0637-7 (cloth)
ISBN 978-1-4875-3398-4 (EPUB)
ISBN 978-1-4875-3397-7 (PDF)

Library and Archives Canada Cataloguing in Publication

Title: Global citizenship education: Challenges and successes / edited by Eva Aboagye and Nombuso Dlamini.
Names: Aboagye, Eva, 1957– editor. | Dlamini, S. Nombuso, 1962– editor.
Description: Includes bibliographical references and index.
Identifiers: Canadiana (print) 20200370634 | Canadiana (ebook) 20200370707 | ISBN 9781487506377 (cloth) | ISBN 9781487533984 (EPUB) | ISBN 9781487533977 (PDF)
Subjects: LCSH: Education and globalization. | LCSH: International education. | LCSH: World citizenship – Study and teaching.
Classification: LCC LC191.G56 2021 | DDC 370.116–dc23

This book has been published with the help of a grant from the Federation for the Humanities and Social Sciences, through the Awards to Scholarly Publications Program, using funds provided by the Social Sciences and Humanities Research Council of Canada.

University of Toronto Press acknowledges the financial assistance to its publishing program of the Canada Council for the Arts and the Ontario Arts Council, an agency of the Government of Ontario.

Canada Council for the Arts Conseil des Arts du Canada

Funded by the Government of Canada | Financé par le gouvernement du Canada | Canada

Contents

Section II: Case Studies

Acknowledgments

Acknowledging the Indeterminate Future: A Note to the Reader

We write this note as the last piece towards the publication of this manuscript. We write at a time of the intersection of multiple contemporary crises and challenges: the global pandemic of COVID-19; the public lynching of Black and Indigenous peoples; demonstrations and protests against social injustices; national and domestic border policing; anti-immigrant sentiments; and so on. Regardless, in the face of these crises, we acknowledge that this is also a period of hope and opportunity. The international responses to the public lynching in the US bring hope to a possibility of reimagining a future that, through global citizenship education, we had already started to re-envision. As we move forward towards a different normality, we want to acknowledge and thank contributors in this volume for engaging in global citizenship education with remarkable futuristic outlooks. We agree with Angela Davis's assertion that the demonstrations of today, these moments of protests, are rehearsals of a revolution.[1] We hope that through this volume scholars of global citizenship education and others will continue these rehearsals through conversations about this insurrection era, of its aftermath, and of a future that offers democratic liberties for all.

To All the People Who Made This Book Possible

As the editors of this volume, we express our sincere thanks to the authors who worked tirelessly to provide important perspectives on the subject of global citizenship education. We thank you for giving us the opportunity to enter into deliberations about the meaning, values, and practices of global citizenship. And importantly, we appreciate your trust in us during the writing and rewriting process, for giving us your words, and for enabling us to share and remake your words for others and for us all. We are also grateful to the reviewers who provided important input and encouragement during the process of making this book. We want to acknowledge Samantha Chin and Cynthia Kwaky-ewah who provided editing and formatting support at various stages of the writing and preparation of the manuscript for submission to the publisher. To our families and friends, we say thank you for the support and encouragement we received that provided the motivation for us to complete this book.

Eva Aboagye and S. Nombuso Dlamini
Toronto, Canada

NOTE

1 "The Fire This Time: Race at Boiling Point," A conversation with Angela Y. Davis, Herman Gray, Gaye Theresa Johnson, Robin D.G. Kelley, and Josh Kun, at UCHRI, 5 June 2020, https://scijust.ucsc.edu/2020/06/05/june05-uchri-boiling-point/

GLOBAL CITIZENSHIP EDUCATION

Introduction

EVA ABOAGYE AND S. NOMBUSO DLAMINI

Why Global Citizenship Education?

The past decade has been marked by diverse sociopolitical, economic, and environmental occurrences that make the subject of global citizenship education more fundamental. On the sociopolitical front, over the past decade, the world has seen shifts from egalitarian to authoritarian leadership across nations. Evidence of this shift exists in the United States where, in 2016, Barack Obama was succeeded by Donald Trump, who built his political campaign and electoral success on racist, Islamophobic, xenophobic, and sexist rhetoric. From the beginning, Trump's presidency has been marked by reversals to democratic arrangements, especially with regards to global economic and international relations (Sennero 2017). The United States is not alone in the rejection of peace oriented global tenacities – the support for Brexit, the rise of nationalism in Hungary and elsewhere, the rise of tariffs, the rejection of international efforts to deal with climate change, and so on indicate a danger to hard-earned world peace.

In the United Kingdom, the Brexit campaign could not have been successful without Boris Johnson's and Nigel Farage's racist, xenophobic, and Islamophobic promises to restore White national and cultural identity in the country. In France, Marine Le Pen's racist, xenophobic, and Islamophobic rhetoric received national approval with her Front National Party (renamed the National Rally Party in June 2018), which swung from 4 per cent in 2007 to placing second in the first run behind Emmanuel Macron in the 2017 French general election. In Sweden the national support for the nationalist, anti-immigrant Sweden Democrats has increased since 2006, transforming it into a party that won forty-nine seats in the 2014 elections, and now is the second most popular political party in Sweden (Sennero 2017). The story is not different in

Denmark, Brazil, Greece, Poland, Hungary, Austria, Italy, the Netherlands, and many other European countries. In some parts of Africa, some African leaders have focused on lesbians, gays, bisexuals, and transgender minorities to incite a moral panic among their conservative backers to divert attention from their leadership failures, as seen in Egypt, Zimbabwe, and Tanzania (Roth 2018).

On the environmental front, climate changes leading to hurricanes, storms, and so forth have brought nations together to align various international solutions. Yet not all environmental fluctuations have been a result of ordinary climate changes; rather, they are a result of the interconnection between governments' policies with economic development. As Mert (2016) states, "Many emerging economies are responding to the pressures of globalization by investing in massive, socially, and ecologically questionable projects, and oppressing democratic opposition to such policies" (13). These mega economic projects threaten the natural environment and its inhabitants. For example, the well-known protests in Gezi Park, Turkey, exposed the complex relationship between the state, capital, and the environment. As narrated in Özkaynak et al. (2015), in 2013 the Turkish government began its plan to redesign Taksim Square, of which Gezi Park is a part as well as being the only green space left in the Beyoğlu neighbourhood in Istanbul's European side. To block the start of construction, a group of activists occupied the park and launched a social media hashtag, #occupygezi, which was responded to by thousands of protesters. On 28 May 2013, these occupiers were violently evicted from the park by Turkish police, marking the beginning of a wave of demonstrations and civil unrest that lasted over four months. In the end, the project was halted, and the Turkey Council of Cities officially approved its cancellation on 6 May 2014.[1]

This was an illustrious case of global environmental justice. Noting its subsequent plurality of focus, Mert (2016) writes, "Another dimension of the equivalential chain was the relationship between the local and the global: climate activist and radio producer Madra (2013) wrote that the local demands of Gezi were linked to the global demands of climate activism" (8). Further, Takism is partially accredited for bringing awareness to the fact that "environmental problems are actually interlinked and largely structural and political rather than technical in nature" (Özkaynak et al. 2015, 111). Still, and importantly for this volume, Takism illustrated how young people can mobilize to counter hegemony or to work towards transformative practice that addresses issues of power and oppression by dominant groups.[2]

There are numerous other incidences that exemplify interconnection between human rights violations and environmental abuses at the global level. For example, in 2011 Human Rights Watch documented a case in China in which several thousand children had suffered permanent mental and physical disabilities as a result of lead poisoning, and in 2012, it documented a case in Nigeria in which more than 400 children had been killed by lead poisoning. In the Philippines, many children are at risk of death or permanent physical disabilities as there is widespread mercury pollution created by artisanal gold mines (Green 2015).

Since we began this book project, these ensuing world events have forced us to incessantly examine the importance of global citizenship education because they present a challenge to core consolidated efforts aimed at promoting a world marked by principles of social justice and equity among interconnected world citizens. In fact, some scholars have cautioned that these events have potential for society to revert to ultra-nationalism, chauvinism, secularism, and other acts that need to be addressed in order to ensure that the next generations do not fall victim to fear mongering and a return to tribalism (Roth 2018). Also, these scholars warn of an earlier time when Europe fell victim to the lure of fascism based on fear and a sense of national superiority. Thus, these world events underscore the importance to imbue students with an understanding of global sensitivities and responsibilities and the pragmatic as well as the social need for global justice. Lastly, these world events have necessitated a closer look at ongoing discussions and questions about the very description of global citizenship education and its role in promoting student activism towards sociopolitical and environmental virtues, globally.

This volume addresses the questions: (1) What is global citizenship education and what are its tenets? (2) What/who is a global citizen and how can we recognize this citizen when the very core of identity is challenged and the fluidity of individualities is now the norm? (3) What should the curriculum on global citizenship education entail and what are the related pedagogies? And relatedly, how do we teach theories and practices of engagement, empathy, and compassion that are needed to address the intricacies of uneven global interconnectedness? Other concerns that are part of the global education debate include assessment, accountability, and ethics. Authors in this volume address these questions through theoretical debates, ethnographic case studies, and reflective personal narratives.

What Is Global Citizenship Education?

Global citizenship education (hereafter GCE) and its related traditions of global teaching and learning have been widely acknowledged as an important area in which injustice can be tackled and the world can be made a more just and sustainable place (Banks 2004; Abdi and Shultz 2008; Peters, Britton, and Blee 2008; Andreotti and De Souza 2012; Tiessen and Huish 2014). However, beyond this acknowledgment, there are a range of ideas about its tenets; that is, there remain questions about what GCE is, what pedagogies should be used, whom it should target, and how to assess outcomes.

Some scholars view GCE as a framework designed to develop in students the ethics of social justice and their potential applicability, globally (Abdi and Shultz 2008; Dower 2003). Others view GCE as a framework that offers learners critical tools to question their histories, context, and sociopolitical responsibilities in globalization (e.g., Peake 2008). To have a global perspective means that individuals have broadened horizons that allow for a critical grasp of humanity. Still, others equate GCE as human rights (Abdi and Shultz 2008) and critical consciousness (Abdi and Carr, 2012), as well as peace education (Verma 2017) and, as addressing multiculturalism and social inequalities related to race, class, and migration (Banks 2017).

In this volume, we build on these varied frames and we shy away from offering a totalizing definition because we are aware that these various descriptions serve particular GCE purposes with described goals. Nonetheless, we find that the UNESCO (2014) definition encompasses all of the above: GCE is "a framing paradigm which encapsulates how education can develop the knowledge, skills, values and attitudes learners need for securing a world which is more just, peaceful, tolerant, inclusive, secure and sustainable" (9). Following this definition, which is commonly used by authors in this volume, global citizenship education's purposes are presented as follows: (1) It equips students with the knowledge to understand and make sense of major issues and process that are shaping the world; (2) it encourages students to adopt a sense of responsibility to address those problems; and, (3) it provides students with skills and competencies that will enable them to work to address those problems (see chapter 11 by Robinson in this volume). In using this definition, we also take seriously the intricacies of current world events and realize that GCE initiatives must be undertaken in relation to these complexities.

We also describe GCE along the views offered by Peters, Britton, and Blee (2008) who present a history that traces global citizenship education from the time of European enlightenment, to European democratic rights, to Western constitutions, to challenges in Western hegemony, and, finally to the "age of terrorism." In the end, they conclude, "global citizenship education must be set against these [world] contemporary realities" (11). We work with this statement to unpack ways that GCE can address identified realities affecting people globally.

Chapters in this volume discuss the history of colonialism and imperialism as a history of growth and development of liberal democracies that gave rise to enlightenment thinkers, the League of Nations, UNESCO, and other institutions that defend general human rights, globally. While these institutions are positioned within democratic ideologies, we must also be cognizant of the history of power and hegemony that led to their formation and of the political and market places that are intertwined with/in their very existence. Elsewhere, Lynette Shultz (2010) writes that access to multiple generalized others is a common feature of the "globalizing times." Drawing from Rizvi and Lingard (2004), she cautions that, "often, it is those already endowed with power and privilege who are given access to even more of the world. These are empowered positions supported by market and political structures that, by design, intentionally limit any projects of redistribution that might dismantle these elite enclaves or even shift their membership" (Shultz 2010, 8). Thus, through looking at GCE programs in post-secondary institutions, for example, Eva Aboagye, in chapter 10 in this volume, discusses the inherent tension between democratic ideals and history-laden practices of hegemony and subordination in the implementation of these GCE programs.

Other scholars, such as those in Banks's (2004) edited volume, offer a definition of GCE that is tied to the limits and possibilities of educating learners towards an effective citizenship while still upholding values of diversity and multiculturalism. The preface states that "effective citizenship education programs promote national unity as well as incorporate important cultural components of diverse groups into national civic culture" (xxii). Chapters in this volume ask questions about the unity of nations in a period of global socio-economic interconnectedness that is, however, experienced unevenly across and within nations. These chapters also raise questions about the identification criteria and processes of incorporating "important components" of diverse groups in a period where group values, traditions, symbols, and practices are under scrutiny.

What/Who Is a Global Citizen?

Citizenship as a key concept in global citizenship education is debatable. As described in the 2014 UNESCO report on GCE, some literature refers to global citizenship as "citizenship beyond borders" or beyond the state; others have referred to it as "planetary citizenship," which is about the world's responsibility to preserve planet Earth; and still others argue that cosmopolitanism might be a better and more encompassing word that allows for diversity of cultures. Despite these differences, there seem to be agreement that global citizenship does not include legal standing; rather, it refers more to community belonging and shared responsibility towards a just humanity. As Vasti Torres states, "Global citizenship is marked by an understanding of global interconnectedness and a commitment to the collective good" (quoted in UNESCO 2014, n.p.).

Historically, the notion of citizenship was linked to the nation and the process of state formation, which was about building a common identity and inculcating patriotism and loyalty to the nation (Green 1990; Nussbaum 2002; Davies, Evans, and Reid 2005). This idea of citizenship has evolved over time and citizens are often expected to achieve a far more complex set of purposes, which broadly reflect changing conceptions of what it means to be a good citizen. To be a good citizen is laden with contradictions that relate to economic and identity matters. To be good citizens now includes the ability to live with others in diverse societies, promote a common set of values of acceptance, human rights, and democracy and, in general, be critically aware of the limits of ethnonationalistic forms of identity (Osler and Starkey 2006). Accordingly, UNESCO (2015) offers this definition: "Global Citizenship refers to a sense of belonging to a broader community and common humanity. It emphasizes political, economic, social and cultural interdependence and interconnectedness between the local, the national and the global" (14). In other words, good citizens are expected to contribute to the promotion of social justice, social reconstruction, and democracy. On the other hand, however, in order to compete in the global economy, states require a more innovative, autonomous, inventive, and reflective workforce. Good citizens are also those who successfully participate in the economic development of themselves, others, and their country. To successfully participate as workers in a shrinking and competitive world economy, citizens must be ambivalent about issues of labour exploitation, for instance. To be a good citizen, then, encompasses a recurring dilemma: good citizens must live and embrace global interconnectedness while concurrently overlooking the oppressive mode of the global economy, among other things. Yet, as demonstrated by the Turkish protests, such modes of oppression do not go uncontested. Still, in defining citizenship, it is important to note how operations of the global economy often function in competition with values of global democracy and, more frequently, against the aims of global citizenship education.

Citizenship as a position located within a set of identity symbols is also complicated. This complexity results from the privileging of the

"Westphalian model of state sovereignty in which rights and obligations are extended to members of a circumscribed territory or state" (Held 2002, quoted in Jorgenson 2010, 24). Sovereignty has the power to confer national identity through birth certificates, passports, and so on, which are signs of identity as well as status, loyalty, rights, and responsibilities. In the present world of transnational communication, cross-border travel, and migration, the Westphalian model of citizenship as imagined sovereignty (Anderson 1983) can no longer account for the cross-national movement of ideas, people, goods, and services, and for the formation of large political bodies such as the European Union. Yet where people live has implications for how citizenship is carried out and experienced. For instance, while students in the developed countries of the West are encouraged to embark on study abroad and international service-learning programs as part of developing their global citizenship, in developing countries, such travel is often induced by war, repression, poverty, and climate change. Such dichotomies necessitate in-depth analysis of how globalization produces complex, changing, and contradictory subjectivities (some gendered and some racialized). Bhabha (1994) refers to the naturalized nation-centred views of citizenship as having an ontological flaw.

Jorgenson (2010) describes the complexity of citizenship (located within identity symbols) as narrated by participants engaged in an experiential, cross-cultural, and international GCE program in a Canadian university. After their three-month placement in Thailand, participants were asked how their experience in the program had affected or shaped their identity as global citizens. Participants were unsure of global citizenship as part of who they were; instead, the travel experience allowed them to connect with and understand more about their Canadian identity rather than connect to places "out there" where their placement had occurred. For one of Jorgenson's participants, reflexively, global citizenship had the potential to reimpose historical oppressions, as illustrated by the response offered to the question about identifying as a global citizen: "there are so many contradictions there for myself to identity with a country that hasn't apologized for its past injustices ... global citizenship for me is contradictory. It goes back to 'what is it that I am imposing on other cultures from my experience of having other culture imposed on me?'" (31). Chapters in this volume attend to issues of power, hegemony, colonialism, and so on and how these are part and parcel of the dilemma and incongruity of this volume's key concepts: global citizenship, global economy, (global) democracy, and education.

What Should the Curriculum on Global Citizenship Education Entail and What Are the Related Pedagogies?

UNESCO (2014) has identified three core conceptual dimensions for global citizenship education, which are aligned with the cognitive, socio-emotional, and behavioural learning domains. Under the cognitive domain, there is the learning that takes place to create "understanding and critical thinking about global, regional and local issues and the interconnectedness and interdependence of different countries and populations" (n.p.). A wide range of core courses and projects in GCE programs provide the learning about local, national, regional, and global issues. As presented in the chapters in this book, these programs include experiential learning that range from local service learning to international service-learning programs, as well as signature learning experiences designed to inculcate in students the commitment to their communities and to ensure a just world.

The second UNESCO-identified dimension is ensuring that students have a sense of belonging to a common humanity, sharing values and responsibilities, empathy, solidarity and respect for differences, and diversity. The third section looks at behavioural skills involving the commitment to act effectively and responsibly at the local, national, and global levels for a more peaceful and sustainable world.

Chapters in this volume build on and illustrate the different ways that all three UNESCO GCE conceptual dimensions can be accomplished. These chapters demonstrate diverse methods that post-secondary institutions use to educate students to be global citizens; as well, authors propose different models and approaches for assessing outcomes. Given the diverse frames of global citizenship education and the ensuing debates about what it means to be a globally educated citizen, these chapters offer two critical GCE contributions. First, they examine the development of global citizenship education as an important field in the humanities in post-secondary institutions through outlining the critical discourses utilized by North American institutions. Second, the chapters present theoretical and empirically informed models of global citizenship education that could be adopted by various post-secondary institutions, globally. Each chapter takes a look at some of the developments in GCE as a field; provides a framework for developing global citizens; or provides examples of how global citizenship education can be or has been implemented in different situations. Put together, chapters in this volume offer a collage of curriculum possibilities for GCE. The contributors seek to address complicated issues of global citizenship education through explicit theoretical analysis and by means of empirical vignettes, historical-institutional illustrations, and policy-oriented critics. Although there is much that is shared among the authors, they have been encouraged to express their distinctive approach to understanding and addressing practices of global citizenship education in their locales. The authors have also been encouraged to offer examples of curriculum goals and lessons that could be incorporated by educators interested in pursuing GCE in post-secondary classrooms. The overall aim is to present an interlocking mosaic of descriptions of different aspects of GCE.

This volume has two sections. Section one has five chapters that examine key theories and concepts of global citizenship education. Section two is made up of five chapters that offer GCE case studies plus a concluding chapter. Case study chapters explore different exempla of initiatives that authors or their associates have done to facilitate experiential learning for students in their local and/or global contexts. Some of the chapters in this section also address ways that education can live up to the UN Sustainable Development Goals (SDGs) and to the formation of a global citizen. The concluding chapter outlines the main ideas in the book, and it futuristically theorizes ways that contemporary events shape the impending route of global citizenship education.

In chapter 1, "The Global Context of Global Citizenship: A Pedagogy of Engagement," Eva Aboagye and S. Nombuso Dlamini present the history of global citizenship education and offer exemplary post-secondary snapshots of effective pedagogy for facilitating global citizens. This chapter offers suggestions of what the processes of GCE should look like and what the accompanying pedagogy could be composed of. It also proposes an instructional process that encourages students to be aware of their role as members of the global community.

In chapter 2, "Bridging the Local and the Global: The Role of Service Learning in Post-Secondary Global Citizenship Education," Sarah Eliza Stanlick discusses the aims and goals of global citizenship education and what is expected in terms of growth and development for students. This chapter uses the transformative learning theory as central to how global citizenship and service learning fit together in a pedagogical paradigm that promotes GCE. In this chapter, global citizenship education is catalogued as a transformative experience in which students are not only learning content knowledge and mechanisms of citizenship but are also expected to develop attributes and values that shift their meaning perspective in relation to the larger world towards more humility, critical thinking, cross-cultural understanding, and orientation towards social justice (de Andreotti 2014; Sperandio, Grudzinski-Hall, and Stewart-Gambino 2010; Peters, Britton, and Blee 2008).

In chapter 3, "Peace Education as Education for Global Citizenship: A Primer," Kevin Kester reviews the entanglement between global citizenship and peace education. The chapter offers an overview of the history of peace education and its use as a pedagogic strategy to promote global citizenship education. By considering the transformative possibilities of peace education and cultures of peace, the chapter explores further the intersections between peace education and global citizenship. The chapter then details a number of enabling factors of successful programs that have been highlighted in other literature, provides an overview of the teaching of peace and global citizenship in post-secondary institutions, and offers a case presentation of peace education graduate studies at the United Nations University for Peace in San Jose, Costa Rica. Finally, the chapter concludes by detailing some possibilities for the evaluation of peace and global citizenship education programs.

In chapter 4, "Citizenship through Environmental Justice: A Case for Environmental Sustainability Education in Pre-Service Teacher Training in Canada," Clinton Beckford presents environmental sustainability education as a critical component of global citizenship. The chapter also gives examples of pressing environmental issues facing humanity and argues that education must play a vital role in resolving these issues by providing citizens with the requisite knowledge and skills for action. The chapter concludes that pre-service initial teacher education should be ground zero for creating an environmentally literate global citizenry.

In chapter 5, "Human Trafficking and Implications for Global Citizenship Education: Gender Equality, Women's Rights, and Gender-Sensitive Learning," Mikhaela Gray-Beerman discusses the relationship between globalization, education, and the gendered nature of human trafficking. The chapter provides an outline of gender sensitive GCE and identifies how it can challenge societal views that marginalize women. The chapter then looks at pervasive gender rights issues within Canada and proposes ways to deconstruct them through education. It also examines the relationship between culture, education, and gender equality, globally. Finally, it looks at the responsibilities of post-secondary institutions towards human trafficking and concludes by illustrating how a GCE curriculum that emphasizes the rights of women and girls can help combat human rights issues like human trafficking.

Chapters 6–10 offer case studies that are illustrative of classrooms and community places where GCE is shown in practice. In chapter 6, "A Case-Study Exploration of Deweyan Experiential Service Learning as Citizenship Development," Catherine A. Bloom and Heesoon Bai begin by reviewing some of the major contemporary global citizenship theorists in order to highlight how these theories gesture towards and support some forms of experiential and service learning, which, they argue, build on John Dewey's theories of experiential learning. This chapter also presents the findings of a qualitative interview study with high school students and teachers who have taken part in service projects. The discussion illustrates the benefits and challenges of citizenship development through experiential curricula.

In chapter 7, "Vacationing beyond the Beaten Path – Checkmate! Examining Global Citizenship and Service-Learning Education through Reflective Practice in Grenada and Jamaica," Karen Naidoo and Marie Benjamin's case study of international service learning illustrates how practitioners can bring constructive critique and growth to the arena of global citizenship education. The chapter begins by offering critical analyses of definitions of global citizenship and service learning, and then it draws examples from events that occurred through service-learning programs on the islands of Grenada and Jamaica. This chapter asks questions about the split positioning of the Global North and Global South. For example, if some places like the Caribbean are seen as "vacation havens" and as places where students from Canada can engage in service learning while "vacationing," how can they also be positioned as deserving community development initiatives such as those mentioned in the UN SDGs? To what extent can individuals engage in service learning and simultaneously be on vacation in (developing) countries where poverty and sociopolitical inequality are rampant? The chapter concludes by examining the ways in which service-learning programming can be used as a tool for community development and knowledge mobilization in more community-centred ways.

In chapter 8, "Promoting Global Citizenship Outside the Classroom: Undergraduate-Refugee Learning in Practice," Gisella Gisolo and Sarah Stanlick present a case study on global service learning in a local US context, focused on community–university partnerships to support refugee settlement in Allentown, Pennsylvania. The chapter is based on a pilot study of reflections from local US students who, as part of their undergraduate studies, engaged in a service-learning component with newly arrived refugees in the United States. The chapter answers the questions: How does service learning in a local context allow for students to practice and apply skills of global citizenship education? Can service learning affect conceptual change in undergraduate first-year students in the way they see themselves as global citizens and in the way in which they perceive their civic self-efficacy? How do undergraduate students exhibit change and growth through their reflective practice? And are such self-reported accounts accurate measures of such change? The chapter illustrates how a global service-learning platform can be programed in the midst of refugee and migrant crises, globally.

In chapter 9, "Social Justice and Global Citizenship Education in Social Work Context: A Case of *Caveat Emptor*," Paul Banahene Adjei describes GCE as social justice education and uses the field of social work to demonstrate the challenges of racial diversity that educators must tackle in order to achieve GCE goals. The author's personal experiences teaching social justice at the Bachelor of Social Work and Master of Social Work levels in a social work program are used to illustrate some of the intricacies of multiculturalism and GCE objectives. The chapter works with the questions: What discursive practices do social work educators need to offer as counter-reading to the liberal notion of social justice that reinscribes dominant ideologies while claiming to support social transformation? What pedagogical strategies do social work educators need in order to address what Gayatri Spivak (1999) calls "sanctioned ignorance" – meaning the way in which "*know-nothingism*" (x, emphasis in the original) about social justice and global citizenship education is justified and even rewarded the social work context? In what ways do social work educators situate their teaching philosophy and classroom deliveries beyond self-interest and an empty sense of obligation as they prepare students to become global citizens? What are the negative undercurrents – tensions, contestations, fear, shame, and anxiety – that come with teaching social justice and global citizenship education in social work classrooms?

In chapter 10, "Global Citizenship Education: Institutional Journeys to Socially Engaged Students in Canada," Eva Aboagye presents the approaches of two institutions that made educating global citizens institutional goals: Centennial College in Toronto, which started a GCE program in 2004, and the University of British Columbia in Vancouver, which started a GCE program in 1997. These institutions have been chosen for examination because they represent the dynamic approaches to GCE that are used by post-secondary institutions in Canada. This chapter's definition of GCE follows that offered by Broom and Bai in chapter 6 of this volume whereby GCE is about the cosmopolitan notion of global citizenship education that is about nation-building, but it is also about diversity, social justice, cultural awareness, and human rights. While there are commonalities in the working of these definitions, this chapter argues that both institutions followed the definition of GCE that is about diversity, social justice, cultural awareness, and human rights. Evidently, the fact that there are various definitions of global citizenship education also means institutions are able to approach it from different perspectives that are value and conflict laden.

In chapter 11, "They Want to Be Global Citizens: Now What? Implications of the NGO Career Arc for Students, Faculty Mentors, and Global Citizenship Educators," Andrew M. Robinson advances our thinking about how to help prepare students for global citizenship-inspired careers by discussing four key topics. First, it offers a partial snapshot of the non-governmental organization (NGO) career arc based on the results of an exploratory survey conducted in 2010 of staff working in the Canadian province of Ontario. Second, beginning with pre-career experiences, the chapter discusses the importance of diverse forms of participation in extracurricular activities, including involvement in campus clubs and volunteering, as well as international internships. Third, the chapter addresses the question of whether a bachelor's degree is sufficient as a credential for entering and advancing within the NGO sector. This third discussion leads to a presentation of typical career patterns of those who work in the NGO sector as well as the positions people hold and the related skills necessary to perform effectively. Fourth, and finally, the chapter discusses the role of gender in the NGO sector.

In the conclusion, Eva Aboagye and S. Nombuso Dlamini bring the volume's GCE themes together and offer ideas on how the transformative nature of GCE can prepare citizens of the world to deal with the complexities of our times. This chapter also discusses this volume's case studies as evidence of a growing recognition of the importance of GCE and the growth of working together that happens alongside the ongoing revival of nationalism, xenophobia, chauvinism, and populism.

NOTES

1 It is worth noting that this victory was not without causalities. Amnesty International (2013) reported that during the three months of uprisings, over 4 million people participated, and of these, 8,000 people were injured, and eleven protesters died because of the violence that ensued.

2 Acknowledged as mobilized by young people and using conventional and non-conventional tools, a participant is quoted in Mert (2016) as saying, "I never thought mothers to be a political group, but when the mayor requested them *to call their children back from the park*, hundreds of them formed a chain around the park which brought me to tears ... Even the teenage girls that I only thought to be petty-bourgeois shopping-addicts were participating en masse! People stopped being scared; I guess they thought 'eight kids were killed in peaceful, democratic protests in

this country, what is the point of being afraid, how much worse can it get?'" (8–9, emphasis added). Another stated, "We wrongly assumed this generation was fundamentally apolitical. When we entered the Park, we loved what the youngsters did with the place! The Y-generation gave us back the hope we lost since the 1980 coup" (7).

REFERENCES

Abdi, A.A., and L. Shultz. 2008. *Educating for Human Rights and Global Citizenship*. Albany: State University of New York Press.

Abdi, A.A., and P. Carr. 2012. *Educating for Democratic Consciousness: Counter Hegemonic Possibilities*. Frankfurt: Peter Lang.

Amnesty International. 2013. *Gezi Park Protests: Brutal Denial of the Right to Peaceful Assembly in Turkey*. London: Amnesty International. https://www.amnestyusa.org/reports/gezi-park-protests-brutal-denial-of-the-right-to-peaceful-assembly-in-turkey/

Anderson, B. 1983. *Imagined Communities: Reflections on the Origin and Spread of Nationalism*. London: Verso.

Andreotti, V.O., and L.M.T.M. De Souza. 2012. *Postcolonial Perspectives on Global Citizenship Education*. New York: Routledge.

Banks, J.A., ed. 2004. *Diversity and Citizenship Education: Global Perspectives*. San Francisco: Jossey-Bass.

– 2017. "Failed Citizenship and Transformative Civic Education." *American Educational and Research Association* 46, no.7: 366–77.

Bhabha, H. 1994. *The Location of Culture*. New York: Routledge.

Davies, I., M. Evans, and A. Reid. 2005. "Globalising Citizenship Education? A Critique of Global Education and Citizenship Education." *British Journal of Educational Studies* 53, no. 1: 66–8. https://doi.org/10.1111/j.1467-8527.2005.00284.x

de Andreotti, V.O. 2014. "Soft versus Critical Global Citizenship Education. In *Development Education in Policy and Practice*, edited by S. McCloskey. London: Palgrave Macmillan.

Dower, N. 2003. *An Introduction to Global Citizenship*. Edinburgh: Edinburgh University Press.

Green, A. 1990. *Education and State Formation: The Rise of Education Systems in England, France and the USA*. London: Macmillan.

– 2015. "Philippines: Children Risk Death to Dig and Dive for Fold." Human Rights Watch. 29 September. https://www.hrw.org/news/2015/09/29/philippines-children-risk-death-dig-and-dive-gold

Jorgenson, S. 2010. "De-centering and Re-visioning Global Citizenship Abroad Programs." *International Journal of Development Education and Global Learning* 3, no. 1: 23–38. https://doi.org/10.18546/ijdegl.03.1.03

Mert, A. 2016. "The trees in Gezi Park: Environmental Policy as the Focus of Democratic Protests." *Journal of Environmental Policy & Planning*, 593–607. https://doi.org/10.1080/1523908X.2016.1202106

Nussbaum, M. 2002. "Education for Citizenship in an Era of Global Connection." *Studies in Philosophy and Education* 21: 289–303. https://doi.org/10.1023/a:1019837105053

Osler, A., and H. Starkey. 2006. "Education for Democratic Citizenship: A Review of Research, Policy and Practice 1995–2005." *Research Papers in Education* 24: 433–66. https://doi.org/10.1080/02671520600942438

Özkaynak, B., C.I. Aydin, P. Ertör-Akyaz , and I. Ertör. 2015. "The Gezi Park Resistance from an Environmental Justice and Social Metabolism Perspective." *Capitalism Nature Socialism* 26, no. 1: 99–114. https://doi.org/10.1080/10455752.2014.999102

Peake, L. 2008 "Editorial: Moving on Up." *Gender, Place and Culture* 15, no. 1: 1–5.

Peters, M., A. Britton, and H. Blee, eds. 2008. *Global Citizenship Education: Philosophy, Theory and Pedagogy*. Rotterdam: Sense Publishers.

Roth, K. 2018. *The Pushback against the Populist Challenge*. New York: Human Rights Watch. https://www.hrw.org/world-report/2018/pushback-against-the-populist-challenge

Sennero, J. 2017. "Anti-Immigrant Sweden Democrats Move into Second Place in Polls." Reuters, 23 March. https://www.reuters.com/article/us-sweden-politics/anti-immigrant-sweden-democrats-move-into-second-place-in-polls-idUSKBN16U1NS

Shultz, L. 2010. "What Do We Ask of Global Citizenship Education? A Study of Global Citizenship Education in a Canadian University." *International Journal of Development Education and Global Learning* 3, no. 1: 5–22. https://doi.org/10.18546/ijdegl.03.1.02

Sperandio, J., M. Grudzinski-Hall, and H. Stewart-Gambino. 2010. "Developing an Undergraduate Global Citizenship Program: Challenges of Definition and Assessment." *International Journal of Teaching and Learning in Higher Education* 22, no. 1: 12–22.

Spivak, G.C. 1999. *A Critique of Postcolonial Reason: Toward a History of the Vanishing Present*. Cambridge, MA: Harvard University Press.

Tiessen, R., and R. Huish, eds. 2014. *Globetrotting or Global Citizenship? Perils and Potential of International Experiential Learning*. Toronto: University of Toronto Press.

UNESCO. 2014. World Conference on Education and Sustainable Development, Aichi-Nagoya, Japan, 10–12 November. http://www.unesco.org/new/en/unesco-world-conference-on-esd-2014/

– 2015. *Global Citizenship Education: Topics and Learning Objectives*. Paris: UNESCO.

United Nations. 2015. "Transforming Our World: The 2030 Agenda for Sustainable Development." UN Resolution A/RES/70/1. Adopted 25 September.

Verma, R. 2017. *Critical Peace Education and Global Citizenship*. New York: Routledge.

SECTION I

Key Theories and Concepts of Global Citizenship Education

1 The Global Context of Global Citizenship: A Pedagogy of Engagement

EVA ABOAGYE AND S. NOMBUSO DLAMINI

There is growing interest and programing in the area of global citizenship education (GCE) in post-secondary institutions. A number of scholars have published books exploring the subject (see, for example, Dower 2003; Banks 2004; Abdi and Shultz 2008; Stearns 2009; Peters, Britton, and Blee 2008; Andreotti and De Souza 2012; Tiessen and Huish 2014; Harshman, Augustine, and Merrifield 2015). The research covers how to define GCE, what the learning outcomes should be, the content, and the learning process itself, as well as curricular and co-curricular activities. Educating students to become global citizens has become important in our rapidly changing and interconnected world, in fact OECD/Asia Society (2018) suggests it might be important for our very survival:

> Inexorable economic, cultural, technological, environmental, and political forces are affecting every society on earth and making nations and peoples more interdependent than ever before. Responding effectively to these forces, lessening their damage or harnessing them for good, will require creative multinational solutions to be negotiated and carried out by individuals who can and do participate simultaneously in local, national, and global civic life. Put simply, if individuals and their communities are to thrive in the future, schools must prepare today's students to be globally competent. (10)

It goes on to say that global competence is necessary for a number of reasons, including employability in the global economy; living cooperatively in multicultural communities; and achieving the United Nations Sustainable Development Goals (SDGs).

There are, however, a number of gaps in our understanding and implementation of GCE, including the definition of the field. Most research in the field attempt to answer the question: What does it mean to be a global citizen and how do students achieve that status? Defining GCE has proved to be challenging as many institutions implement it in different ways. As Peters, Britton, and Blee (2008) assert, "There can be no one dominant notion of global citizenship education as notions of 'global,' 'citizenship,' and 'education' are all contested and open to further argument and revision" (11). Since citizenship is the focus of global citizenship education, it is worth exploring the notion of citizenship here. Dower and Williams (2002) define citizenship as "membership, determined by formal factors such as place of birth, parentage or an act of naturalization, of a political community (generally a nation-state)" (xix), which comes with rights, duties, and responsibilities. Individuals in the nation-state are educated to exercise the rights, duties, and responsibilities expected of them. This definition can be extended to the broader world, which would result in other global-citizenship-related questions: Do all global citizens know their rights, duties, and responsibilities as citizens of the global community; and as educators, how can we educate students to be effective members of the global community? Do expectations of us as members of the global community only apply when we are outside of our nation-state or are they all encompassing to the local and global?

Golmohamad (2008) points out that the first purpose of GCE is to cultivate an integrative mindset, offering encounters with diverse people and settings where possible; and the second is to channel knowledge and experience gained to some purposeful contribution, encouraging choices of vocations or careers and acts of service where it is possible to work for the betterment of the whole society. Aligned with Golmohamad's ideas, the United Nations defines the goal of GCE as "nurturing respect for all, building a sense of belonging to a common humanity and helping learners become responsible and active global citizens" (United Nations n.d.). The OECD/Asia Society (2018) captures the end goal of GCE as educating people to be globally competent and define it as: "Global competence is the capacity to examine local, global, and intercultural issues; to understand and appreciate the perspectives and world views of others; to engage in open, appropriate, and effective interactions with people from different cultures; and to act for collective well-being and sustainable development" (5).

Humes (2008) points out that despite the lack of a clear definition, the idea of global citizenship education has allowed educators to reintroduce discussions of the big issues of our time in the classroom, which include issues that are being discussed in the UN SDGs such as inequality, poverty, hunger, health, education, gender equality, energy, climate change, peace, and justice.

This chapter presents the history of global citizenship education; as well, it offers exemplary post-secondary snapshots of effective pedagogy for facilitating global citizens. The overall goal for this chapter is to provide the why, how, and what in GCE and to move the dialogue towards the articulation of a core curriculum in global citizenship education; that is, the chapter looks at what the processes of GCE should look like and what the accompanying pedagogy could be composed of. It also proposes a pedagogical process that encourages students to be aware of their role as members of the global community.

Global Citizenship Education: The Discourse

GCE has become important because of the changing nature of global relations and the awareness of the interconnectedness of the world. In *Teaching for Global Competence in a Rapidly Changing World*, the OECD/Asia Society (2018) points out that global competence in the world today is necessary for a number of reasons, including for employability in the global economy; for living cooperatively in multicultural communities; for young people to communicate and learn effectively and responsibly with old and new media; and for achieving the UN SDGs (10). There is growing recognition of the need for this generation to take care of one another in society and to take care of our resources for the next generation. Organizations like Oxfam, UNESCO, the United Nations, and now the OECD have at various times led the charge of encouraging educational institutions to implement programs to encourage the development of students who are both locally and globally aware.

Advances in technology have also brought the world closer together, for example, the uprisings and rebellions in the Arab countries in 2010–11 (commonly referred to as the Arab Spring) and the political unrest in Venezuela in 2019 were brought immediately to the world's phones, computers, and televisions for all to see. The aftermath of the 9/11 terrorist attacks and the images of genocides, refugees, and starving children have created that sense of a global community where we cannot ignore what goes on in other parts of the world. Climate change and environmental issues are visible for all to see. In addition, globalization, the process whereby governments are engaged in economic and political activities beyond their own borders and that impact nations outside their own, means there is a sense of responsibility for what happens outside of our doors. Global issues like inequality, environmental sustainability, threats of terrorism, gender inequality, and poverty have become important to discuss, and for educational institutions to not only make students aware of these issues but also to encourage a sense of becoming critical participants in resolving these issues.

Educational institutions from elementary to post-secondary levels, as well as intergovernmental organizations like the United Nations, UNESCO, OECD, and the non-governmental organizations like Oxfam have been engaging with the question of GCE and exploring ways to incorporate it in the learning environment. There are many aspects of curriculum, teaching, and learning that need to be undertaken in order to achieve this goal. Further, all activities aimed to achieve this goal must utilize a pedagogy of engagement with society, a pedagogy that cultivates shared responsibility to the community both local and global.

One of the basic purposes of post-secondary education has always been to develop civic knowledge in students (Jacoby and Associates 2009). Educational institutions provide a socializing role in society and part of it is teaching individuals to be effective and responsible members of their community or nation. As the focus of post-secondary institutions moved more to professional development, their role in developing civic consciousness declined. Fallis (2014) has discussed the current dialogue on whether universities should return to their civic duties and has concluded that as renewed commitment takes hold in the post-secondary sector, it has become important to explore what the curriculum and learning processes should be in order to achieve civic responsibilities.

A number of authors (Dower and Wiliams 2002; Banks 2008; Falk 2002) have discussed citizenship in terms of the nation-state and government and society's interest in developing people to be effective members of their countries. With industrialization, there was a need to prepare people for necessary industrial-based skills; consequently, educating for the industrial and technological system took precedence over teaching members of society to be civic minded. This resulted in more of a focus in post-secondary institutions in the 1980s on professional development and less on the more general and civic education of the past. With globalization, international politics, human rights, inequality, safety, and security around the world, a focus has returned to how we create students who understand our interconnected world and can be effective members of that world. This has resulted in an interest in extending the concept of citizenship to the global level.

The increasing interest in global citizenship education is a move to return to the 1960s when the focus of post-secondary education was on civic education, with an added interest in getting students to challenge and take action on what they perceived as injustice, and on other global issues (DeVititis and Sasso 2016). It is a response to a general feeling that the younger generation is drifting away from their responsibility to society (Fallis 2014).

The focus and goals of civic, global, or citizenship education are often tied into development on the global level (Holden 2000). For example, in the post–world war era, developments in globalization and internationalization contributed to an interest in focusing education on creating international understanding (Hicks 2003). In order to better appreciate others, the focus was on learning about other regions of the world and other cultures. This was in line with education for citizenship at the national level. The focus for states was ensuring that citizens understood their roles and responsibilities. In the 1960s the focus was on world studies, which was mainly used to study other regions and other nations and to include global issues in the curriculum. The current focus is on seeing the world as one and on seeing one another as belonging to one world.

Different philosophical camps and disciplinary areas look at global citizenship education concepts in ways that reflect the field in which they are located. Pike (2008) summarized some of the work that was done in different disciplines as follows:

> At the theoretical level, there is no shortage of models and visions of education for global citizenship. Among these are Heater's concept of the "multiple citizen" (Heater, 1990); Selby's description of "plural and parallel citizenship" (Selby, 1944); and Herbert's construction of "a new flexible citizenship" (Hebert, 1997). From the field of multicultural education, Lynch (1992) suggests that "education for active global democracy" is the real challenge for educators; and Banks (2001) depicts "globalism and global competency" as the sixth and ultimate stage in individual's development of cultural identity. From peace education perspective comes Boulding's idea of "building a global civic structure" (Boulding, 1988). Nussbaum (1996) makes a strong case from a philosophical viewpoint for teaching children to see themselves as global citizens in her defense of "cosmopolitan education." (223)

Also, philosophical and ideological approaches impact the way different academics view GCE. Some scholars, like Cameron (2014), propose that GCE should be grounded in cosmopolitanism and should include the positive and negative requirements of citizenship. Cameron states that cosmopolitanism can make important contributions to global citizenship, it provides universal obligations of all humans towards all other humans, and also provides emphasis on the personal responsibility of all humans to be aware of the consequences of their actions, direct or indirect, intended or unintended, which may radically restrict or delimit the choices of others.

Another philosophical approach sees GCE as multiculturalism (Banks 2004; Pashby 2012). Pashby's (2012) definition of global citizenship states: "As an ideal, the concept of educating for global citizenship encourages students to adopt a critical understanding of globalization, to reflect on how they and their nations are implicated in local and global problems and to engage in intercultural perspectives" (9).

UNESCO (2015) has philosophically approached global citizenship as identity and belonging to a broader and common community. It emphasizes "political, economic, social and cultural interdependency and interconnectedness between the local, the national and the global" (14). Given the diversity of approaches to GCE for post-secondary institutions, therefore, we need to ask the question, How do we find a common focus, definition, and curriculum? The goal being to get students to think beyond their immediate community and to begin to embrace their role, responsibilities, and rights in the global community. In the end, GCE needs to encompass a number of these diverse approaches. Given the current world political climate, it is important for students to feel connected both locally and globally, to be culturally aware and to critically engage with the issues of our time.

There are international organizations that have explored GCE and have created GCE related initiatives. This includes the United Nations Academic Impact Initiative that was set up in 2010. Its aim is to align institutions of higher education with the goals of the United Nations in supporting and contributing to the UN's goals that encourage GCE. There is also UNESCO's Global Education First Initiative that was launched in 2012. One of the priorities under this initiative is global citizenship, and it looks at the challenges the world faces and calls for an education that would lead to changes in how we think and act for the dignity of our fellow human beings. Oxfam has also developed specific initiatives for global citizenship education, by looking closely at outcomes and creating resources for use at the local level. The newly developed UN Sustainable Development Goals (SDGs) also has a section on global citizenship education. It is an all-embracing goal that challenges educational institutions to do more to prepare people to be citizens of the world. As noted earlier, in 2018 the OECD/Asia Society also came out with a report emphasizing the importance of GCE for individuals and for the world as a whole.

Global Citizenship Education: The History in Post-Secondary Institutions

The focus on global citizenship education at the post-secondary level has taken on a new importance. Osler and Starkey (2006) point out that the interest in global citizenship has been the result of a number of factors, including global injustice and inequality; globalization and migration; concerns about civic and political engagement; the end of the cold war and anti-democratic and racist movements; and environmental degradation. Global citizenship education can take many forms and, in fact, many educational institutions have approached global citizenship education in their own way.

In Canada, the school systems have embraced global citizenship education in their curriculum. Provincial governments in Canada at the elementary and secondary levels have taken the lead in focusing on educating students to be global citizens. For example, the Province of Ontario together with the teachers' association of the province created a document on curriculum for global citizenship education for teachers (Elementary Teachers' Federation of Ontario 2010). Schattle (2008) states that Canada and the United States have taken the lead in developing global citizenship programs, which is evident from the extensive GCE research coming from these countries.

Commenting on the United States, Osler and Starkey (2006) state that the students of the 1960s were followed by a more subdued student population on campus, leading some to think that maybe the post-1960s generation of students have been less engaged with their world. However, there are studies that indicate the opposite, signalling that students are actively involved in civic action even if not to 1960s levels. For instance, Finley (2011) reports from a study of 12,000 college students that more than 75 per cent of students had participated in civic engagement while in college, of which 30 per cent were course based.

Musil (2009) offers a history of GCE in the United States and presents the work done by the National Leadership Council for Liberal Education and America's Promise (LCLEAP) as a pioneering organization in the field. Musil listed four broad essential learning outcomes that the LCLEAP wanted students to acquire in GCE. These were civic knowledge and engagement both local and global; intercultural knowledge and competence; ethical reasoning and action; and foundations and skills for lifelong learning.

While global citizenship education is only a recent development, there has always been a commitment to civic education. As Musil (2009) notes, involvement in both local and global communities has a long-standing history with post-secondary institutions in the United States. A scan of current programs in post-secondary institutions in the United States shows a wide range of courses and co-curricular activities. Not only are institutions committed to training students to be global citizens but employers in the United States are demanding this as a skill in their employees. Employers are increasingly looking for employees who will be able to function in an interdependent and global work place. Musil (2009) reports that a national poll in 2007 reported that 76 per cent of employers want colleges to place more emphasis on the intercultural competencies that lead to teamwork skills in diverse groups, and 72 per cent want more emphasis on global knowledge.

The Association of American Colleges and Universities (n.d.) reports that different institutions in the United States have included some civic and global learning in their learning outcomes for students. These outcomes are described in such phrases as "demonstrate stewardship of local, national, and global communities by cultivating awareness of: interdependence among those communities; issues within those communities; and organizations and skills that address such issues" (Utah Valley University); "students will take courses under the themes of Global Crossroads and Diversity and Traditions and Movements that Shape the world" (Hawai'I Pacific University); and "to develop competencies for responsible global citizenship" (Central College).

In the UK, global citizenship education, especially at the lower levels of the education system, has been part of teaching, learning, and research since the 1960s (Hicks 2003). Global citizenship education in the UK has its origins in the world studies movement. This movement covered promoting the knowledge, attitudes, and skills that enabled people to live responsibly in a multicultural and interdependent world. In 1997, Oxfam UK developed a curriculum for global citizenship education that was based on previous global learning studies and combined knowledge and attitudes with a sense of responsibility. Hicks (2003) outlines the Oxfam UK curriculum as having three main components: (1) promoting background knowledge to global issues and addressing issues in social justice, peace and conflict, diversity, sustainable development, globalization and interdependence; (2) teaching the definite skills needed to learn to become global citizens, including critical thinking skills, argumentation, cooperation, and conflict resolution, and the ability to challenge injustice; and (3) teaching values and attitudes needed to be recognized as a global citizen, including values such as commitment to equality, respecting diversity, concern for the environment, and a sense of identity and self-esteem.

Global Learning and Global Citizenship Education

There is some linkage between the development of GCE and global learning. Hicks (2003) discusses some of the developments in global learning that took place at the World Council for Education in World Citizenship where the focus was mainly on creating international understanding. According to Hicks, a participatory pedagogy was developed with influences from Johan Galtung, Paulo Freire, and Carl Rogers. World studies was designed to provide knowledge, attitudes, and skills that enabled individuals to live in our multicultural and independent world in a responsible manner. It can be described as a precursor to global citizenship education. World studies, however, was about learning and understanding the local and not really about engaging with the rest of the world. A framework for exploring world studies was developed that had four main components: poverty, oppression, conflict, and the environment. Hicks goes on to explain that in the 1980s Pike and Selby examined global education by taking a fresh look at its components. They looked at what the aims of global education should be and developed a framework that would see students acquire systems consciousness; perspective consciousness; health and planet awareness; involvement consciousness; and preparedness and process mindedness. Global learning has many forms and expected outcomes, some of which are discussed by Richardson (2008) and outlined later in this chapter. In addition, Hovland (2014) adds more information about global learning with a focus on what students learn through curricular and co-curricular experiences.

The North-South Centre of the Council of Europe (2008), for example, provided a framework on what the knowledge, skills, and attitudes for global education should encompass. The Centre suggests that the content areas should cover knowledge of the globalization process and the development of world society; knowledge of the history and philosophy of universal concepts of humanity; and knowledge about commonalities and differences. It also lists a number of specific skills that range from critical thinking to dealing with science and modern technology. On values and attitudes, the Centre suggests self-esteem, self-confidence, self-respect, and respect for others; social responsibility; environmental responsibility; open-mindedness; visionary attitudes; proactive and participatory community membership; and solidarity.

GCE evolved from a world studies and global learning focus, encompassing ideas from both. For example, the goals of global citizenship education in Canada have evolved from one level to the other and from one period to the next. This evolution is aptly captured by Richardson

Table 1.1. The five imaginaries of global citizenship education

Imaginary	Subject area	Goal of the program
Imperial	Students under this imaginary of global citizenship education learn about the world and their country's role in the world as well as their own position in the world.	The focus of global citizenship education under this imaginary is in developing in students, a pride in their country and developing and re-enforcing a national identity.
Bipolar	The world under this imaginary is divided into two ideological camps – communism and capitalism. Students are taught about communism in order to create a better understanding of a rival system.	The focus is to create a better understanding of the two systems and to provide to students the value of the capitalist system.
Multipolar	This imaginary relates to the era of the creation of the United Nations and other multilateral agencies. An emphasis is placed on the values of international cooperation, multilateralism and interdependence.	The focus here is to teach students about the interdependence of the world. It is also to help students develop skills and attitudes to help them engage in the world.
Ecological	The emphasis here is on the concerns about the survival of the planet and also the need to embrace diversity.	The focus is to create a transformative experience that will help students evaluate their own values. The hope is to have students who will take action to solve the problems of the world.
Monopolar	This imaginary brings us back close to the Imperial Imaginary. Here the focus is on seeing the world as a global market place and to learn to be competitive in it.	The focus is on getting students to see the world as one and to encourage them to become competitive in it.

Source: Richardson (2008).

(2008) in his description of what he terms the "different 'imaginaries" of GCE over the years, which he said "do not represent a linear process – rather in many cases, they overlap and intersect – but each has its own understanding of the purpose of global citizenship education, its own worldview and its own value structure" (119). His five imaginaries (shown in table 1.1) give a clear description of the different aspects of global citizenship education, which are also cited in Brigham and Aboagye (2013).

Each of these "imaginaries" have had some successes and some failures during their time. Notable failures have been the "Imperial" period, which resulted in colonialism, and the "Bipolar" period, which resulted in a rise of the accumulation of materials and machinery of war. The current approach to GCE shares parts from the "Multipolar," "Ecological," and "Monopolar" focus. It fits into the conceptions of global citizenship education that looks at providing the knowledge and skills that individuals need to be responsible members of the world. It doesn't make students competitive but rather makes them effective and responsible members of the global community. A look at the framework provides society's main focus at the time in terms of its relationship with the rest of the world. Under these "imaginaries," we see a focus on knowledge and on skill development that depends on prevailing needs. What is missing is the bigger picture of us as one humanity.

Global Citizenship Education: Different Approaches

Shultz (2007) examines three approaches to education for global citizenship at post-secondary institutions. The first is the neo-liberal approach, which is linked to global economic participation and enables the individual to acquire knowledge and skills necessary for transnational mobility. Examples of this approach include study abroad programs and the internationalization of the curriculum. Second is the radical approach, which is characterized by opposition to global and multinational institutions like the International Monetary Fund (IMF) and which encourages students to be critical of existing systems. The increased activism on university and college campuses of the 1960s and early 1970s exemplifies the effects of this approach to globalization and global relations. The third is the transformational approach, which focuses on factors that have led to new kinds of exclusion and inclusion and disparity locally, nationally, and globally. The global citizen with this approach seeks to engage with others based on a common humanity, a shared planet, and a shared future. Recent interests in post-secondary institutions tend to follow this transformational approach.

Shultz and Jorgenson's (2012) review of the literature lists a number of initiatives in post-secondary institutions on global citizenship education. They point out that despite the common commitment to educate students for global citizenship, no two programs of global citizenship education are alike. Each institution of higher education has created its own unique initiative consisting of various forms of policy, programing, prerequisites, credentialing, and student and community involvement (7).

According to Preece (2008), global citizenship education has been introduced in other parts of the world, including in Australia, East Asia, Africa, and the Pacific region. She points out that citizenship education is bound by national histories as well, and this is evident in how the different countries have approached it. Her article paints a picture of a close link between citizenship education and nation states especially in non-Western countries. She concludes that there are questions asked about the legitimacy of Western notions of citizenship and human rights education in non-Western countries. As we explore GCE in post-secondary institutions, we have to be cognizant of the fact that citizenship and commitment to national development may be viewed differently in different countries. For non-Western countries, it might be more crucial for students to be trained about their roles and responsibilities to their countries and the importance of taking action for change at the local level than at the global level.

Another approach that has been proposed is that we focus on engagement of students in the classroom about actions of a global citizenship (Brigham and Aboagye 2013). This approach has components that include theory or the learning objectives; content that covers the course of study; experiences including study abroad, service learning, and civic engagement; methodology covering strategies and techniques; and assessment including processes used to establish and document student learning outcomes. We want to take the pedagogy a step further by looking at the actual processes that are used in creating global citizenship.

Creating global citizens is often guided by the following questions: Do we create students as future citizens who view themselves as mere objects in history, or do we create learners who view themselves as dynamic political agents of personal and social improvement? (Hyslop-Margison and Sears 2008). Also, How can we encourage young people to become engaged with the nature and scale of the challenge that globalization represents in ways that make a difference to the way they act? (Humes 2008). Commenting on this later question, Humes (2008) points out that global citizenship deals with issues of wealth and poverty; equality and justice; access and exclusion; rights and democracy; and freedom and authority – all of which are important to global citizenship and are issues that need to be discussed.

Richardson (2008) lists two perspectives to global citizenship education:

1. One that is grounded in an ecological awareness of the fundamental interrelatedness of all aspects of the Earth and of the importance of physical and cultural diversity;
2. And a second one that is founded on individualism and neo-liberal economic ideas that suggest that despite superficial differences individuals have the same fundamental wants and needs and that by serving their own self-interest, ultimately the interests of the planet are also served. (10)

In the context of the first perspective, the purpose of global citizenship education is to help students develop the knowledge and skills that will allow them to be competitive and successful in the global arena. The second perspective was the driving force behind a lot of the study abroad and international programs in the past. However, the field of global citizenship education, while incorporating this perspective, is mainly focused on the first perspective of helping students to develop a sense of interconnectedness, empathy, and an appreciation of diversity and difference. While it is easier to provide a core curriculum and pedagogy and processes for the second perspective, the first continues to be a struggle.

To meet the demands of Richardson's first perspective, Brigham and Aboagye (2013) suggest that a range of courses must be offered as part of global citizenship programs or as standalone courses. These courses can be grouped into three categories: the core global citizenship courses; courses on sustainability and environmental issues; and courses on ethnic and cultural issues.

The first category, core global citizenship courses, will have content such as global issues, social justice issues, human rights, democratic principles, and equity and equality. A quick review of courses and programs on global citizenship in Canada shows some similarities in that all the institutions that have global citizenship education programs have core courses covering a range of social justice issues, cultural or language courses, and human rights. Here we would like to propose that for the post-secondary sector, the core courses should comprise the following:

- Learning what global citizenship means in the current context;
- Understanding the historical context of society and social development and globalization;
- Learning about one's identity and appreciating diversity;
- Developing a critical democratic perspective on global issues; and
- Developing skills to take action to address global issues/activism/ or learning to be an activist.

Most programs in post-secondary institutions will have one or two or three of these components. We are proposing that all GCE programs have all three of these as their core components, as well as service-learning components or other co-curricular activities. In addition, there is a need for textbooks that are readily recognized for these courses.

The second category focuses on sustainability and the environment. Concern with proper stewardship of our planet is so well developed that one cannot really be a global citizen without having some understanding of environmental care and sustainability. The environmental movement has provided a plethora of literature (see also Beckford in chapter 4 of this volume) that makes it easy for educators to identify core topics and related teaching methods. In Canada, the school sector has been active in educating students on the proper stewardship of the environment; as a result, most students are environmentally aware or aware of sustainable development before they get to the post-secondary level. Courses taught at the school level are about sustainability of the environment and global warming. These courses create environmental consciousness and provide students with the skills and possible solutions to environmental issues. Also, the UN Sustainable Development Goals are a great source for educating students at the high school level on environmental sustainability.

The third category focuses on ethnic and cultural issues. These can range from courses on identity, ethnicity, culture, and language to music and the arts. These courses are designed to provide students with knowledge of overall concepts and debates on diversity.

The field of global citizenship education has developed over time, and, despite lack of program consensus among institutions, there are some exemplary initiatives that are worth documenting. These initiatives include the works of the world studies movement; the Centre for Global Education at the University of York; Oxfam in the United Kingdom; work by intergovernmental agencies like the UN, UNESCO, and OECD; the work by institutions in the United States, including the Association of American Colleges and Universities; and the work done by colleges and universities in Canada, including Centennial College and the University of British Columbia. These initiatives have contributed to the formulation of a consistent set of core courses or outcomes across global citizenship education. Notably, Centennial College identified outcomes that address all of the above three major areas of focus in global citizenship education (see chapter 10 by Aboagye in this volume). The outcomes include:

1. Identify one's roles and responsibilities as a global citizen in personal and professional life;
2. Identify beliefs, values, and behaviours that form individual and community identities and the basis for respectful relationships;
3. Analyse issues of equity at the personal, professional, and global level;
4. Analyse the use of the world's resources to achieve sustainability and equitable distribution at the personal, professional, and global level;

5. Identify and challenge unjust practices in local and global systems;
6. Support personal and social responsibility initiatives at the local, national, or global level.

Classroom Learning, Experiential Initiatives, and Programing

Literature on in-class processes or engagement-based learning processes and tools of analysis that encourage critical analysis of global citizenship issues are scarce. Therefore, it is important that GCE looks at related pedagogical approaches in other disciplines. Pedagogies of engagement that can inform GCE include those presented by researchers like Sloam (2011), Eberlein et al. (2008), and Smith et al. (2005). Similarly, Parsons's (2012) work can offer GCE some insight on conversational pedagogies; Subedi (2013) on decolonizing pedagogies; Shulman (2005) on signature pedagogies; and Schertz (2006) on empathy pedagogies. All these pedagogical approaches provide the environment for students to critically engage with what they are learning. While these pedagogies would be useful for global citizenship education, it is also important to evaluate their effectiveness before adopting them.

GCE has moved from simply understanding global issues, or learning about other cultures, or embracing diversity to a place where students are taught how to directly engage in global issues. To do this, students need critical analysis skills as well as familiarity with equity and social justice. There are many tools for critical analysis related to global citizenship and equity education. Hackman (2005) offers tools in the classroom for an engaged student population and suggests that first and foremost are classroom materials that present information from multiple, non-dominant perspectives. Once these materials are established, GCE educators should use tools that open students' minds to a broader range of experiences, which are centred on a critical analysis of the effects of power and oppression. Additionally, there are components of this education that take place outside through service-learning and international service-learning projects.

Most global citizenship programs have a component that requires students to either undertake a service-learning trip of varying lengths or study abroad, or requires students to work within the community on projects that usually have a global or diversity component (e.g., requires students to learn a second language). As reported by Cameron (2014), "One of the frequently stated goals of experiential learning programs in Canadian and American universities is to foster the values, aptitudes, and abilities of global citizenship among student participants" (21). Experiential learning is considered important in enabling students to learn and understand other cultures and other people and to provide a better understanding of global issues. In Tiessen and Huish's (2014) edited volume, authors explore international service learning and the role it plays in educating global citizens. Similarly, authors in section two of this volume critically present a diverse range of experiential learning opportunities for students. These chapters paint a picture of the different ways in which the experiential component of global citizenship education is approached. In the face of varying GCE learning outcomes, questions remain about whether experiential learning initiatives should be embedded in the curriculum and be developed as a consistent program requirement.

There is growing evidence indicating students' interest in engaging in GCE's experiential component. College and university campuses have become sites for student-run non-profit organizations that are all seeking to change the world in one way or the other. In Canada, these programs include community development projects at the local, national, and international levels. These groups include AISEC, Journalists for Human Rights, Youth Challenge International, Free the Children, and Engineers Without Borders, which all have chapters or members on college and university campuses. Post-secondary institutions are also developing service-learning programs for their students as well as partnering with non-governmental organizations to provide service-learning opportunities for their students. In addition, some of the programs have capstone projects and independent projects, as well as global and community projects. All of these are options that faculty can consider as they develop curriculum for GCE.

Conclusion

In the current global environment where no nation can be an island and where technology has brought us even closer, this chapter has provided reasons why we need to educate students to be good global citizens and to be aware of the issues of this world. The current UN SDGs are ambitious goals aimed at helping us all live a more sustainable life and this includes taking care of people and the planet. In fact, as pointed out by OECD, our very survival might depend on it. The chapter examined why we need a global citizenship education in our interconnected world. It looked at examples of what is being done in both curricular and co-curricular activities for global citizenship education in post-secondary institutions. It has proposed core courses for global citizenship education as well as experiential learning activities.

As this chapter has shown, and many researchers have pointed out, GCE continues to evolve. The good news is that on surveying global citizenship courses and programs around the world, we see patterns that include core global citizenship courses; courses on sustainability and the environment; and ethnic and cultural courses, as well as service-learning components and some project expectations. Still, there is a need to review our understanding of a pedagogy of engagement and evaluate how effective it is in the pursuit of the outcomes for global citizenship education.

REFERENCES

Abdi, A.A., and L. Shultz. 2008. *Educating for Human Rights and Global Citizenship*. Albany, NY: SUNY Press.

Andreotti, V.O., and L.M.T.M. De Souza. 2012. *Postcolonial Perspectives on Global Citizenship Education*. New York: Routledge.

Association of American Colleges and Universities. n.d. "Global Learning Outcomes." https://www.aacu.org/global-learning/outcomes

Banks, J.A. 2004. *Diversity and Citizenship Education: Global Perspectives*. San Francisco: Jossey-Bass.

– 2008. "Diversity, Group Identity, and Citizenship Education in a Global Age." *Educational Researcher* 37, no. 3: 129–39. https://doi.org/10.3102/0013189x08317501

Brigham, M., and E. Aboagye. 2013. "Signature Pedagogy for Global Citizenship Education." *The Journal of the World Universities Forum* 5, no. 4: 31–46. https://doi.org/10.18848/1835-2030/cgp/v05i04/56815

Cameron, J.D. 2014. "Grounding Experiential Learning in 'Thick' Conceptions of Global Citizenship." In *Globetrotting or Global Citizenship: Perils and Potential of International Experiential Learning*, edited by R. Tiessen and R. Huish. Toronto: University of Toronto Press.

DeVititis, L.J., and P.A. Sasso. 2016. *Higher Education and Society*. New York: Peter Lang.

Dower, N. 2003. *An Introduction to Global Citizenship*. Edinburgh: Edinburgh University Press.

Dower, N., and Williams, J. 2002. *Global Citizenship: A Critical Introduction*. New York: Routledge.

Eberlein, T., J. Kampmeier, V. Monderhout, R.S. Moog, T. Platt, P. Varma-Nelson, and H.B. Whilte. 2008. "Pedagogies of Engagement in Science: A Comparison of PBL, POGIL, and PLTL." *Biochemistry and Molecular Biology Education* 36, no. 4: 262–73. https://doi.org/10.1002/bmb.20204. Medline:19381266

Elementary Teachers' Federation of Ontario. 2010. *Educating for Global Citizenship*. Toronto: ETFO.

Falk, R. 2002 "An Emergent Matrix of Citizenship: Complex, Uneven, and Fluid." In *Global Citizenship: A Critical Introduction*, edited by N. Dower and J. Williams. New York: Routledge.

Fallis, G. 2014. "Reclaiming the Civic University in Academic Affairs." Academic Matters, June. http://www.academicmatters.ca/2014/06/reclaiming-the-civic-university/

Finley, A. 2011. *Civic Learning and Democratic Engagements: A Review of the Literature on Civic Engagement in Post-Secondary Education*. New York: United States Department of Education.

Golmohamad, M. 2008. "Global Citizenship: From Theory to Practice, Unlocking Hearts and Minds." In *Global Citizenship Education: Philosophy, Theory and Pedagogy*, edited by M.A. Peters, A. Britton, and H. Blee. Rotterdam: Sense Publishers.

Hackman, W.H. 2005. "Five Essential Components for Social Justice Education." *Equity and Excellence in Education* 38: 103–9. https://doi.org/10.1080/10665680590935034

Harshman, J., T. Augustine, and M. Merryfield. 2015. *Research in Global Citizenship Education*. Charlotte, NC: Information Age Publishing.

Hicks, D. 2003. "Thirty Years of Global Education: A Reminder of Key Principles and Precedents." *Education Review* 55, no. 3: 265–75. https://doi.org/10.1080/0013191032000118929

Holden, C. 2000. "Learning for Democracy: From World Studies to Global Citizenship." *Theory into Practice* 39, no. 2: 74–80. https://doi.org/10.1207/s15430421tip3902_3

Hovland, K. 2014. *Global Learning: Defining, Designing, Demonstrating*. Washington, DC: Association of American Colleges and Universities.

Humes, W. 2008. "The Discourse of Global Citizenship." In *Global Citizenship Education: Philosophy, Theory and Pedagogy*, edited by M.A. Peters, A. Britton, and H. Blee. Rotterdam: Sense Publishers.

Hyslop-Margison, E.J., and A.M. Sears. 2008. "Challenging the Dominant Neo-Liberal Discourse: From Human Capital Learning to Education for Civic Engagement." In *Global Citizenship Education: Philosophy, Theory and Pedagogy*, edited by M.A. Peters, A. Britton, and H. Blee. Rotterdam: Sense Publishers.

Jacoby, B., and Associates, eds. 2009. *Civic Engagement in Higher Education: Concepts and Practices*. San Francisco: Jossey-Bass.

Musil, C.M. 2009. "Educating Students for Personal and Social Responsibility: The Civic Learning Spiral." In *Civic Engagement in Higher Education: Concepts and Practices*, edited by Jacoby and Associates. San Francisco: Jossey-Bass.

North–South Centre of the Council of Europe. 2008. *Global Education Guidelines: Concepts and Methodologies on Global Education for Educators and Policy Makers*. Lisbon: NSCCE.

OECD/Asia Society. 2018. *Educating for Global Competence in a Rapidly Changing World*. Paris: OECD. http://doi.org/10.1787/9789264289024-en

Osler, A., and H. Starkey. 2006. "Education for Democratic Citizenship: A Review of Research, Policy and Practice 1995–2005." *Research Papers in Education* 24: 433–66. https://doi.org/10.1080/02671520600942438

Parsons, J. 2012. "Conversational Pedagogies and the Gift of Diversity." *Encounter: Education for Meaning and Social Justice* 25, no. 4: 41–4.

Pashby, K. 2012. "Questions for Global Citizenship Education in the Context of the 'New Imperialism': For Whom, by Whom." In *Postcolonial Perspectives on Global Citizenship Education*, edited by V.O. Andreotti and L.M.T.M. De Souza. New York: Routledge.

Peters, M.A., A. Britton, and H. Blee. 2008. "Introduction: Many Faces of Global Civil Society: Possible Futures for Global Citizenship." In *Global Citizenship Education: Philosophy, Theory and Pedagogy*, edited by M.A. Peters, A. Britton, and H. Blee. Rotterdam: Sense Publishers.

Pike, G. 2008. "Reconstructing the Legend: Educating for Global Citizenship." In *Educating for Human Rights and Global Citizenship*, edited by A. Abdi and L. Shultz. Albany, NY: SUNY Press.

Preece, J. 2008. "A Social Justice Approach to Education for Active Citizenship: An International Perspective." In *Global Citizenship Education: Philosophy, Theory and Pedagogy*, edited by M.A. Peters, A. Britton, and H. Blee. Rotterdam: Sense Publishers.

Richardson, G. 2008. "Conflicting Imaginaries: Global Citizenship Education in Canada as a Site of Contestation." In *Global Citizenship Education: Philosophy, Theory and Pedagogy*, edited by M.A. Peters, A. Britton, and H. Blee. Rotterdam: Sense Publishers.

Schattle, H. 2008."Education for Global Citizenship: Illustrations of Ideological Pluralism and Adaptation." *Journal of Political Ideologies* 13, no. 1: 73–94. https://doi.org/10.1080/13569310701822263

Schertz, M. 2006. "Empathic Pedagogy: Community of Inquiry and the Development of Empathy." *Analytic Teaching* 26, no. 1: 8–14.

Shulman, L.S. 2005. "Signature Pedagogies in the Professions." *Daedalus* 134, no. 3: 52–9. https://doi.org/10.1162/0011526054622015

Shultz, L. 2007. "Educating for Global Citizenship: Conflicting Agendas and Understandings." *Alberta Journal of Educational Research* 53, no. 3: 248–58.

Shultz, L., and S. Jorgenson. 2012. "Global Citizenship Education in Post-Secondary Institutions: What Is Protected and What Is Hidden under the Umbrella of GCE?" *Journal of Global Citizenship and Equity Education* 2, no. 1: 1–22.

Sloam, J. 2011. "A Pedagogy of Engagement in Higher Education." Paper presented to the American Political Science Association 2011 Annual Meeting, 1–4 September.

Smith, K.A., S.D. Sheppard, D.W. Johnson, and R.T. Johnson. 2005. "Pedagogies of Engagement: Classroom-Based Practices." *Journal of Engineering Education* 94, no. 1: 87–101. https://doi.org/10.1002/j.2168-9830.2005.tb00831.x

Stearns, P.N. 2009. *Educating Global Citizens in Colleges and Universities: Challenges and Opportunities.* New York: Routledge.

Subedi, B. 2013. "Decolonizing the Curriculum for Global Perspectives." *Educational Theory* 63, no. 6: 621–38. https://doi.org/10.1111/edth.12045

Tiessen, R., and R. Huish, eds. 2014. *Globetrotting or Global Citizenship? Perils and Potential of International Experiential Learning.* Toronto: University of Toronto Press.

UNESCO. 2015. *Global Citizenship Education: Topics and Learning Objectives.* Paris: UNESCO.

United Nations. n.d. "Global Citizenship Education." Academic Impact Initiative. Accessed 14 April 2020. https://academicimpact.un.org/content/global-citizenship-education

2 Bridging the Local and the Global: The Role of Service Learning in Post-Secondary Global Citizenship Education

SARAH ELIZA STANLICK

Global citizenship is an interdisciplinary topic consisting of intertwining theories and practices. It is individual and collective, practiced globally and locally, and can consist of both thoughts and actions. Further, the essence of global citizenship education is to develop a critical lens in our post-secondary students that challenge power structures, confound norms, and reimagine one's role as it relates to the larger world. Thus, the complexity of global citizenship education presents a significant challenge – and opportunity – to educators who are not only developing the content knowledge for their students, but also developing aspects of character, critical inquiry, and civic agency. As a working definition of global citizenship education (GCE), for the purposes of this chapter, I have adapted the framework of Oxfam's global citizenship curriculum to name GCE as a transformative education framework that emphasizes the cultivation of learners to be aware of the wider world and their role and agency in the world, to respect and value diversity, to commit to social justice, to participate in local and global efforts, to work towards equitable and sustainable peace, and to be responsible for their own actions (Stanlick 2015; Oxfam 1997, 2006). In light of its complicated nature, educators must take care to plan and implement learning experiences that nurture and expand student growth into meaningful action towards responsible global citizenship. One curricular device that is particularly effective in providing students such global perspective and experiences is service learning. Service learning is described by the Canadian Alliance for Community Service-Learning (CACSL) as a network of an educational approach that integrates service in the community with intentional learning activities. Within effective CACSL efforts, members of both educational institutions and community organizations work together towards outcomes that are mutually beneficial (Hayes 2006). The CACSL is a national network that is credited with being a force in the institutionalization of service learning in Canada

(Aujila and Hamm 2018). In the global citizenship curriculum, service learning can serve as a high-impact, experiential mechanism for learners to make sense of their place in the global landscape. Service learning is an outcropping of the theoretical and pedagogical construct of experiential learning and can be an effective mediator of transformative change (Kiely 2005; Kolb, Boyatzis, and Mainemelis 2000; Kolb 1984). Service learning can be categorized as an experiential learning practice with civic and community engagement at the fore (Jacoby 2014; Bringle and Hatcher 1996). While service learning is often simply viewed as the incorporation of service into a planned curriculum, a more structured framework for service learning can be found in the work of Bringle, Clayton, and Hatcher (2013). Adapting from their more robust definition (see page 222), service learning is:

> Service-learning, as a component of civic engagement, can be defined as a course or competency-based, credit-bearing educational experience in which students:
>
> (a) participate in mutually identified service activities that benefit the community, and
> (b) reflect on the service activity in such a way as to gain further understanding of course content, a broader appreciation of the discipline, and an enhanced sense of personal values and civic responsibility.

Service learning is an emerging addition to global citizenship education (GCE) and will continue to play a valuable role in GCE curriculum as it becomes more formalized in post-secondary settings. By surveying the literature on service learning, transformative learning, and global citizenship, educators can better understand the relationship between service learning and global citizenship education, its roots, applications, and effect on learner development. From the theoretical underpinnings of service learning and global citizenship to empirical research this chapter discusses the existing research that has informed our understanding of service learning's efficacy in developing traits of global citizenship.

Theoretical Framework: Transformative Learning, Global Citizenship, and Service Learning

Transformative Learning

Before delving into the specific implementations and outcomes of service learning and global citizenship, educators must first understand the unique aims and goals of global citizenship education and what is expected in terms of growth and development for students. Transformative learning theory for adult learners is one way to understand how global citizenship and service learning fit together in a pedagogical paradigm. Global citizenship education is categorized by and large as a transformative experience in which students are not only learning content knowledge and mechanisms of citizenship but are also expected to develop attributes and values that shift their meaning perspective in relation to the larger world towards more humility, critical thinking, cross-cultural understanding, and orientation towards social justice (de Andreotti 2014; Sperandio, Grudzinski-Hall, and Stewart-Gambino 2010; Peters, Britton, and Blee 2008). Oxfam (1997, 2006) offers a curriculum that emphasizes certain knowledge, skills, and attitudes that fall into the following categories: agency, social justice and equity, diversity, sustainable development, and peace and conflict. In short, global citizenship education not only develops a professional identity but also a different way of being for the learner.

Early definitions of transformative learning suggest that it is a learning process by which, through critical self-reflection and discourse, a learner can shift their identity, beliefs, and actions (Mezirow 1981). Through the cognitive rational approach of transformative learning (Mezirow 1997; Taylor, 2007; Cranton 1994, 2006), learners undergo a process of disorientation, critical reflections on their assumptions, dialogue, and action on new meaning perspectives created through the transformative process. Mezirow (1991) developed a framework to understand more deeply the roles of transformative learning in individual learner development. Through Mezirow's cognitive rational approach (CRA), learners are faced with disorienting dilemmas that force them to re-evaluate previously held beliefs and assumptions. The process of the experiential and course-related events that occur fall into the category of "disruptive" or "disorienting" events necessary for the transformation to occur (Mezirow 1991; Cranton 1994, 2006). Such events introduce experiences and information so intense or contrary to held beliefs that they shift the meaning perspective of the learner towards a different worldview. Figure 2.1 offers my graphical interpretation of Mezirow's (1991) process of critical reflection by which disorienting, high-impact experiences (e.g., service learning) lead to transformation of attitudes, beliefs, and actions.

Global Citizenship

Similar to learners' transformative learning processes, global citizenship is at its core an orientation of one's self in the globalizing world (Noddings 2005). A global citizen is someone who "can live and work

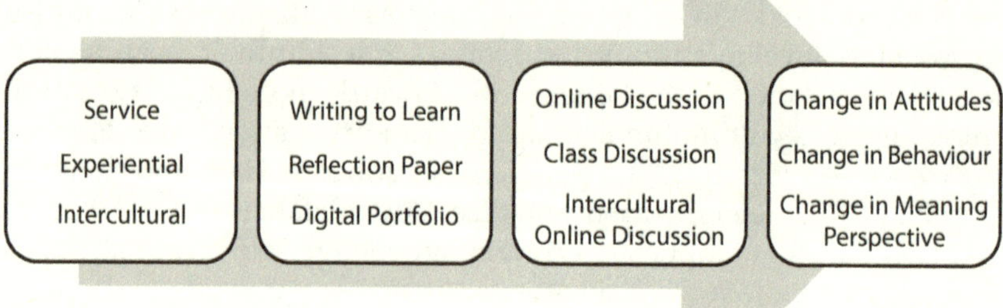

Figure 2.1. Learning process via global citizenship and service learning

effectively anywhere in the world, and a global way of life would both describe and support the functioning of global citizens" (3). The modern global citizen, as described by Riley (2006), is "reflective, informed, and involved."

The increasing numbers of students who have a global experience that ranges from more traditional study abroad to international internships indicate the growing number of global citizens. According to the 2018 Open Doors Report, study abroad is on a steady incline with 332,727 students having studies abroad in 2016–17, an increase of 2.3 per cent (IIE 2018). This is a result of a number of influences – more funding for international experiences, more options and diversity in experiences, and a realization of the benefits of study abroad for professional and personal development. The addition of global citizenship as a distinct goal within the UN's Sustainable Development Goals (SDGs), coupled with trends of global citizenship education adoption in higher education, and an increased emphasis on global citizenship education through the United Nations Academic Impact program, indicate momentum for more institutions to adopt such programs. Additionally, institutions must now focus on refining and maintaining curriculum that ensures ethical, reciprocal practices towards global citizenship education and student development. And, within that curriculum, there must be an intentional bridge from theory to practice, allowing students to interact in real world contexts (Hartman et al., 2013; Altbach and Knight 2007; Kiely 2004). For instance, the theoretical framework of Fair Trade Learning (FTL) can be applied to decision-making in everything from the decision of what program or experience to pursue to the assessment and evaluation of the learning done in those contexts. Hartman, Paris, and Blache-Cohen (2014) emphasize FTL in community-engaged international volunteerism, establishing best practices that prioritize community voice and local expertise, exemplify empowerment and transformative reciprocity, and maximize benefit and learning for all who are involved.

Along with thinking on study abroad programs, undergraduate curricula has incorporated texts, materials, reflections, and experiences to prepare students for active global citizenship in ways that are critical and value-driven (Mbugua 2010). Study abroad and service abroad trips are beginning to better understand the impact on local communities, the importance of developing critical perspective in students, and the lasting effects of those transformative experiences on participants and hosts alike (Stanlick and Hammond 2016; Hartman, Paris, and Blache-Cohen 2014).

Global citizenship education courses aim to be transformative through a curriculum that typically includes service learning, experiential learning, and traditional instructional experiences (Brigham 2011; Lewin 2009). Richardson (2008) asserts that the process of learning about social studies leads to "wider and more sophisticated understanding of self and community" (115). Gaudelli (2013) emphasizes a critical view of global citizenship education and cites the need for curriculum and experiences that bridge the local-global gap for student engagement. Such criticism highlights the need for connecting experiences that relate both to the learner's lived experience and the wider world, a reminder that global citizenship is as much a worldview and active practice at home as much as it is in travels abroad, and that not everyone has the same context for global citizenship or how it is practiced cross-culturally. While there has been an increased emphasis on researching study abroad experiences (Crabtree 2008), historically, the focus in international education was heavily weighted on experiences that took students outside of their home country. However, there was often a disconnect between the global and the local, which contributed to a misconception that international experiences were something to be done "out there." Students are increasingly participating in experiential learning opportunities within the confines of their coursework, and bringing a global perspective to their local work within the university.

Service Learning

Service learning is a highly popular curricular tool in higher education, as evidenced by the proliferation of institutionalized service-learning offices and experiences highlighted in the report *A Crucible Moment*. For instance, statistics from the American Association of Community Colleges cite that 60 per cent of community colleges offer service learning with another 30 per cent actively developing programs (National Task Force on Civic Learning and Democratic Engagement 2012). As part of GCE, service learning is experiencing a surge in valuation and development (National Task Force on Civic Learning and Democratic Engagement 2012; Bringle and Hatcher 2010). Institutions in the United States and Canada have implemented the practice across disciplines, learner types, and settings (Wade 2008; Jagla 2008; Bringle and Hatcher 1996). From elementary to post-secondary education to professional certifications, service learning is finding its place in curricula that emphasize not only content knowledge but also the development of individual learner character attributes and self-efficacy (Wade 2008; Jagla 2008). The purpose for such initiatives varies widely from Dewey's (1916) assertion that democracy is learned through good works to Bielefeldt et al. (2011) lauding the use of service learning as a tool for solidifying professional skills. For the purpose of global citizenship education, service learning is a viable and beneficial educational practice for learner transformation as related to GCE attributes and to emphasize civic participation.

Service learning promotes individual learner development through reflection and self-awareness, including building capacity for self-authorship and agency (Jones and Abes 2004). For undergraduates in a post-adolescent stage, establishing identity, purpose, and independence are all key motivators for learning and character development (Torres, Jones, and Renn 2009; Chickering 1964; Chickering and Reisser 1993). Thus, service learning meets the needs of a diverse set of learners, and each developmental experience is uniquely captured through reflection (Hatcher, Bringle, and Muthiah 2004).

As Gardner (2000) has written extensively, learners acquire knowledge and skills in vastly different ways, exhibiting multiple intelligences that can be harnessed by different tasks and pedagogies. Table 2.1 illustrates the ways in which service learning can leverage those different types of intelligence for learner growth. Service learning gives learners the agency, confidence, and engagement necessary to improve retention and recall of information while giving applicable skills for future endeavours, as well as the flexibility to fit their individual learning styles.

Table 2.1. Service-learning attributes for Gardner's multiple intelligences theory

Learning styles	Characteristics	Service-learning illustration
Logical/ mathematical	Logic, reasoning, abstraction, and critical thinking	Critical assessment of social injustice, global issues, and/or current affairs that have left need for service
Spatial	Spatial intelligence and ability to visualize in the mind	Planning and exercising of artistic or spatial
Linguistic	Verbal capabilities, reading, writing, storytelling, memorization	Constructing written pieces, exploring history and issues around service project; storytelling as a function of place
Bodily/ kinesthetic	Motor skills and "making"	Creating tangible objects as a service to a community; using mechanical skills to aid underserved who do not have the skills or finances to hire those skills
Musical	Auditory learning	Musical interventions for hospital patients in underserved areas; sharing of music between cultures and understanding societal importance
Interpersonal	Interactions with others	Working in teams towards a common goal; building relationships through service
Intrapersonal	Introspective	Reflecting on one's experience in the service; taking time to step back and think about one's own role in the world
Naturalistic	Relating information to one's surroundings	Appreciation for nature, geography, and landscapes based on where service takes place; connecting community planning and space to social issues
Existential	Spiritual or otherworldly elements; relationships to spiritual life	Religious call to service; speaks to some students' individual moral or religious traditions

Source: Gardner (2000).

High-Quality Service Learning

Service learning has been implemented in a variety of settings and levels of quality, and as a result, there has been debate over what makes a positive service-learning experience (Bringle, Hatcher, and Muthiah 2010; Eyler and Giles 1999). Dewey (1933) stated, "The belief that all genuine education comes about through experience does not mean that all experiences are genuinely or equally educative" (247). As such, when

Table 2.2. Attributes and practice of high-quality service learning

Attribute	In practice
Integrated learning	Seamless integration between service experience and curricular materials (e.g., readings)
Community service	Meaningful service experiences in a community, local or global
Collaborative development and management	Service partners, learners, and educators working together to negotiate and deepen the experience
Civic engagement	Emphasis on service and its connection to citizenship and civic life; a worldview not an isolated experience
Contemplation	Reflective activities designed to help learners process the experience and shift meaning perspective
Evaluation and disclosure	Survey and dialogue about the experience with all invested partners

Source: Smith et al. (2011).

planning a service-learning experience, educators must heed standards and best practices for planning and implementing service learning for maximum efficacy.

As a result of this debate, Smith et al. (2011) developed a model of high-quality service-learning experiences (HQSLEs) that addresses this challenge. HQSLEs are defined by six hallmarks: integrated learning, community service, collaborative development and management, civic engagement, contemplation, and evaluation and disclosure (Smith et al. 2011). If an HQSLE is designed and executed, students will be able to understand and apply curricular content, exhibit a commitment to social good, have increased motivation for good works/volunteerism, and help them to professionally develop (Furco and Root 2010; Levitt and Schriehans 2010; Terry and Panter 2010). Table 2.2 is adapted from the work of Smith et al. (2011) and outlines the critical components for an HQSLE with an explanation of what that looks like in practice.

Knowledge, Skills, and Attitudes of the Global Citizen

Many service-learning studies frame their analysis in cognitive outcomes such as content knowledge – for example, understanding of mathematics, public policy, social justice (Bradford 2005; Simons et al. 2010). For global citizenship education, however, the outcomes are in

Table 2.3. Knowledge, skills, and attitudes for global citizenship competency

Knowledge and understanding	Skills	Attitudes and values
Social justice and equity Diversity Globalization and interdependence Sustainable development Peace and conflict	Critical thinking Ability to argue effectively Ability to challenge injustice and inequalities Respect for people and things Co-operation and conflict resolution	Sense of identity and self-esteem Empathy Commitment to social justice and equity Value and respect for diversity Concern for the environment and commitment to sustainable development Belief that people can make a difference

Source: Oxfam (2006).

both the acquisition of knowledge but also the transformation of perspective and character (Althof and Berkowitz 2006; Noddings 2005). While a universally accepted definition of global citizenship does not exist, central tenets of global citizenship education such as empathy, ambiguity tolerance, value and respect for diversity, and an orientation towards social justice are all qualities that are emphasized in curricula (de Andreotti 2014; Brigham 2011; Sperandio, Grudzinski-Hall, and Stewart-Gambino 2010). Content knowledge for global citizenship learners includes history, citizenship, and civic principles education (Banks, 2007).

Oxfam (2006) created a curriculum that stressed attributes that can be categorized as knowledge, skills, and attitudes that quality global citizenship education should develop and nurture in learners. The Oxfam curriculum has been widely adopted in a variety of education settings, and its efficacy has been cited by global citizenship scholars. Scholars such as Merryfield (2008), Davies (1999), and Kirby and Crawford (2012) have all cited the Oxfam definition and have used it as the basis of their work. Table 2.3 outlines these categories and their attributes.

For this multifaceted, interdisciplinary topic, learning endeavours demand scaffolded experiences that interact with real-world situations and theoretical concepts. In addition to meeting academic objectives, service learning can also address the character education issues that global citizenship demands (Wade and Saxe 1996). Service learning can take place in both local and international contexts, with undergraduate students working in collaborations that lead to global civil society/ social action for global change (Annette 2002).

Post-secondary education is a unique time of growth where students are the most receptive to new ideas and are spending a majority of their attention on identity development (Perry 1999; Chickering 1964; Chickering and Reisser 1993). This young adulthood presents a time when students are separating from the lessons learned from authority figures (parents, teachers, etc.) and creating their own space and identity in the world. This relation to the global citizenship curriculum is significant, as the curricula prompts students to create an identity in Nussbaum's (1997) framework as a citizen of humanity. For undergraduates in a post-adolescent stage, establishing identity, agency, and meaning are all key motivators for learning and character development (Torres, Jones, and Renn 2009; Chickering 1964; Chickering and Reisser 1993).

Developing Global Citizenship Competencies through Service Learning

One of the most critical roles of service learning in undergraduate education is developing the tools and skills for civic engagement and active citizenship. Local, national, or global, citizenship education imparts upon students the skills necessary to participate fully in their community and understand the full responsibility of citizenship to keep a community thriving. Merryfield (2000) emphasized that "increasing diversity and inequity within the United States along with the globalization of the world's economic, political, technological, and environmental systems have forever changed the knowledge and skills young people need to become effective citizens" (429). These skills that are outlined by Merryfield are those that are not classroom-bound but part of a larger complex skill set needed to thrive in a globalized world and practiced in communities local and global.

Service learning is an educational endeavour that tackles a real-life problem in a students' community in order to remedy that situation (Snowman, McCowan, and Biehler 2009). The National Council for Social Studies (Wade 2007), which advocates service learning as an essential component to social studies curriculum, believes that service learning can enhance the ability for social studies teachers to engender the next generation of active and informed citizens. They go so far as to affirm that students who participate in service learning are more likely to be committed to improving society and working within the democratic process. In global citizenship education, the concept of citizenship is emphasized, but in this case as an effort that transcends borders. Citizenship education, nevertheless, is an important component of the content knowledge that is gained in the GCE classroom. It creates the opportunity for students to explore the rights and responsibilities that accompany global citizenship identity, while also naming and understanding the many complexities of the concept of citizenship.

One byproduct of global citizenship education is meaningful social change, using education as a way to create understanding and equality in society. Dewey (1916) asserts that democracy begins at home through good works to concretizing content knowledge gained. Active citizenship, a central value to global citizenship education, demands that learners take steps to affect change in their local or global community through sustained service. Such service, in an academic setting, takes place via the construct of service learning.

Developing Global Citizenship Attributes through Service Learning

Empathy and Intercultural Competence

Empathy is a well-established factor in global citizenship education, as it covers the development of intercultural understanding and the ability to internalize the need to address inequality. From understanding between cultures and individuals to conflict and coexistence studies, global citizenship curriculum aims to bring about empathetic thinking of students through experiences that create connections and increase the acceptance of others.

Empathy can be better developed in an experiential context when learners are dealing with real people and can connect textbook lessons to weighty, real-world situations (Moon 2013). Service learning is an effective curricular tool to develop empathy, as learners work with communities to understand historical, social, and structural issues that have influenced the development of a community (Bringle, Hatcher, and Muthia 2010; Battistoni, Longo, and Jayanandhan 2009). Furthermore, empathy can be built when students engage in service learning and reflection (Terry and Panter 2011); they experience a virtual global citizenship classroom that uses intercultural exchanges online; and they experience an increase in empathy, intercultural teamwork, acceptance, and knowledge of GCE (Patterson, Carrillo, and Salinas 2012). Service learning has also been shown to significantly increase the expression of empathy in reflective writing (Wilson 2007).

The Association of American Colleges and Universities (AACU) – which is comprised of both American and Canadian institutions – established a framework for learning endeavours that are intense, experiential, and, in most cases, transformative. These practices are denoted as high-impact practices (HIPs) and include service learning as an example of an experience that is transformative via the intensity, curriculum, and real-world repercussions (Brownell and Swaner 2010). As cited previously, this stage of post-secondary education is unique for learner development and maximum learner impact (Chickering 1964; Chickering and Reisser 1993; Kegan 1994). As such, high impact curricular tools such as service learning can prove an intense and transformative experience that changes the meaning perspective of the undergraduate learner (Kuh 2008).

Closely linked to empathy, intercultural understanding is another aspect of global citizenship education that is developed in service-learning environments. Naidoo (2008) finds service learning is an effective tool of internationalization by both encouraging cooperation between different communities and providing students enriching cross-cultural experiences. Intercultural communication and the ability to reflect on interactions that take place in service-learning environments increase intercultural understanding in undergraduate learners (Austin and Anderson 2008). Finally, the construct of international service learning also provides students with opportunities to interact in environments vastly different from their own, developing skills of intercultural understanding, open-mindedness, and tolerance for ambiguity (Clark et al. 2013; Kassam et al. 2013).

Ambiguity Tolerance, Agency, and Resilience

As Nodding's (2005) definition affirms, global citizens are individuals who are adaptable and able to thrive across social, cultural, and political contexts. When we think about attributes or measurements that might capture this type of growth in students, ambiguity tolerance emerges as a clear fit. Ambiguity tolerance is defined as the ability for individuals to "accept a state of affairs capable of alternate interpretations, or of alternate outcomes: e.g., feeling comfortable (or at least not feeling uncomfortable) when faced by a complex social issue in which opposed principles are intermingled" (English and English 1958, 24).

Agency and self-confidence through ambiguity tolerance are clear learner attributes to be developed in global citizenship education. According to Richardson (2008), self-efficacy is the "technology" that aids and fosters democracy and citizenship in individuals, noting that when that confidence and comfort with a changing world is present, individuals can be more effective citizens. She posits that when individuals are in control of their citizenship education and exercise, democratic thought and application, they can be fully realized.

The idea of individual responsibility and the active citizen is an essential tenet of global citizenship education, promoting engagement with the world at-large in a way that is dynamic and purposeful (Hollister, Mead, and Wilson 2006). Such a citizen is an outcropping of liberal individualism, which emphasizes the individual's role in civic life (Annette 2009). Encouraging a personal and social responsibility viewpoint empowers students to see their role as a player on the world stage and that they can contribute in a meaningful way to the world and community around them. Individual self-efficacy as it relates to social justice and citizenship education can also be tied back to transformational learning as it is an individual process that is shaped, connected, and understood through self-reflection and meaning perspective shift (Davies 2006).

Noddings (2005) states that global citizens are those who can be dropped in any place in the world and adapt to the situation as a result of a global citizenship self-identity and the attributes that accompany that identity. Thus, such an individual would have a high tolerance for ambiguity and the ability to adapt and thrive in new environments. Global citizens are expected to be adaptable and open to new experiences that come as a result of working in global capacities (Doerr 2013). Experiential and service learning develops ambiguity tolerance as it prepares students for real-world situations where rules and expectations are not always clearly defined (Huber 2003).

Social Justice Orientation

Social justice orientation has also been highlighted as an emphasis for global citizenship education, as the assumption is that students will think critically about injustice and be compelled to act based on principles (Sleeter 2013; Oxfam 1997, 2006). Hughes et al. (2012) found that service learning in undergraduate settings was an effective strategy for raising awareness of social justice issues such as income inequality and poverty. They emphasize that such education is a first step towards creating better understanding of such social justice issues in hopes of creating long-term advocates and policymakers who would address such social problems. In teacher education settings, studies have found that learners have developed identities as educators through "deconstructing lifelong attitudes" to better confront injustices and promote socially just practices in the classroom (Baldwin, Buchanan, and Rudisill 2007).

Kuh, O'Donnell, and Reed (2013) found that high-impact experiences such as service learning can reach a large, diverse population and maximize learning success for learners who are traditionally underserved (e.g., first-generation college students, underrepresented groups in higher education). High-impact experiences for underserved students such as service learning can develop skills and open opportunities previously unavailable. A second byproduct of this type of educational experience is orienting students from underserved populations to see inequities and their agency for creating solutions to such social and global problems.

Longitudinal studies have shown that international service-learning experiences with a social justice focus have affected meaningful perspective shift and commitment to ongoing social justice aims in undergraduates (Kiely 2004). Battistoni, Longo, and Jayanandhan (2009) expand upon the idea of service as a developer of national civic ideals and affirm that acting globally in one's community through service learning can promote global citizenship in undergraduates. Kenny (2002) summarizes case studies from a wide range of higher education settings and concludes that service-learning is a type of "outreach scholarship" that strengthens civil society and promotes ideals of social justice in the wider community.

Reflection and Service Learning: A Critical Component

Reflection serves many roles in the service-learning context – as mediator of experience, processor of disorienting events, and as an assessable record of student development and learning. Daudelin (1997) defines reflection as "a process of stepping back from an experience to ponder, carefully and persistently, its meaning to the self through the development of inferences" (36). Reflection is the most popular assessment tool for measuring individual growth and learning in service learning as well as for the success of such programing (Blumenfeld 2010; Cord and Clements 2010).

In Mezirow's (1991) model of the cognitive rational approach for transformative learning, critical reflection is an essential mediator for individual transformative learning. Critical reflection, to differentiate, is defined by Mezirow (1990) as "critique of the presuppositions on which our beliefs have been built" (1). Beyond the process of stepping back, the learner challenges assumptions held and, as such, experience meaningful perspective change in a way that reorients their worldview and sense of self in that world. King and Kitchener (1994) state that critical reflection is "the process an individual evokes to monitor the epistemic nature of problems and the truth value of alternative solutions" (12). For global citizens, the ability to challenge norms, think critically, and construct solutions to global problems is essential, and the critical reflection is the process by which they connect those experiences and develop that advocacy identity.

Reflection also serves as an effective qualitative assessment of a service-learning program. Student reflection can reveal what transformative learning took place, capture meaning perspective shifts, and, if done frequently and through the experience, it can help a student process and negotiate the experience for maximum satisfaction and learning. Lear and Abbott (2009) affirm the importance of aligning expectations in learners from the first meeting through the end of the service, while continually taking opportunities to align expectations through reflection. They found that guided reflection allowed learners to air negative impressions and simple misunderstandings, which then aided improvements in programing and curricular objectives for learner satisfaction and future iterations of the program.

Assessing Service-Learning Outcomes

Service learning in the realm of global citizenship education is a complex, experiential opportunity that yields a variety of student outputs and opportunities for evaluation and assessment. They also should be programs that are empowering and reciprocal for all stakeholders. This means that there are many actors, inputs, and variables that can affect the measurement of student learning and what impacts that development. The complexity of these programs can present a quandary to educators and educational researchers as they work in settings that have real-world consequences and complications, while trying to sort out which variables are affecting change in the learners.

From the viewpoint of an administrator, there are two subjects for assessment that exist in this scenario: the success of the program and its impact on the community and individual learner growth. To assess growth, tasks that exhibit Wiggins, Wiggins, and McTighe's (2005) six facets of understanding would be designed. These tasks would involve the students explaining, interpreting, applying, gaining perspective, empathizing, and gaining self-knowledge through their work and reflection. Accounting for the importance of learner-centred assessment, reflective assignments are used to understand the learner's processing of the experience and growth (Webber 2012). Reflection is the most common assessment for service learning (Eyler and Giles 1999; Eyler 2002).

Either through written papers, diaries, blogs, or portfolios, most service-learning projects have a component requiring students to exhibit their growth and change through individual reflection. Additionally, students can be surveyed at the beginning and end of semesters using psychometric measures to get quantifiable data on the service-learning impact. For programatic assessment (i.e., presentation to the Course and Curriculum Committee), surveying would be applied for insight into the experience of the educators and community change (Minkler and Wallerstein 2003). This information can be triangulated with student reflection and assessment information, providing a holistic view of the service-learning program's impact, opportunities for improvement, and strengths to be retained for the future.

Examples for Educators: Service Learning and Global Citizenship

There are many ways in which service learning is implemented in the global citizenship classroom. The versatility of service learning to engage different learner types, skill sets, and competency levels is yet another positive attribute of the pedagogy. Students arrive in the classroom with vastly different prior knowledge, previous experiences, learning styles, and attitudes that affect the way in which they will receive global citizenship ideals. While some settings for global citizenship education include students who have self-selected into the program, other institutions are developing global citizenship as a core factor in their general curriculum. A few of the more formalized global citizenship projects incorporating service learning are illustrated here:

- Through the UN volunteers program, an online platform that matches individuals around the world with non-profits in need of specialized skills, individual students or whole classrooms can become connected with an international non-profit in need of administrative and project assistance. By volunteering their own skill set, students can assist these groups and communities in need without leaving the classroom. Students can bring an invaluable perspective on the organization they are assisting and the challenges faced by people in their area of service, thus broadening the worldview of the participating students. Any individual can volunteer through the portal (https://www.unv.org/), and educators can use the platform as a connector to projects that would be appropriate in skill, training, and level for students in a service-learning program.

- Photovoice (https://photovoice.org/) projects have been another popular service endeavour that connects global-local themes and photography (Joubert 2012; Baldwin and Chandler 2010). The projects often put cameras in the hands of learners and ask them to document their experience in their community or abroad. Joubert (2012) found that such experiences engendered self-efficacy in young learners, gave them voice in a way that other assignments did not, and gave them the confidence to act as agents of change in their communities. Baldwin and Chandler (2010) used the Photovoice framework to encourage critical reflection on environmental issues and citizenship, promoting an advocacy orientation in learners. One must be also cognizant of ethical photography standards and work with students prior to their service-learning experience to understand the potential for exploitation or invasion of privacy (Gharib 2017).
- "Project Ulysses" is an integrated service-learning program that emphasizes global leadership skills development (Pless, Maak, and Stahl 2011). Teams of learners are sent to developing nations, working in collaboration with communities, NGOs, and development organizations on much-needed projects for the communities. Surveys of project participants have found lasting shifts in global citizenship attributes and meaning perspectives, including empathy, responsibility, self-efficacy, and social justice orientation.

At Lehigh University, which has a specialized global citizenship certificate program, students engage in service learning throughout their four years. As described in Gisolo and Stanlick (2012), students undertake organized service learning through work with a local refugee resettlement organization. Students have curricular preparation through readings and written assignments to develop understanding of the political and structural issues that cause resettlement. They then work with the local organization to support educational opportunity and cross-cultural, collaborative learning to help aid the transition of refugees in the local community, welcome new neighbours, and increase understanding of larger world issues while building empathy and civic agency. Throughout the experience, students reflect and draw connections between their service and the materials they have surveyed as part of the course.

Conclusion

For student learning, global citizenship education transcends the boundary of content knowledge into the area of character development. Students not only learn about the political, social, and economic interconnectedness of the world but also develop a sense of their individual relationship to the world. Further, global citizenship education that is transformative and empowering – engagement that happens in collaboration with stakeholders outside the boundaries of the university – has the capacity to change systems of oppression or injustice.

With this challenge, educators must find ways to engage students not only in the material they read, but challenge them to examine their relationship and involvement in the world at large. Through service learning, students are uniquely poised to make change alongside these essential partners in their communities and practice the "competencies" of global citizenship that have been emphasized in the literature and by established global citizenship education practitioners. Finally, just as much as GCE has the opportunity to change individuals, it has the potential to change systems. If the curriculum and experiential components of global citizenship can open eyes to systems of injustice, or one's own critical or complacent role in those systems, the impossible task of transforming the world suddenly becomes possible.

REFERENCES

Altbach, P.G., and J. Knight. 2007. "The Internationalization of Higher Education: Motivations and Realities." *Journal of Studies in International Education* 11, nos. 3–4: 290–305. https://doi.org/10.1177/1028315307303542

Althof, W., and M.W. Berkowitz. 2006. "Moral Education and Character Education: Their Relationship and Roles in Citizenship Education." *Journal of Moral Education* 35, no. 4: 495–518. https://doi.org/10.1080/03057240601012204

Annette, J. 2002. "Service-Learning in an International Context: Frontiers." *The Interdisciplinary Journal of Study Abroad* 8, no. 1: 83–93.

– 2009. "Active Learning for Active Citizenship: Democratic Citizenship and Lifelong Learning." *Education, Citizenship and Social Justice* 4, no. 2: 149–60. https://doi.org/10.1177/1746197909103934

Aujla, W., and Z. Hamm. 2018. "Establishing the Roots of Community Service-Learning in Canada: Advocating for a Community First Approach." *Engaged Scholar Journal: Community-Engaged Research, Teaching, and Learning* 4, no. 1: 19–37.

Austin, R., and J. Anderson. 2008. "Building Bridges Online: Issues of Pedagogy and Learning Outcomes in Intercultural Education through Citizenship." *International Journal of Information and Communication Technology Education (IJICTE)* 4, no. 1: 86–94.

Baldwin, S.C., A.M. Buchanan, and M.E. Rudisill. 2007. "What Teacher Candidates Learned about Diversity, Social Justice, and Themselves from Service-Learning Experiences." *Journal of Teacher Education* 58, no. 4: 315–27. https://doi.org/10.1177/0022487107305259

Baldwin, S.C., and L. Chandler. 2010. "'At the Water's Edge': Community Voices on Climate Change." *Local Environment* 15, no. 7: 637–49. https://doi.org/10.1080/13549839.2010.498810

Banks, J.A. 2007. *Diversity and Citizenship Education: Global Perspectives*. San Francisco: Jossey-Bass.

Battistoni, R.M., N.V. Longo, and S. Jayanandhan. 2009. "Acting Locally in a Flat World: Global Citizenship and the Democratic Practice of Service-Learning." *Journal of Higher Education Outreach and Engagement* 13, no. 2: 89–108.

Bielefeldt, A.R. 2011. "Incorporating a Sustainability Module into First-Year Courses for Civil and Environmental Engineering Students." *Journal of Professional Issues in Engineering Education and Practice* 137, no. 2: 78–85.

Blumenfeld, E.R. 2010. "Reflections on Student Journals and Teaching about Inequality." *Journal of Poetry Therapy* 23, no. 2: 101–6.

Bradford, M. 2005. "Motivating Students through Project-Based Service-Learning." *Technological Horizons in Education* 32, no. 6: 29–30.

Brigham, M. 2011."Creating a Global Citizen and Assessing Outcomes." *Journal of Global Citizenship and Equity Education* 1, no. 1: 15–43.

Bringle, R.G., and J.A. Hatcher. 1996. "Implementing Service-Learning in Higher Education." *The Journal of Higher Education* 67, no. 2: 221–39.

Bringle, R.G., J.A. Hatcher, and P.H. Clayton, eds. 2013. *Research on Service-Learning: Conceptual Frameworks and Assessments*. Sterling, VA: Stylus Publishing.

Bringle, R.G., J.A. Hatcher, and R.N. Muthiah. 2010. "The Role of Service-Learning on the Retention of First-Year Students to Second Year." *Michigan Journal of Community Service-Learning* 16, no. 2: 38–49.

Brownell, J.E., and L.E. Swaner. 2010. *Five High-Impact Practices: Research on Learning Outcomes, Completion and Quality*. Washington, DC: Association of American Colleges and Universities.

Chickering, A.W. 1964. "Dimensions of Independence." *The Journal of Experimental Education* 32, no. 3: 313–16.

Chickering, A.W., and L. Reisser. 1993. *Education and Identity*. San Francisco: Jossey-Bass.

Clark, C., C. Faircloth, R. Lasher, and M.K. McDonald. 2013. "Alternative Spring Break Jamaica! Service-Learning and Civic Engagement in a Developing Country." *Global Partners in Education Journal* 3, no. 1: 49.

Clayton, P.H., R.G. Bringle, and J.A. Hatcher, eds. 2013. *Research on Service-Learning: Conceptual Frameworks and Assessments*. Sterling, VA: Stylus Publishing.

Cord, B., and M. Clements. 2010. "Reward through Collective Reflection: An Autoethnography." *E-Journal of Business Education & Scholarship of Teaching* 4, no. 1: 11–18.

Crabtree, R.D. 2008. "Theoretical Foundations for International Service-Learning." *Michigan Journal of Community Service-Learning* 15, no. 1: 18–36.

Cranton, P. 1994. "Self-Directed and Transformative Instructional Development." *The Journal of Higher Education* 65, no. 6: 726–44.

– 2006. "Fostering Authentic Relationships in the Transformative Classroom." *New Directions for Adult and Continuing Education* 109: 5–13.

Daudelin, M.W. 1997. "Learning from Experience through Reflection." *Organizational Dynamics* 24, no. 3: 36–48. https://doi.org/10.1016/s0090-2616(96)90004-2

Davies, L. 2003. *Education and Conflict: Complexity and Chaos*. London: Routledge.

– 2006. "Global Citizenship: Abstraction or Framework for Action?" *Educational Review* 58, no. 1: 5–25. https://doi.org/10.1080/00131910500352523

de Andreotti, V.O. 2014. "Soft versus Critical Global Citizenship Education. In *Development Education in Policy and Practice*, edited by S. McCloskey. London: Palgrave Macmillan.

Dewey, J. 1916. *Democracy and Education*. New York: Macmillan.

– 1933. *How We Think: A Restatement of the Relation of Reflective Thinking to the Educational Process*. Lexington, MA: Heath.

Doerr, N.M. 2013. "Do 'Global Citizens' Need the Parochial Cultural Other? Discourse of Immersion in Study Abroad and Learning-by-Doing." *Compare: A Journal of Comparative and International Education* 43, no. 2: 224–43. https://doi.org/10.1080/03057925.2012.701852

English, H.B., and A.C. English. 1958. *A Comprehensive Dictionary of Psychological and Psychoanalytical Terms: A Guide to Usage*. Washington, DC: APA.

Eyler, J. 2002. "Reflection: Linking Service and Learning – Linking Students and Communities." *Journal of Social Issues* 58, no. 3: 517–34. https://doi.org/10.1111/1540-4560.00274

Eyler, J., and D.E. Giles Jr. 1999. *Where's the Learning in Service-Learning? Jossey-Bass Higher and Adult Education Series*. San Francisco: Jossey-Bass.

Furco, A., and S. Root. 2010. "Research Demonstrates the Value of Service llearning." *Phi Delta Kappan* 91, no. 5: 16–20. https://doi.org/10.1177/003172171009100504

Gardner, H.E. 2000. *Intelligence Reframed: Multiple Intelligences for the 21st Century*. London: Hachette UK.

Gaudelli, W. 2013. "Critically Theorizing the Global." *Theory & Research in Social Education* 41, no. 4: 552–65.

Gharib, M. 2017. "Volunteering Abroad? Read This Before You Post That Selfie." *NPR News*. 26 November. https://www.npr.org/sections/goatsandsoda/2017/11/26/565694874/volunteering-abroad-read-this-before-you-post-that-selfie

Gisolo, G., and S.E. Stanlick. 2012. "Promoting Global Citizenship outside the Classroom: Undergraduate-Refugee Service-Learning at Lehigh University." *Journal of Global Citizenship & Equity Education* 2, no. 2: 98–122.

Hartman, E., R. Kiely, J. Friedrichs, and C. Boettcher. 2013. *Building a Better World: The Pedagogy and Practice of Global Service-Learning*. Sterling, VA: Stylus.

Hartman, E., C.M. Paris, and B. Blache-Cohen. 2014. "Fair Trade Learning: Ethical Standards for Community-Engaged International Volunteer Tourism. *Tourism and Hospitality Research* 14, no. 1–2: 108–16. https://doi.org/10.1177/1467358414529443

Hatcher, J.A., R.G. Bringle, and R. Muthiah. 2004. "Designing Effective Reflection: What Matters to Service-Learning." *Michigan Journal of Community Service-Learning* 11, no. 1: 38–46.

Hayes, E. 2006. *Community Service-Learning in Canada: A Scan of the Field*. Ottawa: Canadian Association for Service-Learning.

Hollister, R.M., M. Mead, and N. Wilson. 2006. "Infusing Active Citizenship throughout a Research University: The Tisch College of Citizenship and Public Service at Tufts University." *Metropolitan Universities Journal* 17, no. 3: 38–54.

Huber, N. 2003. "An Experiential Leadership Approach for Teaching Tolerance for Ambiguity." *Journal of Education for Business* 79, no. 1: 52–5. https://doi.org/10.1080/08832320309599088

Hughes, C., R. Steinhorn, B. Davis, S. Beckrest, E. Boyd, and K. Cashen. 2012. "University-Based Service-Learning: Relating Mentoring Experiences to Issues of Poverty." *Journal of College Student Development* 53, no. 6: 767–82. https://doi.org/10.1353/csd.2012.0076

Institute of International Education (IIE). 2018. *Open Doors Report 2018*. New York: IIE. https://www.iie.org/Research-and-Insights/Publications/Open-Doors-2018

Jacoby, B. 2014. *Service-Learning Essentials: Questions, Answers, and Lessons Learned*. New York: John Wiley & Sons.

Jagla, V. 2008. "Service-Learning Prepares Teachers to Meet the Needs of Diverse Learners." *International Journal of Learning* 15, no. 6: 1–7. https://doi.org/10.18848/1447-9494/cgp/v15i06/45830

Jones, S.R., and E.S. Abes. 2004. "Enduring Influences of Service-Learning on College Students' Identity Development." *Journal of College Student Development* 45, no. 2: 149–66.

Joubert, I. 2012. "Children as Photographers: Life Experiences and the Right to Be Listened to." *South African Journal of Education* 32, no. 4: 449–64. https://doi.org/10.15700/saje.v32n4a677

Kassam, R., A. Estrada, Y. Huang, B. Bhander, and J. B. Collins. 2013. "Addressing Cultural Competency in Pharmacy Education through International Service-Learning and Community Engagement." *Pharmacy* 1, no. 1: 16–33. https://doi.org/10.3390/pharmacy1010016

Kegan, R. 1994. *In Over Our Heads: The Mental Demands of Modern Life*. Cambridge, MA: Harvard University Press.

Kenny, M., ed. 2002. *Learning to Serve: Promoting Civil Society through Service-Learning*. Vol. 7. New York: Springer.

Kiely, R. 2004. "A Chameleon with a Complex: Searching for Transformation in International Service-Learning." *Michigan Journal of Community Service-Learning* 10, no. 2: 5–20.

– 2005. "A Transformative Learning Model for Service-Learning: A Longitudinal Case Study." *Michigan Journal of Community Service-Learning* 12, no. 1: 5–22.

King, P.M., and K.S. Kitchener. 1994. *Developing Reflective Judgment*. San Francisco: Jossey-Bass.

Kirby, M.M., and E.O. Crawford. 2012. "The Preparation of Globally Competent Teachers: A Comparison of American and Australian Education Policies and Perspectives." *Global Partners in Education Journal* 2, no. 1: 12–24.

Kolb, D.A. 1984. *Experiential Learning: Experience as the Source of Learning and Development*. Upper Saddle River, NJ: Prentice-Hall.

Kolb, D.A., R.E. Boyatzis, and C. Mainemelis. 2000. "Experiential Learning Theory: Previous Research and New Directions." In *Perspectives on Cognitive, Learning, and Thinking Styles*, edited by R.J. Sternberg and L.F. Zhang. Mahwah, NJ: Lawrence Erlbaum Associates.

Kuh, G.D. 2008. *High Impact Educational Practices: What They Are, Who Has Access to Them, and Why They Matter*. Washington, DC: Association of American Colleges and Universities.

Kuh, G.D., K. O'Donnell, and S. Reed. 2013. *Ensuring Quality and Taking High-Impact Practices to Scale*. Washington, DC: Association of American Colleges and Universities.

Lear, D., and A. Abbott. 2009. "Aligning Expectations for Mutually Beneficial Community Service-Learning: The Case of Spanish Language Proficiency, Cultural Knowledge, and Professional Skills." *Hispania* 92: 312–23.

Levitt, C., and C. Schriehans. 2010. "Adding a Community University Educational Summit (CUES) to Enhance Service-Learning in Management

Education." *Journal of Instructional Pedagogies* 3. https://eric.ed.gov/?q=reflection&ff1=locCalifornia&pg=7&id=EJ1097116

Lewin, R. 2009. *The Handbook of Practice and Research in Study Abroad: Higher Education and the Quest for Global Citizenship*. London: Routledge.

Mbugua, T. 2020. "Fostering Culturally Relevant/Responsive Pedagogy and Global Awareness through the Integration of International Service-Learning in Courses." *Journal of Pedagogy* 1, no. 2: 87–98. https://doi.org/10.2478/v10159-010-0011-8

Merryfield, M.M. 2000. "Why Aren't Teachers Being Prepared to Teach for Diversity, Equity, and Global Interconnectedness? A Study of Lived Experiences in the Making of Multicultural and Global Educators." *Teaching and Teacher Education* 16, no. 4: 429–43. https://doi.org/10.1016/s0742-051x(00)00004-4

– 2008. "Scaffolding Social Studies for Global Awareness." *Social Education* 72, no. 7: 363–6.

Mezirow, J. 1990. "How Critical Reflection Triggers Transformative Learning." *Fostering Critical Reflection in Adulthood* 1, no. 20: 1–6. https://doi.org/10.4324/9781351033305-1

– 1991. *Transformative Dimensions of Adult Learning*. San Francisco: Jossey-Bass.

– 1997. "Transformative Learning: Theory to Practice." *New Directions for Adult and Continuing Education* no. 74: 5–12. https://doi.org/10.1002/ace.7401

Minkler, M., and N. Wallerstein. 2003. *Community-Based Participatory Research for Health*. San Francisco: Jossey-Bass.

Moon, J.A. 2013. *A Handbook of Reflective and Experiential Learning: Theory and Practice*. New York: Routledge.

Naidoo, L. 2008. "Crossing Borders: Academic Service-Learning as a Pedagogy for Transnational Learning." *International Journal of Learning* 15, no. 3: 139–45. https://doi.org/10.18848/1447-9494/cgp/v15i03/45676

National Task Force on Civic Learning and Democratic Engagement. 2012. *A Crucible Moment: College Learning and Democracy's Future*. Washington, DC: Association of American Colleges and Universities.

Noddings, N., ed. 2005. *Educating Citizens for Global Awareness*. New York: Teachers College Press.

Nussbaum, M.C. 1997. *Cultivating Humanity: A Classical Defense of Reform in Liberal Education*. Cambridge, MA: Harvard University Press.

Oxfam. 1997. *A Curriculum for Global Citizenship*. London: Oxfam GB.

– 2006. *Education for Global Citizenship: A Guide for Schools*. London: Oxfam GB. http://www.oxfam.org.uk/education/gc/files/education_for_global_citizenship_a_guide_for_schools.pdf

Patterson, L.M., P.B. Carrillo, and R.S. Salinas. 2012. "Lessons from a Global Learning Virtual Classroom." *Journal of Studies in International Education* 16, no. 2: 182–97.

Perry, W.G. 1999. *Forms of Intellectual and Ethical Development in the College Years: A Scheme.* San Francisco: Jossey-Bass.

Peters, M.A., A. Britton, and H. Blee. 2008. *Global Citizenship Education: Philosophy, Theory and Pedagogy*. Rotterdam: Sense Publishers.

Pless, N.M., T. Maak, and G. K. Stahl. 2011. "Developing Responsible Global Leaders through International Service-Learning Programs: The Ulysses Experience." *Academy of Management Learning and Education* 10, no. 2: 237–60. https://doi.org/10.5465/amle.10.2.zqr237

Richardson, G.H. 2008. "Conflicting Imaginaries: Global Citizenship Education in Canada as a Site of Contestation." In *Global Citizenship Education: Philosophy, Theory and Pedagogy,* edited by M.A. Peters, A. Britton, and H. Blee. Rotterdam: Sense Publishers.

Riley, D.R. 2006. "Teaching Global Citizenship: Reflections on the American Indian Housing Initiative." *New Directions for Teaching and Learning,* no. 105: 51–61. https://doi.org/10.1002/tl.224

Simons, L., L. Fehr, N. Blank, H. Connell, R. DeSimone, D. Georganas, G. Manapuram, and D. Thomas. 2010. "A Comparative Analysis of Academic-Based Service-Learning Programs: Students' and Recipients' Teachers' Perspectives." *Metropolitan Universities* 20, no. 3: 77–92.

Sleeter, C. 2013. "Teaching for Social Justice in Multicultural Classrooms." *Multicultural Education Review* 5, no. 2: 1–19. https://doi.org/10.1080/2005615x.2013.11102900

Smith, B.H., J. Gahagan, S. McQuillin, B. Haywood, C.P. Cole, C. Bolton, and M.K. Wampler. 2011. "The Development of a Service-Learning Program for First-Year Students Based on the Hallmarks of High Quality Service-Learning and Rigorous Program Evaluation." *Innovative Higher Education* 36, no. 5: 317–29. https://doi.org/10.1007/s10755-011-9177-9

Snowman, J., R. McCowan, and R. Biehler. 2009. *Psychology Applied to Teaching*. Boston, MA: Houghton Mifflin.

Sperandio, J., M. Grudzinski-Hall, and H. Stewart-Gambino. 2010. "Developing an Undergraduate Global Citizenship Program: Challenges of Definition and Assessment." *International Journal of Teaching and Learning in Higher Education* 22, no. 1: 12–22.

Stanlick, S.E. 2015. "Quality and Directionality of Global Citizenship Identity Development in the Context of Online and Offline Reflections during an Introductory Global Citizenship Course." PhD diss., Lehigh University.

Stanlick, S.E., and T.C. Hammond. 2016. "Service-Learning and Undergraduates: Exploring Connections between Ambiguity Tolerance, Empathy, and Motivation in an Overseas Service Trip." *The International Journal of Research on Service-Learning and Community Engagement* 4, no. 1: 273–89.

Taylor, E.W. 2007. "An Update of Transformative Learning Theory: A Critical Review of the Empirical Research (1999–2005)." *International Journal of Lifelong Education* 26, no. 2 (2007): 173–91. https://doi.org/10.1080/02601370701219475

Terry, A.W., and T. Panter. 2011. "Students Make Sure the Cherokees Are Not Removed … Again: A Study of Service-Learning and Artful Learning in Teaching History." *Journal for the Education of the Gifted* 34, no. 1: 156–76.

Torres, V., S.R. Jones, and K.S. Renn. 2009. "Identity Development Theories in Student Affairs: Origins, Current Status, and New Approaches." *Journal of College Student Development* 50, no. 6: 577–96. https://doi.org/10.1353/csd.0.0102

Wade, R.C. 2007. *Community Action Rooted in History: The CiviConnections Model of Service-Learning*. Silver Spring, MD: NCSS.

– 2008. "Service-Learning." In *Handbook of Research in Social Studies Education*, edited by L.S. Levstik and C.A. Tyson. New York: Routledge.

Wade, R.C., and D. Saxe. 1996. "Community Service-Learning in the Social Studies: Historical Roots, Empirical Evidence, Critical Issues." *Theory and Research in Social Education* 24, no. 4: 331–59. https://doi.org/10.1080/00933104.1996.10505783

Webber, K.L. 2012. "The Use of Learner-Centered Assessment in US Colleges and Universities." *Research in Higher Education* 53, no. 2: 201–28.

Wiggins, G., G.P. Wiggins, and J. McTighe. 2005. *Understanding by Design*. Alexandria, VA: ASCD.

Wilson, J. 2007. "Service-Learning and the Development of Empathy in US College Students." *Education & Training* 53, nos. 2/3: 207–17.

3 Peace Education as Education for Global Citizenship: A Primer[1]

KEVIN KESTER

The UNESCO *Declaration and Integrated Framework of Action on Education for Peace, Human Rights and Democracy* provides an overview of the broad objectives of peace education:

> The ultimate goal of education for peace, human rights and democracy is the development in every individual of a sense of universal values and types of behavior on which a culture of peace is predicated. It is possible to identify even in different socio-cultural contexts values that are likely to be universally recognized ... Education must develop the ability of non-violent conflict-resolution. It should therefore promote also the development of inner peace in the minds of students so that they can establish more firmly the qualities of tolerance, compassion, sharing and caring.
>
> (UNESCO 1995, section 2, n.p.)

This declaration adopted at the 44th session of the International Conference on Education was initially endorsed by the General Conference of UNESCO at its 28th session in 1995, and was later presented by the Ministers of Education calling for member states and UNESCO to integrate education for peace, human rights, and democracy into their national activities. After its adoption, the declaration was promoted by the Ministers of Education in conjunction with UNESCO, with the intent of integrating the values of democracy, human rights, and peace into formal and nonformal learning contexts. This was intended to develop the full personality of the child and promote a values-based education that fosters intercultural understanding towards global peace. In the same document, it was proclaimed that education for international citizenship must be a core facet of achieving this education for peace.

In addition to the quote that begins this chapter, further on, the 1995 *Declaration* states that the content of education should "strengthen the formation of values and abilities such as solidarity, creativity, civic responsibility, the ability to resolve conflicts by non-violent means, and critical acumen." Hence,

> it is necessary to introduce into curricula, at all levels, true education for citizenship which includes an international dimension ... The whole of education must transmit this message and the atmosphere of the institution must be in harmony with the application of democratic standards. Likewise, curriculum reform should emphasize knowledge, understanding and respect for the culture of others at the national and global level and should link the global interdependence of problems to local action. (UNESCO 1995, 10–11)

In a nutshell, this 1995 declaration underscores the interconnection between global citizenship education and peacebuilding education for pedagogical purposes as well as for civic peacebuilding, globally (Banta 2017; Bickmore 2014; Brantmeier 2011, 2013; Hicks 1988; Reardon and Cabezudo 2002; Snauwaert 2009; Toh and Cawagas 2017; see also chapter 1 by Aboagye and Dlamini in this volume).

In the pages that follow, this chapter will interrogate this interconnection between global citizenship and peace education. The chapter begins by offering an overview of peace education as a pedagogic strategy to promote global citizenship, which will be followed by a brief discussion of the history of peace education. Thereafter, it will present transformative possibilities of peace education and cultures of peace as critical intersecting components of building global citizenship. The chapter then details a number of enabling factors of successful programs that have been highlighted in other literature, provides an overview of the teaching of peace and global citizenship in post-secondary institutions, and offers a case presentation of peace education graduate studies at the United Nations University for Peace in San Jose, Costa Rica. It concludes by detailing some possibilities for the evaluation of peace and global citizenship education programs.

Peace Education as Pedagogy for Peacebuilding and Global Citizenship

It is possible to situate peace education as part of the larger field of peace and conflict studies, which may be subdivided into peace research, peace studies, peace education (hereafter referred to as PE), and peace activism. Global citizenship is at the centre of the field of PE (Osler and Starkey 2018; Page 2008; Reilly and Niens 2014; Snauwaert 2009).

PE has roots in the work of several educators, including John Dewey (1916), Maria Montessori (1949), Paulo Freire (1970), Johan Galtung (1975), Elise Boulding (1988), Betty Reardon (1988), Betty Reardon and Dale Snauwaert (2015), Swee-Hin Toh (2004), and Swee-Hin Toh and Cawagas (2017). In addition, critical humanist authors and peace activists, such as Mahatma Gandhi and Martin Luther King Jr., influenced PE thought through their practices of social critique, civil disobedience, and active nonviolence. Although some of the following are contestable, various heads of states have also influenced practices in PE through their connections with peace institutes, including former president of East Timor Jose Ramos-Horta, former president of Costa Rica Oscar Arias, His Holiness the Dalai Lama, and His Majesty King Hussein of Jordan. The writings of Henry David Thoreau, Leo Tolstoy, and William James are used in post-secondary institutions to teach peace lessons, as is the theoretical work of Margaret Mead (1928), Michel Foucault (1969, 1975), Gene Sharp (1973), Albert Bandura (1977), and Howard Zinn (2006). Peace education has several conceptual frameworks that underscore the development of programs and content, much emanating from the aforementioned thinkers (Kester 2008, 2017a).

As a values-oriented field that aims to cultivate in learners the knowledge, attitudes, skills, and behaviours upon which a culture of peace is predicated (UNESCO 1995; Fountain 1999), PE serves as a reflexive educational and community approach to social change. In this sense, education is viewed as a social investment, not merely a personal means to a vocation. Betty Reardon (1999a) stated: "The development of learning that will enable humankind to renounce the institution of war and replace it … with the norms of a peaceful society [as articulated in] the Universal Declaration of Human Rights (UDHR) remains a core of the peace education task" (31–2). As such, peace educators teach about contemporary social, political, economic, ecological, and ethical problems, exploring the root causes of conflict and facilitating the exploration of nonviolent social strategies to manage social discord without resort to violence.

Hence, educators for peace seek to nurture intercultural understanding and global citizenship through developing respect for oneself, others, and the larger environment of which all are a part (Earth Charter 2000; Lee 2019; Reardon 1988; Shiva, Kester, and Jani 2007; Toh and Cawagas 2017). One dominant objective of the field is to nurture cultures of peace that challenge the assumption that violence is innate to the human condition and that violence emanates from our common animal ancestors (Adams 2000). PE is receiving increasing attention due to its policy and values-centred alignment with the work of UNESCO,

UNICEF, and other international organizations, including the Hague's "Appeal for Peace" (1999) and the Earth Charter (2000).

Contemporary scholars have written about the philosophy, politics, and pedagogy of PE in the twenty-first century (Bajaj 2015; Bickmore 2013, 2015; Brantmeier 2011; Cremin 2016; Jenkins 2007; Page 2008). Some of these scholars offer a critical PE approach (e.g., Bajaj 2008; Bajaj and Brantmeier 2011; Zembylas and Bekerman 2013), while some offer critiques of how the PE field is implicated in the production of social and cultural violence (e.g., Cremin 2016; Gur Ze'ev 2001; Kester and Cremin 2017; Pupavac 2001; Zembylas and Bekerman 2013). The latter scholars call for efforts to make PE more fundamentally fit for the twenty-first century. Aboagye and Dlamini (in chapter 1 in this volume) also raise concerns about the legacy of imperialism and colonialism in the field of global citizenship education, noting the decolonizing citizenship pedagogy work of Subedi (2013) and Fontan (2012), who have written on efforts to decolonize peace and PE.

A Brief History of Peace Education

European philosophical thought greatly influenced PE when it became institutionalized in the 1950s and 1960s in Western Europe and the United States (Harris and Morrison 2013; Ramsbotham, Woodhouse, and Miall 2011). Johan Galtung, a Norwegian sociologist, is often credited as the "Father of Peace Studies" (Ikeda 2002). He founded the International Peace Research Institute (PRIO) in 1959, which in 1964 began the first academic journal devoted to peace studies – the *Journal of Peace Research*. In 1964, Galtung also co-founded the International Peace Research Association (IPRA), which today houses the influential *Journal of Peace Education* and the Peace Education Commission. As a peace scholar, Galtung is known for promoting the dialectic between "negative peace," or the absence of war, and "positive peace," or the presence of cultural values and institutional practices that sustain peace cultures and nonviolence. His theory of "structural violence" is also widely used (Galtung 1988, 1996).

During the same time that Galtung was initiating the movement for peace research in Europe, several educators in the United States were mobilizing networks for peace in North America. Notable among these academics are Kenneth Boulding, Elise Boulding, and Betty Reardon. Kenneth and Elise Boulding – an economist and sociologist, respectively – were active Quakers and peace activists (Morrison 2005). The Bouldings, along with Johan Galtung, were instrumental in the development of IPRA, and, importantly, in gaining its consultative status to the UN Economic and Social Council (ECOSOC). Elise Boulding additionally served on the congressional panel that led to the creation of the United States Institute of Peace (USIP) in Washington, DC, an institute that is responsible today for numerous conflict resolution programs in public schools across the United States (Morrison 2005).

Additionally, many contemporary scholars cite Betty Reardon of Teachers College, Columbia University as the "Mother of Peace Education," particularly as a leading pioneer in the design of education for peace programs addressing militarism and patriarchy within higher education (Harris 2004; Kester 2010b; Reardon and Snauwaert 2014; Stomfay-Stitz 1993). Reardon sought to construct formal education programs that taught expressly for peace, whereas Galtung and Kenneth and Elise Boulding conducted peace research and established civil society organizations for peace activism within communities. In this respect, Reardon oversaw the establishment of the PE concentration in master's and doctoral programs at Teachers College, Columbia University in 1981. She also founded the International Institute for Peace Education (IIPE) in 1982. IIPE annually brings together researchers, educators, and activists across the globe to study peace and conflict issues in local learning communities. In its nearly forty-year history, IIPE has been held in various locations across North and South America, Europe, and Asia (Jenkins 2008). Reardon was also instrumental in forming the Global Campaign for Peace Education at the Hague Agenda, a civil society conference held in the Hague in 1999. In 2002, she served as a lead consultant in the formation of the master's program in Peace Education at the United Nations University for Peace in Costa Rica. Reardon remains an active author and practitioner in the field.[2]

In Canada, specifically, Kathy Bickmore has had a strong presence in PE for nearly forty years, and the late Anne Goodman established adult education programs and professional networks for PE. Goodman taught, and Bickmore continues to teach, PE courses at the Ontario Institute for Studies in Education, University of Toronto (OISE/UT). Bickmore was additionally involved along with Reardon in the development of the Peace Education master's degree program at the UN-mandated University for Peace (UPEACE) in Costa Rica (Jenkins 2004).

There are numerous other post-secondary institutions, in addition to OISE/UT and UPEACE, offering PE programs around the world, including those with a religious orientation, such as Notre Dame in the United States (Catholic), Bradford in the UK (Quaker), Soka University in Japan (Buddhist), and those with a secular approach like the University of Sydney, United Nations University, University for Peace, and George Mason University. In addition, there are those institutions embodying forms of local Indigenous knowledge, such as the University of Jos in Nigeria, or the University of Otago in New Zealand. A review of worldwide universities offering programs in PE reveals PE departments clustered around Western Europe, North America, and Australia, and some inclusion of PE as part of international relations, education, languages, or law departments. There is also a grouping of PE programs, with more of a cultural studies emphasis in Spanish-speaking countries, notably Colombia, Costa Rica, and Spain.[3]

Peace Education and Global Citizenship

In particular, many PE programs have thrived in university departments that seek to facilitate intercultural understanding and global citizenship, and many global citizenship programs position their work as a form of PE (Osler and Starkey 2018; Reimers et al. 2016; Reimers and Chung 2010). In fact, the history of the field suggests that many of the earlier programs began as anti-war teaching and learning initiatives that sought to mitigate hostility towards other societies through an increased understanding of diverse cultures and ways of life (Howlett and Harris 2010; Stomfay-Stitz 1993). The development of these programs coincided with the evolution of international organizations and were often initiatives of these organizations, such as the League of Nations, International Bureau of Education, and later the United Nations, all of which sought to prevent war and foster mutual respect. The UN organization included specific mandates for education to promote peace, which eventually became manifest in the establishment of UNESCO, the United Nations University, and the University for Peace (Kester 2017a, 2017b).

On 10 December 1948, the UDHR was adopted and it stated, "Everyone has the right to education … Education shall be directed toward the full development of the human personality and to the strengthening of respect for human rights and fundamental freedoms. It shall promote understanding, tolerance and friendship among all nations, racial or religious groups, and shall further the activities of the United Nations for the maintenance of peace" (UNGA 1948, Article 26: 1 & 2). The explicit linkage of human rights to peace in the UDHR provides a reference point for many peace educators working toward peace through education about and for human rights. Under this purview, and with the emergence of other human rights frameworks (e.g., Convention on the Elimination of All Forms of Discrimination Against Women and Convention on the Rights of the Child), many higher and adult education programs have added human rights instruments into their peace curricula. The promotion of a peace and human rights approach was further buttressed with the rise of transnationalism and global citizenship in the 1970s (UNESCO 1974). In this vein, two important books in the 1980s later emphasized education for peace as education for global citizenship. They were Elise Boulding's *Building a Global Civic Culture: Educating for an Interdependent World* and Betty Reardon's *Comprehensive Peace Education: Educating for Global Responsibility*, both published in 1988. At the core of Boulding and Reardon's human rights education frameworks is the emerging sense of a one-world community. Peace and social justice, global citizenship, transnationalism, human dignity and global solidarity are central values to their PE and global citizenship approaches (Boulding 1988; Reardon 1988; Reardon and Cabezudo 2002; Snauwaert 2009, 2011).

In the 1990s, PE took a turn towards even greater integration with human rights education. Important achievements at this time include the passing of the Convention on the Rights of the Child (UNGA 1989), the Vienna Declaration and Program of Action (UNGA 1993), and the Declaration and Integrated Framework on Action for Education for Democracy, Human Rights and Peace (UNESCO 1995). Reardon also published *Educating for Human Dignity* (1995) and *Tolerance: The Threshold of Peace* (1997) at this time. The human rights approach to peace and citizenship education remains popular (Palaiologou and Zembylas 2018).

The evolution of PE in Canada at the end of the twentieth century is documented in the Council of Ministers of Education report (2001), which offers debates on peace and education at this time. The report details how some educators and institutions perceive PE as not critical because it is believed to be already included in current mainstream schooling. Ahmad (2003) similarly argues that democratic citizenship and PE have always been included within public schooling in the United States. It could be assumed that this argument holds for similar liberal democratic states, such as the UK and Australia.

The end of the 1990s garnered a shift from the language of human rights towards the language of non-violence, a culture of peace and back to global citizenship. This shift is noticeable in the declarations of the International Year for a Culture of Peace (2000) and the Decade for a Culture of Peace and Non-Violence for the Children of the World (2000–10). In the midst of the culture of peace decade, the University for Peace established its Master of Arts Program in Peace Education in 2004. Shortly thereafter there was another trend moving in the direction of Education for Sustainable Development (2005–14); and, in 2012, former UN secretary-general Ban Ki-Moon established the Global

Education First Initiative to promote global citizenship education. This initiative has three main priorities: (1) to put every child in school, (2) to develop quality education, and (3) to promote global citizenship education.[4] This Global Education First Initiative – like education for sustainable development, education for a culture of peace, human rights education, and intercultural education – emphasizes civic engagement and participatory action in society, among various other social, political, and cultural values. The Global Education First Initiative continues to function in the post-2015 global development arena, although it has been significantly slowed since Antonio Guterres became UN secretary-general in January 2017. Its agenda is primarily carried on through the formal and nonformal activities of partnership agencies, such as UNESCO's Asia-Pacific Centre of Education for International Understanding, which hosts the Global Citizenship Education Clearinghouse (see Banta 2017).

Hugh Starkey, Audrey Osler, Daniel Schugurensky, and Kathy Bickmore are four other scholars deeply engaged in research into the association space(s) between citizenship education, democracy, peace, and social justice. Osler and Starkey (2015, 2018), for their part, discuss the linkages between citizenship learning and PE, where they emphasize the values of cosmopolitanism and human dignity to be integral to global citizenship and PE. Daniel Schugurensky's work, on the other hand, explores the intersections between citizenship learning and participatory democracy. Schugurensky (2010) and No, Schugurensky, and Brennan (2017) emphasize four key components of active citizenship education: namely, identity, civic virtues, social capital, and personal agency. Bickmore (2014, 2015) interrogates the gaps and potential linkages between young people's lived experiences of citizenship, democracy, and peace and what young people are taught in public schools around the world in the way of content and pedagogy.

More recently, global citizenship and PE work have taken on new dimensions that seek to respond to the social changes and political challenges in three interrelated areas: (1) within post-conflict and conflict-affected contexts (Kirk 2007; Novelli and Higgins 2016; Reilly and Niens 2014); (2) in response to forced migration and educational mobilities (Dvir et al. 2018; Islam 2019; Kyuchukov and New 2016; Lee 2019; Yemini et al. 2018); and (3) in addressing the post-2016 post-truth period in "stable" democracies (Kahne and Bowyer 2017; Kester et al. 2019; Peters 2017, 2019). A defining characteristic of the former is the realization that education and the aspiration for access to education drives conflict. Also it recognizes that conflict is either addressed or avoided in the classroom in favour of value-free global educational norms. Post-truth is characterized as a period of public doubt, anti-intellectualism, altfacts, and general mistrust of knowledge, which has crucial ramifications for educational institutions and educators promoting evidence-based policy and peacebuilding initiatives (Kester 2018; Peters 2017). In response, PE and global citizenship education efforts have encouraged enhanced endeavours towards peace, conflict, media literacy, and critical thinking. The UN and various agencies have funded research and advocacy to address these areas, for example, the $200 million UNICEF funded Peacebuilding, Education and Advocacy Program and its Research Consortium on Education and Peacebuilding (Novelli, Lopes Cardozo, and Smith 2015; Smith and Ellison 2015). Although the names of the initiatives and educational projects change over the years, the foci remain more or less the same across the varied fields of inquiry, which is the creation of a just and nonviolent society through consciousness-raising education, peacebuilding dialogue, and social action for the nurturance of cultures of peace.

Towards Transformative Learning and Cultures of Peace

Since the late 1980s, several educators have amalgamated various dimensions of PE under the umbrella term "cultures of peace" (Adams 1989a, 2000; Boulding 2000; Cabezudo and Haavelsrud 2013; Goodman 2002; Lum, 2017; Reardon 1999b; Toh 2004; Toh and Cawagas 2017; Wenden 2012). In this frame, the overarching goal of education for peace is both the reduction of violence and the transformation of mindsets that emphasize cultures of war into peace cultures. In other words, through a culture of peace lens, peace educators explore cultures of violence more deeply and aim to transition cultures of violence to cultures of peace. To realize this aspiration, programs purposefully educate for critical awareness, cultural solidarity, empowerment, and transformation towards a culture of peace. They do this through creating students who are responsible citizens, open to other cultures, respectful of differences, and able to resolve conflicts nonviolently (Kester 2008). In respect to the transformation of a culture of war to a culture of peace, UNGA (1999) describes a culture of peace as

> a set of values, attitudes, traditions and modes of behavior and ways of life based on, among others, respect for life, ending of violence and promotion and practice of non-violence through education, dialogue and cooperation; full respect for and promotion of all human rights and fundamental freedoms; commitment to peaceful settlement of conflicts; and adherence to the principles of freedom, justice, democracy, tolerance, solidarity,

> cooperation, pluralism, cultural diversity, dialogue and understanding at all levels of society and among nations. (2–3)

Furthering this agenda, an important document that grounds the movement for cultures of peace is The Seville Statement on Violence, which is a declaration by psychologists and medical practitioners stating that violence is not an innate characteristic of the human condition (Adams 1989a). These practitioners challenge the biological fatalism that underscores many peoples' justifications for violent conflict, defense spending and fear of others. The Seville Statement is organized around five scientific propositions; it argues that it is scientifically incorrect to say the following:

1. We have inherited a tendency to make war from our animal ancestors.
2. War or any other violent behavior is genetically programmed into our human nature.
3. In the course of human evolution there has been a selection for aggressive behavior more than for other kinds of behavior.
4. Humans have a "violent brain."
5. War is caused by "instinct" or any single motivation. (Adams 1989a, 328–9)

In this vein, Mikhail Gorbachev proclaimed:

> When disarmament is discussed a common thesis is that man is violent by nature and that war is a manifestation of human instinct. Is war the perpetual concomitant of human existence then? If we accept this view, we shall have to reconcile ourselves with continuous development and accumulation of ever more sophisticated weapons of mass destruction. Such thinking is unacceptable. It is reminiscent of times when more sophisticated weapons were invented and used to conquer other peoples and enslave and pillage them. That past is no model for the future. (quoted in Adams 1989b, 113)

Adams goes on to declare:

> The Seville Statement confronts an active resistance in the mass media and related social institutions more than it confronts an inherent ignorance or "psychological inertia" in ordinary people. The myth that war is part of human nature does not appear to be so much an inherent component of "common sense" so much as it is the end result of a campaign of psychological propaganda that has been promulgated in the mass media in order to justify political policies of militarism. (1989b, 120)

Gorbachev insisted that a new model for the future is needed. In this respect, peace educators seek to propose alternative possibilities through futures-envisioning exercises (Boulding 1988; Hicks 1988, 2004; Jenkins 2016). Through philosophical inquiry – asking the questions, Where are we now? Where did we come from? How did we get here? Where do we want to go? And how do we get there? – educators are promoting a category of transformative learning (Berry 1988, 1999; O'Sullivan 1999). As Stanlick in chapter 2 of this volume states, transformative learning is a deep cultural and philosophical adjustment through which peoples come to see life and living through new lenses. Values and attitudes are transformed, for example, from competition, consumerism, and a-historicism to cooperation and shared resources, and through this transformation new possibilities begin to emerge for a society based on common principles, needs, interests, and shared visions. O'Sullivan (1999) writes: "Truly, we live in a momentous time of survival and we are in desperate need of a broad historical system of interpretation to grasp our present situation. Although we cannot predict the future, we must nevertheless make educated guesses about where our present state of affairs is leading" (16).

Anne Goodman, former professor of community-based peacebuilding at the University of Toronto, writes that cultures of peace encompass diverse and integrally connected projects and actions as well as the principles that underscore the work of peacemakers. She contends that there are numerous paths towards peacebuilding that educators and students may participate in. These include working to abolish nuclear weapons, generating alternative sustainable energy, challenging the global market economy, working towards disarmament, conducting conflict resolution training in conflict zones, working for more democratic political institutions, advocating for more women in decision-making roles at all levels of political and economic institutions, and trying to get PE into schools. All of these endeavours converge with the process of education as educators and students reflect on the lessons learned through participation (Goodman 2002).

Goodman (2002) also delineates between the "official" and "unofficial" aspects of cultures of peace (187–8). She explains that the official cultures of peace mission is outlined and promulgated by UNESCO and the UN, while unofficial components are driven by grassroots efforts in local communities such as peace gardens, peace circles, peace zones, advocacy networks, and local educators for peace. Examples of these regional networks include the Canadian Voice of Women and the anti-nuclear movements of the past sixty years in North America, Europe, and Asia, as well as the more recent Occupy movements in the United

States and student demonstrations in Quebec. Additional initiatives for broad-based PE include the current civil society initiative in Canada for a Canadian Department for Peace,[5] with its ongoing efforts based on Bill C-447 to Establish the Department at the Canadian House of Commons, and the Global Campaign for Peace Education,[6] established in 1999. Nonformal and grassroots PE efforts complement and, in many cases, may drive support for formal PE in schools and universities (Lopes Cardozo and Maber 2019). As the PE field continues to spread, there is an increasing demand for investigation into what kind of impact PE is having on learners and whether or not the programs are contributing to more peaceful societies (Danesh 2008; Felice, Karako, and Wisler 2015; Harris 2003, 2008; Nevo and Brem 2002).

Enabling Factors of Successful Programs

There are a number of enabling factors that support successful PE programs. Program designers and educators may draw on these enabling conditions to ensure effective educational interventions. Allport (1954) formulated a *contact hypothesis* that pinpoints under what conditions prejudice is reduced and mutual understanding is fostered. His hypothesis is over sixty years old, yet it still informs many practices of PE (Felice, Karako and Wisler 2015; Salomon and Nevo 2001; Tal-or, Boniger, and Gleicher 2002). Allport (1954) argues that conditions necessary for intergroup contact to be effective include (a) supportive environment, (b) equal status among participants, (c) close and sustained contact, and (d) cooperation. In other words, trainers and participating members of peace programs need to be committed to the entire agenda. They must take full moral and financial responsibility for the training and the physical and ecological environment in which the learning takes place. For training to have a sustained effect, members of the larger community, other departments in the school, and outside community organizations also need to reflect the goals and values of training. This is a complex and complicated endeavour, particularly in regions of prolonged intractable conflict (Feuerverger 2001).

Paulo Freire (1970) is one scholar-practitioner whose work engaged communities in Brazil, including those within prolonged intractable conflicts, in efforts towards social transformation through education. Today, many global citizenship and peace educators around the world draw on the work of Freire to guide educational programs concerned with social justice, equality, and peacebuilding in and through education. Freire's pedagogy offers tremendous guidance on how to establish and maintain a culture of respect and equality in the classroom. After a supporting environment of equal status has been established, it is then possible to move forward with close prolonged contact that may foster continued international understanding and cooperation. This community could be enveloped with a common goal and sense of purpose, which will assist in fostering cooperation in the learning community. Kester and Booth (2010) also assert that at least one important element needs to be added to Allport's model: (e) the revelation and dialogue on power dynamics present in communities, which mirror greater societal norms and political institutions.[7]

Another important condition of building PE communities is the recognition of multiple forms of identity. Tal-Or, Boninger, and Gleicher (2002) note how discussing identity may help form peaceful environments where learners begin to reconstitute notions of *in-group* and *out-group*. This consequently leads to dialogue on concepts of othering, a process that may or may not lead to the production of *super-ordinate* identities. They describe super-ordinate identities where Black and White share identities as US citizens, or Muslim and Hindu share a South Asian identity. These super-ordinate identities when facilitated well may lead to discussions of shared values and common futures, where historically competitive relationships may convert to cooperative partnerships. Arie Nadler (2002) also highlights enabling factors of successful programs that include (a) deliberately designed equality, (b) interpersonal trust, (c) awareness and respect for the various cultural beliefs and practices present in the training, and (d) addressing real, pressing, and common problems (137–8). Nadler, therefore, includes the need to include "real and common problems" in the training. This ensures contextually relevant training and serves to expand on the conditions developed by Allport (1954) and Tol-Or, Boninger, and Gleicher (2002).

With enabling conditions in mind, there are myriad ways to ensure they are met to facilitate successful learning. First, the values associated with PE could be infused throughout the curriculum and across disciplinary boundaries (Apple 1969; Cremin and Bevington 2017; Pike and Selby 1988; Reardon and Cabezudo 2002). For example, educators could use dialogue circles to foster equality and trust and to deconstruct assumptions of the Other in a variety of classroom situations (Bohm 1996; Cremin and Bevington 2017). Practitioners could also use social justice theatre to develop trust among participants (Boal 1992), or the jigsaw teaching technique, which manufactures a sense of equal status and responsibility among learners (Kester 2010a). Futures-envisioning activities might also assist learners to define shared values and common visions for the group (Boulding 1988; Hicks 1988; Jenkins 2016).

These activities, along with enabling factors could help in the creation of sound education for peace programs. More on this follows in regard to PE in post-secondary institutions.

Teaching Peace and Global Citizenship in Post-Secondary Institutions

As stated earlier, the bulk of PE efforts in post-secondary institutions are within international relations, history, law, education, and language departments. This is due mostly to relevant topical areas, such as power, justice, identity, and social order. Additionally, there are several PE programs that address questions of conflict and peace through interdisciplinary teaching and learning, and that cut across typical disciplinary boundaries (Donahoe and Wibben 2018). Within such programs, knowledge is presented through inquiry and debate rather than through a rigid set of a particular disciplinary framework. Together, the educator and students co-construct new knowledge in response to contemporary issues and envisioning alternative future arrangements for the particulars of their context. Such PE is often linked to international normative documents, such as the UN decades old Millennium Development Goals (MDGs), and is facilitated through participatory methods, critical pedagogy, and cooperative learning techniques, such as exercises and role-play to teach conflict management skills, empathy, and critical listening, meditation, and creative problem-solving. Courses frequently involve practice-based components that allow students to develop these skillsets.

Other PE programs are devoted towards promoting social justice through critical media literacy in nationalist, anti-globalist, and post-truth times (Peters 2018). Courses in such programs use debates, simulations, and policy-writing/critical journalism as pedagogical tools. In these courses, skills such as active listening, creativity, critical thinking, empathy, and problem solving, are seen as fundamental to supporting sustainable cultures of peace. These skills are core for PE at all levels (Horner et al. 2015), but are especially relevant to post-secondary institutions that are preparing citizens and professionals to grapple with the contemporary challenges of globalization, political polarization, migration, post-truth, and nuclear threats across diverse sectors and levels of society. Finally, PE programs engage students to reflect on the meaning and relevance of the peace and conflict lessons beyond the classroom. To implement PE beyond the classroom requires the use of pedagogical tools such as case studies, service learning, community engagement, and internships (Boal 1992; Cremin and Bevington 2017).

Hence, post-secondary PE involves interdisciplinary inquiry rooted in the local and practical with an aim towards critical global consciousness. To illustrate how PE works in post-secondary spaces, this chapter presents an example of PE and global citizenship in one post-secondary institution.

Peace Education as Global Citizenship in Action: The UN Mandated University for Peace

This section describes a model of PE developed largely from the work of many actors behind the scenes at the UN and Betty Reardon at Teachers College Columbia University. The program is the United Nations University for Peace (UPEACE) MA Program in Peace Education in Costa Rica (Kester 2017a).

In 1980, the United Nations General Assembly adopted resolution 35/55 for the founding of a higher education institution dedicated solely to the study and pursuit of sustainable global peace. That resolution led to the establishment of the UPEACE Graduate School of Peace and Conflict Studies, with headquarters in San Jose, Costa Rica.[8] The university has liaison offices in New York and Geneva, and regional programs in Africa, the Middle East, Central Asia, Asia-Pacific, Latin America, and the Caribbean. UPEACE with its worldwide reach and impact could be argued to be the leading international institution in the global movement toward education for peace and international understanding. There are other leading institutions that have departments and centres focused on peace research, such as the University of Bradford, George Mason University, and Notre Dame. However, UPEACE is the only institution dedicated solely to the study of peace.

The mission of the UPEACE, as agreed by the UN General Assembly and stated in its Charter, is "to provide humanity with an international institution of higher education for peace, with the aim of promoting among all human beings the spirit of understanding, tolerance and peaceful coexistence, to stimulate cooperation among peoples and to help lessen obstacles and threats to world peace and progress, in keeping with the noble aspirations proclaimed in the Charter of the United Nations" (UNGA 1980, Article 1). UPEACE was not the first institution of the UN to be established and dedicated to the pursuit of peace through education. Others include UNESCO, the United Nations Institute for Training and Research (UNITAR), and the United Nations University (UNU) in Tokyo, Japan. UPEACE was, however, until 2009 the only educational institute of the United Nations to offer degree programs.[9] The UN secretary-general serves as honorary president of UPEACE, a position currently held by Antonio Guterres of Portugal.

The university is mainstreaming education for peace and sustainable development objectives in alignment with the SDGs (2015–30), the UN International Decade for a Culture of Peace and Nonviolence for Children of the World (2001–10), and the Decade for Education for Sustainable Development (2005–14), as well as gender mainstreaming in alliance with UN Security Resolution 1325 (2000). As part of these declarations and resolutions, UN organizations and member states are encouraged to emphasize education for nonviolence, a global culture of peace, sustainable ecological development, and gender equity into their policy priorities (Kester 2017a; Lum 2017). At its San Jose campus, also home to the Earth Charter Center for Education for Sustainable Development,[10] UPEACE is mainstreaming PE, sustainable development, and gender education in its programs.

These priorities impact the campus culture. Students at UPEACE interact with concepts of social justice, human rights, and peacebuilding through exploration of the values, beliefs, and worldviews present among cultures of the diverse student body. The more than 200 students that study at UPEACE's main campus represent nearly sixty nations. This manifests itself in a multicultural approach to PE, which embodies a symbiotic relationship between education for peace and international education where both multicultural education and PE aim to raise global awareness and intercultural respect. At UPEACE, graduate students deconstruct (and/or re-construct) their previously held prejudices and beliefs about other cultures and formulate models for greater cooperation in the future. Interrogating values, beliefs, and universal human rights inevitably leads to contested visions for how the world ought to be, particularly in multicultural communities; thus, introspection and dialogue on social justice and human rights is in part dependent on constructive and compassionate facilitation processes (Bickmore 2013, 2015; Cremin and Bevington 2017). This is where the culture of the university plays an educative role as a whole-school approach to education for peace and global citizenship (Kester 2017a). In the classroom these issues are explored through a broad curriculum, including the following courses within the PE concentration:

- Foundation in Peace and Conflict Studies
- Peace Education: Theory and Practice
- Cultures and Learning: From Violence Towards Peace
- Practices of Conflict Management and Peacebuilding
- Language, Media and Peace

- Human Rights Education
- Education for Sustainable Development
- Gender and Education
- Education in Emergencies

Beyond the classroom, issues of human rights, social justice, democracy, and peace take place in university-wide symposia, conferences, service-learning projects in local communities, informal conversations over lunch and dinner, and university-facilitated social interactions. This model of PE is being implemented in multiple centres of UPEACE within Asia, Africa, and Europe. Culturally sensitive, PE as global citizenship learning offers a model of education that promotes peace, justice, and democracy through radical inquiry and compassionate listening. How are such programs evaluated?

Evaluation of Programs

Nevo and Brem (2002) summarized a body of research on PE programs that were conducted from 1981 to 2000. The publications were identified through a search of PsyLit and ERIC databases and PE websites. The authors began by categorizing programs into "facets" pertaining to the purposes of programs, age of participants, didactic approaches, duration of programs, research design, and methods of measurement. The most important findings of Nevo and Brem include that not enough attention in PE programs is given to behavioural development. Most programs, on the contrary, appeal to rationality, not emotions, which could be perceived as problematic when emotions and psychology are so central to conflict resolution. Few programs work with participants beyond one year, and most evaluations of programs conclude that they are effective with few critical perspectives. They also found that programs that attempt to reduce violence are less effective than PE programs that emphasize intercultural understanding. Additionally, shorter programs (with a total duration counted in weeks and months) are more effective than longer programs that extend beyond a year. These findings have serious implications for PE developers.

UNICEF Egypt (1995) has furthermore outlined behavioural indicators for PE programs. UNICEF Egypt categorizes behavioural indicators as *knowledge* objectives, *skill* objectives, and *attitude* objectives. The *knowledge* objectives include knowledge of prevailing gender norms and stereotypes with indicators such as participants labelling the concept of stereotype when presented with bias and providing examples of prejudices. The *skill* objectives include development of communication skills, including attentive and active listening, restating the events of a story, refraining from creative liberty (i.e., changing the actual events of the story), and paraphrasing concepts back to the speaker. The *attitude* objectives include willingness to take action with indicators such as knowing one's agency and control over things in one's own environment (e.g., personal and natural), identifying a range of choices in the face of conflict, choosing constructive and collaborative action, and expressing satisfaction with having taken action and achieving the desired outcomes. If these attitudinal and behavioural indicators are witnessed among students during and after the program (measured preferably against pre-tests and post-tests), then it is possible to quantify changes among learning participants in evaluating the impact of programs. The Brookings Institution (2017) in partnership with the Education First Initiative collated a set of assessment and evaluation tools similarly used in global citizenship education around the world. They write, "Today, global challenges such as climate change, migration, and conflict will require people to do more than just think about solutions. They will require effective action by both individuals and communities. Education for global citizenship is one means to help young people develop the knowledge, skills, behaviors, attitudes, and values to engage in effective individual and collective action at their local levels" (ix).

Other scholars contend that in evaluating programs, the emphasis should be on monitoring pedagogy, not students (Hicks 1988; Setiadi et al. 2017; Toh, Cawagas, and Durante 1993; O'Sullivan 1999). Churchill and Omari (1981), for example, provide a list of criteria for program evaluation that seeks to assess programs in relation to PE program goals, indicators, students' learning, teaching skills, and associational networks. They propose general criteria for evaluation that monitors the education program's "relevancy and worth of the projects in light of evolving needs" (11) as well as the program's consistency with PE objectives. They also question the "worth of the activities in relation to expenditures (financial and human), taking into account eventual opportunity costs to participants" (11). Finally, Churchill and Omari assess criteria indicating the worth of the program to participants. They ask how the program has increased positive effects on participating schools, education in the country, and international relations. Their model operationalizes program value through assessing students' and educators' post-program attitudes towards international understanding, education innovation, and educational partnerships. More recently, Felice, Karako, and Wisler (2015) similarly state that "there is a need for specific tools and approaches for evaluation that take into genuine consideration the objectives and formats of peace education programs" (xxii). The UNESCO International Institute for Capacity Building in Africa, for example, has developed recommendations and specific tools for working toward peacebuilding through transformative pedagogy and assessment in educational settings affected by conflict (UNESCO-IICBA 2018). Going forward, PE scholars and practitioners must continue to develop context-specific and conflict-sensitive evaluation tools.

Conclusion

In conclusion, PE as global citizenship aims to confront and resist violence in and across diverse communities. PE focuses on education about peace, education for peace, and education through peace and civic action, while addressing the knowledge and skills needed to nurture cultures of peace and active citizenship. The content of programs includes diverse worldviews, nonviolent methods of social transformation, political economy of peacebuilding, case studies of peacemakers and democratic movements, human rights and responsibilities, sustainability education, disarmament education, and global justice. The pedagogy of PE for global citizenship is student-centred and directed towards solving "real and pressing issues" in contemporary politics and international affairs. Conditions that foster successful programs include a supportive environment, equal status among participants, close and sustained contact, interpersonal trust, cultural awareness, critical thinking, and dialogue on real and pressing issues. Furthermore, shorter intercultural understanding programs seem to be more effective than longer programs seeking to reduce violence in schools and communities. Indicators of success include attentive and active listening, paraphrasing, and identifying a range of choices in the face of conflict. Finally, the overall goal of PE is to transform conflict through dialogue and nonviolence towards the creation of sustainable, civic, and peaceful communities.

NOTES

1 This chapter is a revised version of an article that appeared under the title "Peace Education Primer," *Journal of Global Citizenship & Equity Education* 2, no. 2 (2012): 62–75.

2 For more information on Betty Reardon's contributions to peace education, see Kester (2010b).

3 For a detailed review of PE in post-secondary institutions see, for example, Kester (2017c) and Harris (1993).

4 See http://www.globaleducationfirst.org/
5 See https://canadianpeaceinitiative.ca. Movements for departments of peace are growing in numerous countries. Departments of peace have already been established in the Solomon Islands (2005), Nepal (2007), and Costa Rica (2009).
6 See https://www.peace-ed-campaign.org/
7 The work of peace educator Mohammed Abu-Nimer (1999, 2007) is useful in dealing with contact across power differentials.
8 See https://www.upeace.org
9 In 2009, UNU in Tokyo and its affiliate institutes also began matriculating students in MA and subsequently PhD programs, focused on sustainability science.
10 See https://www.earthcharter.org/

REFERENCES

Abu-Nimer, M. 1999. *Dialogue, Conflict Resolution and Change: Arab-Jewish Encounters in Israel.* Albany, NY: SUNY Press.

Abu-Nimer, M., and M. Shafiq. 2007. *Interfaith Dialogue: A Guide for Muslims.* Washington, DC: International Institute of Islamic Thought.

Adams, D. 1989a. "The Seville Statement on Violence and Why It Is Important." *Journal of Humanistic Psychology* 29, no. 3: 328–37. https://doi.org/10.1177/0022167889293003

– 1989b. "The Seville Statement on Violence: A Progress Report." *Journal of Peace Research* 26, no. 2: 113–21.

– 2000. "Toward a Global Movement for a Culture of Peace." *Peace and Conflict: Journal of Peace Psychology* 6, no. 3: 259–68. https://doi.org/10.1207/s15327949pac0603_9

Ahmad, I. 2003. "Education for Democratic Citizenship and Peace." Accessed 15 December 2013. http://files.eric.ed.gov/fulltext/ED475576.pdf

Allport, G. 1954. *The Nature of Prejudice.* Cambridge, MA: Addison-Wesley.

Apple, M. 1969. *Ideology and Curriculum.* New York: Routledge.

Bajaj, M. 2008. "'Critical' Peace Education." In *Encyclopedia of Peace Education.* Charlotte, NC: Information Age Press.

– 2015. "'Pedagogies of Resistance' and Critical Peace Education Praxis." *Journal of Peace Education* 12: 154–66. https://doi.org/10.1080/17400201.2014.991914

Bajaj, M., and E. Brantmeier. 2011. "The Politics, Praxis, and Possibilities of Critical Peace Education." *Journal of Peace Education* 8: 221–4. https://doi.org/10.1080/17400201.2011.621356

Bandura, A. 1977. *Social Learning Theory.* Englewood Cliffs, NJ: Prentice-Hall.

Banta Jr., R. 2017. "Innovative Approaches to Global Citizenship Education: APCEIU's Experience." *Childhood Education* 93, no. 6: 446–56. https://doi.org/10.1080/00094056.2017.1398544

Berry, T. 1988. *The Dream of the Earth*. San Francisco: Sierra Club Books.

– 1999. *The Great Work: Our Way into the Future*. New York: Random House.

Bickmore, K. 2013. "Peacebuilding through Circle Dialogue pprocesses in Primary Classrooms: Locations for Restorative and Educative Work." In *Restorative Approaches to Conflict in Schools: Interdisciplinary Perspectives on Whole School Approaches to Managing Relationships*, edited by E. Sellman, H. Cremin, and G. McCluskey. London: Routledge.

– 2014. "Citizenship Education in Canada: 'Democratic' Engagement with Differences, Conflicts, and Equity iissues?" *Citizenship Teaching and Learning* 9, no. 3: 257–78. https://doi.org/10.1386/ctl.9.3.257_1

– 2015. "Incorporating Peace-Building Citizenship Dialogue in Classroom Curricula: Contrasting Cases of Canadian Teacher Development." In *Building Democracy in Education on Diversity*, edited by R. Malet and S. Majhanovich. Rotterdam, Netherlands: Sense Publishers.

Boal, A. 1992. *Games for Actors and Non-Actors*. London: Routledge.

Bohm, D. 1996. *On Dialogue*. New York: Routledge.

Boulding, E. 1988. *Building a Global Civic Culture: Education for an Interdependent World*. New York: Teachers College Press.

– 2000. *Cultures of Peace: The Hidden Side of History*. New York: Syracuse University Press.

Brantmeier, E. 2011. "Toward Mainstreaming Critical Peace Education in US Teacher Education." In *Critical Pedagogy in the 21st Century: A New Generation of Scholars*, edited by C. Malott and B. Portillo. Charlotte, NC: Information Age.

– 2013. "Toward a Critical Peace Education for Sustainability." *Journal of Peace Education* 10: 242–58. https://doi.org/10.1080/17400201.2013.862920

Brookings Insitution. 2017. *Measuring Global Citizenship Education: A Collection of Practices and Tools*. Washington, DC: Center for Universal Education at Brookings.

Cabezudo, A., and M. Haavelsrud. 2013. "Rethinking Peace Education." *Journal of Conflictology* 4: 3–13. https://doi.org/10.7238/joc.v4i1.1521

Churchill, S., and I. Omari. 1981. *Evaluation of the UNESCO Associated Schools Project in Education for International Cooperation and Peace*. Paris: UNESCO.

Council of Ministers of Education, Canada. 2001. "Education for Peace, Human Rights, Democracy, International Understanding and Tolerance." Ottawa: Council of Ministers of Education. http://www.cmec.ca/Publications/Lists/Publications/Attachments/32/pax.en.pdf

Cremin, H. 2016. "Peace Education Research in the Twenty-First Century: Three Concepts Facing Crisis or Opportunity?" *Journal of Peace Education* 13: 1–17. https://doi.org/10.1080/17400201.2015.1069736

Cremin, H., and T. Bevington. 2017. *Positive Peace in Schools: Tackling Conflict and Building Cultures of Peace in the Classroom*. London: Routledge.

Danesh, H.B. 2008. "The Education for Peace Integrative Curriculum: Contents, Concepts, and Efficacy." *Journal of Peace Education* 5, no. 2: 157–74. https://doi.org/10.1080/17400200802264396

Dewey, J. 1916. *Democracy and Education*. New York: Free Press.

Donahoe, A., and A. Wibben. 2018. "Peace and War in the Classroom." *Peace Review* 30, no. 3: 265–9.

Dvir, Y., P. Morris, and M. Yemini. 2018. "What Kind of Citizenship for Whom? The 'Refugee Crisis' and the European Union's Conceptions of Citizenship." *Globalisation, Societies and Education* 17, no. 2: 208–19. https://doi.org/10.1080/14767724.2018.1525284

Earth Charter. 2000. "About Us." http://earthcharter.org/about-us/

Felice, C.D., A. Karako, and A. Wisler. 2015. *Peace Education Evaluation: Learning from Experience and Exploring Prospects*. Charlotte, NC: Information Age Press.

Feuerverger, G. 2001. *Oasis of Dreams: Teaching and Learning Peace in a Jewish-Palestinian Village*. New York: RoutledgeFalmer.

Fontan, V. 2012. *Decolonizing Peace*. Doerzbach, Germany: Dignity Press.

Foucault, M. 1969. *The Archeology of Knowledge*. Paris: Gallimard.

– 1975. *Discipline and Punishment: The Birth of the Prison*. Paris: Gallimard.

Fountain, S. 1999. *Peace Education in UNICEF*. New York: UNICEF.

Freire, P. 1970. *Pedagogy of the Oppressed*. New York: Continuum.

Galtung, J. 1975. *Peace: Research, Education, Action*. Vol. 1 of *Essays in Peace Research*. Copenhagen: Christian Ejlers.

– 1988. *Peace and Social Structure: Essays in Peace Research*. Vol. 6 of *Essays in Peace Research*. Copenhagen: Christian Eljers.

– 1996. *Peace by Peaceful Means: Peace and Conflict, Development and Civilization*. London: Sage.

Goodman, A. 2002. "Transformative Learning and Cultures of Peace." In *Expanding the Boundaries of Transformative Learning*, edited by Edmund O'Sullivan, Amish Morrell, and Mary Ann O'Connor. New York: Palgrave.

Gur Ze'ev, I. 2001. "Philosophy of Peace Education in a Postmodern Era." *Educational Theory* 51: 315–36. https://doi.org/10.1111/j.1741-5446.2001.00315.x

Hague. 1999. "Appeal for Peace." The Hague Agenda. UN Ref A/54/98.

Harris, I. 1993. "Peace Studies in the United States at the University and College Levels." In *Peace Education: Global Perspectives*, edited by A. Bjerstedt. Stockholm: Almquist and Wiksell International.

– 2003. "Peace Education Evaluation." Paper presented at the Annual Meeting of the American Educational Research Association, 21–5 April, Chicago, IL.
– 2004. "Peace Education Theory." *Journal of Peace Education* 1, no. 1: 5–20. https://doi.org/10.1080/1740020032000178276
– 2008. "The Promise and Pitfalls of Peace Education Evaluation." In *Transforming Education for Peace*, edited by Jing Lin, Edward Brantmeier, and Christa Bruhn. Charlotte, NC: Information Age Publishing.
Harris, I., and M.L. Morrison. 2013. *Peace Education*. 3rd ed. Jefferson, NC: McFarland and Company.
Hicks, D. 1988. *Education for Peace*. London: Routledge.
– 2004. "Teaching for Tomorrow: How Can Future Studies Contribute to Peace Education?" *Journal of Peace Education* 1, no. 2: 165–78. https://doi.org/10.1080/1740020042000253721
Horner, L., L. Kadiwal, Y. Sayed, A. Barrett, N. Durrani, and M. Novelli. 2015. *Literature Review: The Role of Teachers in Peacebuilding*. Amsterdam, The Netherlands: UNICEF.
Howlett, C.F., and I. Harris. 2010. *Books, Not Bombs: Teaching Peace since the Dawn of the Republic*. Charlotte, NC: Information Age Publishing.
Ikeda, D. 2002. "Johan Galtung – Father of Peace Studies." *SGI Quarterly Magazine*. http://www.sgi.org/resources/sgi-quarterly-magazine/
Islam, M.T. 2019. "(Re)Searching for the Development of a Conceptual Model of Education for Citizenship in the Context of Young People's Globalised Mobility in Higher Education." *Globalisation, Societies, and Education* 17, no. 2: 194–207. https://doi.org/10.1080/14767724.2019.1583093
Jenkins, T. 2004. "Comprehensive Programme and Course Planning Frameworks for the University for Peace Master's Degree Programme in Peace Education." In consultation with B. Reardon and J. Gerson. Revised by A. Brenes. New York: Teachers College Columbia University.
– 2007. *Community-Based Institutes on Peace Education (CIPE): Organizer's Manual*. New York: IIPE.
– 2008. "The International Institute on Peace Education: Twenty-Six Years Modeling Critical, Participatory Peace Pedagogy." *Factis Pax* 2, no. 2: 166–74.
– 2016. "Transformative Peace Pedagogy: Fostering a Reflective, Critical, and Inclusive Praxis for Peace Studies." *Factis Pax: Journal of Peace Education and Social Justice* 10, no. 1: 1–7.
Kahne, J., and B. Bowyer. 2017. "Education for Democracy in a Partisan Age: Confronting the Challenges of Motivated Reasoning and Misinformation." *American Educational Research Journal* 54, no. 1: 3–34. https://doi.org/10.3102/0002831216679817
Kester, K. 2008. "Developing Peace Education Programs: Beyond Ethnocentrism and Violence." *Peace Prints: Journal of South Asian Peacebuilding* 1, no. 1: 37–64.

– 2010a. "Education for Peace: Content, Form, and Structure – Mobilizing Youth for Civic Engagement." *Peace & Conflict Review* 4, no. 2: 58–67.
– 2010b. "Betty Reardon Creates the International Institutes on Peace Education." In *History of Education: Selected Moments of the 20th Century*, edited by D. Schugurensky. http://www.oise.utoronto.ca/research/edu20/moments/1982bettyreardon.html
– 2017a. "The Case of Educational Peacebuilding inside the United Nations Universities: A Review and Critique." *Journal of Transformative Education* 15 no. 1: 59–78. https://doi.org/10.1177/1541344616655888
– 2017b. "The Contribution (or not) of UN Higher Education to Peacebuilding: An Ethnographic Account." *Globalisation, Societies and Education* 15, no. 4: 464–81. https://doi.org/10.1080/14767724.2017.1303364
– 2017c. "The United Nations, Peace and Higher Education: Pedagogic Interventions in Neoliberal Times." *Review of Education, Pedagogy and Cultural Studies* 39, no. 3: 235–64. https://doi.org/10.1080/10714413.2017.1326273
– 2018. "Postmodernism in posttruth times." *Educational Philosophy and Theory* 50, no. 14: 1330–1. https://doi.org/10.1080/00131857.2018.1461417
Kester, K., and A. Booth. 2010. "Education, Peace and Freire: A Dialogue." *Development* 53, no. 4: 498–503. https://doi.org/10.1057/dev.2010.86
Kester, K., and H. Cremin. 2017. "Peace Education and Peace Education Research: Toward a Concept of Poststructural Violence and Second-Order Reflexivity." *Educational Philosophy and Theory* 49, no. 14: 1415–27. https://doi.org/10.1080/00131857.2017.1313715
Kester, K., T. Tsuruhara, and T. Archer. 2019. "Peacebuilding Education in Posttruth Times: Lessons from the Work of Betty A Reardon." In *Exploring Betty A. Reardon's Perspective on Peace Education: Looking Back, Looking Forward*, edited by D. Snauwaert. New York: Springer.
Kirk, J. 2007. "Education and Fragile States." *Globalisation, Societies and Education* 5, no. 2: 181–200. https://doi.org/10.1080/14767720701425776
Kyuchukov, H., and W. New. 2016. "Peace Education with Refugees: CaseSstudies." *Intercultural Education* 27, no. 6: 635–40. https://doi.org/10.1080/14675986.2016.1259092
Lee, F. 2019. "Cultivating a Culture of Peace and Empathy in Young Children while Empowering Refugee Communities." *Childhood Education* 95, no. 1: 16–23. https://doi.org/10.1080/00094056.2019.1565751
Lopes Cardozo, M., and E. Maber, eds. 2019. *Sustainable Peacebuilding and Social Justice in Times of Transition: Findings on the Role of Education in Myanmar*. New York: Springer.
Lum, J., ed. 2017. *Peace Education: Past, Present and Future*. London: Routledge.
Mead, M. 1928. *Coming of Age in Samoa*. New York: Harper Perennia.
Montessori, M. 1949. *Education and Peace*. Oxford: CLIO.

Morrison, M.L. 2005. *Elise Boulding: A Life in the Cause of Peace*. Jefferson, NC: McFarland.

Nadler, A. 2002. "Post-Resolution Processes: Instrumental and Socio-emotional Routes to Reconciliation." In *Peace Education: The Concept, Principles, and Practices Around the World*, edited by G. Salomon and B. Nevo. Mahwah, NJ: Lawrence Erlbaum.

Nevo, B., and I. Brem. 2002. "Peace Education Programs and the Evaluation of Their Effectiveness." In *Peace Education: The Concept, Principles, and Practices Around the World*, edited by Gavriel Salomon and Baruch Nevo. Mahwah, NJ: Lawrence Erlbaum.

No, W., D. Schugurensky, and A. Brennan. 2017. By *the People: Participatory Democracy, Civic Engagement, and Citizenship Education*. Phoenix, AZ: Participatory Governance Initiative.

Novelli, M., M. Lopes Cardozo, and A. Smith. 2015. *A Theoretical Framework for Analyzing the Contribution of Education to Sustainable Peacebuilding: 4Rs in Conflict-Affected Contexts*. Amsterdam, The Netherlands: UNICEF.

Novelli, M, and S. Higgins. 2016. "The Violence of Peace and the Role of Education: Insights from Sierra Leone." *Compare: A Journal of Comparative and International Education* 47, no. 1: 32–45. https://doi.org/10.1080/03057925.2015.1119650

Osler, A., and H. Starkey. 2015. "Education for Cosmopolitan Citizenship: A Framework for Language Learning." *Argentinian Journal of Applied Linguistics* 3, no. 2: 30–9.

– 2018. "Extending the Theory and Practice of Education for Cosmopolitan Citizenship." *Educational Theory* 70, no. 1: 31–40. https://doi.org/10.1080/00131911.2018.1388616

O'Sullivan, E. 1999. *Transformative Learning: Educational Vision for the 21st Century*. London: Zed Books.

Page, J. 2008. *Peace Education: Exploring Ethical and Philosophical Foundations*. Charlotte, NC: Information Age Publishing.

Palaiologou, N., and M. Zembylas. 2018. *Human Rights and Citizenship Education: An Intercultural Perspective*. Newcastle upon Tyne, UK: Cambridge Scholars Publishing.

Peters, M. 2017. "Education in a Post-Truth World." *Educational Philosophy and Theory* 49, no. 6: 563–6. https://doi.org/10.1080/00131857.2016.1264114

– 2018. "The Information Wars, Fake News and the End of Globalization." *Educational Philosophy and Theory* 50, no. 13: 1161–4. https://doi.org/10.1080/00131857.2017.1417200

– 2019. "The Threat of Nuclear War: Peace Studies in an Apocalyptic Age." *Educational Philosophy and Theory* 51, no. 1: 1–4. https://doi.org/10.1080/00131857.2017.1367876

Pike, G., and D. Selby. 1988. *Global Teacher, Global Learner*. London: Hodder and Stoughton.

Pupavac, V. 2001. *Cultures of Violence Theories and Cultures of Peace Programs: A Critique*. Leicester, UK: Perpetuity Press.

Ramsbotham, O., T. Woodhouse, and H. Miall. 2011. *Contemporary Conflict Resolution*. 3rd ed. Cambridge: Polity Press.

Reardon, B. 1988. *Comprehensive Peace Education: Educating for Global Responsibility*. New York: Teachers College Columbia University Press.

– 1995. *Educating for Human Dignity*. Philadelphia: University of Pennsylvania Press.

– 1997. *Tolerance – the Threshold of Peace*. Paris: UNESCO.

– 1999a. "Peace Education: A Review and Projection." *Peace Education Reports No. 17*. Malmo, Sweden: School of Education, Malmo University.

– 1999b. "Educating the Educators: The Preparation of Teachers for a Culture of Peace." Peace Education Miniprints, No. 99. Malmo, Sweden: Preparedness for Peace.

Reardon, B., and A. Cabezudo. 2002. *Learning to Abolish War*. New York: Hague Appeal for Peace.

Reardon, B., and D. Snauwaert. 2014. *Betty A. Reardon: A Pioneer in Education for Peace and Human Rights*. New York: Springer International.

– 2015. *Betty A. Reardon: Key Texts in Gender and Peace*. New York: Springer.

Reilly, J., and U. Niens. 2014. "Global Citizenship as Education for Peacebuilding in a Divided Society: Structural and Contextual Constraints on the Development of Critical Dialogic Discourse in Schools." *Compare* 44, no. 1: 53–76. https://doi.org/10.1080/03057925.2013.859894

Reimers, F., V. Chopra, C. Chung, J. Higdon, and E.B. O'Donnell. 2016. *Empowering Global Citizens: A World Course*. North Charleston, SC: CreateSpace.

Reimers, F., and C. Chung. 2010. "Education for Human Rights in Times of Peace and Conflict." *Development* 53, no. 4: 504–10. https://doi.org/10.1057/dev.2010.82

Salomon, G., and B. Nevo. 2001. "The Dilemmas of Peace Education in Intractable Conflicts." *Palestine-Israel Journal of Politics, Economics and Culture* 8, no. 3. http://www.pij.org/details.php?id=843

Schugurensky, D. 2010. "Citizenship Learning for and Through Participatory Democracy." In *Learning Citizenship by Practicing Democracy: International Initiatives and Perspectives*, edited by E. Pinnington and D. Schugurensky. Newcastle upon Tyne, UK: Cambridge Scholars Publishing.

Setiadi, R., S. Kartadinata, Ilfiandra, and A. Nakaya. 2017. "A Peace Pedagogy Model for the Development of Peace Culture in an Education Setting." *The Open Psychology Journal* 10: 182–9. https://doi.org/10.2174/1874350101710010182

Sharp, G. 1973. *Politics of Nonviolent Action*. Boston: Porter Sargent.
Shiva, V., K. Kester, and S. Jani. 2007. *The Young Ecologist Initiative Water Manual: Lesson Plans for Building Earth Democracy*. New Delhi: Navdanya.
Smith, A., and C. Ellison.2015. *The Integration of Education and Peacebuilding: A Review of the Literature*. Amsterdam, The Netherlands: UNICEF.
Snauwaert, D. 2009. "The Ethics and Ontology of Cosmopolitanism: Education for a Shared Humanity." *Current Issues in Comparative Education* 12, no. 1: 14–22.
– 2011. "Social Justice and the Philosophical Foundations of Critical Peace Education: Exploring Nussbaum, Sen, and Freire." *Journal of Peace Education* 8, no. 3: 315–31. https://doi.org/10.1080/17400201.2011.621371
Stomfay-Stitz, A. 1993. *Peace Education in America, 1828–1990. Sourcebook for Education and Research*. London: Scarecrow Press.
Subedi, B. 2013. "Decolonizing the Curriculum for Global Perspectives." *Educational Theory* 63, no. 6: 621–38. https://doi.org/10.1111/edth.12045
Tal-Or, N., D. Boninger, and F. Gleicher. 2002. "Understanding the Conditions and Processes Necessary for Intergroup Contact to Reduce Prejudice." In *Peace Education: The Concepts, Principles, and Practices around the World*, edited by G. Salomon and B. Nevo. Mahwah, NJ: Lawrence Erlbaum.
Toh, S.H. 2004. "Education for International Understanding toward a Culture of Peace: A Conceptual Framework." In *Education for International Understanding toward a Culture of Peace: Teachers Resource Book*, edited by V.F. Cawagas. Seoul, South Korea: UNESCO-APCEIU.
Toh, S.H., and V.F. Cawagas. 2017. "Building a Culture of Peace through Global Citizenship Education: An Enriched Approach to Peace Education." *Childhood Education* 93, no. 6: 533–7. https://doi.org/10.1080/00094056.2017.1398570
UNESCO. 1974. "Recommendation Concerning Education for International Understanding, Cooperation and Peace and Education Relating Human Rights and Fundamental Freedoms." Paris: UNESCO.
– 1995. *Declaration and Integrated Framework of Action on Education for Peace, Human Rights and Democracy*. Paris: UNESCO.
UNESCO-IICBA. 2018. *Transformative Pedagogy for Peacebuilding: A Guide for Teachers*. Addis Ababa: UNESCO-IICBA.
UNGA. 1948. "Universal Declaration of Human Rights." General Assembly Resolution 217A (III).
– 1980. "Charter of the University for Peace." General Assembly Resolution 35/55.
– 1989. "Convention on the Rights of the Child." General Assembly Resolution 44/25.
– 1993. "Vienna Declaration and Program of Action." A/CONF.157/23.

– 1999. "Declaration and Programme of Action on a Culture of Peace." General Assembly Resolution 53/243.

UNICEF. 1995. "Education for Peace Project: Description of Activities Conceived within the Project's Plan of Action 1995–1997." Egypt: UNICEF.

Wenden, A. 2012. *Educating for a Culture of Social and Ecological Peace*. Albany, NY: SUNY Press.

Yemini, M., H. Goren, and C. Maxwell. 2018. "Global Citizenship Education in the Era of Mobility, Conflict and Globalisation." *British Journal of Educational Studies* 66, no. 4: 423–32. https://doi.org/10.1080/00071005.2018.1533103

Zembylas, M., and Z. Bekerman. 2013. "Peace Education in the Present: Dismantling and Reconstructing Some Fundamental Theoretical Premises." *Journal of Peace Education* 10: 197–214. https://doi.org/10.1080/17400201.2013.790253

Zinn, H. 2006. *A Power Governments Cannot Suppress*. San Francisco: City Lights.

4 Citizenship through Environmental Justice: A Case for Environmental Sustainability Education in Pre-service Teacher Training in Canada

CLINTON BECKFORD

In 1978, UNESCO noted that the urgency about environmental problems first expressed at the Stockholm Conference in 1972 remained. Those sentiments are still accurate in 2018. Environmental degradation continues unabated in many parts of the world, climate change and variability could have existential implications for many countries across the world, and extreme natural hazards and disasters seem to be intensifying. At the same time, knowledge and awareness of these issues require improvement. This is critically important if the citizenry of countries around the world are to build adaptive capacity to the myriad of interconnected environmental, economic, and socio-cultural issues. Furthermore, research shows that there is a lack of environmental competence among pre-service teacher candidates and gaps in teacher training curriculum regarding environmental education (Alvarez-Garcia, Sureda-Negre, and Comas-Forgas 2015). This view is supported by Franzen (2017), Ashmann and Franzen (2015), and Ashmaan (2010), who argue that, despite the fact that pre-service education has been identified as an area to be targeted for preparation of environmentally literate citizens, most teachers continue to graduate without environmental education expertise.

This chapter makes four fundamental points. First, citizenship education is important. Second, environmental sustainability education (ESE)[1] should be a fundamental pillar given the grave environmental challenges facing humankind. Third, education must play a vital role in resolving these issues by providing citizens with the requisite knowledge and skills for action and this requires a reorientation of education. Fourth, given the critical role of education, pre-service teacher education is the logical place to start. Put another way, initial teacher education should be ground zero for creating an environmentally literate global citizenry.

Environmental Sustainability Education (ESE) Is a Critical Component of Global Citizenship

Conceptualizing Citizenship

Citizenship is a contested and controversial issue in academic discourse, particularly in terms of what citizen education should entail. Definitions of citizenship tend to vary greatly, depending on who is defining it and what their purpose is. A common trend often observed is the conflating of citizenship with civics. This conflating is worth exploring briefly in order to provide clarity, which is needed for a proper context for the discussion in this chapter. Civics is an academic discipline concerned primarily with teaching the rights and responsibilities of citizens of a society, particularly in respect to their legal rights under their constitution or similar guiding principles. As a contested concept, citizenship has been variously defined and is contextual mainly from political standpoints. According to Citizenship Education Foundation Inc., "Citizenship education is the study of the rights and duties of a citizen, and the application of the rights and duties to our responsibilities as [citizens]" (CEFI n.d., 3). Citizenship, then, is the result of effective civics education (CEFI n.d.) and, in its purest form, implies the lifelong application of, and adherence to, the rights and responsibilities as they pertain to a given society. In the case of Western democratic countries, it would involve living in a pluralistic democracy.

GOALS AND COMPETENCIES FOR EFFECTIVE CITIZENSHIP

Goals of citizenship education and perspectives about desired citizenship competencies are not necessarily universal. Instead, they are contextual and relate to the values and goals of a particular country or society. Some of the more common goals for Canada include educating engaged citizens, producing lifelong learners, and turning out citizens committed to the goals and values of global citizenship (CEFI n.d.). A review of literature indicates numerous and differing views about citizenship competencies. For this specific discussion, the competencies outlined for the Canadian province of Saskatchewan are adopted. They list five "essential citizenship competencies" (ECCs) necessary for citizenship education for students, namely, enlightened, empowered, empathetic, ethical, and engaged.

These essential competencies or desired citizen characteristics may be described as the profound; that is, enduring, features at the core of citizenship knowledge and practice. Although they are identified individually, they are not isolated; they act in concert and are generally understood to be integrated rather than mutually exclusive, and are equally important.

GLOBAL CITIZENSHIP

Global citizenship represents the knowledge, competencies, values, and attitudes that develop a global awareness and the human agency that empowers local and global action towards a more peaceful, equitable, and sustainable world (UNESCO 2014; Reade et al. 2013). Goleman, Bennett, and Barlow (2012) stress the importance of teachers' roles in helping young people develop an ecological intelligence that is crucial for twenty-first-century sustainability. Reade et al. (2013) highlight the need for leadership skills and an understanding of global complexity and interconnectedness. Global citizenship applies the principles of citizenship to contemporary global issues based on a recognition of the connectedness of humanity and the interdependence of the Earth's physical systems and human and environmental, economic and social interactions.

In an increasingly globalized world, conceptualizations of citizenship now transcend local, regional, and national geographies to include global communities. Global citizenship is, therefore, the goal of contemporary citizenship education, certainly in open societies. Tacit in this definition is the view that citizenship education and study is intentional and explicit. It involves the critical dimensions of rights, responsibilities, respect, equity, justice, and participation.

Global Citizenship and ESE

This chapter submits that ESE should be a major pillar of global citizenship education. The myriad of environmental issues facing humanity today makes this an absolute imperative. Environmental challenges and the concerns they cause are not new. Governments, NGOs, and United Nations organizations have been sounding the alarm for decades now. In the early days, concerns about issues like deforestation and pollution in various forms dominated the discussion and debate about the environment. In the last two and a half decades, concerns about climate change and variability and the perceived threats to life on Earth as we know it have been front and centre. Global warming and its main consequence of rising sea levels have become part of the lexicon, even in non-academic contexts.

The Intergovernmental Panel on Climate Change, the foremost authority on the subject, has consistently warned about the dangers posed by climate change. Today while there are still skeptics about the role of human activity in climate change and particularly global warming, there is very little credible dissent about the presence of climate change. The unpredictability of weather, the increased intensity of climatic hazards, and the increased frequency of catastrophic meteorological events have permeated the consciousness of people across the world. The implications for human welfare, including poverty and food security, are dire.

This chapter submits that an educated citizenry, with an awareness and understanding of the role of human activity in environmental change and the attitudes to do something about it, is critical to arresting climate change. Climate change, like many other environmental problems, is transnational, which means that a global interdependent effort is needed to solve what could very well be an existential crisis. It is in this context that a rationale for ESE at all levels of education becomes clear.

Education's Vital Role in Developing an Environmentally Literate Global Citizenry

What Is Environmental Sustainability Education (ESE)?

To answer this question, let us first look at the two parts of this concept, environmental education on the one hand, and sustainability education on the other. According to the Office of the Superintendent of Public Instruction (OSPI and EEAW 2010):

> Environmental education is a learning process that increases peoples' knowledge and awareness about the environment and associated challenges, develops the necessary skills and expertise to address the challenges, and fosters attitudes, motivations, and commitments to make informed decisions and take responsible action. (2)

As UNESCO (1978) postulates:

> The ultimate aim of environmental education is to enable people to understand the complexities of the environment and the need for nations to adapt their activities and pursue their development in ways which are harmonious with the environment ... Environmental education must also help create an awareness of the economic, political and ecological interdependence of the modern world. (12)

Meanwhile, OSPI and EEAW note, "Sustainability education is a learning process that supports academic success and lifelong learning, and develops a responsible citizenry capable of applying knowledge of ecological, economic, and socio-cultural systems to meet current and future needs" (2010, 2). When these two concepts are integrated, ESE may thus be defined, as a conceptual framework in which environmental and sustainability issues are integrated into teaching and learning. There is no universal consensus about what constitutes ESE, but key dimensions include people, prosperity, peace, and the planet (National Roundtable on Environmental Sustainability Education in Teacher Education 2016). These elements are interconnected in symbiotic complexity.

In this sense, it could be argued that ESE is important to achieving sustainable development and consequently is a significant component of ESD. This can be seen when we examine the United Nations Development Goals of 2015, which outlined a set of targets with the broad aim of ending global poverty, protecting the environment, and promoting world peace (United Nations 2015). Goals 6, 7, and 12–15 of the 17 big goals of this new sustainable development agenda directly or indirectly relate to environmental sustainability. The relevant goals are about the protection, use, and maintenance of the world's waters, seas, and forests.

All these goals attest that sustainable development invariable have a significant ecological and environmental component. As such, sustainable development is "underpinned by … development *in harmony with nature, meeting the needs of the present generation without compromising the ability of future generations to meet their own needs*" (UNECE 2012, n.p.; emphasis added). The link between ESD and ESE is further underscored when we examine the range of concepts and topics suggested for ESD.[2]

Sustainable development is understood to comprise several dimensions, one of which is the environment. UNESCO (2005) suggests that the environmental dimension encompasses such elements as natural resources, climate change, rural transformation, sustainable urbanization, and hazard or disaster management. According to UNDPI (1997), the core themes of education for sustainability include lifelong learning, interdisciplinary education, partnerships, multicultural education, and empowerment. UNECE suggests that these and the other ESD concepts can be supported by engaging learners in active citizenship projects (UNECE 2012).

The point is made therefore, that a number of terminologies have been used in the literature on this topic. A recent review analysis of environmental education in teacher education, found that the term environmental education (EE) was most often used. The review found 899 cases of EE use in the research literature (Alvarez-Garcia, Sudere-Negre, and Comas-Forgas 2015). They also found 282 cases of the use of the term ESD sparked perhaps by the declaration of the Decade of Education for

Sustainable Development in 2005. The authors did not make any reference to the use of the term ESE, which is a more recent term used by some instead of environmental education (EE). In the context of the current discussion, ESE and EE are conceptualized and operationalized as interchangeable. The terms are also interchangeable with education for environment and sustainability (EES) as the following definition of EES will confirm: "The Education for Environment and Sustainability program is to support academic success and life-long learning, and to develop a responsible citizenry capable of applying knowledge of ecological, economic, and socio-cultural systems to meet current and future needs" (Washington State, Office of the Superintendent of Instruction 2016). This statement describes the goal of environmental and sustainability education for students in the State of Washington in the United States.

In summary, the concept of environmental sustainability education has its roots in the older concept of environmental education (EE), which is still used by many (perhaps even most) today (see Alvarez-Garcia, Sudere-Negre, and Comas-Forgas 2015). The term ESE, then, reflects a transition to a more modern term that has become an integral part of the global development agenda. This is marked by the inclusion of the word "sustainability." The terms EE and ESE might therefore be used interchangeably.

Brief History of Education about the Environment

According to the United States Environmental Protection Agency (EPA, n.d.): "Environmental education is a process that allows individuals to explore environmental issues, engage in problem solving, and take action to improve the environment. As a result, individuals develop a deeper understanding of environmental issues and have the skills to make informed and responsible decisions." Environmental education as an academic pursuit is not new, and may be traced back to as early as the 1950s; however, it came to global prominence in the 1970s. The first manifestation of this prominence was the Belgrade International Workshop on Environmental Education (BIWEE) in 1975, which established a set of guiding principles for EE (UNESCO 1978). These guidelines and the BIWEE itself could be considered as the antecedents of the Tbilisi Declaration in 1977. The Tbilisi Declaration was the result of the first intergovernmental conference on environmental education. The Tibilisi Declaration stated:

> Environmental education must adopt a holistic perspective which examines the ecological, social, cultural and other aspects of particular

> problems ... the problems it addresses should be those familiar to the learners in their own home, community, and nation and it should help the learners acquire the knowledge, values and skills necessary to help solve these problems ... require changes to be made in some well-established approaches to teaching, especially in formal education. (UNESCO 1978, 12)

It established a set of guidelines and outlined goals and principles for EE, which were identified as follows:

(a) to foster clear awareness of, and concern about, economic, social, political and ecological interdependence in urban and rural areas;
(b) to provide every person with opportunities to acquire the knowledge, values, attitudes, commitment and skills needed to protect and improve the environment;
(c) to create new patterns of behaviour of individuals, groups and society as a whole towards the environment. (UNESCO 1978, 26)

The Tbilisi Declaration outlined several objectives for environmental education. These were categorized under (1) awareness, (2) knowledge, (3) skills, (4) attitudes, and (5) participation. The following key principles were also articulated by UNESCO in the Tibilisi Declaration:

Environmental education should:

- consider the environment in its totality – natural and built;
- be a continuous lifelong process beginning at the pre-school level;
- be interdisciplinary in its approach;
- examine major environmental issues at different spatial scales;
- focus on current and historical perspectives;
- explicitly consider environmental aspects in plans for development and growth;
- focus on development of critical thinking and problem-solving skills in learners;
- utilize diverse learning environments and a broad array of educational approaches with emphasis on experiential learning. (UNESCO 1978, 27)

The Tbilisi Declaration noted that, since the Belgrade Workshop, some efforts had been made in many countries to implement EE programs. For example, formal education systems introduced environmental components into traditional school subjects and developed teaching materials, and in higher education special courses, seminars, and training sessions on environmental topics were being introduced along with environmental studies courses (UNESCO 1978). Environmental competitions, exhibitions, and lectures were also held in some countries.

A decade after the Tbilisi Declaration, the Bruntland Commission Report, "Our Common Future," set forth a global development agenda, which linked development to environmental sustainability (United Nations 1987). The development agenda emphasize the need for ethical environmental stewardship for the benefit of current and future generations. Whereas the Tbilisi Declaration had not explicitly mentioned the concept of sustainability, the Bruntland Commission Report placed it at the centre of the development agenda and, in that respect, laid the foundation for sustainability education.

The Bruntland Commission Report was followed in 1992 by the United Nations Conference on Environment and Development (UNCED) in Rio de Janeiro, Brazil (United Nations 1992). Dubbed the "Earth Summit," the signature accomplishment of UNCED was the establishment of Agenda 21. Environment figured prominently in Agenda 21 and so did "environmental education," the terminology which was then in vogue. Agenda 21 offered a way forward for formal EE and public awareness with recommendations for integrating EE into education programs (United Nations 1992). The concept of sustainability was a prominent feature of Agenda 21 given its overarching goal of engendering sustainable development, which the Bruntland Commission defined as development that meets the needs of current generations without compromising the ability of future generations to meet theirs (United Nations 1987).

Today, there is general agreement that, relatively speaking, not enough progress has been made in enhancing environmental education in formal education both at the school and post-secondary levels. According to Gough (2016): "Despite efforts over the past 40 plus years, environmental sustainability is still on the margins of the curriculum in most countries. While there is much evidence that children enjoy learning *about* and *in* the environment, many teachers remain reluctant to teach environmental sustainability, and governments frequently marginalize the area" (83).

The global landscape is uneven when it comes to environmental sustainability education. Some countries have made quite good progress while others have not. For example, Australia is now seen as a model for environmental education programing at all levels of the education system. In Europe, the United Kingdom is a leader in the field. There are individual programs in Canada and the United States but not a lot of state or province-wide institutionalized programs. There are a number of professional organizations focused on environmental education in both Canada and the United States; nevertheless, the ideals of the Tbilisi Declaration have not yet been fully actualized in a global context. The reasons for this are many, varied, and localized, but two critical reasons exist at the micro level; that is, in teacher education. First, EE is a low priority because of an already crowded curricula. Second, the lack of environmental courses in basic education adds to this low prioritization because of the question, why train environmental education teachers if there are no teaching jobs in the field.

Contemporary ESE

ESE is a multidimensional concept that is a combination of educational activities related to ecological, economic, and social dimensions (European Education Research Association n.d.). Sustainability issues – such as climate change, systemic thinking, world trade, global distribution of wealth and resources, life quality, quality of environment, health, intercultural communication, and depletion of natural resources – are some of the key concepts of concern in ESE study.

Makrakis (2011) defines education for sustainability as "the learning needed to maintain and improve our quality of life and the quality of life of generations to come. It is about equipping individuals, communities, groups, businesses and government to live and act sustainably, as well as giving them an understanding of the environmental, social and economic issues involved" (411). This is a holistic, interdisciplinary, and cross-disciplinary vision of education capable of fostering requisite knowledge and skills for a sustainable future based on changes in values, behavior, and lifestyles (Makrakis 2012). According to the National Roundtable on Environmental Sustainability Education in Pre-service Teacher Education (NRESE-TE 2016), held in Peterborough, Ontario, in 2016: "ESE is underpinned by principles that support sustainable living, respect for all life, and human wellbeing. Environmental protection and restoration, natural resource conservation and sustainable use, addressing unsustainable production and consumption patterns, and the creation of just and peaceful societies are also important principles underpinning ESE."

Environmental and sustainability education (ESE) should empower people to make informed decisions for environmental integrity, sustainable economic viability, and a just society for present and future generations, while respecting cultural diversity. It is organized around critical and central themes: planet, people, prosperity, and peace. "These themes are characterized by uncertainty, complexity and a high degree of systemic interconnection, ESE requires participatory teaching and learning methods like critical thinking and making decisions in a collaborative way in order to empower learners to take action for sustainability and ecological integrity" (NRESE-TE 2016). ESE learning involves learning to ask critical questions; learning to clarify one's own values; learning to envision more positive and sustainable futures; learning to think systemically; and learning to respond through applied learning. Traditional approaches to schooling are no longer suitable and appropriate. Twenty-first century challenges and opportunities and twenty-first century learners require different approaches. The status quo K-12 and teacher education are inappropriate and inadequate (NRESE-TE 2016).

There are many perspectives on what the focus of ESE should be. The following are some of the key principles suggested by the NRESE-TE (2016):

- human and environmental interactions, with a focus on interconnectedness of people and places, individual and collective decision-making, society, economy, environment and civic responsibility-stewardship of the environment
- evidenced based and informed actions regarding environmental sustainability issues
- increased awareness among learners of their rights and responsibilities and their impact and footprint as individuals and communities
- valuing different ways of knowing and ES knowledges
- environmental and sustainability issues are social issues linked to personal civic responsibility
- opportunities for learners to reflect on and interrogate their own lifestyle and practices and the strictures that promote these lifestyles

ESE IN CANADA

Environmental education in Canada occurs in diverse contexts and sites and utilize many approaches, which make up formal and informal ESE programs and is characterized by lack of shared understanding of ESE/EE in Canada (Inwood and Jagger 2014). Inwood and Jagger (2014) suggest that the structure of education in Canada, which is characterized by provincial responsibility for education, is a hindrance in this regard. The meaning of ESE/EE or what it entails is highly contested with multiple conceptualizations. Terms like EE, Outdoor Education, Experiential Education, Adventure Education, among others, are often discussed as ESE/EE and are encountered often in the literature on ESE in Ontario.

Status of ESE in Ontario. According to Inwood and Jagger (2014), environmental education has been unevenly integrated across the curriculum over the last twenty years in Ontario. Environmental science courses were first introduced in the Ontario curriculum by the Ontario Ministry of Education (OME) in 1973 (Houghton et al. 2002, quoted in Inwood and Jagger 2014). This continued until 2000 when environmental science, which had been offered as an elective in secondary schools, was discontinued when the OME opted for the infusion of environmental education in other subjects particularly geography and science, instead of a stand-alone course. The failure of the infusion model led to calls for a more structured approach to environmental education in the province by non-profit ESE groups, organizations, and associations. The groups that lead the call include the Ontario Association of Geography and Environmental Educators (OAGEE), Canadian Network for Environmental Education and Communication (EECOM), the Council of Outdoor Educators of Ontario (COEO), the Ontario Society for Environmental Education (OSEE), Environmental Education Ontario (EEON), and Evergreen.

Many schools and school boards across the province implemented environmental education initiatives without much institutional supportive from the OME. These efforts were recognized by the Working Group on Environmental Education (2007): "For many years, promising elements of environmental education have been reflected in Ontario's curriculum, and supported by innovative programs and partnerships developed by school boards and schools across the province. In the absence of a comprehensive framework for environmental education however, these efforts remain fragmented and inconsistent" (1). In 2009 and flowing from the recommendations of the Working Group on Environmental Education, the OME unveiled its policy framework for EE in Ontario schools. The framework identified specific roles for stakeholders such as the Ministry of Education, school boards, and schools. It does not mention a role for teacher education programs while "encouraging teachers to develop the knowledge, skills, and perspectives that will enable them to teach confidently about environmental issues" in order to support student learning (OME 2009, 11).

Pre-service Teacher Education: Ground Zero for ESE

Environmental Sustainability Education in Teacher Education (ESE-TE)

ESE-TE is teacher education that promotes development of responsible, knowledgeable, and active citizens; emphasizes the importance of all aspects of environmental well-being; promotes development of knowledge, attitudes, values, and actions to support a sustainable future; and models positive social and environmental change (NRESE-TE 2016). ESE-TE engages pre-service teachers in explorations of the foundations of ESE and examining and developing strategies and approaches for the engagement of pre-service teacher candidates in ESE. The aim is to develop teachers capable of providing learning experiences to students that emphasize the global nature of environmental problems and their individual and collective responsibility to sustainable behaviours as global citizens.

STATUS OF ESE IN INITIAL TE IN CANADA

Although growing in recent years, research about ESE in Canadian teacher education programs remain sparse. The 2002 study by Lin is still one of the seminal works in this regard despite being written more than a decade and half ago. Lin's study was a long overdue update on the state of EE in Canadian teacher education after the work of Towler (1981). Towler's analysis painted a dire picture of the situation and Lin (2002) suggested that very little had changed in the EE in teacher education landscape since then. Her research indicated that only twelve of thirty-five teacher education programs were offering methodology courses in environmental education and another six integrated environmental education into other courses. According to Lin, environmental elements included in EE courses focused on ecology, outdoor education, and conservation. It was also found that environmental education instructors hardly contributed to research and scholarship in the field. In essence, environmental education was a low priority in teacher education programs, as lack of funding, lack of time, already overcrowded curricula, lack of interest (and expertise) remained significant stumbling blocks.

Some changes have occurred since Lin's (2002) study, but the picture is still not clear because of lack of reliable data. Inwood and Jagger (2014) argue that the inclusion of ESE in initial teacher education programs varies greatly across Canada. For example, some universities in Saskatchewan and British Columbia do offer ESE as a major component in teacher education but many initial teacher education programs across the country did not offer ESE courses at the time. This is also the case in Alberta (Alberta Council for Environmental Education 2012).

Perhaps due to growing panic about global environmental change, especially climate change and variability, the last six years have brought more urgency to the issue of environmental sustainability education in teacher education in Canada. In 2012, the Council of Ministers of

Education Canada (CMEC) commissioned a study to investigate the presence of ESD in teacher education programs. The goal was to see where Canada was in the context of the UN Decade of Education for Sustainable Development (UNDESD) from 2005 to 2014. Then in 2014, Inwood and Jagger, professors at the Ontario Institute for Studies in Education at the University of Toronto (OISE/UT), published *DEEPER: Deepening Environmental Education in Pre-Service Education Resource*. The publication was the result of a provincial roundtable of sixty participants from twelve Ontario universities in May 2013. The aim of the resource is " to support and inspire faculty, staff and students to broaden and deepen the implementation of environmental education in initial teacher education programs across the province" (Inwood and Jagger 2014, 7). The desired outcome was to deepen and broaden environmental education discourse among teacher educators locally, nationally and even internationally. *DEEPER* provides a vision of and an introduction to environmental education that can serve as a framework for academic exploration of the field. Newcomers to the field will find the bank of environmental education resources provided to be particularly useful.

As noted above, the National Roundtable on Environmental Sustainability Education in Teacher Education was convened at Trent University in Peterborough, Ontario, in 2016. The roundtable was a gathering of educational stakeholders concerned about the lack of teaching expertise in the area of ESE and laid out a road map for addressing the problem through the strengthening of ESE in teacher education. The results of the roundtable were captured in the Otonabee Declaration, which states, "We urge leaders in Canadian faculties of education, ministries of education, boards of education, and bodies that regulate the teaching profession to make Environmental and Sustainability Education a mandatory component of initial teacher education." This recognition of the need for ESE instruction in initial teacher education is not new. This was also one of the most significant observations of the Tbilisi Declaration (UNESCO 1978), and UNESCO has subsequently called for a reorientation of teacher education to address sustainability education (UNESCO 2006).

The Otonabee Declaration set out a Canadian National Action Plan for enhancing ESE in Canadian teacher education programs. The action plan incorporated the following four dimensions:

1. Establish a new national organization to support ESE in Pre-Service Teacher Education in Canada
2. Assess the state of ESE in Pre-Service Teacher Education in Canada

3. Develop supports for ESE in Pre-Service Teacher Education in Canada
4. Advocate for the crucial importance of ESE in Pre-Service Teacher Education in Canada

Many jurisdictions across the province have implemented environmental programs in their K–12 systems but most pre-service teachers receive no formal ESE training in their education programs. The result is a lack of expertise to effectively teach ESE. This limitation was cited by the Working Group and Environmental Education in Ontario in 2007and again by the 2016 roundtable. They argued, that despite curriculum reorganization of the K–12 education, and establishment of many EE initiatives in schools, there were substantial gaps "between these current practices and a comprehensive approach to environmental education in Ontario schools. Evidence of this gap exists at every level of the system" (Working Group on Environmental Education 2007, 2).

The urgency of the issue of ESE-TE is reflected in ongoing efforts by the Association of Canadian Deans of Education (ACDE), an organization of deans of both faculties of education and domestic teacher education programs across Canada. The ACDE has initiated the process of developing a "Deans' Accord on Environmental and Sustainability Education in Teacher Education," which may be viewed as a manifestation of its recognition of ESE-TE as an important imperative, and its support and commitment for ESE programing in pre-service teacher education in Canada.

The recommendations of the Working Group on Environmental Education emphasize the significant role they ascribe to teachers, and hence teacher education. The following recommendations are directly related to teacher education:

> 22. Collaborate with Ontario teachers' federations and affiliates, school boards, the Ontario College of Teachers, faculties of education, subject associations, and other stakeholders to develop and implement a strategy for ongoing professional development for teachers.
>
> 23. Provide ongoing professional development for teachers with a focus on content/knowledge, teaching in the environment, and using environmental themes to contextualize learning.
>
> 25. Provide provincial/regional training sessions for educators to build capacity and share effective practices, in collaboration with school boards, teachers' federations, faculties of education, subject associations, and other stakeholders.

26. Develop and support workshops and summer institutes on cross-curricular environmental education.

27. Consult with the Ontario College of Teachers about the need for an Additional Qualification course in cross-curricular environmental education.

28. Develop resources for teachers, using a variety of media including sample units of study, course profiles, teaching guides, and electronic resources such as e-learning modules and webcasts.

31. Establish a working group in collaboration with the Ministry of Training, Colleges and Universities, Ontario teachers' federations and affiliates, the Ontario College of Teachers, faculties of education, and other stakeholders to develop and implement a strategy for effective pre-service training in environmental education for all teacher candidates, including environmental education as a teachable subject. (Working Group on Environmental Education 2007, 16)

RE-ORIENTING INITIAL TEACHER EDUCATION IN ONTARIO TO INCORPORATE ENVIRONMENTAL SUSTAINABILITY EDUCATION

Role of Teacher Education in ESE. The role of teacher education in creating an environmentally literate citizenry is well established in the literature. Research indicates that education also provides the motivation, justification, and social support for pursuing and applying education for sustainability (UNESCO 2006; Lawale and Bory-Adams 2010). Winter-Simat, Wright, and Choi (2017) share these sentiments, arguing that personal and societal transformation must be a priority of formal education if the ecological effects of anthropological activities are to be reduced. This is supported by a significant body of recent research on ESE-TE (see, for example, Sureda-Negre et al. 2014; Tuncer et al. 2014; Andersson et al. 2013; Tal 2010; McKeown 2013).

ESE requires the reorientation of education towards environmental sustainability and by extension, sustainable development. This demands a more central role for environmental science and environmental studies more generally to bring them into the mainstream (DiGiuseppi 2013; Russell and Fawcett 2012). According to Makrakis (2012): "Rethinking and revising education to address the knowledge, skills, perspectives, and values related to sustainability is of paramount importance to current and future societies. This implies a review of existing curricula … with the aim to develop interdisciplinary and cross-disciplinary understanding and knowledge of social, cultural, economic, and environmental sustainability" (91). Makrakis (2008) identified two of the major forces driving education in the early twenty-first century as:

1. The increasing demand for new educational approaches and pedagogies that foster transformative and lifelong learning, and
2. The reorientation of educational curricula to address sustainable development (SD).

Makrakis (2012) has postulated that "education systems, at all levels, and especially Higher Education and Teacher Education bear their own responsibility for building a more sustainable future. If higher education fails to educate students for sustain-ability, future teachers and leaders cannot be qualified agents for sustainable development" (90). If sustainability is to be achieved through education, teachers who are well prepared and committed to the principles of sustainability must be a critical part of the process (Makrakis 2010; UNESCO 2006, 2017).

Visioning ESE-TE in Ontario and Canada.

> Initial teacher education in Ontario can and should empower teacher candidates to become responsible, knowledgeable, and active citizens who support and model positive social and environmental change in the communities in which they work and live. This requires a clear commitment on the part of … and faculties of education to environmental sustainability and citizenship education as a mandatory component of all initial teacher education programs in the province.
> (Inwood and Jagger 2014, 21)

The preceding is part of the vision for environmental education that proceeded from the Ontario roundtable meeting in 2013. The vision speaks specifically to the Province of Ontario but has lessons for other Canadian provinces and international jurisdictions as well. The vision continues:

> All teacher candidates should have the opportunity to learn in, about and for the environment as part of their initial teacher education program. They should learn with an emphasis on experiential, holistic, enquiry-based pedagogies in the natural and built environments in which they live … teacher candidates need to engage in interdisciplinary study to explore the environmental challenges of contemporary society; develop collaborative problem-solving and creative and critical thinking skills to address these challenges; build on their sense of empathy and care; and practice modeling and applying these skills with their students. By re-orienting initial teacher education

> to focus on sustainable future for all, teacher candidates will have the knowledge, skills and attitudes necessary to provide environmental education for their students, schools, and communities, and work towards societal well-being locally and globally. (Inwood and Jagger 2014, 21)

The North American Association of Environmental Educators (NAAEE 2010) identified several essential understandings for environmental education, namely systems, interdependence, importance of where one lives (a sense of place), integration and infusion, roots in the real world, and lifelong learning. These are not necessarily universally accepted, and the core competencies that should be included in ESE at all levels of education and for societies at large are a matter still being discussed in the ESE/EE literature. Hopkins and McKeon (2005) suggest that pre-service teachers' education need to provide an understanding of the relational nature of society, economy, and environment (quoted in Inwood and Jagger 2014). The NAAEE states that teacher candidates should learn about the nature of environmental education, develop environmental literacy, learn to integrate environmental education into school curricula and assessment, and pursue professional development in environmental education (NAAEE 2007). The UNCEE (2012) outlines four core competency areas – learning to learn, learning to do, learning to be, and learning to live together. The vision for environmental education in Ontario espoused in the publication *DEEPER*, categorize some twenty core competencies for Ontario pre-service candidates under knowledge, attitude, and action. UNESCO has weighed in on this issue as well, postulating that:

> To begin the process of reorienting teacher education to address sustainability, faculties of education around the world must draw their own thematic guidelines based on descriptions and ideals of sustainability … faculties of education must decide which themes to emphasize within their curriculums, programs, practices, and policies to ensure that teacher-education programs fit the environmental, social, and economic conditions and goals of their communities, regions, and nations. (UNESCO 2005, 15)

Discussion

Environmental sustainability education constitutes a comprehensive lifelong education that is responsive to contemporary environmental challenges and changes. It prepares citizens with knowledge and awareness of environmental issues and their global nature, and it develops in citizens an understanding of and interconnectedness of social, economic, and environmental issues in major problems of the contemporary world (Inwood and Jagger 2014; Liu et al. 2015; Makrakis 2011,

2012; European Education Research Association n.d.; NRESE-TE 2016; UNESCO 2006). Effective ESE is holistic and multidisciplinary, integrating inquiry-based and problem-solving strategies focused on responsible decision-making and responsible actions, which are the hallmarks of effective participatory citizenship.

According to Makrakis (2012), ESE must promote sustainable thinking and living and this requires changes in learning and behaviours. It should be holistic, with economic, social, and environmental factors considered in relation to each other (UNESCO 2005). Thus, ESE should help learners to learn how to live sustainably. In the context of teacher education, it follows that ESE should inspire learners to interrogate their own environmental attitudes and actions.

Solutions to environmental sustainability problems require a thorough analysis of these issues, and this is where research in ESE becomes vital. Empirical research in ESE is vital to the advancement of the field as it will enhance conceptual and methodological development but research is considered to be weak at this time. In a review of EE in teacher education, Alvarez-Garcia, Sureda-Negre, and Comas-Forgas (2015) reported an overall paucity of research in this area. Inwood and Jagger (2014) call on faculty researchers to link their environmental teaching to their research agendas.

However, there are serious questions about the realistic goals of ESE under the current educational structure and societal mindsets. In this regard, a number of fundamental questions were raised by Inwood and Jagger (2014):

> How can environmental education be successfully implemented in educational systems when it contradicts the culture of consumption, consumerism, inequity, and globalization often promoted in those systems? Can environmental education be taught in a transformative way if our education systems are still mired in transmission-based approaches? Can environmental education exist within the current educational structures that are often more supportive of economy over ecology? How can we teach in a way that is profoundly educational, yet challenges prevailing cultural norms? (60)

The fundamental challenge, then, is how can education and environmental education be reimagined and how can teacher education be reoriented to effectively prepare new teachers and in-service teachers too, to teach about environmental sustainability? ESE requires the reorientation of education towards environmental sustainability and, by extension, sustainable development. Inwood and Jagger (2014) suggest that environmental educators need to "walk the talk."

Other important issues need to be resolved as well. Some of these are related to the role of education and what constitute effective or quality teaching. What should be the goal of ESE for teacher candidates? What is the role of activism in ESE-TE? According to the United States EPA (n.d.), "Environmental education does not advocate a particular viewpoint or course of action. Rather, environmental education teaches individuals how to weigh various sides of an issue through critical thinking and it enhances their own problem-solving and decision-making skills." If this viewpoint is put into practice in ESE, can the desired outcomes be achieved for environmental sustainability? Is that our role as educators? This issue is addressed by Inwood and Jagger (2014). They wondered if space should be made for teacher candidates to become activists. "And if we enable them to take action, do we expect them to make change, or is it more important that we expose them to types of learning and understanding that only arise through the embodied experience of doing something?" (61). This chapter argues that participation should be considered to be an important dimension of environmental literacy because acquiring knowledge and awareness about environment and sustainability is unhelpful to active citizenship if this knowledge and awareness is never used. The implication is that knowledge and awareness must be applied to make a difference. Taking responsible environmental action would therefore be a necessary component of sustainable behavior and active citizenship. The myriad of pressing environmental problems today demand problem-solving approaches. This should perhaps be distinguished from "activism," a concept that has decided political overtones and negative connotations for many individuals.

ESE might not teach activism but, armed with the knowledge and awareness acquired through ESE, some teacher candidates may be motivated to take action that might rightly be seen as activism. UNESCO (1978) proclaimed that EE could not be effective without creating a citizenry with the tools to participate in environmental improvement. Hollweg et al. (2011) describe an environmentally literate citizen as one who, among other things, "makes informed decisions concerning the environment; is *willing to act* on these decisions … and *participates in civic life*" (2–3, emphasis added). The point is that ESE should lead to environmental advocacy and environmental advocacy could be manifested in many different ways by different individuals. The real issue, according to Inwood and Jagger (2014), is how can participation and action be promoted without coercion and the imposition of instructors' positions and priorities on students? Perhaps this is the point that the earlier EPA quote was addressing.

There are still other unresolved issues to consider too. How can faculties of education address the multi-barriers that hinder meaningful and coherent ESE inclusion in pre-service teacher education curricula? Significant barriers that have been identified include deficiencies in faculty member knowledge and interest, unreceptive institutional cultures, and the fact that EE competencies are not required for teacher certification (Ashman 2010; Franzen 2010, 2017). How will faculties of education reimagine curricula to make room for ESE in an already crowded curriculum? And how should this be done? Should ESE be mandatory for all teacher candidates or teacher candidates in certain disciplines? Or should it be an elective available to all? Should it be delivered through discrete or stand-alone ESE courses, or should it be ESE across the curriculum where it is infused in other subjects? These are open questions, but it bears pointing out that research has shown that the infusion model has not had a successful record in ESE. Puk and Behm (2003) in discussing outcomes of environmental education and ecological literacy in Ontario, postulate that the environmental education was diluted by the infusion model. Environmental science was often infused in science and geography, but the evidence showed that teachers of these subjects gave environmental content only short shrift.

However, before any of this even becomes relevant, seismic changes are required in pre-service teacher education in Canada and Ontario. ESE must become a significant part of initial teacher education curricula. This requires support from administrative leadership and faculty champions committed to ESE, and willing to advocate for its meaningful inclusion in the curriculum. A few universities in Canada have made ESE a mandatory component of their pre-service teacher education program and could be studied as possible models for achieving this by other education programs. For example, Lakehead University in Thunder Bay, Ontario, started a mandatory SES course for all teacher candidates in 2015 and Simon Fraser University in Vancouver, British Columbia, offers a minor in environmental education. Both the University of Regina and the University of Saskatchewan have identified ESE as a major component of their teacher education programs (Inwood and Jagger 2014).

In the context of the grave ecological problems facing humanity today, ESE-TE should be considered a fundamental component of global citizenship education. The nexus between ESE and citizenship is partly found in their common principles to:

- Engage and support all learners
- Enhance cultural competence-inclusive, equitable, social justice – these are key to effective citizenship
- Prepare learners for operating in a multicultural and global world
- Focus community orientation – collaboration, service

- Application of learning for living sustainably. (OSPI and EEAW 2010)

The effective incorporation of ESE into teacher education requires teacher education curriculum revision aimed at:

1. Empowering future teachers to develop their instructional skills actively and experientially, in a variety of learning environments, both individually and collaboratively.
2. Providing an authentic learning environment so that future teachers engage in concrete tasks within realistic and problem-solving learning scenarios.
3. Emphasizing ways, that technology can facilitate and enhance future teachers' professional roles. (Makrakis 2012, 92)

The gravity of global environmental concerns makes this a critical imperative.

Conclusion

In concluding this discussion, it is prudent to consider the challenge for incorporating global citizenship education through ESE in post-secondary education. From the preceding discussion, it is clear that education and higher education, and teacher education more specifically, can play a major role in global sustainability and development agendas. However, there is skepticism about the possibilities of this happening, and a consensus that the current approaches to education largely will not bring about the desired outcomes of ESE. It is felt that a paradigm shift is required: that education in general and teacher education more specifically needs to be reoriented towards effective delivery of ESE. Winter-Simat, Wright, and Choi (2017) call for a shift in education to a "transformative ecocentric learning paradigm" (5). This fosters ecological thinking and a relational view of the world. The desired outcome would be the development of global citizens who make sustainability a natural part of their lives. Learners are engaged in an integrated way where humans are positioned not as superior beings, but as participants within the Earth's interconnected and interdependent ecological community (Winter-Simat, Wright, and Choi 2017). This is important as "awareness of the world as a web of connected complex adaptive systems in which they participate rather than manipulate or dominate, develops an ecological intelligence that can lead students to a broader worldview and more sustainable lifestyles" (Golman, Bennett, and Barlow 2012, n.p.). According to Winter-Simat, Writght, and Choi (2017):

> Although there are emerging initiatives around the world to align education with the perceived needs of the 21st century, two major problems arise. First, the conflicting structures and values of the existing education paradigm will limit their effectiveness. Further, as long as the dominant educational paradigm remains embedded and complicit with a market driven and mechanistic dominant culture, it will struggle to promote change to a system in which it is invested. Second, preparing young people or a future based on the progression of the current unsustainable economic paradigm only furthers ecological crises. (2)

There is a need for ESE in both pre-service and in-service education. With reorientation of pre-service education, future teachers would have increased competence, but practicing teachers who did not have those experiences in their initial teacher preparation will need professional development and additional qualifications courses. Shifts in thinking are required in key areas of teacher education – curriculum, philosophy, and pedagogy. More importantly perhaps, it might also require a shift in the culture of higher education (Bowers 1997). Enhancing awareness of the importance of ESE in TE is needed in faculties of education. ESE must become one of the many competing priorities in TE. Greater institutional support for ESE is required in universities and faculties. This means funding ESE courses and activities and hiring more faculty with ESE expertise.

NOTES

1 The term ESE is confusing to some because of the use of other terms such as education for sustainability eevelopment (ESD), environmental education (EE), and education for environmental sustainability (EES). ESE, EE, and EES may be rightly seen as different names for the same process and thus interchangeable. ESD, on the other hand, is not necessarily synonymous with ESE, EE, or EES. ESD is best seen as a broader and overarching concept. In this sense ESE/EES might be seen as an important dimension of ESD. ESD is grounded in "the urgent need to recast our ways of living, away from ones that rely on the unsustainable consumption of resources, the degradation of ecosystems and the exploitation of people" (United Nations Economic Commission for Europe 2012, 4).

2 Suggested ESD concepts include environmental sustainability (ES) concepts such as citizenship, biological and landscape diversity; environmental protection; ecological principles and an ecosystem approach; natural resource management; climate change; personal and family health (e.g.,

HIV/AIDS, drug abuse); environmental health (e.g., food; water quality; pollution); corporate social responsibility; Indigenous knowledge; production and/or consumption patterns; economics; rural/urban development, environmental technology; and sustainability assessment (UNECE Strategy for ESD and the UNESCO International Implementation Scheme for the United Nations Decade for Education for Sustainable Development [2005–2014], quoted in UNECE 2012).

REFERENCES

Alberta Council for Environmental Education. 2012. "Advancing Pre-Service Environmental Education in Alberta: A Discussion Paper." Canmore, AB: ACEE .

Alvarez-Garcia, O., J. Sureda-Negre, and R. Comas-Forgas. 2015. "Environmental Education in Pre-Service Teacher Training: A Literature Review of Existing Evidence." *Journal of Teacher Education for Sustainability* 17, no. 1: 72–85. https://doi.org/10.1515/jtes-2015-0006

Andersson, K., S.C. Jagers, A. Lindskog, and J. Martinsson. 2013. "Learning for the Future? Effects of Education for Sustainable Development (ESD) on Teacher Education Students. *Sustainability* 5, no. 12: 5135–52. https://doi.org/10.3390/su5125135

Ashmann, S. 2010. "In What Ways Are Pre-Service Teachers being Prepared to Teach K-12 Students about the Environment? An Investigation of Wisconsin's Teacher Education Programs." Produced under a 2008–2009 grant from the Wisconsin Environmental Education Board, Stevens Point, WI.

Ashmann, S., and R.L. Franzen.2015. "In What Ways are Teacher Candidates being Prepared to Teach about the Environment? A Case Study from Wisconsin." *Environmental Education Research* 23, no. 3: 299–323. https://doi.org/10.1080/13504622.2015.1101750

Bowers, C. 1997. *The Culture of Denial: Why the Environmental Movement Needs a Strategy for Reforming Universities and Public Schools*. Albany, NY: SUNY Press.

Citizenship Education Foundation Inc. (CEFI). n.d. "Citizenship and Citizenship Education." Concentus: Citizenship Education Foundation. Accessed 24 June 2020. https://www.concentus.ca/citizenship-and-citizenship-education/

Council of Ministers of Education Canada. 2012. "Education for Sustainable Development in Canadian Faculties of Education." https://www.iisd.org/pdf/2013/esd_canadian_faculties.pdf

DiGiuseppe, M. 2013. *Bringing Environmental Science into the Mainstream: Crucial Learning for the 21st Century*. Whitby, ON: McGraw-Hill Ryerson.

European Education Research Association. n.d. "Environmental and Sustainability Education Research, ESER." Accessed 25 June 2020. https://eera-ecer.de/networks/30-environmental-and-sustainability-education-research-eser/

Franzen, R.L. 2010. "Faculty Perspectives on Environmental Education Teacher Training." Unpublished manuscript. Department of Teaching and Learning, Northern Illinois University, DeKalb, IL.

– 2017. "Environmental Education in Teacher Education Programs: Incorporation and Use of Professional Guidelines." *Journal of Sustainability Education*16. http://www.susted.com/wordpress/content/environmental-education-in-teacher-education-programs-incorporation-and-use-of-professional-guidelines_2018_01/

Goleman, D., L. Bennett, and Z. Barlow. 2012. *Eco Literate: How Educators are Cultivating Emotional, Social, and Ecological Intelligence*. San Francisco: Jossey-Bass.

Gough A. 2016. "Environmental Sustainability in Schools." In *Global Learning in the 21st Century*, edited by T. Barkatsas and A. Bertram. Rotterdam: Sense Publishers. https://doi.org/10.1007/978-94-6300-761-0_6

Hollweg, K.S., J. Taylor, R.W. Bybee, T.J. Marcinkowski, W.C. McBeth, and P. Zodio. 2011. *Developing a Framework for Assessing Environmental Literacy*. Washington, DC: North American Association for Environmental Education. http://www.naaee.net/sites/default/files/framework/EnvLiteracyExeSummary.pdf

Hopkins, C., and R. McKeown. 2005. "Guidelines and Recommendations for Reorienting Teacher Education to Address Sustainability." Paris: UNESCO Education Sector.

Inwood, H., and S. Jagger. 2014. *DEEPER: Deepening Environmental Education in Pre-Service Education Resource*. Toronto: University of Toronto, Ontario Institute for Studies in Education.

Lawale, S., and A. Bory-Adams. "The Decade of Education for Sustainable Development: Towards Four Pillars of Learning." *Development* 53, no. 4: 547–50. https://doi.org/10.1057/dev.2010.76.

Lin, E. 2002. "Trend of Environmental Education in Canadian Pre-Service Teacher Education Programs from 1979 to 1996." *Canadian Journal of Environmental Education* 7, no. 1: 199–215.

Liu, S.-Y., S.-C. Yeh, S.-W. Liang, W.-T. Fang, and H.-M. Tsai. 2015."A National Investigation of Teachers' Environmental Literacy as a Reference for Promoting Environmental Education in Taiwan." *The Journal of Environmental Education* 46, no. 2: 114–32.

Makrakis, V. 2008. "An Instructional Design Module of ICT that Empowers Teachers to iintegrate Education for Sustainable Development across the Curriculum. In *Proceedings of the 6th Panhellenic Conference with International*

Participation on Information and Communication Technologies in Education, edited by C. Angeli and N. Valanides. Vol. 1. Cyprus: University of Cyprus.

– 2010. "Strategies to Reinforce the Role of ICT in Teaching and Learning for Sustainability." In *Tomorrow Today*, edited by M. Witthaus, K. Candless, and R. Lambert. Leicester: Tudor Rose.

– 2011. "ICT-Enabled Education for Sustainable Development: Merging Theory with Praxis." In *Proceedings of the 4th Conference on e-Learning Excellence in the Middle East*, edited by M. Youssef and S.A. Anwar. Dubai, UAE: Hamdan Bin Mohammed e-University.

– 2012. "Reorienting Teacher Education to Address Sustainable Development Through WikiQuESD." In *Research on e-Learning and ICT in Education*, edited by A. Jimoyiannis. New York: Springer. https://doi.org/10.1007/978-1-4614-1083-6_7

McKeown, R., with USTESD Network. 2013. "Reorienting Teacher Education to Address Sustainability: The U.S. Context." White Paper Series, No. 1. Indianapolis, IN: United States Teacher Education for Sustainable Development Network.

National Roundtable on Environmental Sustainability Education in Teacher Education (NRESE-TE). 2016. "Action Plan." Peterborough, ON: Trent University. http://eseinfacultiesofed.ca/pdfs/events-pdfs/National%20Action%20Plan%20(July%202016).pdf

North American Association of Environmental Educators (NAAEE). 2007. "Standards for the Initial Preparation of Environmental Educators." Washington, DC: National Council for Accreditation of Teacher Education.

– 2010. "Excellence in Environmental Education: Guidelines for Learning (K-12)." https://naaee.org/eepro/publication/excellence-environmental-education-guidelines-learning-k-12

Office of the Superintendent of Instruction (OSPI). 2016. "Education for Environmental Sustainability. Washington State." http://www.k12.wa.us/EnvironmentSustainability/default.aspx

Office of the Superintendent of Instruction (OSPI) in Cooperation with Environmental Education Association of Washington (EEAW). 2010. "Environmental and Sustainability Education: Professional Development Guidelines. Public Review Draft." Olympia, WA: OSPI.

Ontario Ministry of Education (OME). 2009. *Acting Today, Shaping Tomorrow: A Policy Framework for Environmental Education in Ontario Schools*. Toronto: OME.

Puk, T., and D. Behm. 2003. "The Diluted Curriculum: The Role of Government in Developing Ecological Literacy as the First Imperative in Ontario Secondary Schools." *Canadian Journal of Environmental Education* no. 8: 215–32.

Reade, C., W.J. Reckmeyer, M. Cabot, D. Jaehne, and M. Novak 2013. "Educating Global Citizens for the 21st Century: The SJSU Salzburg

Program." *The Journal of Corporate Citizenship* no. 49: 100–16. https://doi.org/10.9774/gleaf.4700.2013.ma.00008

Russell, C., and L. Fawcett. 2012. "Moving Margins in Environmental Education." In *International Handbook of Research on Environmental Education*, edited by R. Stevenson, M. Brody, J. Dillon, and A. Wals. New York: Routledge.

Sureda-Negre, J., M. Oliver-Trobat, A. Catalan-Fernández, and R. Comas-Forgas. 2014. "Environmental Education for Sustainability in the Curriculum of Primary Teacher Training in Spain." *International Research in Geographical and Environmental Education* 23, no. 4: 281–93. https://doi.org/10.1080/10382046.2014.946322

Tal, T. 2010. "Pre-Service Teachers' Reflections on Awareness and Knowledge Following Active Learning in Environmental Education." *International Research in Geographical and Environmental Education* 19, no, 4: 263–76. doi: 10.1080/10382046.2010.519146https://doi.org/10.1080/10382046.2010.519146

Towler, J.O. 1981. "A Survey of Canadian Pre-Service Training in Environmental Education." *Journal of Environmental Education* 12, no. 2: 11–16. https://doi.org/10.1080/00958964.1981.10801893

Tuncer, G., J.W. Boone, O.Y. Tuzun, and C. Oztekin. 2014. "An Evaluation of the Environmental Literacy of Pre-Service Teachers in Turkey through Rasch Analysis." *Environmental Education Research* 20, no. 2: 202–27. https://doi.org/10.1080/13504622.2013.768604

UNESCO. 1978. "Intergovernmental Conference on Environmental Education. United Nations Environmental Program." http://www.gdrc.org/uem/ee/tbilisi.html

– 2005. "Guidelines and Recommendations for Reorienting Teacher Education to Address Sustainability, UNESCO Education for Sustainable Development in Action." Technical Paper No. 4. http://unesdoc.unesco.org/images/0014/001433/143370e.pdf

– 2006. *Higher Education for Sustainable Development Education. UN Decade, 2005–2014 Section for Education for Sustainable Development (ED/PEQ/ESD).* Paris: UNESCO.

– 2014. *Global Citizenship Education: Preparing Learners for the Challenges of the 21st Century*. Paris: UNESCO. http://unesdoc.unesco.org/images/0022/002277/227729E.pdf

– 2017. *Education for Sustainable Development Goals: Learning Objectives. UNESCO Education Sector and the Global Education 2030 Agenda*. Paris: UNESCO. http://unesdoc.unesco.org/images/0024/002474/247444e.pdf

United Nations. 1992. United Nations Conference on Economic Development – Agenda 21. https://sustainabledevelopment.un.org/content/documents/Agenda21.pdf.

– 2015. "Transforming Our World: The 2030 Agenda for Sustainable Development Rome: United Nations General Assembly." Sustainable Development Goals

Knowledge Platform. https://sustainabledevelopment.un.org/post2015/transformingourworld

United Nations Department of Public Information (UNDPI). 1997. "Earth Summit + 5: Programme for the Further Implementation of Agenda 21." New York: UNDPI.

United Nations Economic Commission for Europe (UNECE). 2012. *Learning for the Future: Competences in Education for Sustainable Development*. United Nations Economic Commission for Europe, Strategy for Education for Sustainable Development. Geneva: UNECE.

United Nations World Commission on Environment and Development. 1987. *Our Common Future*. Oxford: Oxford University Press.

United States Environmental Protection Agency (EPA). n.d. "What Is Environmental Education?" Accessed 24 June 2018. https://www.epa.gov/education/what-environmental-education

Winter-Simat, N., N. Wright, and J.H. Choi. 2017. "Creating 21st Century Global Citizens. A Design-Led Systems Approach to Transformative Secondary Education for Sustainability." Paper presented at EAD 12 | 2017 Design for Next conference, 12–14 April, Rome, Italy.

Working Group on Environmental Education. 2007. "Shaping Our Schools, Shaping Our Future: Environmental Education in Ontario Schools. Report of the Working Group on Environmental Education." Toronto: Ontario Ministry of Education.

5 Human Trafficking and Implications for Global Citizenship Education: Gender Equality, Women's Rights, and Gender-Sensitive Learning[1]

MIKHAELA GRAY-BEERMAN

This chapter discusses the need for the inclusion of gender-sensitive learning in global citizenship education (GCE). It begins by examining the relationship between globalization, education, and human trafficking. This section will provide an outline of gender-sensitive GCE and identify how it can challenge societal views that marginalize women. The chapter then looks at pervasive gender rights issues within Canada, and proposes ways to deconstruct them through education. On an international scale, the chapter examines the relationship between culture, education, and gender equality. Finally, it will look at the responsibilities of post-secondary institutions to view human trafficking as an international problem and combat it through focused educational efforts that promote gender-sensitive GCE with teachers, students, and researchers. The chapter suggests that a GCE curriculum that emphasizes the rights of women and girls can help combat human rights issues like human trafficking.

Globalization, Education, and Human Trafficking

The world has become more interconnected, and the speed of travel and the accessibility of transportation have increased dramatically. Technology has allowed us to share and attain knowledge at a mass level. Also, cross-continental trade is presently the norm as commercial goods have become easily available in countries across the world, which is a practice commonly referred to as globalization.

Globalization affects local policies and practices in education. There are many institutions contributing to discussions on global education, including "the World Bank, the Organization for Economic Cooperation and Development, the World Trade Organization, the United Nations, and UNESCO" (Spring 2008, 330). Regional organizations such as the

European Union, the Organization of American States, and the African Union are also engaged in this topic. Global education can influence attitudes, develop caring individuals, and prepare generations to promote a world of peace. "There is no more powerful transformative force than education – to promote human rights and dignity, to eradicate poverty and deepen sustainability, to build a better future for all, founded on equal rights and social justice, respect for cultural diversity, and international solidarity and shared responsibility, all of which are fundamental aspects of our common humanity" (UNESCO 2015b, 4). The globalization of education can be used to make the world a better place and influence positive change.

In addition to implications on education, globalization involves trade between nations and allows access to goods and services across borders. "International trade is integral to the process of globalization. Over many years, governments in most countries have increasingly opened their economies to international trade" (World Trade Organization 2008, xiii). During the period from 1950 to 2007, international trade grew on average by 6.2 per cent (15). Trade continues to grow today and advances in technology are shaping the global economy in new ways.

A question that arises when considering globalization is whether an interconnected world helps promote social justice, human rights, and a sustainable world or if it increases inequalities, inhumane criminal activity, and environmental crisis. This chapter centres on the limits of this world togetherness by examining human trafficking as a bourgeoning global criminal activity. "Transnational criminals have been major beneficiaries of globalization. Human smuggling and trafficking have been among the fastest growing forms of transnational crime because current world conditions have created increased demand and supply" (Shelley 2010, 2). As a result of these societal changes and advances in technology, it is estimated that there are more people in forced labour today than any time in human history. Human trafficking undervalues and exploits adults and children in both developing and developed nations; this is a global issue. There is not an area of the world that is safe from this exploitive crime. "Human trafficking affects every country of the world, as countries of origin, transit or destination – or even a combination of all" (United Nations Office on Drug and Crime n.d.a).

There are many competing definitions of human trafficking and a lack of consensus among governments, non-governmental organizations, and various stakeholders on what the crime entails. As a result, information and data collected are often incomparable because the lens through which exploitation is viewed differs. For example, Article 3 of the United Nations Protocol to Prevent, Suppress, and Punish

Trafficking in Persons Especially Women and Children (also known as the Palermo Protocol) defines human trafficking as

> the recruitment, transportation, transfer, harbouring or receipt of persons, by means of the threat or use of force or other forms of coercion, of abduction, of fraud, of deception, of the abuse of power or of a position of vulnerability or of the giving or receiving of payments or benefits to achieve the consent of a person having control over another person, for the purpose of exploitation. Exploitation shall include, at a minimum, the exploitation of the prostitution[2] of others or other forms of sexual exploitation, forced labour or services, slavery or practices similar to slavery, servitude or the removal of organs. (United Nations Human Rights Office of the High Commissioner 2000, 2)

The Palermo Protocol is one of three protocols that are a part of the United Nations Convention against Transnational Organized Crime (United Nations Office on Drugs and Crimes, n.d.b). The Protocol came into effect on 25 December 2003 and "is the first global legally binding instrument with an agreed definition on trafficking in persons" (United Nations Office on Drugs and Crimes, n.d.b, n.p.). The International Labour Organization (ILO) highlights that "forced labour refers to situations in which persons are coerced to work through the use of violence or intimidation, or by more subtle means such as accumulated debt, retention of identity papers or threats of denunciation to immigration authorities" and notes that "most situations of slavery or human trafficking are ... covered by ILO's definition of forced labour" (International Labour Organization 2014, n.p.). The Canadian government defines human trafficking as "the recruitment, transportation, harbouring and/ or exercising control, direction or influence over the movements of a person in order to exploit that person, typically through sexual exploitation or forced labour. It is often described as a modern form of slavery" (Government of Canada 2012, 4). The differentiations in how the issue is defined by various stakeholders contributes to the human trafficking data crises, which will be discussed later in this chapter. Within this chapter, the Canadian definition of human trafficking is used to frame the discussion with a predominant focus on sexual exploitation and sex trafficking due to the fact that the majority of human trafficking cases in Canada involve people who have been trafficked domestically for the purposes of sexual exploitation (Royal Canadian Mounted Police 2013, 5).

The number of trafficked persons globally is staggering. The number of women and girls being exploited is even more shocking. The ILO and Walk Free Foundation predict that in 2016, there were 40.3 million people, 5.4 out of every 1,000 people worldwide, who were being exploited through human trafficking (International Labour Organization and Walk Free Foundation 2017, 21). Women and girls account for 71 per cent of the 40.3 million persons being trafficked (10). Globalization has increased the demand and accessibility of sexual services, perpetuating the growth of the trafficking of persons in both local and global contexts. When examining sexual exploitation, 99 per cent of the persons trafficked are women and girls (22). Why are women and girls grossly overrepresented in sex trafficking and sexual exploitation? What underlying beliefs and attitudes towards gender are contributing to the trafficking of women and children? These questions are not being adequately addressed by many of those interested in making the world a better place. Education can play a vital role in combatting the trafficking of persons by building leaders who value the life of each human being, see and respect the equality of genders, and work together to eradicate the degradation of women and girls. Further, gender-sensitive GCE in post-secondary institutions could also play an important role in addressing human trafficking.

Similar to other chapters in this volume (e.g., chapter 10 by Aboagye), this discussion demonstrates that post-secondary institutions can shape the next generation of leaders and activists to be caring global citizens who promote the rights of women. The next section will examine the role of gender-sensitive GCE and human trafficking in Canada and abroad to demonstrate that post-secondary institutions have a responsibility to ensure that the world's future leaders are prepared to create a more just and equitable world. Gender-sensitive GCE can create systematic change and help redress human rights issues like gender inequality that contributes to the trafficking of persons.

Gender-Sensitive Global Citizenship Education

Global citizenship education that emphasizes human rights and women's rights provides a lens for students to see beyond themselves through encountering and wrestling with the challenges that oppress and cause division among citizens around the globe. "Global Education is education that opens people's eyes and minds to the realities of the world, and awakens them to bring about a world of greater justice, equity and human rights for all" (O'Loughlin and Wegimont 2002, quoted in McDonnell, Solignac-Lecomte, and Wegimont 2003, 40). This kind of education will help students view one another with dignity and respect, which is an essential concept in order to understand and address issues like human trafficking. Questions that need to frame discussions within GCE include: What is a person's worth? Can you assign a dollar amount to someone's life? Understanding that a person is valuable because they are is a concept, which could help students learn, internalize and uphold the important idea that no human being is a commodity to be bought and sold. In addition, discussing these ideas through a women's rights perspective in the classroom would help students combat the ideology that women are inferior to men. Male superiority, or toxic masculinity, perpetuates the idea that women are of lesser value. Global citizenship education promotes equity for all and can redress systemic beliefs that underlie the issue of trafficking.

The majority of people who are trafficked are women and most offenders of trafficking are men. It is important to highlight, however, that there are men who are trafficked and women who are traffickers. In fact, women trafficking other women is the norm in some countries (United Nations Office on Drugs and Crime, n.d.c).

As Greve (2014) notes, the attention given by the media and reports on this issue often makes it appear that people who are trafficked are solely women and it overlooks the exploited population of men which is problematic. However, since the overwhelming majority of people who are trafficked are women and girls, GCE needs to include an explicit emphasis on women's rights in addition to acknowledging the exploitation of men and boys in trafficking. In addition, the LGBTQ2+ community is often targeted by traffickers for the purposes of exploitation and needs to be included in gender-sensitive GCE discussions. "'A gender-sensitive, global citizenship education' has the 'potential to help women actively contribute to cross-national global thinking, it provides a space for addressing gender-related issues and it embraces a pedagogical philosophy that empowers students by encouraging them to engage critically with contemporary concerns'" (Arnot 2004, quoted in Lister 2008, 13). Education provides a pathway for reconstructing societal views that degrade, disrespect, and exclude women. As Paul Banahene Adjei highlights in chapter 8 of this volume, teachers need to ensure that students build new knowledge about social justice and oppression, as well as unlearn what they already know. The British Council report indicates that education for global citizenship "will tackle not just gender inequality and the rights of women, but some of the fundamental ideas in a society over who is a 'citizen,' and what the rights of those 'citizens' are" (Davies 2000, quoted in Lister 2008, 12). By including women's rights prominently in the classroom, girls will feel empowered and boys will learn the important concepts of respect and inclusion. "The first step in challenging gender-based exclusion is for women 'to become aware that their exclusion is an injustice and that things can change'" (Lister 2008, 16, quoting Meer with Sever 2004).

The UNESCO Office Bangkok released a 2014 report, *Learning to Live Together* (LTLT), which identifies the importance of gender equality in the curriculum. "While gender equality is a greater challenge for some countries than it is for others, ensuring gender equality is recognized at the policy level and ensuring it is reinforced through curriculum, teaching and assessment policies is essential to the fostering of LTLT in education systems" (80). Through gender-sensitive GCE and addressing underlying systemic issues of sexism and patriarchy in the classroom, beliefs that propagate the issue of human trafficking can be transformed.

The United Nations Human Rights Office of the High Commissioner report *Human Rights and Human Trafficking* (2014, 42) affirms that long-term measures are needed to address the social, cultural, and structural causes of violence against women, which is clearly demonstrated and reproduced when examining the issue of human trafficking. UNESCO (2015a, 16) has identified gender equality as a priority in the *2015 Global Citizenship Education: Topics and Learning Objectives* report: "Global citizenship education can support gender equality through the development of knowledge, skills, values and attitudes that promote the equal value of women and men, engender respect and enable young people to critically question gendered roles and expectations that are harmful and/or encourage gender-based discrimination and stereotyping" (16). A gender-sensitive approach to global citizenship education makes space for critical conversations about the equal value of all human beings. If girls can see themselves as being valuable and as individuals with intrinsic worth, their vulnerabilities to being trafficked could be reduced. According to the Canadian Women's Foundation (2014, 27), one of the biggest risk factors for being trafficked is being a girl. Another risk factor is wanting to be loved (34). As Arnot and Ghaill (2006) write, "Young women ... need to be guided into good personal choices, helped to overcome misconceptions about the limits on their options, and taught that they can do anything. In these ways they can then become responsible for their future, lead and integrate their communities, and act as role models for others" (273). It is hoped that through unlearning limits imposed on gender and relearning truths about the equality of all persons, fewer people will be vulnerable to trafficking. If boys could see girls as valuable and as individuals with intrinsic worth, the demand to purchase and sell them could be reduced. Girls and boys who see one another as equals is an important starting place to combat human trafficking.

Beyond critical thinking and shifting mindsets, a gender-sensitive approach to global citizenship education helps students understand their civic responsibility locally, nationally and globally. This will hopefully lead to developing agents of change who are prepared to take action to combat global inequities. Chapter 11 by Andrew Robinson in this volume defines global citizenship education as follows: (1) It equips students with knowledge to understand and make sense of major issues and processes that are shaping the world; (2) it encourages students to adopt a sense of responsibility to address those problems; and (3) it provides students with skills and competencies that will enable them to work to address those problems. This definition highlights that through global citizenship education, students will be provided the necessary resources and tools to know how to respond to injustice and human rights issues. The trafficking of persons is becoming a common problem amongst youth globally; therefore, GCE is needed as a preventative measure to teach about human trafficking, as well as to equip students to join the fight to end it. According to a 2016 report, over 21 per cent of individuals trafficked for commercial sexual exploitation were children under the age of eighteen years old (International Labour Organization and Walk Free Foundation 2017, 40).

Human trafficking requires an understanding of the human rights violations that are prevalent at all three levels of global citizenship (local, national, and global). Educators must raise students' awareness of various forms of injustices and prepare them to be globally responsible; also, students must learn to act in a way that helps promote peace. If students are taught about gender, human trafficking, and the implications of violating others, it will reduce demand and vulnerabilities, and open discussions on how to create meaningful change in order to make a better future for all.

The Canadian Context

The trafficking of persons is a problem in Canada. I began to learn about the realities of trafficking in my home country eight years ago, when my mother shared a story with me. When she was in grade school, her best friend Dawn[3] went missing. Years later, they reunited. Dawn had been trafficked for the purposes of sexual exploitation at the age of fourteen. She was removed from Ontario (through the United States) and sold in Vancouver, British Columbia. I was shocked and deeply disturbed when I heard this story of child exploitation and injustice. Questions raged through my mind: Does this type of exploitation still exist in our society, or was this a one-time tragic situation? If it does still exist, what is being done to end human trafficking here in Canada? Who are the trafficked persons today? Through research and education, I quickly learned that today the issue is not only ongoing but also growing.

Over 90 per cent of people who are trafficked in Canada are from within Canada's borders (Canadian Women's Foundation 2014, 12). The most common recruitment age in Canada is thirteen or fourteen years old (24). Eighty-three per cent of persons accused of human trafficking in Canada between 2009 and 2014 were male, 41 per cent of whom were between the ages of eighteen and twenty-four (Karam 2016, 4). Ninety-three per cent of police-reported individuals who were exploited through human trafficking during this same period of time were female. Forty-seven per cent of trafficked persons were between the ages of eighteen and twenty-four and, shockingly, one-quarter of these individuals were under the age of eighteen (3). A significant number of young-adult males in Canada are exploiting young-adult females. This fact highlights that human trafficking is a gender issue, and there is a desperate need for it to be addressed within Canadian schooling.

There is a lack of data on the number of Indigenous women impacted by the sex industry and sex trafficking, however, "individual studies in Canada's urban centres point to a disproportionately high number of Aboriginal women" involved in the sex industry (Sikka 2009, 10). As Barrett (2013) notes in the Task Force on Trafficking of Women and Girls in Canada report entitled *An Assessment of Human Trafficking in Canada*, "It is currently not known what percentage of these girls and women are in sex trafficking situations versus 'survival sex' situations, where they are compelled to sell or exchange sex for shelter, food or drugs, but not by a third party" (14).[4] It is estimated that 70 per cent of sexually exploited youth and 50 per cent of sexually exploited adults in Winnipeg are Indigenous (Seshia 2005, 16). The Indigenous community makes up only 4 per cent of Canada's population, yet estimates indicate that over 50 per cent of people trafficked in Canada are Indigenous. This highlights the gross overrepresentation of Indigenous women and girls who are impacted by human trafficking. There are various factors that influence why Indigenous peoples are vulnerable to being trafficked in Canada. Indigenous youth from remote areas move to large urban centers seeking better access to education, health, and family services (Sikka 2009, 13). Due to "their lack of employment-related skills and lack of experience living in an urban centre" these youth are susceptible to being trafficked (Oxman-Martinez, Lacroix, and Hanley 2005, 11).

In addition, the ongoing exploitation and violence against Indigenous women and girls is linked to colonial roots. As Hunt (2016) writes, a "more complex understanding of trafficking and colonialism is necessary if colonial violence is to be taken seriously within sex workers rights movements, and if Indigenous communities are to truly begin to address the particular vulnerability and violence faced by our relations in the sex trade as part of the continuum of violence faced by Indigenous girls and women" (26). The complexity that Hunt refers to points to the importance of viewing human trafficking through an interdisciplinary lens that includes race, gender, and socio-economic barriers: "Indeed, sexual violence is seen as a hallmark of colonial progress and is a central force in creating racial and gendered hierarchies through colonial legal categories. It is within this context of ongoing, systematic, and longstanding sexualized violence that Indigenous women's involvement in trading and selling sex occurs" (32). Decolonizing education is required in order to support and empower Indigenous youth. What does gender-sensitive global citizenship education look like within an Indigenous framework and context? How can the long history of colonial exploitation and violence against Indigenous women and girls be redressed through GCE? Indigenous peoples are especially vulnerable to being trafficked; what kind of educational tools and resources could be employed to appropriately address human rights issues like human trafficking through GCE within Indigenous communities? These are critical questions that are worthy of investigation.

An aspect of education that must be considered when addressing human trafficking is ensuring that gender-sensitive GCE is provided to men and boys, not just girls. As the Global Education Monitoring Report Team (2016) puts it, "Gender inequality affects us all. Achieving gender equality must involve us all" (12). In Janice Wallace's (2007) paper "Inclusive Schooling and Gender," she shares a story her colleague told her that illustrates the misperceptions of women in Canada and gender inequality among school-aged children:

> During a preliminary school visit, [Wallace's colleague] and the students were walking down the hall behind two young boys who ... were probably in grade two. One of the young boys took a surreptitious look over his shoulder at the large group of strangers following him down the hall and in a loud whisper, nervously asked: "Who are they?" His friend whispered back: "The girls are here to learn how to be teachers and the boys are here to learn how to be principals." (71)

The belief that women are subordinate to men still exists within today's Canadian society, even among and within the mindsets of children.

These biases and misconstrued beliefs about gender roles and the oppression of women and girls must be redressed. This inequality can be further observed through the representation of women in the workforce. According to chapter 11 by Andrew Robinson in this volume, "women are proportionately underrepresented among executive directors" in the non-profit sector in Ontario, Canada. His study found that 50 per cent of women held top executive positions, which is surprising because 70 to 80 per cent of the workers in this sector are female. In addition to gender gaps in employment, Canadian women are subject to a higher likelihood of experiencing violence in their lifetime. The Canadian Women's Foundation (2016) lists shocking statistics that emphasize the need to address gender-based violence and advocate for the rights of women and girls in Canada:

- "Half of all women in Canada have experienced at least one incident of physical or sexual violence since the age of 16."
- "67% of Canadians say they have personally known at least one woman who has experienced physical or sexual abuse."
- "Approximately every six days, a woman in Canada is killed by her intimate partner. Out of the 83 police-reported intimate partner homicides in 2014, 67 of the victims – over 80% – were women."
- "On any given night in Canada, 3,491 women and their 2,724 children sleep in shelters because it isn't safe at home." (1–2)

Gender inequality is one of the factors that is contributing to the growth of trafficking in Canada. There is no doubt that there is a correlation between sexism, violence against women, and the trafficking of persons. Attitudes and beliefs about the value of women need to be challenged in Canada. Kizhaay Anishinaabe Niin, named for an Ojibway phrase that means "I am a Kind Man," is an initiative by Indigenous men in Ontario to address "the problem of men's violence and abuse against women in Indigenous communities" (see http://iamakindman.ca). Part of the "I am a Kind Man" initiative includes "raising awareness and an understanding of the causes of violence against women." According to the Minister for the Status of Women, there could be as many as 4,000 cases of missing or murdered Indigenous women in Canada (Tasker 2016). The Canadian federal government stated in its 2014 Action Plan that "the Status of Women Canada will 'work with First Nations, Inuit and Métis communities and stakeholders'" on projects that "will raise awareness through education and related activities to increase understanding about the impacts of violence; engage Aboriginal men and boys to prevent violence; and empower Aboriginal women and girls to speak out about violence" (Feinstein and Pearce 2015, 19). These initiatives point to the need to expand existing efforts and explore opportunities to include gender-sensitive global citizenship education in Canada that includes concepts of respect and inclusion, gender equity and empowerment, and the ongoing impact of colonial violence in the classroom. Gender-sensitive GCE embraces the "important African philosophy of Ubuntu, which, in simplified terms, is 'seeing our humanity through the humanity and the needs of others'" (Abdi and Shultz 2007, 10). Teaching students to care for the needs of women and girls as an aspect of global citizenship can change societal structures of domination and subordination that foster the exploitation of women. We must learn to see ourselves in one another – and beyond seeing, we must empathize with the needs and lived realities of individuals whose experiences are different from our own. Compassion may lead to positive actions, which could help remedy injustices like human trafficking in our world.

Beyond Canada's Borders

"Research suggests that women and children have been among the largest losers of globalization" (Shelley 2010, 17). As a result of the 2008 global financial crises, in some countries girls were pulled out of school in order to work to support their families (298). The crisis began when the price of housing in the United States plummeted, first impacting the American financial sector, and then overseas when prices of shares dropped around the globe (Havemann 2010). Families depended on girls to make an income even though they had a lack of skill and education, which made them more susceptible to human trafficking (Shelley 2010, 17). According to the Committee on the Elimination of Discrimination against Women (CEDAW 1992, para. 14), "Poverty and unemployment increase opportunities for trafficking in women" and forms of sexual exploitation "are incompatible with the equal enjoyment of rights by women and with respect for their rights and dignity." Gender-sensitive GCE can address the systemic and societal norms that have created a culture of the degradation of women globally.

In many parts of Africa, Latin America, and Asia, girls and women often obtain employment in sectors where they are vulnerable to labour and sexual exploitation (Shelley 2010, 54). In some countries, low socioeconomic conditions as well as lack of supports and access to education may influence families to view exploitation as part of the system in which they must operate to survive. By providing access to knowledge, particularly to communities with low literacy rates, ideas about gender equality and human trafficking can begin to shape attitudes and cultural beliefs that not only enable this issue to exist but are contributing to its growth. "There are such long traditions of debt bondage, forced marriages, and trafficking into prostitution that in many Asian countries neither the victim nor the trafficker is significantly stigmatized, helping perpetuate these practices" (149). These traditions raise questions about the global application of UN policies of children and women's rights. For example, when I was conducting research in India in 2017 I was told of a women's trafficking story where her parents were charged for trafficking her. Afterwards, she got married and started a family of her own. One day, her brother came to visit and then re-trafficked her (Gray 2018, 98). This example illustrates possible cultural perceptions and ideologies that contribute to the exploitation of women. Importantly, this highlights the need to consider the question: What role should global citizenship education play in examining traditions that are context- and culture-bound? Should citizens who are external to those contexts contribute in this examination, and if so, what processes and actions are worth embracing?

Efforts are being made globally to bring gender inequality to the forefront of education. For example, a ten-year initiative by the MasterCard Foundation supports the education of 15,000 young people, most of whom are from Africa. The educational program helps students "to become 'socially transformative leaders,' driving change and making a positive social impact in their communities." A measurement indicator within the program is the level at which a student "understands and expresses positive attitudes towards differences of gender" (UNESCO 2014, 35). This MasterCard initiative builds global citizens who understand the value of women and girls, which helps address the systemic issues and cultural belief systems that are part of the root cause of human trafficking. GCE is a tool that can be used to break down the societal norms that exploit women across the world. Perhaps one of the expected outcomes of GCE ought to be whether the individual has understood and embraced the global importance of a gender-sensitive attitude and perspective.

In addition to educating youth through gender-sensitive GCE, faculties of education in post-secondary institutions play an important role in building globally responsible citizens. Teacher trainees have the opportunity to impact the next generation through gender-sensitive teaching strategies and GCE that emphasizes women's rights. Teacher trainees will be the future leaders who shape the minds of young people in primary and secondary schools. They have the power to influence positive change and challenge gender binaries, through which issues like human trafficking can begin to be addressed.

A course subject entitled "Social Dimensions of Teaching" is a part of the pre-service teacher education curriculum in the Philippines. Within the course, teacher trainees can select three one-unit seminars, one of which is on "gender, peace and human rights" (UNESCO Office Bangkok 2014, 56). The course also includes an entire section on gender and development, which is composed of the following sub-sections: gender and equality, gender and power, and gender and education towards development (102). Similarly, a course called "The Global Citizen and Education" was developed by Liverpool Hope University in the United Kingdom for second-year students in education studies. Women's rights is one of the issues covered in the course, and students are responsible for developing workshops on global citizenship for Grade 8 students at a local public school (Jorgenson and Schultz 2012, 13). World University Service of Canada (2014, 14) has a project in South Sudan that in addition to pedagogy instruction includes gender awareness training for teachers. These examples reinforce the importance of exposing teachers-in-training to concepts of gender equality. Valuing all human beings as equal, and emphasizing the importance of valuing women and girls, is an integral part of being a global citizen. Teacher's colleges have a responsibility to ensure that teacher trainees model a global citizenry that embraces gender sensitivities. By building future leaders who understand and value the importance of women's issues, they can empower their students to see the world from a lens of equality. Perhaps boys and girls who view one another as equals, and who care about addressing global injustice, will be less likely to contribute to the demand of trafficked persons or be vulnerable to trafficking – a critical preventative measure. Through gender-sensitive teaching, students may understand the role they can play in using their voice to enact change in the world by raising awareness and taking action.

The Data Crisis and Opportunity for Post-Secondary Institutions

There is an inadequacy of comprehensive and reliable data on human trafficking, which is influenced by the very nature of trafficking as characterized by secrecy and danger (UNESCO 2007, 33). According to Antonio Maria Costa, the former executive director of the United Nations Office on Drug and Crime, there is a knowledge crisis, and governments and social scientists need to commit to improving information-gathering and information-sharing on human trafficking (United Nations Office on Drugs and Crime 2009, 7). Further, there is a dismal lack of research focused specifically on the globalization of human trafficking and implications for education. There is a significant need for accurate and diverse research on human trafficking on this issue in Canada and globally.

As indicated through the story of my own learning about the existence of human trafficking in Canada, there is a lack of general public awareness of the human trafficking that is taking place within Canada; consequently, most people fail to understand that it is a domestic issue as much as a global one. For example, a report issued by the British Columbia Ministry of Justice (2013, 8) found that human trafficking is not well understood within the province of British Columbia and the Canadian public. Post-secondary institutions have the opportunity to raise awareness on systematic issues of the degradation of women in society within Canada and globally. They can develop an understanding of how human trafficking works and its impact on the lives of those who are trafficked. Research can create the impetus for policies and for change. Post-secondary institutions can build curricula and promote community values that teach the next generation of students how to be globally responsible. As Minter and Thompson (1968) wrote some decades ago, "the university will change society through individuals rather than through corporate action. 'Out from its citadel will go educated, men and women with passion to remake the world ... From it will emanate ideas and knowledge that will be revolutionary in their impact'" (3, quoting Carnegie Foundation for the Advancement of Teaching 1967). The societal changes and attitudinal shifts required to eradicate human trafficking include preparing globally responsible students within higher education institutions, who use scholarship and research to create informed change through policy and curriculum development.

Canada was among the first countries to implement the United Nations Protocol to Prevent, Suppress and Punish Trafficking in Persons, especially Women and Children (Government of Canada 2012, 1). A national document that derived from this protocol is the *National Action Plan to Combat Human Trafficking,* which was published by the federal government in 2012. The plan's proposed prevention strategy highlights the following actions: "promote training for front-line service providers; support and develop new human trafficking awareness campaigns within Canada; provide assistance to communities to identify people and places most at risk; distribute awareness materials at Canadian embassies and high commissions abroad; and strengthen Child Protection Systems within the Canadian International Development

Agency's programs targeting children and youth" (Government of Canada 2012, 11).

It appears that, although this strategy was launched eight years ago, anecdotal information shows that general awareness is still low. There is an immense amount of work that needs to be done to understand the issue and to educate the public. The House of Commons Standing Committee on Justice and Human Rights launched a national investigation on human trafficking in Canada and released a report entitled *Moving Forward in the Fight Against Human Trafficking in Canada* (Standing Committee on Justice and Human Rights 2018). The report outlines the significant measures that are needed to combat trafficking locally.

The first recommendation states: "That the Government of Canada take appropriate measures to increase public awareness of human trafficking. This should include campaigns directed to the general population and targeted towards specific groups, such as the hospitality industry, taxi, limousine drivers and ride-sharing services, such as Uber and Lyft. It should also be directed towards more vulnerable groups or persons, such as Indigenous and racialized communities, and children. These campaigns should also be reaching out to young people through social media" (1). The eighth recommendation states: "That the Minister of Justice work with the provinces and territories to improve data gathering and information sharing among all stakeholders involved in the fight against human trafficking in Canada and work towards creating a national database containing such data and information" (2). The report goes on further to highlight that "the Committee also recognizes that the absence of a standardized method to collect data on human trafficking for civil society and governments is posing a barrier to the improvement of our understanding of human trafficking" (57).

Post-secondary institutions can help fill this gap by supporting research and data collection to create evidence-informed approaches to educate and respond to the issue. Taylor and Fransman (2004) write that higher learning institutions "have the real potential to become key actors in promoting not only transformative learning at an individual level, but also wider social, institutional and discursive change" (9–10). In addition, universities and colleges have the opportunity to encourage students to be global leaders who enable change through scholarship and practice. This data is necessary to spread awareness about the realities of human trafficking within our society. Global citizenship education that goes beyond learning to empathize with others through reading materials within a course must also include long-term educational strategies of action, including sustainable service-learning components. If educational programs on global citizenship are going to truly create meaningful conversation on gender binaries and change attitudes towards the rights of women, data collection and research is needed to create informed curriculum on the violence against women, including human trafficking.

Public awareness also needs to be raised globally on trafficking and exploitation. Shelly (2010) describes this pressing need:

> Although public awareness of, and concern over the trafficking of women and children (and irregular migration in general) has never been greater among governments, international agencies and NGOs, the knowledge base is still relatively weak. After almost a decade of attention, research on trafficking for sexual exploitation has not moved much beyond mapping the problem, and reviews of legal frameworks and policy responses. Despite repeated calls in international documents, including from the European Union and Council of Europe, the vast majority of states are still unable to provide reliable data as to the number of cases, the [survivors] and their characteristics and the perpetrators. (216)

Governments need to be called to action to fund post-secondary research in this area globally. Funding research focused on human trafficking and violence against women would encourage universities and colleges to focus more effort on gender equality and the rights of women. This shift would encourage the development of curricula that teach students to be globally responsible citizens who are aware of the needs of women and girls. Alongside gender-sensitive GCE that reduces demand and vulnerabilities of individuals being trafficked, there must be deeper understanding and more accurate data on the issue of human trafficking.

Questions that need to be addressed through research include:

- What are the systemic issues such as violence against women and gender inequalities that influence trafficked persons?
- What does global citizenship mean/represent to women who have been exploited through sex trafficking?
- What does a gender-sensitive global citizenship education look like from the perspective of women and girls who have been trafficked for sex?
- How can demand be addressed through educating men about ideas around gender that are perpetuating the growth of sex trafficking in Canada?

Research on these questions will help analyse the type of educational system, awareness strategies, preventative measures, and reintegration methods that are needed in order to eradicate human trafficking, as well as inform supports for women and girls who have been trafficked. Also, data will help inform gender-sensitive global citizenship curriculum and educational policy that has the potential to influence the minds of future generations towards positive change.

Human trafficking is multifaceted and there is not one approach that will solve the exploitation of women and girls. There has been a focus on research that analyses the psychological and legal aspects of human trafficking. We need research on prevention, protection, rehabilitation, and training: a holistic educative approach. Canada could lead on the subject of combating human trafficking through establishing a human trafficking research centre through a reputable and leading academic institution. This centre would allow scholars to

> collaborate and develop an approach to fight human trafficking through an interdisciplinary lens: youth homelessness, psychology, counselling, economic, law, feminist theorists, international development, education etc. From movement therapy to Indigenous issues to gender based-violence scholars, a research Centre would render the possibility of creating an effective qualitative and quantitative analysis of human trafficking in Canada. (Gray 2018, 149).

Further, human trafficking needs to be understood in relation to interconnected systemic, social, and structural factors. As Howard (2012) suggests,

> As yet, few researchers have engaged with the way individuals and institutions live within trafficking discourse and policy, with the way inter- and intra-institutional dynamics are reflected in them, with the way these interact with and are influenced by those "target communities" upon whom they act, or with the way that each are structured by wider, more fundamental forces within the social formation. The result has been a propagation of simplistic explanatory tropes that attribute the persistence of problematic paradigms primarily to policy-maker ignorance or malevolence. (28)

Research needs to move away from isolated perspectives and towards more critical theory to adequately address a world in which women are viewed as commodities.

Considerations and the Way Forward

Human trafficking is growing rapidly and steps need to be taken to combat the issue through preventative measures such as gender-sensitive GCE. There is need for curriculum that embodies global citizenry and emphasizes gender inequalities within Canada and beyond. Curriculum that emphasizes a gender-sensitive approach to GCE has the potential to shape individuals to contribute meaningfully to society in order to create a more just and equitable world. Through addressing systemic issues such as patriarchy, sexism, and Canada's history of colonialism, students will be able to join the fight to end violence against women, including human trafficking. Training in teacher's colleges should also include gender-sensitive teaching strategies; that is, strategies about how to teach GCE that highlights gender inequalities and violence against women. These efforts would help break down the oppressive societal systems that influence the growing number of sexually exploited women and girls. Patriarchal ideologies need to be challenged and an awareness of the global problem of gender inequality needs to be discussed in the classroom. Post-secondary institutions can support and conduct research, develop gender-sensitive global citizenship curriculum, and build up the next generation to respect and uphold the rights of women and girls.

The Toronto Police indicate that children as young as twelve years old are being trafficked in Canada.[5] In addition, over 26 per cent of people trafficked in Canada are children under the age of eighteen.[6] Such information underscores the importance of elementary and high schools teaching about human trafficking as an integral preventative measure. Where do youth acquire the knowledge that their life matters and has importance? How are our youth learning that the lives of those around them have worth? Escalating suicide rates and the mental health crisis among youth in our nation highlight the loneliness and isolation many individuals are experiencing. Low self-confidence, loneliness, and feeling isolated are risk factors for being trafficked – how many of our youth are at risk?

In addition to health and well-being, economic issues have been said to make women and girls vulnerable to human trafficking. For instance, university students are susceptible to being trafficked partly due to the high costs of post-secondary tuition. From conversations with community members, research, and my work as a volunteer, I have learned of a student who was trafficked through a university residence building. I was told of an international student who was trafficked while in the midst of her studies. It is unclear how universities and colleges are addressing this issue on their campuses. It is also unclear if academics are acknowledging the oppressive and exploitive issue of commercial sexual exploitation that is impacting some of their students. How are post-secondary institutions addressing patriarchy when talking about consent? Can the work administrators do to create conversations about consent on campuses go deeper to unpack toxic masculinity and examine human rights violations like trafficking? We often exclude sex trafficking and commercial sexual exploitation in dialogue regarding violence against women because awareness is lower and the issue is often misunderstood. Universities and colleges could embed conversations about gender inequality and address the topic of human trafficking within these spaces.

Through teaching gender-sensitive global citizenship education and building future teachers who are gender-sensitive global citizens, as well as through conducting research and developing curriculum that emphasizes the rights of women, human trafficking can be combated on the educational front. Gender-sensitive GCE prepares morally responsible citizens who respect one another and take action to fight injustices like human trafficking. It seeks to address systemic issues of gender-based violence and gender inequality, which are root causes of human trafficking. Education is a powerful tool that can be used to shape views and condition citizens to be gender sensitive. The current executive director of UNODC, Yury Fedetov, said in the *Global Report on Trafficking in Persons 2012*, "human trafficking is a widespread crime in the early 21st century, it cannot be allowed to continue into the 22nd century" (United Nations Office on Drugs and Crime 2012, 1). And, as I stated in earlier writing, "Although globalization is a contributing factor to the growth in the trafficking of persons" it also provides educators "with the opportunity to work together in new and innovative ways, *sans frontiers*, to end human trafficking" (Gray 2018, 150).

NOTES

1 Part of the literature discussed in this chapter appears in Gray (2018).
2 Language used within quotes embedded in the chapter reflects the authorship of the cited source. The author of this chapter acknowledges that there are sensitivities in how and what language is used when describing the trafficking of persons and that conflating work in the commercial sex industry with human trafficking is problematic.
3 Pseudonym used.
4 It is worth noting that this report also draws from previous research

conducted in this area; it includes a footnote on page 14 that reads: "See W. Oppal, Foresaken: The Report of the Missing Women Commission of Inquiry, vol. 1 (British Columbia: 2012) at 110 (noting that 'survival sex work, if seen on a continuum of choice to engage in sex work, is one step removed from sexual slavery/trafficking in which a woman is forced into prostitution and far removed from the highly-paid sex trade')."

5 See https://www.cbc.ca/news/canada/toronto/human-trafficking-toronto-1.5126939

6 See https://www150.statcan.gc.ca/n1/pub/85-005-x/2018001/article/54979-eng.htm

REFERENCES

Abdi, A., and L. Shultz. 2007. "Schooling and Social Justice: A Human Rights and Global Citizenship Perspective." In *Education for Social Justice: From the Margin to the Mainstream*. Ottawa: Canadian Teacher's Federation.

Arnot, M., and M.M.A. Ghaill, eds. 2006. *The RoutledgeFalmer Reader in Gender & Education*. Milton Park, UK: Routledge.

Barrett, N.A. 2013. *An Assessment of Sex Trafficking in Canada*. Toronto: Canadian Women's Foundation. http://www.canadiancentretoendhumantrafficking.ca/wp-content/uploads/2016/10/Assessment-of-Sex-Trafficking-in-Canada.pdf

British Columbia Ministry of Justice. 2013. *BC's Action Plan to Combat Human Trafficking 2013–2016*. Victoria: British Columbia Ministry of Justice.

Canadian Women's Foundation. 2014. *"NO MORE" Ending Sex Trafficking in Canada – Report of the National Task Force on Sex Trafficking of Women and Girls in Canada*. Toronto: Canadian Women's Foundation. http://canadianwomen.org/sites/canadianwomen.org/files//CWF-TraffickingReport-Auto%20%281%29_0.pdf

– 2016. "Fact Sheet: Moving Women Out of Violence." Updated August 2018. https://www.canadianwomen.org/wp-content/uploads/2017/09/FactSheet-VAWandDV_Feb_2018-Update.pdf

Committee on the Elimination of Discrimination against Women (CEDAW). 1992. "General Recommendations Made by the Committee on the Elimination of Discrimination against Women." United Nations Entity for Gender Equality and the Empowerment of Women. http://www.un.org/womenwatch/daw/cedaw/recommendations/recomm.htm

Feinstein, P., and M. Pearce. 2015. *Review of Reports and Recommendations on Violence against Indigenous Women in Canada: Master List of Report Recommendations Organized by Theme*. Vancouver: Legal Strategy Coalition on Violence Against Indigenous Women.

Global Education Monitoring Report Team. 2016. *Creating Sustainable Futures for All: Global Education Monitoring Report, 2016 – Gender Review*. Paris: UNESCO. http://unesdoc.unesco.org/images/0024/002460/246045e.pdf

Government of Canada. 2012 *National Action Plan to Combat Human Trafficking*. Ottawa: Her Majesty the Queen in Right of Canada. https://www.publicsafety.gc.ca/cnt/rsrcs/pblctns/ntnl-ctn-pln-cmbt/ntnl-ctn-pln-cmbt-eng.pdf

Gray, M. 2018. "SOLD: The Human and Economic Costs of Selling Women and Girls." MEd diss., York University.

Greve, A. 2014. "Human Trafficking: What about the Men and Boys?" Human Trafficking Center, 18 September. http://humantraffickingcenter.org/men-boys/

Havemann, J. 2010. "The Great Recession of 2008–09." *Encyclopædia Britannica*. https://www.britannica.com/topic/Great-Recession-of-2008-2009-The-1661642

Howard, N. 2012. "It's Easier if We Stop Them Moving: A Critical Analysis of Anti-Child Trafficking Discourse, Policy and Practice – The Case of Southern Benin." PhD diss., Oxford University.

Hunt, S. 2016. "Representing Colonial Violence: Trafficking, Sex Work, and the Violence of Law." *Atlantis* 37, no. 2: 25–39. http://journals.msvu.ca/index.php/atlantis/article/view/3042/pdf_37

International Labour Organization (ILO). 2014. "The Meanings of Forced Labour." https://www.ilo.org/global/topics/forced-labour/news/WCMS_237569/lang--en/index.htm

International Labour Organization and Walk Free Foundation. 2017. *Global Estimates of Modern Slavery: Forced Labour and Forced Marriage*. Geneva: International Labour Organization. http://www.ilo.org/wcmsp5/groups/public/---dgreports/---dcomm/documents/publication/wcms_575479.pdf

Jorgenson, S., and L. Schultz. 2012. "Global Citizenship Education (GCE) in Post-Secondary Institutions: What Is Protected and What Is Hidden under the Umbrella of GCE?" *Journal of Global Citizenship & Equity Education* 2, no. 1: 1–22. http://journals.sfu.ca/jgcee/index.php/jgcee/article/viewFile/52/25

Karam, M. 2016 *Trafficking in Persons in Canada, 2014*. Ottawa: Statistics Canada.

Lister, R. 2008. "Inclusive Citizenship, Gender and Poverty: Some Implications for Education for Citizenship." *CitizeEd, Citizenship Teaching and Learning* 4, no. 1: 3–19. http://citeseerx.ist.psu.edu/viewdoc/download?doi=10.1.1.574.1991&rep=rep1&type=pdf

McDonnell, I., H. Solignac-Lecomte, and L. Wegimont, eds. 2003. *Public Opinion and the Fight against Poverty*. Paris: OECD Publishing. https://doi-org /10.1787/9789264199996-en

Minter, W.J., and I. Thompson. 1968. *Colleges and Universities as Agents of Social Change*. Boulder, CO: Western Interstate Commission on Higher Education.

Ontario's Ministry of Children, Community and Social Services. n.d. "Ontario's Strategy to End Human Trafficking." Last modified 29 February 2019. https://www.mcss.gov.on.ca/en/mcss/programs/humantrafficking/index.aspx

Oxman-Martinez, J., M. Lacroix, and J. Hanley. 2005. *Victims of Trafficking in Persons: Perspectives from the Canadian Community Sector*. Research and Statistics Division, Department of Justice Canada, August. http://www.justice.gc.ca/eng/rp-pr/cj-jp/tp/rr06_3/rr06_3.pdf

Royal Canadian Mounted Police. 2013. *Domestic Human Trafficking for Sexual Exploitation in Canada*, October. http://publications.gc.ca/collections/collection_2014/grc-rcmp/PS64-114-2014-eng.pdf

Seshia, M. 2005. *The Unheard Speak Out: Street Sexual Exploitation in Winnipeg*. Canadian Centre for Policy Alternatives, October. http://policyalternatives.ca/sites/default/files/uploads/publications/Manitoba_Pubs/2005/The_Unheard_Speak_Out.pdf

Shelley, L.I. 2010. *Human Trafficking: A Global Perspective*. New York: Cambridge University Press.

Sikka, A. 2009. *Trafficking of Aboriginal Women and Girls in Canada*. Institute on Governance, Aboriginal Policy Research Series. https://iog.ca/docs/May-2009_trafficking_of_aboriginal_women-1.pdf

Spring, J. 2008. "Research on Globalization and Education." *Review of Educational Research* 78, no. 2: 330–63. https://doi.org/10.3102/0034654308317846

Standing Committee on Justice and Human Rights. 2018. *Moving Forward in the Fight Against Human Trafficking in Canada*. Ottawa: House of Commons.

Tasker, J.P. 2016. "Confusion Reigns over Number of Missing, Murdered Indigenous Women." *CBC News*, 16 February. http://www.cbc.ca/news/politics/mmiw-4000-hajdu-1.3450237

Taylor, P., and J. Fransman. 2004. *Learning and Teaching Participation: Exploring the Role of Higher Learning Institutions as Agents of Development and Social Change*. Brighton, UK: Institute of Development Studies.

UNESCO Office Bangkok. 2014. *Learning to Live Together*. Bangkok: UNESCO Office Bangkok. http://unesdoc.unesco.org/images/0022/002272/227208e.pdf

United Nations Educational, Scientific, and Cultural Organization (UNESCO). 2007. *Human Trafficking in South Africa: Root Causes and Recommendations*. Paris: UNESCO. http://unesdoc.unesco.org/images/0015/001528/152823e.pdf

– 2014. *Global Citizenship Education. Preparing Learners for the Challenges of the 21st Century*. Paris: UNESCO. http://unesdoc.unesco.org/images/0022/002277/227729e.pdf

– 2015a. *Global Citizenship Education. Topics and Learning Objectives*. Paris: UNESCO. http://unesdoc.unesco.org/images/0023/002329/232993e.pdf
– 2015b. *Rethinking Education in a Changing World towards a Global Common Good?* Paris: UNESCO. https://unesdoc.unesco.org/ark:/48223/pf0000232555
United Nations Human Rights Office of the High Commissioner. 2000. "Protocol to Prevent, Suppress and Punish Trafficking in Persons Especially Women and Children, supplementing the United Nations Convention against Transnational Organized Crime." Adopted 15 November. http://www.ohchr.org/EN/ProfessionalInterest/Pages/ProtocolTraffickingInPersons.aspx
– 2014. *Human Rights and Human Trafficking*. New York: United Nations. http://www.ohchr.org/Documents/Publications/FS36_en.pdf
United Nations Office on Drugs and Crime. 2009. *Global Report on Trafficking in Persons*. Vienna: UNODC. http://www.unodc.org/documents/Global_Report_on_TIP.pdf
– 2012. *Global Report on Trafficking in Persons 2012*. New York: United Nations. https://www.unodc.org/documents/data-and-analysis/glotip/Trafficking_in_Persons_2012_web.pdf
– n.d.a "Human Trafficking FAQs." Accessed 7 December 2016. http://www.unodc.org/unodc/en/human-trafficking/faqs.html#Which_countries_are_affected_by_human_trafficking
– n.d.b. "United Nations Convention against Transnational Organized Crime and the Protocols Thereto." Accessed 14 March 2019. https://www.unodc.org/unodc/en/organized-crime/intro/UNTOC.html
– n.d.c. "UNODC Report on Human Trafficking Exposes Modern Form of Slavery." Accessed 24 December 2016. http://www.unodc.org/unodc/en/human-trafficking/global-report-on-trafficking-in-persons.html
Wallace, J. 2007. "Inclusive Schooling and Gender." In *Education for Social Justice: From the Margin to the Mainstream*. Toronto: Canadian Teachers' Federation.
World Trade Organization. 2008. *World Trade Organization Report 2008: Trade in a Globalizing World*. Washington, DC: World Bank. https://www.wto.org/english/res_e/booksp_e/anrep_e/world_trade_report08_e.pdf
World University Service of Canada. 2014. *2013-2014 Annual Report*. Ottawa: WUSC. https://s3.amazonaws.com/assets.wusc.ca/NEW%20website/04%20About%20Us/Annual%20reports%20%26%20financials/2013-2014%20AnnualReport_06b.pdf

SECTION II

Case Studies

6 A Case-Study Exploration of Deweyan Experiential Service Learning as Citizenship Development

CATHERINE A. BROOM AND HEESOON BAI

Developing good citizens is one of the root theoretical justifications and purposes of public schooling and social studies. Much discussion exists, however, over what good citizenship entails and how it can best be achieved. One approach – experiential learning and its associated service learning – is currently popular in a number of disciplines. It is argued to be an invaluable way of developing students' citizenship through experience-based learning. The first part of this chapter concerns itself with the theoretical grounding of experiential and service learning. We begin by reviewing briefly some of the major contemporary global citizenship theorists. As we shall see, many of these contemporary theories gesture towards and support some forms of experiential and service learning, which builds on earlier philosophers' work. Thus, our next move is to explore a key philosophical figure behind experiential learning: John Dewey. Dewey's theories of experiential learning are still unmatched today in providing strong theoretical foundations for experiential and service-learning pedagogies.

The second part of this chapter presents the findings of a qualitative interview study with high school students and teachers who have taken part in service projects. The discussion illustrates the benefits and challenges of citizenship development through experiential curricula and concludes with recommendations that aim to strengthen this form of learning.

In this case study we consider how experiential learning can foster a sense of global citizenship in youth. We conclude our chapter by considering the strengths of youth's experiences when embedded in effective reflection and discussion for developing their civic-mindedness. As well, the strengths of the experience can be further developed when we acknowledge the challenges that remain for such experiences, such as how to create opportunity for all youth to access the experience and to ensure that it is not limited to economically privileged youth who go out to help "poor" others. Another related issue is consideration of the safety of global experiential opportunities, as some contexts may have risks for students. Our educational recommendations focus on the significance of reflection, discussion, and accordion/discordant experiences, dovetailing nicely with the discussion in chapter 7 by Naidoo and Benjamin in this volume. At the same time, we acknowledge the insight from chapter 2 by Stanlick in this volume that global citizenship education can also be local (as a way of countering the concerns of critical theorists). Stanlick describes the positive benefits of a service-learning project with refugees in the community, illustrating that through in-service learning global citizenship can be developed locally. Global citizenship education through experiential learning doesn't have to become a means of perpetuating neocolonial narratives of global Western dominance.

Theoretical Grounding

Contemporary Theories of Global Citizenship

Contemporary work in global citizenship is a broad, complex, and contested field of study. Much discussion exists over what good citizenship is, what it entails, and how it can best be achieved. In this section, we will review some of theorists of global citizenship in order to illustrate its key concepts, which largely focus around how we can understand and live in our rapidly changing and globalizing world. Understanding relates to our philosophies and values, to the ways in which we make sense of our local and global world. Living relates to how we choose to act and engage within local and global spaces. Together, these theories by and large point towards experiential learning for citizenship education.

One group of theorists frame citizenship through a cosmopolitan perspective that aims to address issues while cultivating personal and/or social connections and addressing diverse perspectives or cultures. For example, Hansen's (2011) cosmopolitan model encompasses "an attentive outlook on life," a way of being, or an orientation to living mindfully in our contemporary world through a balance between "reflective openness" to other points of view and "reflective loyalty" to community values and traditions (xiv). Appiah (2007), similarly, presents a framed and balanced discussion of cosmopolitanism and an argument for how we can cultivate identification with the larger human community while also maintaining our local connections. He describes how much we share in common with others, while acknowledging our cultural differences. He encourages openness to diverse perspectives and authentic dialogues, which allow us to reframe our thinking and embrace pluralism. He recognizes the complexity of cross-cultural dialogues, due to the manner in which knowledge is partial and values can be differentially understood, but believes that we can still come to agreement on necessary actions. Indeed, these conversations can expand our conceptual boundaries. He cautions us to distinguish between an authentic cosmopolitanism and an inauthentic one that is not rooted in openness and respect but rather is pushing forward one vision, or agenda, such as that of religious fundamentalists. He also raises questions about how far our behaviour as cosmopolitans extends, acknowledging that our ethical obligations to act towards "strangers" are bounded. He encourages us to understand the root causes of global issues and work to address these.

Nussbaum (1997) also aims to create cosmopolitan citizens – that is, individuals who identify themselves as citizens of the world, who view themselves as part of a larger human community that stretches beyond national borders. Nussbaum presents an educational program, describing a curriculum that includes Socratic dialogue, logic, philosophy, and cross-cultural – or intercultural – studies. She aims to create citizens who believe in the equality of all people and justice in the world generally and who participate actively in debates and discussions in order to support healthy democratic societies.

Other theorists take a more critical stance, having us question ourselves, our histories, and our contexts in our search for a global citizenship. For example, Pike (2008) draws the concepts of multiplicity, conflict resolution, and minority groups into his vision of a global perspective. Having a global perspective is understood to mean that individuals have broadened horizons, that their loyalty and allegiance go beyond one nation to embrace all of humanity in an inclusive manner. Individuals with a global perspective have knowledge and awareness of current global realities and of the connections and interdependence between us all. They work to instigate long-term solutions to global issues using critical thinking. They are motivated, feel personal responsibility, and creatively imagine alternatives. They use contemporary tools and technologies to act from a distance. They aim to develop community and value sustainability. Educators can use local experimental education, critical media literacy, discussions on ethics, and activities that develop conflict resolution skills to broaden their students' perspectives and allow for complexity and multiplicity and, thus, the potential for students to develop global citizenship.

Andreotti (2006) explores these concepts further by deconstructing how global citizenship can become a continuation of Western individuals' colonial mindsets and actions through, for example, a missionary-like zeal to go out and "save" non-Western people and make them more like Westerners. Western governments and companies also engage in actions that increase global social and economic inequities. She recommends that individuals explore their own values and actions through critical dialogue and consider how they themselves may be implicated in both creating and sustaining conditions of inequality around the world through unequal power in the cultural, political, and economic domains. For example, international bodies such as the World Trade Organization often work to support the interests of Western countries and companies. Global citizenship, she argues, can be labelled an elitist project when we consider who can move and act in international spaces and whose cultural knowledge, traditions, and actions are considered to be "universal." Thus, it requires critical exploration of its underlying roots, concepts, actions, and implications.

Theorists have also connected global citizenship to human rights (Abdi and Shultz 2008) and critical consciousness (Abdi and Carr 2012), as well as peace education (Verma 2017) and continued social inequalities related to race, class, and migration (Banks 2017) that consider the tensions between contemporary multicultural societies, the assimilationist aims of nation-states, and individuals' feelings of belonging and efficacy. Work has also explored youth's civic mindsets as the products of their readings of their contexts in interaction with their values, knowledge, and perspectives acquired through lived experiences (Broom 2016).

Dewey and the Philosophical Foundations of Experiential Learning

Philosophers of the twentieth century have argued that the aim of education is the creation of good citizens, which includes knowledge learning, ethical education, and the disposition to act on right morals for the betterment of their societies. They have theorized how good citizens can be developed through education. One of the key thinkers of the twentieth century was John Dewey. For Dewey (1916), experiential, project-based learning would shape individuals who could contribute positively to a continuously developing democratic society. His theory laid the foundation for experiential learning and democratic education out of which current service-learning theories and methods have developed. In this section, we will explore Dewey's philosophy to better support and implement experiential service learning.

Dewey had a broad conception of education, viewing it as a social process, as learning that occurs in both informal and formal (school) settings through experiences. Informal settings within both the family and social group have a significant impact on the development of individuals. Schools also have a role to play in societies where informal learning is insufficient to master the depth and breadth of social knowledge and where they can help to further develop students' capacities, temper bad acquired habits, and increase their understanding and connections to each other through a "common subject matter [that] accustoms all to a unity of outlook" (Dewey 1916, 26). A shared program of study provides students with the possibilities of developing similar outlooks and dispositions; that is, it develops the groundwork for a common community consciousness.

However, schools have a major shortcoming for Dewey: they are subject to the danger of becoming places of dried out, overly abstracted knowledge that is meaningless to students, for learning is not a process of "telling" (direct teacher instruction) but rather of "doing" (student-centred learning). As life is a process of continuous growth and learning through experience, schooling should also be living and should provide students with the conditions that nurture their continued growth. Teachers should begin by understanding where their students are at and what they understand, and then develop an environment that simulates their students' development. This leads to individuals' (and by extension, society's) "progressive" or continual growth. As Dewey (1916) states: "While a careful study of the native aptitudes and deficiencies of an individual is always a preliminary necessity, the subsequent and important step is to furnish an environment which will … shape the experiences of the young so that instead of reproducing current habits, better habits shall be formed, and thus the future adult society be an improvement on their own" (87, 92). He argues that the best pedagogy is the "continuous reconstruction of experience" (93). Experiences are interactions between individuals and their social and physical environments, which provide opportunities for learning through reflection: "To 'learn from experience' is to make a backward and forward connection between what we do to things and what we enjoy or suffer from things in consequence … Under such conditions, doing becomes a trying; an experiment with the world to find out what it is like; the undergoing becomes instruction – discovery of the connection of things" (164).

As knowledge is created in these situations, it is living. Knowledge formation follows a process similar to that of scientific hypothesizing: incomplete understanding leads to hypotheses that one further refines through inquiry, research, and testing. Knowledge is, thus, socially and historically constructed and open to future refinement and amendment. Best teaching practices engage students in experiences that are meaningful to them and lead to issues (or problems) that the students address through conducting research and developing and testing tentative answers. They embed subject learning in authentic experiences emerging from daily social life. A vital feature of this education is making "experience intelligent" (Rocheleau 2004) through democratic (or social) inquiry, discussion, and reflection. The aim of this education is to create individuals with shared common interests – that is, with a shared valuation of the public good – who freely cooperate with a number of social groups and, as a result of the many "complicated conversations" (Stoddard and Cornwell 2003) that result from this open and respectful interaction, continue their own (and society's) growth.

Having discussed Dewey's theory and the aim of developing critical global citizenship, we now turn to explore service learning as a method of developing global citizens. This exploration is done through looking at our case studies of Nicaragua and Kenya, which follow other youth service-learning projects developed using Dewey's theory of experiential learning (see, for example, Speck and Hoppe 2004; Kolb 1984; Zull 2002; Pritchard and Whitehead 2004). These approaches involve students in authentic community learning experiences that are integrated with classroom content learning and reflection. The experiences are developed through reciprocal community relationships that meet authentic community needs (Pritchard and Whitehead 2004). They can occur inside and outside of school, at both the local community and wider cross-cultural level.

The Significance of Community-Based Citizenship

Our world faces many problems, including environmental degradation and individualism (Beck and Beck-Gernsheim 2006), which are the products of human action. Such action denies the potential of people to transform our world for the better, a capacity some scholars describe as "humanity" (Broom 2010). The latter involves living ethically and engaging in moral activities of value that are embedded in a recognition of our shared human nature. These activities improve the social community for all and actualize individual human potential. Well-known scholars, including Dewey and Aristotle, have argued that individuals can best be educated to act with humanity through experiential learning: "It is well said, then, that it is by doing just acts that the just man is produced, and by doing temperate acts the temperate man; without doing these, no one would have even a prospect of becoming good" (Aristotle n.d., chap. 4).

In other words, community or service-learning experiences can help to develop a number of educational objectives, including "personal and interpersonal development; understanding and applying knowledge; engagement, curiosity, and reflective practice; critical thinking; perspective transformation; and citizenship" (Eyler and Giles 1999, ix). These can be assessed through achievement at college or university and as expressed attitudes and behaviours. In this chapter, we focus on expressed attitudes and behaviours.

Emerging from community or service-learning theory is a question: Is experience-based learning an effective method of nurturing students' sense of community consciousness (and thus their humanity)? The next section of this chapter describes the findings of a research project that analysed the interrelationships between high school students' experiential projects and the ideal described. We end the chapter with recommendations that aim to strengthen experiential learning as a pedagogical tool. The findings and recommendations are of value to educators at all levels, from elementary school to universities.

A Case-Study Exploration of Service Learning and Humanity

In the winter and spring of 2010, twenty high school students who had taken part in service were interviewed by one of the authors of this chapter; ethically, both authors were at arm's-length from the students.[1] Of the twenty interviewees, thirteen students had gone to Nicaragua and seven to Kenya. More females than males were interviewed. The students were in Grade 12 for the Nicaragua trip (ages fifteen to seventeen), and in Grades 10 to 12 for the Kenya trip. Both trips were optional. The Nicaragua experience was embedded in a course on global education, and the Kenya trip preparation happened outside of class time. Each interview was structured around seven open-ended questions that gave students flexibility in their answers and lasted from fifteen minutes to half an hour. (See the appendix for the questions as well as sample representative answers, divided by students in each country, Nicaragua or Kenya.) The questions were developed by the chapter authors, based on their experiences in the GCE field and with the aim of highlighting the theoretical frame that informs this chapter. The interviews were anonymous. Students' answers were qualitatively analysed by the principal investigator and grouped into themes using content analysis, which involved studying and interpreting student and teacher interviews by identifying commonly repeated concepts. The interpretation also had a phenomenological angle in the sense that studying the interview data used horizontalization and linked the significant and repeated concepts that were identified to common themes that described the "what" and "how" elements of students' service-learning experiences (Creswell 1998). Four teachers who organized service activities were also interviewed following the same procedures.

The student and teacher findings are presented separately, as the researchers understand that teachers and students differ in their ages, orientations, and relations to the experiential projects. The student interviews focused on understanding students' perspectives on the trips; the teacher interviews explored the teachers' aims and methods, as well as details of their trip planning and organization. The students participated in service projects. Some went to Nicaragua, where they worked with a couple to build a sustainable village for orphaned children. They contributed to building structures in the village (such as a milking pad for cows and water troughs). Trips to both countries were about ten days long, and were organized by travel agents and international foundations with local experience who liaisoned between the students and teachers' needs and interests and local community needs. Other students went to Kenya where they helped to build a school kitchen and garden. Both groups also interacted with orphans and took part in some sightseeing trips.[2]

STUDY LIMITATIONS

The data was collected from interviews. Limitations related to this include: (1) the shortcomings of self-reported data, and (2) the number of interviews. Self-reported data has the advantage of allowing participants to talk about experiences that happened at different times and places and in natural settings (in addition to the experimental settings). Problems with using self-reported data include participants describing events in a socially desirable way, being biased in how they remember information, or creating memories that include selective information (Segrin and Flora 2011). We attempted to manage these limitations through interviews with both teachers and students, making connections to literature, and conducting semi-structured interviews that allowed the interviewers to seek further clarification when necessary. As to the second limitation, not all youths agreed to participate in interviews. It is possible that youths who agreed to be interviewed were those who enjoyed the experience and wanted to discuss it, while those who had less positive views may not have wanted to share these views. Future research can consider how to tap into varied student perspectives on these types of experiences.

STUDENT REMARKS

Prior to participating in the trip, students had little knowledge of the countries they were to visit. This made some students feel nervous and stressed. Although they were prepared for the trips by teachers, most students held stereotypes of the people, countries, and cultures. The majority imagined the countries to be poor both economically and culturally and perhaps hostile and dangerous. They were also not sure what to expect regarding the people. Most of the students, particularly those who went to Nicaragua, were positively surprised after they arrived: they found the people to be warm, kind, appreciative, and welcoming; the culture to be colourful and vibrant; and the natural environment beautiful: "It was honestly the most amazing place I've ever been, some parts were so beautiful and pure" (student, interview). Another student stated, "I loved every bit of Nicaragua, the heat, the people, the culture, the sites. We slept outside and couldn't have had a better bedroom. The showers were outside, which is interesting because there were a lot of bugs. The beach was amazing" (student, interview). Students found the culture to be far richer than they imagined, and the people to be happy, hardworking, and welcoming. Students were interested to learn about different cultural values, such as a strong family focus and a different conception of time, and enjoyed the active cultural life.

Students also mentioned that they valued the way Nicaraguan and Kenyan people enjoyed life, despite having less monetary wealth than North Americans: "They made me appreciate what we have here. They're always happy there and they have nothing" (student, interview). Those who went to Kenya found it easier than they expected and found most of the people welcoming and helpful, but some came home still feeling that the place was unsafe. One student mentioned, for example, how armed police escorted the students to and from their worksites and how police were at their hotel all the time. Others, on both trips, were surprised by the physical poverty, or by the amount of "Westernization" and the decline of the traditional cultures and languages they saw: "Coca-Cola was everywhere," one student mentioned. They came to understand cultures as fluid and open to change. In all cases, one of the students' main insights was increased ("eye-opening") cross-cultural knowledge and awareness, as well as increased acceptance and respect for different ways of being in the world – "not to judge by first sight" (student, interview). They viewed all countries "with a different mindset" (student, interview) but all people as "no different than us" (student, interview).

STUDENTS' INDIVIDUAL GROWTH THROUGH SERVICE-LEARNING CURRICULUM

All students valued the experience of hands-on, applied learning. They felt it was a different kind of learning from that found in their classrooms. The ability to be in a different place that one could personally take in through one's senses – to see, feel, taste, hear, and smell another place for oneself – was particularly valued. This embodied learning experience opened students to new realities in a manner that was not possible through information-based learning in the closed and isolated space of the school: "It made what we read in textbooks, etc., a reality" (student, interview). They felt they learned information that could not have been learned in class.

They all discussed developing new insights about people, culture, the world, and life for themselves, and they appreciated this individualized learning. They learned about environmental issues such as wastage and political issues such as corruption. They felt that they grew as people ("it's character-building" [student, interview]) and that they increased their empathy and knowledge of our world. They appreciated the good work of some people and organizations, and enlarged their efficacy to bring change ("how you can change the world"; how "help goes a long way"; how "everyone can help everyone"; and how "if you want to do something just do it and don't worry about the bad" [students, interviews]). They expanded their critical awareness of themselves and how their actions impact on others, as well as their feeling of community with (and for) others. They realized how relationships with people, in addition to materialism, are essential for happiness and came to "treasure life" (student, interview). They developed a sense of agency: "I learned that I'm going to have to do more for my fellow man ... it also just made me want to be better and more helpful everyday" (student, interview). Other students realized "how much [they] love to help people in need," (student, interview) and how "the world has good in it" (student, interview). They felt happy helping others. The students thus felt that they developed humanity (connections to others) and happiness. For some, helping others fulfilled them on a spiritual level.[3] These comments may reflect some of Andreotti's (2006) concerns over the "missionary" nature of experiential, global learning experiences. Youths will benefit from deconstructing these feelings through critical dialogue.

Students also stated that they improved their people skills by learning how to work collaboratively with others, trusting them, and accepting different worldviews and people "for who they are" (student, interview). They realized the challenges of community building and explored ways of achieving it through open communication that included listening to others, problem and conflict resolution, and confidence-building. They developed more positive attitudes and their confidence and sense of responsibility and self-sufficiency as young adults. Others stated that they cultivated their leadership skills and that they saw a lack of global leadership ("Someone needs to take charge and do something" [student, interview]). For some, the trip was life changing: "I learned so many lessons that changed my life" (student, interview). Some students even stated that they changed their career and life goals as a result of the trip and found their "life passion," which connected to doing service-based work (student, interview).

Teachers' Reflections on Their Service-Learning Pedagogy

Despite the amount of work involved, all of the teachers organized the experiential activities because they appreciated the opportunity and benefits of service work, and valued the pedagogy. Some felt that the educational experience provided students with possibilities for growth through reflection. The main aim for the teachers was the moral and ethical dimensions of the trips, in terms of their potential to nurture student growth as students explored the meaning of life and the value of global citizenship. A key question for one inspirational teacher was: "What does a successful life look like?" (teacher, interview).

All teachers used external travel agencies (such as Developing World Connections) and groups, such as International Children's Care and Comfort the Children International, to aid them in arranging details of the trips, and felt that this took away some of the organizational stress. They felt confident in the abilities of these groups to plan details and appreciated their local knowledge. The teachers stated that they felt they had community support, including from parents, many of whom did not ask many questions about the trip or appear concerned: they trusted the teachers and the school. Teachers did not express much anxiety about organizing the trips, as they felt they were worthwhile and well organized, and they had confidence in their students.

All teachers worked to prepare the students for the trips by holding discussions and workshops prior to the service work. They discussed with their students what they could expect in terms of culture, economic poverty, and environment, as well as what their expectations were for students. They asked the students to respect people and their varied life situations. One teacher assigned students topics about the trip to research and present to their peers during orientation meetings, and invited guest speakers on topics such as the history, language, and culture of the area. Another teacher, who organized local community service projects, devolved organization to the students: they worked in groups to choose and plan their activities, with teacher guidance and support. These projects were encased in class lessons that explored ethics, such as the challenges of judging moral actions.

After the trips, teachers helped students to make meaning out of their experiences through discussion and reflection activities in open, honest, and supportive forums, as well as through projects on key topics such as sustainability and ethics. Teachers wanted their students to critically reflect on their own and society's social values and the purpose of life itself. Post-trip reflection was a key element for one teacher, who felt that most of the learning occurred once the students were home again and struggled to integrate the experience into their lives. Dewey (1916) also commented on the value of reflecting with these words: "Thought or reflection … is the discernment of the relation between what we try to do and what happens in consequence. No experience having a meaning is possible without some element of thought" (170). That is, associated with the concepts of constructivist learning theory that developed from Dewey's problem-based model of learning and Bruner's (1987) work, learning is understood to be concept based. Students learn through connecting new material to the concepts they already have. The teacher can help students reshuffle their concepts through the presentation of new information that does not fit comfortably with students' current concepts. This cognitive dissonance provides spaces for changed thought, in a manner similar to Vygotsky's (2004) theory of teacher scaffolding of student learning. In the case of the students in this study, the cognitive dissonances provided by the trip fuelled changed thinking for many students.

Teachers had students apply for the trips and used sorting criteria to decide which students they would take on the trips with them. They stated that they selected students who they felt would benefit from the experience (that is, those who were perceived to be reflective, open-minded, relational, and resilient) as well as students who were reliable and responsible. They did not want to have behavioural problems show up. As teachers felt responsibility for the students, they wanted to ensure that they could rely on the students they took. Passion and interest in service were more important than grades for all teachers. Indeed, one teacher stated that the experience could be particularly difficult and challenging for high-achieving students who were not as relational and oriented towards experiential learning.

One teacher mentioned concerns about how the selection process limited the experience to a particular kind of student, and thus made an effort to expand the experience by accepting varied students.[4] The teacher found that not only did the students behave during the trip, but that they also demonstrated growth, maturity, and, at times, unknown talents such as artistic ability. The teacher also engaged students in group fundraising projects prior to the trip. Another teacher provided service work for all students in their regular academic classes and attempted to deal with motivational issues by finding service experiences that matched students' interests.

During the trips the teachers thought that the experiential curriculum for their students was best "taught" through the stepping back of the teacher. That is, their pedagogy was one of mediating and facilitating personal interaction between student and experience. The teacher was there as a guide and a mentor. This kind of pedagogy had the potential for magnifying the individual ethical agency of the students, as their lived experiences were opened to the endless possibilities of personal meaning-making through the skillful mediation and facilitation of the teachers. Teachers viewed leadership as an act of relinquishment, of giving power to the students themselves, in order to provide them with opportunities to grow, to develop an understanding of life, to make meaning through the "testing" of experiences, and to "find" themselves. Teachers found that the students matured when they were given this responsibility. During the trips, the teachers interwove service with some local sightseeing opportunities. They also included group discussions on issues and experiences that furthered reflection and social cohesion and respect among group members and provided journal writing opportunities for self-reflection.

The teachers felt the experience positively affected students with the "right mindsets" (teacher, interview) by helping them to develop deeper, and transformed, knowledge of life and themselves, community- and civic-mindedness, the ability to live with uncertainty and change (i.e., adaptability), the development of increased awareness of what is of value in life, and the development of a number of skills, such as social skills. They valued the experience for helping to break down students' stereotypes of place (how stunning the physical place was), culture (how complex, how similar, yet different), people (how kind and warm people can be), and poverty (what does poverty mean?). Students developed open-mindedness (Hare 1979), which is essential to cultivating citizenship.

Teachers reflected that the pedagogy changed students' understanding of the world by transforming their own lived reality: school learning and life learning became integrated and meaning-making became knowledge. Teachers appreciated the changes they saw in their students, some of whom wanted to continue to do further service work. They also saw students develop new cross-cultural friendships, and they valued the realness of the experience. One stated, for example, how students had a chance to visit the family of a child with AIDS who was supported by the school. The teacher stated that to actually see and play with the child in person made the reality "hit home" for students in a manner that isn't possible in the impersonalized, segregated walls of the school. The pedagogy engaged students by making learning personally meaningful.

Teachers also encountered challenges in delivering service-learning pedagogy, some of which included school administrative structures (such as district policies or lack of support among some administrators), the significant time commitment on top of all the regular duties of teaching, managing all the organizational details (e.g., paperwork), language and cultural differences, the difficulty of developing and coordinating community connections, and the trouble and frustration of having certain types of students (such as academically driven perfectionists) open themselves up to experiences that had transformative potential. Some of these teachers described the challenge of students who "failed" the experience by not opening themselves up to change and reflection. One teacher also felt challenged by the immensity of the global issues experienced and the difficulty of helping everyone.

Necessary Conditions for Pedagogical Success

Research participants, both teachers and students, found the experiential-based, service-learning experiences to be effective and valuable in developing students' citizenship, as theorized by Dewey.[5] They stated that it transformed students' understanding of life as well as developed empathy, or engagement, in the life situations of others. The trips thus had ethical importance because they facilitated development of the connections that bind us all together and the power of action to bring positive change. Generally, then, the trips were authentic examples of Deweyan experiences.

Our analysis, however, revealed that certain factors are required for such trips to be pedagogically successful and identified some areas of concern. To begin, all students stated that the teacher was crucial to the success of the experience; the teacher "was the course." They respected and valued their teachers, who they saw as providing them with support and encouragement to grow. The students described the organizing teachers as people who modelled citizenship: they understood students' individual personalities and strongly encouraged them to step outside of their comfort zones by giving them focused problems to solve and bringing relevant issues to their attention. These teachers intuitively grasped the fine but crucial line between freedom and discipline, responsibility and trust. At the same time, the teachers provided spaces for reflective exploration of lived experiences that led to deepened comprehension and new insights, and helped students to feel respected and valued as individuals. Further, the teachers prepared the students well for the trips beforehand, teaching them the history of the nation and preparing them for the conditions they would see (such as poverty) and have to cope with (such as heat). For example, the Nicaraguan trip combined a Grade 12 board-approved course on global studies with the service-learning experience. This was valuable in providing learning guided by a teacher in class in combination with individualized experiential learning during the trip.

However, some areas of concern did emerge from the interviews as well. Five of these are described next, along with recommendations for addressing them. As we shall see, these shortcomings also relate to the Deweyan theory used to frame this chapter.

Areas of Concern

Who Benefits?

All students who participated in the interviews stated that they were glad they took part in the service learning, as they benefited from the experience in numerous ways. One student stated it was "the best three weeks of my life" (student, interview). However, they also stated that they did not feel all students would benefit from such work. They stated that some of the students complained about the trip and didn't want to complete the physical work, that some students were too selfish or self-absorbed to learn from the trip, and that some students were isolated by their peers. Students thus felt that students had to be particular kinds of people to benefit; in particular, students were seen to need to be open-minded and interested in going. They said that no one should be forced to go.

The problem, then, is how to provide the valuable experience embedded in the trip to students who are not already open and drawn to service learning because their sense of citizenship (in the sense of feeling a sense of connection to, concern for, and desire to help other people) may not be as strong as that of other students. Similar to students in chapter 7 by Naidoo and Benjamin in this volume, students stated that they became interested in the trip because of the allure of travel, the positive comments made by their peers, a desire for a new experience, curiosity, and/or their family philosophy of care for others. High school students are well known for their valuation of peer comments. Some students might be encouraged to participate through peer encouragement, but this does not solve the problem of how to help them to be open to the experience. The teacher's influence might help, as well as teaching methods, but family philosophy and conditions seem to matter critically: structural societal issues are definitely a factor. However, if individuals can be transformed, they can go on to change their social environments for the better as adults. Expanding the service-learning experience to more students would be beneficial to all individuals and to all society.

The Deweyan theoretical framework used in this chapter could be strengthened through an increased sensitivity to the multiple characters and personalities of students in school, some of whom are not open or predisposed to learning, especially experiential learning. Dewey recognized that individuals had varied personalities and that they were influenced by their family backgrounds. His solution lay in making education relevant to these students. In this case, however, relevance may not be sufficient to engage students in the experience, as it was voluntary. The authors recommend that all students should be invited to participate in the trips and that certain teaching methods be used to reach out to these students.

Methods that may help to make the experience valuable to all participants include providing students with a caring space of belonging, seeing and discussing alternative life realities, believing in these students, and giving students responsibilities. Secondly, trip guidelines can be illustrated to be in the interest of all. They can aim at developing a common community spirit that is citizenship. Kalbach and Forester (2006) describe the successful teaching practices of a high school teacher at an alternative school. They provide similar recommendations that include building relationships; empowering students in the Deweyan tradition that conceives the teacher's role as that of a guide, facilitator, or mentor; helping students develop personal connections to the material studied and feel a sense of engagement with it; and exploring meanings through critical dialogue on content in a welcoming and inclusive community of learning.

Possible methods of fostering the open-mindedness necessary for cultivating compassion and community-mindedness include creating cognitive dissonance and allowing students to "see" themselves as others see them and to develop understanding of how "no man is an island," as John Donne's celebrated poetic line states, through discussions that foster reflection on the manner in which we are all dependent on each other. Cognitive change can occur through reading, speaking, and writing activities that incorporate techniques such as displacement (exploring word and concept choice to uncover multiple perceptions of meaning) and critical questioning that identifies connections, contradictions, and tensions in different perspectives to "develop a multilayered foundation for their perspective. From this, [students] are able to understand how their reality may mirror, differ from, or be at odds with" those of others (Kalbach and Forester 2006, 78). Other methods include cooperative learning, hands-on activities, teacher modelling, and peer instruction, all of which place learning and leadership in the hands of students (Tam et al. 2001). Needlessly to say, the service-learning experience should remain one of choice: forcing students to take part will deny its value.

Access

Students had to pay thousands of dollars for the trips. Many students paid by working part-time jobs and getting help from their parents. Some of the students, consequently, stated that they felt access was a problem, as students who could not afford to raise the funds for the trip were not able to take part. Dewey argued for openness and inclusion of all learners in school, for it was through the processes of interaction with, discussion of, and debates over multiple points of views and perspectives that students developed their democratic spirits. The access problem can be addressed by collaborative funding activities. For example, the Kenya trip group conducted fundraising and used the money raised to support their service work. Perhaps fundraising could also be done to provide students from less wealthy families with the opportunities to go. Support might also be found through community sponsorship or by linking with local non-profit agencies that conduct service work in the areas travelled to.

Long-Term Behavioural Change?

While the students clearly valued the experience and developed new knowledge and insights about life from their service learning, the question remains as to how permanent the changes made in students' actual behaviours were. For a couple of students, the changes were definitely enduring, as the students have changed their life plans as a result of the trips. However, others seem to have gone back to their pre-trip behaviours. When one student was asked whether her behaviours with regards to environmental action had changed, her answer was that she was certainly aware of the issues; she said, "I think about it" (student, interview). Thinking and doing can be two different things. Indeed, one could argue that knowing and not doing is more problematic than not knowing and not doing. For service-learning pedagogy to be completely effective, explorations need to occur as to how it can permanently change students' mode of being. This concern is also relevant to Dewey's theory. Dewey argued that education could develop citizens who contributed to a continually growing democracy. He did not explain, however, how teachers could ensure that their teaching would create permanent changes in their students' behaviours. We argue that the educational process should not end with the experience, but rather that continued, interactive, and thoughtful experiences should continue the process of educational growth throughout students' lives. That is, education is not over with the end of schooling. In relation to these trips, this process can begin through post-trip discussions about long-term action. Providing opportunities for continued involvement through the formation of an "alumni club" that continues community service work and critical reflective dialogue is another option. Further, mentorship is an excellent tool for continued engagement. Students who have taken part can become mentors for those planning to go on other trips.

Perception of the Other

In all their reflections, students stated the benefits of the trip from their points of view only. They specifically had to be asked to describe how they thought those to whom they provided service benefited from the service, or how they believed individuals in the culture they visited viewed them as service providers. In both cases, students paused and had to think about their answers to these questions. Students would benefit, in other words, from reflective dialogue on the meaning of the service experience for the people for whom the service is provided. Further, many of the students viewed the Nicaraguan and Kenyan people to be less developed than Canadians. In other words, they maintained a Western modernist worldview of the West as most developed, without considering that Western colonial and post-colonial countries have been responsible for leading actions that exacerbate world issues such as environmental degradation and increased divisions of wealth. The students would thus also benefit from exploring the meaning of "development" and "Westernization" and the purpose of service for those for whom the activities were carried out (Stoecker and Tryon 2009). This also relates to Dewey's theory. Dewey's work argued for an open and inclusive democratic society in which all types of learners (both manual and intellectual) studied together in a program that weaved together and valued both programs. However, he said little of students from varied cultural backgrounds, tending to the argument that all students should study a common curriculum and so become "American citizens." For the twenty-first century, we should expand Dewey's openness to varied learners and varied cultures where cultural groups are treated with equal respect and value. The process of education can include multiple, multicultural perspectives. Through exposure to these multiple cultures and the democratic processes of debate and discussion, students and society can benefit. We can also expand Dewey's nation-based program to one that is global in scope, viewing all peoples as part of a global democracy.

A Class and Ethnicity Issue

As indicated previously, all students identified themselves as "middle class." Why did no working-class students take part? Perhaps access has a role to play, but family beliefs about service work and how money is spent might play a role as well. A key issue thus remains: How can service learning be expanded to include working-class students? Further, students of varying ethnicities took part in the trip, but none (to our knowledge) were First Nations students. Organizers of service-learning projects should consider how they can expand experiences to students of varying backgrounds and classes, as respectful inclusion of all in collaborative projects is a foundational principle of Deweyan citizenship and democratic societies.

Conclusion

Student and teacher interviews demonstrate that experiential/service-learning projects can nurture students' sense of connection and care for others, important dimensions of citizenship as theorized by Dewey. However, this was only the case if the learning projects embedded in the trips were carefully structured and if students were open to the experiences. The most important "lessons learned," as stated by the majority of students, were cross-cultural awareness and acceptance of cross-cultural difference; appreciation for North America's privileged lifestyle; and individual efficacy. These are all key components of global citizenship. However, questions remain. In particular, students self-selected themselves to participate if they were open to the experience or already valued helping others. The experience thus became a self-affirming one. How can those who are not open to such trips be invited and given the space to experience this potentially transformative pedagogy?[6] Further, and significantly, is this experiential pedagogy equally effective for all kinds of students?

Finally, how can this pedagogy bring about enduring change in students' thoughts and actions? These are key questions that remain after this research study and can serve as the basis for future research. Recommendations to address some of these potential shortcomings were described in the final part of the paper, and revolve around the need to expand the potential benefits of this experience-based learning to a wider selection of students and to provide possibilities for change through positive modelling, care, belief in potential, the giving of leadership, and teacher-guided reflection on experiences that have initiated cognitive dissonance.

Implications for Higher Education

While the research focused on service-learning experiences undertaken by Grade 12 high school students, the findings are equally relevant to universities, many of which are coming to focus more specifically on global citizenship as one of their key values or goals. This paper adds to our understanding of what global citizenship entails as well as of the pedagogical approaches that may promote it. Experiential education is equally valuable for university students and entails the same process of recursive dialogue and reflection. Ways of integrating global citizenship education in higher education include classroom activities and trips; policy statements that support research and funding initiatives; campus-wide GCE initiatives; and programs such as Go Global.

Classroom trips and activities can include service initiatives run by professors and instructors as part of their classroom learning experiences. Like the service-learning activity in Nicaragua described in this chapter, an instructor can plan and include an experiential service-learning activity in their course, modelled on Pritchard and Whitehead (2004). Prior to the trip, faculty can provide students with pre-departure preparations; this can include such things as in-class readings and discussions on the nation or place to be visited, along with work on service learning, equity, or global citizenship. The students would then engage in the service-learning activity (which can be either global or local) while at the same time reflecting on their learning through further in-class discussions and activities. Students could write papers that connect their experience with their learning. As one example, in one of their classes, graduate students worked with the first author to identify an area of local need and then organized a service activity related to it. The graduate students felt that loneliness among senior citizens was the issue they wished to address, for which they planned visits to a senior citizens' home. In these visits, senior citizens shared special events of their lives that mattered to them, which the graduate students wrote into a book of memories they later presented to the seniors. This experience benefited both the students (in a number of ways, including the building of empathy and relationships and increased knowledge of historical events) and those to whom the service was provided (through connection-building and the sharing of events of significance to them).

Secondly, post-secondary institutions can make commitments to support service learning through policy and mission statements, which can then influence the institution's actions and activities. For example, if an institution states that it values service learning, it can provide office space, funding, and support for events, which allow it to happen. It can facilitate initiatives by instructors and students, and help to build service-based relationships in local and global contexts. As an example, scholars can support local farmers in improving their crop yields through sharing their learning from research-based projects. Policy statement support can also lead to supporting the funding of a service-learning office that can help to organize and facilitate service-learning opportunities for instructors and students. For example, Go Global at the UBC Okanagan campus provides information and support to students who wish to engage in service-learning opportunities internationally.

Like high school programs, post-secondary institutions should consider the challenges raised regarding concerns over social justice and equity through critical reflections and considerations regarding care, relationships, and empowerment in the development of their classroom activities, policy statements, and actions, which may unpack the potentially neocolonial discourse and practices related to global citizenship education facilitated by experiential service learning. As a starting point, institutions can consider that there should be mutual benefits and equitable relationships in the development of service-learning initiatives and partnerships.

Appendix: Comparison of Findings by Country (Nicaragua: Thirteen Students; Kenya: Seven Students), Using Most Commonly Repeated Words/Phrases

1. Please describe the international service project you took part in. Consider: where you went, what you did, and for how long, plus any additional details you might want to add.
   Nicaragua: making a sustainable village by building milking pads for cows or a cattle corral; digging out water troughs; helping at an orphanage; sightseeing
   Kenya: building a school kitchen and garden; playing with children at an orphanage; sightseeing
2. What were your thoughts about the country you travelled to, and the trip itself, before going there? That is, how did you imagine it to be? Consider: the people, living conditions, environment, and any other factors in your answer.
   Nicaragua: expected poverty; country to be hostile, scary, dirty, and hot; unsure what to expect; nervous
   Kenya: thought it would be difficult to travel there (food/accommodation would be poor, hot, dry, dangerous); nervous; curious to learn about another place; not sure what to expect or whether should go
3. Did your thoughts about the country, and the service, change after completing your service project? If yes, describe how. Then, please answer why you think your thoughts did or did not change.
   Nicaragua: changed view of the country: friendly, happy, kind people and rich, active culture; beautiful landscape; and changed/more global view of the world; changed life goals; loved the service work; more modern/Westernized than expected
   Kenya: thoughts changed a little; reality was hard; lots of work; difficulty; a little more comfortable after it started; police at the hotel all the time; Westernization was apparent; got easier; great organization helping others; some people are scary/dangerous, others are very nice and helpful
4. What did you learn by taking part in this project?
   Nicaragua: the importance of relationships; self-sufficiency; life lessons; collaboration/team and other skills; there are good people in the world; if you want to do something, just do it; about myself and other cultures/the world; growing as a person; happiness isn't related to money; how help goes a long way and is internally satisfying; appreciate what Canada has; acceptance

of others and community mindedness; how my actions affect others; about global issues
Kenya: responsibility; like helping others; some people really need help and some are trying to help; someone needs to take leadership to help others; people there are no different than us; to be active; everyone can help a little; leadership; open-mindedness; appreciation for what we have

5. Are you glad that you took part in the project? Why or why not?
   Nicaragua: yes: it was life changing; want to go back; learned a lot; fulfilling; loved it; biggest experience of my life; learned more than from texts; learn your own way/yourself; bonded as a group; opened my eyes (no students said no)
   Kenya: yes: it changes/develops you; develop leadership skills; see another part of the world; learn about the importance of action; understand others better (no students said no)
6. Do you think other students will benefit from taking part in projects like this? Why or why not?
   Nicaragua: yes: hands-on learning/experience-based learning is the best way; don't force people but make accessible to all and encourage all to go; personal experience learning is better; it's character-building; have to be open-minded and a personal choice to go; most will benefit if run by the same teacher; depends on the person (some changed forever; others not)
   Kenya: yes: allows you to interact with others; learning experience; everyone will change and be more open-minded and appreciate; don't force but encourage participation; develop cultural awareness, maturity, and bonding with others; everyone will benefit
7. Why did you decide to take part in the trip?
   Nicaragua: like helping people; friends; wanted to travel; slide show about it; thought it would be fun and different to being in school
   Kenya: wanted to see the reality of Kenya; friends; teacher encouraged; wanted to help others; different type of learning to that of school

NOTES

1 While the data was collected in 2010, the findings are still relevant today as they inform our thinking about an educational theory that has predominated thinking about pedagogy since the early twentieth century. There has been and continues to be interest in Dewey's foundational work and thinking about how students can best learn and be engaged in their learning.

2 The community projects were identified and organized by the foundations and included hands-on work, supplemented with opportunities to interact with locals, ongoing reflection in groups, and some local sightseeing. Relationships were developed and nurtured on a continual basis. Both researchers are university scholars who are "outside" of the projects: they did not participate in the planning or execution of the trips and are not affiliated with the schools in any way. The principal investigator's research focuses on citizenship and the second author's work focuses on moral philosophy.
3 Both trips were carried out at secular schools and did not include any mention or proselytizing in any form of organized religions.
4 General characteristics of "good" students include such features as participating actively in class, having a good attitude, and being open-minded.
5 The research participants were invited to take part in the interviews by the researchers, and these interviews happened after school. The students individually agreed to be interviewed. These are most likely to be the students who found the experience to be valuable. Students themselves (as well as teachers) mentioned that a few of the participants on the trips did not appear to enjoy or benefit from the trips.
6 This statement assumes that this experiential pedagogy can be valuable and potentially engaging and transforming for all students. Future research can be carried out with the aim of identifying whether this assumption is valid or not.

REFERENCES

Abdi, A., and P. Carr. 2012. *Educating for Democratic Consciousness: Counter Hegemonic Possibilities*. New York: Peter Lang.

Abdi, A., and L. Shultz. 2008. *Educating for Human Rights and Global Citizenship*. Albany, NY: SUNY Press.

Andreotti, V. 2006. "Soft Versus Critical Global Citizenship Education." *Policy and Practice: A Development Education Review* 3: 40–51. https://doi.org/10.1057/9781137324665.0009

Appiah, K. 2007. *Cosmopolitanism: Ethics in a World of Strangers*. New York: W.W. Norton.

Aristotle. n.d. "The Nicomachean Ethics." Nothingistic.org. Accessed July 2010. http://nothingistic.org/library/aristotle/nicomachean/nicomachean09.html

Banks, J. 2017. *Citizenship Education and Global Migration: Implications for Theory, Research and Teaching*. Washington, DC: American Educational Research Association.

Beck, U., and E. Beck-Gernsheim. 2006. "Beyond Status and Class?" In *Education Globalization and Social Change*, edited by H. Lauder et al. Oxford: Oxford University Press.

Broom, C. 2010. "Conceptualizing and Teaching Citizenship as Humanity." *Citizenship, Social and Economics Education: An International Journal* 9, no. 3: 147–55. https://doi.org/10.2304/csee.2010.9.3.147

Broom, C., ed. 2016. *Youth Civic Engagement in a Globalized World: Citizenship Education in Comparative Perspective*. New York: Palgrave Macmillan.

Bruner, J. 1987. "Structures in Learning." In *Curriculum Planning: A New Approach*, 5th ed., edited by G. Hass. Boston: Allyn and Bacon.

Creswell, J.W. 1998. *Qualitative Inquiry and Research Design: Choosing Among Five Traditions*. London: Sage.

Dewey, J. 1916. *Democracy and Education*. New York: The Free Press. http://en.wikisource.org/wiki/Democracy_and_Education

Eyler, J., and D. Giles. 1999. *Where's the Learning in Service Learning?* San Francisco: Jossey-Bass.

Hansen, D. 2011. *The Teacher and the World: A Study of Cosmopolitanism as Education*. New York: Routledge.

Hare, B. 1979. *Open-Mindedness and Education*. Montreal: McGill-Queen's University Press.

Kalbach, L., and L. Forester. 2006. "The Word and the World: A Lesson on Critical Literacy and its Impact on Student Achievement and Self Esteem." In *Curriculum and Teaching Dialogue*, vol. 8, edited by Barbara Slater Stern. Grenwich: IAP.

Kolb, D. 1984. *Experiential Learning: Experience as the Source of Learning and Development*. Englewood Cliffs, NJ: Prentice Hall.

Nussbaum, M. 1997. *Cultivating Humanity: A Classical Defense of Reform in Liberal Education*. Cambridge, MA: Harvard University Press.

Pike, G. 2008. "Reconstructing the Legend: Educating for Global Citizenship." In *Educating for Human Rights and Global Citizenship*, edited by A. Abdi and L. Shultz. Albany, NY: SUNY Press.

Pritchard, F., and I. Whitehead III. 2004. *Serve and Learn: Implementing and Evaluating Service-Learning in Middle and High Schools*. Mahwah, NJ: Routledge.

Rocheleau, J. 2004. "Theoretical Roots of Service-Learning: Progressive Education and the Development of Citizenship." In *Service-Learning History, Theory, and Issues*, edited by B. Speck and S. Hoppe. Westport, CT: Praeger Publishers.

Segrin, C., and J. Flora. 2011. *Family Communication*. 2nd ed. New York: Routledge.

Speck, B., and S. Hoppe. 2004. *Service-Learning History, Theory, and Issues*. Westport, CT: Praeger Publishers.

Stoddard, E., and G. Cornwell. 2003. "Peripheral Visions: Toward a Geoethics of Citizenship." *Liberal Education* 89, no. 3. http://www.aacu.org/liberaleducation/le-su03/le-su3fperspective.cfm

Stoecker, R., and E.A.Tryon, eds. 2009. *The Unheard Voices: Community Organizations and Service Learning*. Philadelphia: Temple Press.

Tam, K.Y., M.K. Rousseau, J.W. Nassivera, and P. Vreeland. 2001. "Holiday in the Museum: An Alternative Program for At Risk High School Students." *Intervention in School and Clinic* 37, no. 2: 77–85. https://doi.org/10.1177/105345120103700202

Verma, R. 2017. *Critical Peace Education and Global Citizenship*. New York: Routledge.

Vygotsky, L.S. 2004. *The Essential Vygotsky*. Edited by R.W. Rieber and D.K. Robinson. New York: Kluwer Academic.

Zull, James. 2002. *The Art of Changing the Brain*. Sterling, VA: Stylus Publishing.

7 Vacationing beyond the Beaten Path – Checkmate! Examining Global Citizenship and Service-Learning Education through Reflective Practice in Grenada and Jamaica

KAREN NAIDOO AND MARIE BENJAMIN

So, you paid for an "all inclusive" package to help the poor. What a splendid idea! How much of that package you signed up will actually go towards the community that you're intending to "give back" to? And how much are you willing to invest for your much-deserved holiday? More and more post-secondary institutions in Canada are promoting to their students the idea of a "global experience" as a valuable part of their education. Besides students having to pay loads of money for their degrees, they are now willing to fork out even more for an internship abroad that will add sparkle to their resumes … In fact, many institutions are embedding the concept of "how to be a global citizen" into their practices and mandates in order to remain competitive.

Promoting the popular ideology of "giving back" to the Global South is not limited to post-secondary institutions; many non-profit organizations are also cashing in big bucks on this very concept. A number of large-scale international development agencies are also promoting the once paid-for internships to now pay-into internships. That's right, as a young person, if you are willing to pay a minimum administration fee, plus accommodation, flight, and other personal expenses, you can have an elite internship with a reputable NGO. With an increasing amount of students having concern over employment opportunities post-graduation, they are often inclined to invest in this avenue with the intent of increasing their work experience and/ or employable skills. Furthermore, the cool backpacking through Europe once a young person completes their degrees are now ancient ideas. Young people are seeking their cultural education in different ways that are all couched under the theme of "helping the Global South." Do these global educational experiences really matter in the larger scheme of things? And how much experience can a student contribute to the host community during their short stay? Are there ways to make international experiences more genuine for the host communities and students alike?[1]

The quest for an international experience through a study or volunteer abroad opportunity is a tool used by post-secondary students who crave to transform their college or university theories into practice. The idea that one can be immersed in a new, unique environment for anywhere between ten and thirty days, as part of a what is often deemed a life-altering experience (Lewin 2009; Keshtiaray et al. 2013), is, to some, appealing. But how many students understand the concept of global citizenship and the opportunities that are within service-learning programs? Similarly, how many volunteer-abroad programs allow a sufficient amount of time for students to prepare for the intense experiences of being in a new community and culture? As active practitioners in service-learning programs that take Canadian students to the Caribbean region and former members of the Canadian non-governmental organization The Lock,[2] we put forth these questions as a means of deconstructing global citizenship education and service-learning practices in international volunteer programs. In so doing, we utilized our experiences in international service-learning programs in the Caribbean as case studies to examine the impact and practice of global citizenship education and service-learning programs. Through these in-depth reflections, we recognize that analysing service learning is one of the most important ways in which practitioners can bring constructive critique and growth to the arena of global citizenship education (Fook, White, and Gardner 2006).

We begin this chapter by offering critical analyses of definitions of global citizenship and service learning; we then draw examples from events that occurred through service-learning programs in the islands of Grenada and Jamaica; and we conclude by examining the ways in which service-learning programing can be used as a tool for community development and knowledge mobilization in more community-centred ways.

Global Citizenship, Study Abroad, and Higher Education

Defining Global Citizenship and Study-Abroad Programs

International experiences and study-abroad programs are theoretically intended to flush out interlocking oppressions, whilst situating power and privilege in a more practical sense. One of the expectations of international exchange programs is finding meaningful and equitable solutions for several global issues, such as poverty, environmental destruction, and child neglect (Goudge 2003; Keshtiaray et al. 2013; Unterhalter 2009; Zemach-Bersin 2009). And although, in theory, international exchanges are designed with good intentions, there are various critiques that must be acknowledged, including but not exclusive to programs being extensions of volunteer tourism and the perpetuation of the colonial gaze. Within these two assertions, international exchanges recreate the dynamic of the outsider infiltrating a foreign space to observe, explore, and engage with the other. In so doing, the very act of participating as a volunteer in an international exchange program recreates the power dynamics that exist in what Edward Said (1985) describes in his conception of otherness. The other is therefore constructed through the lens of European values, assumptions, and cultural codes. Consequently, Said argues that the other is often described in a negative reflection and is dehumanized. In our case study, the Caribbean is positioned within the colonial imagination, obscuring its history, culture, and the politics of power (Ford-Smith 1995; Van Eeden 2004). Therefore, in this chapter, we ask the question: How can international exchanges offer equitable experiences when there is a historical imbalance of power between the Global North and the Global South?[3]

One of the concepts entrenched in the expectations of international student experiences is the ability to develop background to become a global citizen. Throughout their education, students are bombarded with subtle messages emphasizing the value of diversity and the role it serves in navigating a globalized job market. As a result of various challenges that come with globalization, including the continuous shift in information and technology, higher educational institutions are working to arm their students with the tools necessary to compete on the global scale (Arvast 2006). Chang (2002) argues that higher education embraces diversity as an "added texture to [students'] education" and that global citizenship becomes a necessary lens for contextualizing diversity (127). Study-abroad programs then become an extension of the classroom that further prepares students to become global citizens, equipping them with the tools to apprehend diversity (Chan 2005). An example of the impacts to global citizenship education is the Global Citizenship Program at Lehigh University described in chapter 8 by Gisolo and Stanlick in this volume as "exploration of service learning outside of the classroom." Gisolo and Stanlick's discussion of the advantages of service learning, particularly the building of cultural experiences, is important for those interested in incorporating GCE into post-secondary curricula. They concluded that the development of various cultural experiences through service-learning programs offer new information that broadens students' worldview.

According to Margaret Brigham (2011), global citizenship is defined in relation to globalization as the "process of increasing interconnectedness between societies" (16; see also Chase et al. 2014; Kelleher and Klein 2006). In this sense, global citizenship education includes learning about exchanges between people, cultures, ideas, technology, and goods and services. Adding to their definition of global citizenship, Oxfam Canada (n.d.) characterizes a global citizen as a person who "advocates for global peace and recognizes social injustices; they are responsible for their own actions and are aware of their role as a citizen of the world" (2). Finally, the Atlantic Council for International Cooperation, Halifax (as quoted in Oxfam Canada n.d.) defines a global citizen as one who has the ability for understanding how the world works, and has an awareness that their own lives are linked in various ways to those who are on the other side of the world. Chapter 11 by Robinson and chapter 5 by Gray-Beerman in this volume also offer explorations of global citizenship education for NGO practitioners and in specialized topics such leadership and human trafficking, respectively.

Brigham (2011) adds that global citizenship education is transformational, shifting students' philosophical views of the world. These transformations "are often international in scope and containing various forms of study abroad, civic engagement or community service" (21). Thus, study-abroad or international placements help bridge the link between the meaning of a global citizen and social experiences. Additionally, study-abroad or international placements allow student-volunteers to immerse in a social context that may be different from their own lived stories. Chapter 6 by Broom and Bai in this volume expands on similar notions of global citizenship education with a discussion of Dewey's conceptualization of experiential learning. Here, Dewey explains global citizenship education as inherently social, a project in education involving institutions as well as students' experiences within various environments. If these experiences are transformative for students embarking on global education, what are the contributions to communities that are intending to host them? How do student-volunteers and their institutions perceive the organizations that are bridging these exchanges with the host community? How can organizations facilitate mutual exchange among the host community, foreign institutions, and students, so that this exchange fosters empathy together with the discussion of each other's view of the world? We assert that to create global citizens there needs to be acknowledgment of the dynamics of the power and privilege one holds, particularly for those in the Global North. Critical analysis of global citizenship should be embedded throughout the development of curriculum for any international organization or post-secondary institution wishing to create an international student-volunteer experience. If this critical analysis is missed, students and their institutions may approach these international service-learning programs assuming the role of the "expert" or "missionary" and may use these roles when entering their host countries or communities.

In post-secondary institutions specifically, there are numerous ways that integrating global citizenship education, not only in curricula but also in program and administration activities, can occur. Global citizenship education can be first included as a complement to programs that prepare students for work-abroad practicums and study-abroad experiences. In several institutions in Ontario, students have the opportunity to complete program placements internationally, and global citizenship education should be included as part of the placement preparation experience. Having global citizenship education as a placement course, general education requirement, or elective is one such way that this can be accomplished practically. Some program examples of fields where this can be most appropriately implemented include teacher's education, international business, anthropology, international development studies, and environmental studies. Moreover, the assumption that global citizenship education can only be utilized in fields where international placements occur seems archaic. As we now live in a globalized world, students who study in any field and end up in a multicultural/diverse workplace can benefit from the skills taught by global citizenship education. In major cities across the world, diversity is prevalent in the workplace such that the skills of cultural sensitivity, cross-cultural communication, and learning about the historical backgrounds of other parts of the world – in particular what is deemed the Global South – can be an integral professional skill (Jorgenson and Shultz 2012).

Administratively, global citizenship education should be included in the administrative processes and training of staff in international student and advising departments. Global citizenship education will undoubtedly be useful in assisting students with preparing for international exchanges, by adding a more nuanced component to preparations for studying, working, or volunteering abroad. In addition, having global citizenship education available as an aspect of staff training in international student and advising departments can assist institutions with developing staff knowledge and resources. The preparation and resources that departments and advisors provide to students are equally imperative in shaping a student's travel-abroad experience. Therefore, GCE is important to program and department administrators and advisors who help students to understand how their programs and careers are positioned in the world or how cultural diversity can expand one's critical thinking abilities. When staff and administrators apply the lessons from global citizenship education, they can in turn help students with broadening their approaches to their own programs and/or study and work experiences when going abroad or staying at home.

Paradise: No Development Necessary

The Caribbean is often assumed as a place that is not in need of development; instead, it is viewed through a one-dimensional lens – a perfect vacation destination, a paradise. This lens is not recent; rather, it is a historical narrative that dates back to its very first "white tourist," Christopher Columbus (Momsen and Torres 2005, 314; Montero 2011). Mimi Sheller (2003) argues that the Caribbean continues to be "an ideal playground for Westerners" (114). Media images, tourist brochures, and various travel websites idealize the Caribbean as a place for the perfect getaway. This exotic place is expected to melt away one's stress as the carefree natives of the islands cater to the vacationers' every need at any point during their holiday (Hernandez-Ramdwar 2016). Honor Ford-Smith (1995) argues that tourist brochures offer the "images of welcoming plantations peopled with friendly 'natives' in uniforms [who] are manipulated to convey the idea of adventure and excitement in a context which is at once primitive, safe and compliment" (382).

The images that construct the Caribbean as a picture-perfect paradise inhabited by happy-go-lucky people are parallel to Talya Zemach-Bersin's (2009) description of how international placements are presented in "similar language [as] tourism or adventure travel" (306). Zemach-Bersin (2006) argues that international placements are not seen as a process of learning; rather they are a fantasy where "foreign destinations and their citizens are products or commodities" (305). She goes further and states, "Just like advertisements, pre-departure understandings of study abroad focus almost entirely on the individual American student's consumer needs" (311). Deconstructing the historical and ongoing views of the Caribbean as a site of consumption through international placements can be difficult, especially if placement administrators endorse similar perceptions.

In addition to the Caribbean's white sandy beaches and crystal blue waters, the region is also marked as a place with high rates of natural disasters and/or crimes (Hernandez-Ramdwar 2016). Tour brochures are pitted against fundraising campaigns to "save" people who are victims of natural disasters and/or victims of corrupt political regimes. Ford-Smith (1995) argues that people in North America and Europe understand the Caribbean only as "a place of reporting violence, consisting of drug cartels, disasters, souvenirs and fragments of memory … these images, which may then be re-deployed in relationships with people of colour living in Europe and North America" (380). The view of the Caribbean becomes a binary dynamic, functioning in a one-dimensional way and strongly influencing how North Americans and

Europeans engage with the region – either for pleasure or as a place that is in constant state of devastation. This is not to say that international development is not taking place in the Caribbean, as there is a flood of NGOs (Podur 2012) offering valuable aid and services to non-tourist destinations. In this chapter, we are addressing the problems of presenting the Caribbean as in need of aid, or a crime-riddled place, while simultaneously serving as a tourist destination. Consequently, we are interested in examining programs that were designed by The Lock's partnership with Canadian higher educational institutions, facilitated both in Grenada and Jamaica. Given the problematic way that the Caribbean is presented, we want to address the implications of programing international service-learning experiences in the Caribbean.

Internationalizing Volunteer and Practicum Experiences

The Lock is a registered Canadian charitable organization established in the mid-2000s. The founding members, first-generation Canadian people of Caribbean heritage, based their mandate on strengthening the capacity of youth in Ontario and in the Caribbean through education and empowerment. The overall mandate seeks to provide resources and opportunities for youth to discover and utilize their full potential, collectively and as individuals. One of the main objectives of the organization is to provide a voice to communities so that international programs and experiences are created as inclusive of these community needs.

We write this reflective chapter as university program coordinators and former members of The Lock who served for approximately five years collectively with the organization. Similar to program coordinators, individuals who volunteer with The Lock engage in the following learning objectives and outcomes and are expected to analyse the local culture, history, government, and economy from a critical perspective; analyse the impact that the tourist industry has on the island, culture, and economy; identify the significance of Caribbean cultural expression from social, political, and global perspectives; develop and facilitate age-appropriate workshops/engagement activities that focus on the identified development themes; and engage in intercultural exchanges and learning opportunities and evaluate the service-learning experience and its impact on their personal and professional growth.

International service learning in the Caribbean became a necessary component of The Lock's endeavour to integrate student-volunteers in global citizenship education. Although service-learning work can definitely be completed within Canada and Toronto, the integration of second-generation Caribbean descendants as student-volunteers within The Lock's programs encouraged the co-founders to complete a vision for the organization that existed since inception. The organization granted opportunities to contribute to a community and gave specific recognition to young people of Caribbean heritage, giving them a chance to authentically connect with a culture that they are disenfranchised from due to their citizenship abroad. In so doing, through the travel-abroad opportunity, student-volunteers were able to see a different perspective on the islands where they chose to work and volunteer.

Service Learning as a Brand

The Lock as an organization adheres to a definition of service learning that focuses on exposing the dynamics of power and privilege that exist in international development work. To do so, student-volunteers are offered critical perspectives on their positioning within international work and a method of decolonizing their understandings of the history of the Caribbean and its social, economic, and political inequities. Hence, the major traits of the service-learning programing include two philosophies: first, acknowledging where the student-volunteers were positioned socially and culturally in the host environment, and second, uncovering the colonial history of the islands by addressing the effects of colonization on development. The organization's knowledge of the remnants of the colonial legacy in the Caribbean region instigated the need to be mindful of not reproducing these colonial legacies in its programing. Moreover, the creation of social justice – oriented international experiences worked hand in hand with the ability to provide effective community development initiatives. These initiatives therefore allow student-volunteers to move beyond seeing themselves as mere volunteer-tourists. Instead, student-volunteers are encouraged to hold the view that they are individuals who can influence, invest, and be involved in the service-learning and community-development processes.

The Lock's international service-learning program allows student-volunteers to obtain valuable work experience while utilizing their skills in their specific program area and engaging in critically reflective social justice curriculum. Service learning for The Lock therefore begins as part of global citizenship education and prior to student-volunteers' departure from Canada, and continues to be a vigorous thread throughout and until the very end of the program. Service learning takes on an active community voice that contributes to the implementation of a service-learning project and engagement with a curriculum focused on social justice while in the host country. A description of The Lock's service-learning approach once in the host community is as follows. First is the act of service itself, which takes place in the form of student-volunteers being involved in a community development project. For instance, in Jamaica, student-volunteers were responsible for teaching in a literacy and youth leadership summer sports camp and helped build an infrastructural project – a pre-school playground. While in Grenada, student-volunteers completed their teaching practicum placements within local educational institutions.

The second aspect of service learning is a social justice curriculum. This curriculum allows the student-volunteers to participate in workshops and activities that question, shape, create, and reconstruct their understanding of international development work, the host environment, and their positions within the host community. For instance, The Lock's service-learning curriculum includes informal, interactive workshops, historic site visits, group activities, and a comprehensive workbook that pushes student-volunteers to be immersed in the host environment. Moreover, student-volunteers learn from local experts on the context in which The Lock's community work takes place. With a blend of mandatory, tourist, and educational workshops, student-volunteers are exposed to numerous topics, some of which include the history of the island; the economic differences between the home and host country; the interconnections between Canada and the host country; local industries that flourish within the host island; and documentaries and workshops that explore international debt and the island's position in the world economy. A typical day in the host community begins at eight in the morning, and the student-volunteers spend four to five hours of their day at the program site (literacy camp, practicum, or infrastructural build). Then, in the evening on two days out of each week, student-volunteers engage in one cultural workshop, service-learning excursion, or social justice–oriented activity/discussion, which focuses on issues that are specific to the host community.

The third aspect is that student-volunteers are also provided with The Lock's service-learning workbook and are encouraged to journal about their experiences during their time away from home. Reflecting on various events allows the student-volunteers opportunity to address the dynamics of power and privilege, resource-rich and resource-scarce dynamics, and other interlocking issues of political economy both locally and globally. Reflection also allows for ways to address guilt, which is often considered an overall consciousness of oppression.

Nickols et al. (2013) confirm that the process of reflection in service learning allows student-volunteers to develop intercultural competence and critical thinking about experiences that challenge previous assumptions. For example, one annual service-learning activity in The Lock's program encourages student-volunteers to use local currency to purchase items that would be customarily purchased while at home. The aim of this activity is not only to allow student-volunteers to manage their finances in the host environment but also to illustrate the difference in costs of living in both places. A post-activity discussion then illustrates how international debt and relationships to global markets can affect the socio-economic status of individuals in the host environment. These activities are created as a means of dismantling notions of the student-volunteers' power and privilege. In doing so, discussions are intended to disrupt previous knowledge about volunteering in an international context, and to connect the student-volunteers to the personal and external contexts that affect international service and community work.

From inception, The Lock worked independently to recruit and host individuals who were interested in volunteering as teachers and program planners in Jamaica. In 2017, however, The Lock commenced partnering with its first Canadian post-secondary institution and provided its initial service-learning project in Jamaica. The creation of organizational relations with a Canadian post-secondary institution was done intentionally as a way to strengthen and expand the organization in terms of program structure, volunteer recruitment, and financial capacity. Since 2017, together with Canadian institutions, The Lock has completed over six service-learning trips within the Caribbean; however, our discussion will include the service-learning programs that involved three Canadian post-secondary institutions in Jamaica and Grenada. In general, a group participating from one institution would typically constitute eight to ten student-volunteers and two faculty members, who identified either as white or minority, abled-bodied, and between eighteen and sixty years old.[4]

Although these higher-learning partnerships were viewed as a means for building organizational, volunteer, and financial capacity, which is important, they leave small organizations vulnerable. The shift from working independently to having institutional partnerships can be identified as the juncture that altered the ability of The Lock to execute its service-learning programs as originally designed. Variables such as volunteer recruitment, program funding, and preparation were now solely in the hands of the partnering institution. Therefore, for some post-secondary institutions, The Lock had little or no influence over how student-volunteers were selected or prepared for an international service-learning program. The lack of involvement of The Lock with the student-volunteers prior to departure was noted especially in the student-volunteers' reactions to service learning in the host community. On the other hand, when The Lock had contact with the student group prior to departure they were more receptive to The Lock's service learning, because The Lock's brand of service learning remained central to its programs. However, the conflict between the different cultural understandings of development work brought forward by partnering with certain Canadian post-secondary institutions was a constant impediment for program success. Some of these conflicts will be addressed throughout the critical reflections explored in the later part of this chapter.

Critical Reflections – Visiting "Irie" Jamaica and "Pure" Grenada[5]

As an organization, The Lock strives to mould its international service-learning programs with three assumptions in mind. First, the host community context is complex, so the service-learning curriculum is designed to illustrate how community development projects can work alongside traditional tourist activities. Second, service-learning programs should be beneficial to the hosting communities through capacity-building and knowledge-mobilizing activities. Finally, service-learning programs should disrupt the preconceptions prevalent in current global citizenship education initiatives, especially those found within post-secondary institutions that allow student-volunteers to see themselves as passive recipients of international experience.

Keeping Up with the News

In The Lock's service-learning programs and projects, the location of the Caribbean being viewed as a vacation destination is part of a philosophy that we grappled with as being part of the organization. In 2013, Grenada's Ministry of Tourism rebranded its tourism campaign to "Pure Grenada" (Benoit 2014). In its sincere form, the campaign aimed at inviting tourists to enjoy the authentic parts of the island – to meet real Grenadians, to have real experiences in the outdoors, and to enjoy the somewhat untouched beauty of the island, which are all aspects that make it an expensive place to "tour." On the other hand, when compared to Grenada, Jamaica is marketed as a place that is affordable in value. According to the Jamaica Tourist Board (n.d.), Jamaica is deliberately positioned as "the most complete, unique and diverse warm weather destination in the world, which offers the best vacation value currently available." Whatever the differences are, both Jamaica and Grenada are viewed as valuable tourist sites that attract student-volunteers and faculty alike in their pursuit for cultural experiences that differ from those of the Global North.

Although these tourism campaigns portray some aspects of both islands, it is important to highlight that both Grenada and Jamaica are also sites of poverty, crime, social and gender inequality, and political corruption. We state this not to shine a negative light on either island, but to illustrate that community development is complex and unveils learning ambiguities and questions. How do we bring a group of outsiders to the Caribbean to deconstruct the idea of a perfect paradise, when student-volunteers specifically choose the Caribbean as a service-learning destination because of this perception? How do we neglect the obviously touristic nature of these service-learning trips without hampering the overall participant experience?

Based on our experiences, when The Lock had a more active role in providing a service-learning curriculum (from 2014 to 2018), the student-volunteers were better equipped to understand small nuances that explained the "whys" of certain things about the host communities. Student-volunteers were also more engaged in the programs once on the ground and took an active role in naming their privileges when working within the communities. For instance, during the first service-learning trip to Jamaica in 2016, The Lock worked actively with one of its partnering post-secondary institutions to plan every stage of the ten-day program. That is, this post-secondary institution worked together with The Lock in preparing student-volunteers and their faculty for the cultural, economic, and geophysical features they would encounter in Jamaica. During this preparation period, student-volunteers could form relationships with The Lock members, which contributed in building trust; as a result, student-volunteers were notably more equipped to decompress difficult notions that are centred on development once they arrived in Jamaica. In addition, The Lock was purposeful in building social justice and global citizenship education into both pre-departure and on the ground service-learning activities. These relations on behalf of The Lock were a way to set the stage for student-volunteers and faculty to develop connections between issues at the micro and macro level and think critically about their personal reasons for wanting to engage in a global exchange.

In one of the pre-departure exercises, student-volunteers and two participating faculty members were asked to follow then-current news reporting in Jamaica over several months. They were allowed to gather information on any issue published (music, education, healthcare, tourism, comics, and sports) as long as the news story was from the week of the pre-departure preparation meetings. The task of this exercise was for student-volunteers and faculty to find the links between issues relevant to Jamaicans and how these issues may be traced back to former colonial laws/policies (and Canada's relationship to the colonial project, when applicable), larger economic decisions (either the International Monetary Fund or local economic policies), and/or larger social structures (family, education, healthcare).

Simple topics such as eating were used to illustrate the connection between colonial practices and present-day food consumption. For instance, the forced and volunteer blending of various cultures, which includes the Indigenous peoples, Africans, Indians, and Europeans, all influenced many of Jamaica's popular dishes such as jerk chicken or ackee and saltfish. Student-volunteers learned that ackee and saltfish were both imported to the island by Europeans during colonialism. The jerking of meat was taught by the Indigenous populations to Africans as a means of learning to survive off the land. Knowing this provided the student-volunteers with more of an appreciation of how history impacts culture and other simple aspects of life. This exercise allowed student-volunteers to become more engaged in the social issues that were, at the time of travel, taking place in Jamaica. As an organization, The Lock stressed the ongoing relationship between Canada and Jamaica and deliberately pushed student-volunteers to gain knowledge about the island that goes beyond Montego Bay, Jamaica's tourist capital. Student-volunteers and faculty were provided information about what local Jamaican students know about Canadian contemporary issues. This illustrates that international work does not exist in a vacuum, because host communities are equally aware of the foreigner's presence as the foreigner is of the host community.

Another example of historically informed learning occurred when a student who was interested in the Jamaican prenatal health system brought in articles that addressed some of these issues, posing questions around lack of attention to women's health in Jamaica. In this incident, we collectively discussed various policies that impacted Jamaica's overall healthcare system such as former structural adjustment programs that were administered by the World Bank in the early 1980s and the West Indian Domestic Workers' Scheme (1955–67), where Caribbean women between the ages of eighteen and forty years (in most cases educated teachers and nurses) were recruited by Canadian working families to work as childcare workers, cooks, maids, and cleaners (Arat-Koc

2001; Calliste 2001; Henry 1968; Lawson 2013). Student-volunteers were able to critically reflect on how these former policies continue to have rippling effects on healthcare practices in Jamaica today.

In both of these examples, student-volunteers were exposed to dialogue that invited them and faculty members to deconstruct their current cultural paradigms of Jamaica and question where the production of their knowledge is rooted. Local news was used as an avenue to discuss the complexities and dynamics of everyday experiences in Jamaican society. One of the goals for The Lock's approach to service learning is demonstrating how politics and various social structures are interlocking, having profound impacts in the home, at the dinner table, and in family practices in the host community. These pre-departure service-learning pieces are reflective, offering student-volunteers additional tools that are outside of the theory addressed in their programs, which are often Eurocentric. We argue that addressing power and privilege upfront in program preparation frames a more decolonized approach to learning and interacting with communities that are outside of the dominant context. Naming power and privilege also creates room for processing of guilt as a result of one's privilege that is viewed beyond the individual as more systematic – removing the "us" versus "them" dynamic.

Dear and Sharpe (2013) state that shifting our ways of teaching to a more self-reflexive approach of examining a community moves the conversation from studying the "other" to a place where those who live in North America can gain a greater appreciation of the various ways that North Americans are implicated in the history and politics of host communities. Chapter 8 by Gisolo and Stanlick in this volume explains that reflections allow student-volunteers "to work through the complexities of global citizenship ... enriching the learning process." We demonstrate in the concluding discussion how these pre-departure experiences shaped the perceptions and interactions of student-volunteers and faculty with the host community, creating a genuine space of learning for community and the international group alike.

Keeping It Local

As program coordinators, we saw that the involvement of the host community is integral, from the initial discussions on how and where the program takes place to the evaluation of the program upon its completion. It is because of this level of host community involvement that we can ensure that the local community's needs are best served, and that capacity and relationships are built within our program sites. When working with partnering institutions, the needs of student-volunteers and host communities may differ. It was through the example of the programs held in Grenada that we observed the most challenges in satisfying both the host community's and participants' needs during the planning process. Furthermore, our positions as part of the local community, and operating with all our native networks as Grenadians or Jamaicans, did in many ways give us autonomy over aspects of the program planning process. As a result, having an insider view or perspective while program planning allowed us, as coordinators, to make certain community-minded decisions.

Many aspects of local decisions and partnerships were an essential integration of The Lock's service-learning brand. For us, student-volunteers needed to make sense of how local non-tourist decisions, like the selection of program site, participant residence, facilitators, and activities, were impactful on a macro-level of meanings of global citizenship and service learning. Ross Lewin (2009) explains that as educators and/or those engaging in international development work, we must be critical of the practices and meanings of global citizenship. If not, he warns that student-volunteers may end up as global consumers, treating the host countries "as nothing but a playground of fun experiences … where the 'natives' are exotic and in need of 'saving'" (xv). It is important to note that most of The Lock's mandatory pre-departure service-learning pieces were modified by the partnering institution, impacting student-volunteers' overall experiences in the host country. Chapter 10 by Eva Aboagye in this volume says that "Signature Learning Experiences are normally developed by institutions to provide student-volunteers with additional learning outside of their core program areas." She goes further to explain that uncertainty is one of the characteristics of signature pedagogy, which "relies on the response of student-volunteers to each other and to the instructor and neither the instructor nor the student knows exactly what is going to happen." Often top-down approaches do not serve as justice to the community, student-volunteers, or faculty. Program planning is often a grassroots-level approach, and if partnering international institutions are disconnected from the needs of the community the relationship remains superficial.

The examples of community-minded decisions in the programming held in Grenada in 2015 and 2016 illustrate our attempts at community transformation. First, we sought educational institutions for the program that were in somewhat underserved communities. The overarching motivations for these decisions were based on allowing the host community to have access to the knowledge, resources, and outlook of the program student-volunteers. In addition, the practicum student-volunteers would have the opportunity to work within diverse types of settings with varying needs and approaches to formal education. Hence, the program sites included a children's orphanage and a primary and a special needs school, which were all located in the same community. Second, the choice to reside in a locally owned guesthouse instead of an all-inclusive hotel was intentional, as the presence of and business provided to locally owned hotels is diminishing on the island. Third, all of our service-learning workshops were delivered by local experts – a child psychologist from Children's Aid provided a workshop on child development in Grenada, the founder of a drumming ensemble led a workshop on Grenadian culture, and the director of the national museum led a workshop on Grenadian history and a walking tour of St. George's. Countless other examples, such as visiting unorthodox and unconventional sites of culture and heritage, purchasing local food products from small-scale vendors, and providing local dishes for student-volunteers as meals, were integral to supporting and in some ways building capacity within the local community.

It can be assumed that the lack of a shared vision of The Lock's approach to service learning with the Canadian partnering institution also inhibited the ability to build capacity for the host community. In some ways, some of the participating student-volunteers were unreceptive or outright disinterested in the opportunities provided to immerse themselves in the host community in ways that furthered global citizenship education learning and sharing knowledge. One such example includes the child welfare workshop that took place prior to the student-volunteers commencing their practicum placements. The local facilitator not only shared important information about the state of child welfare in the island but also presented an emerging technique of art therapy that she was currently using in her own sessions with children in care. The participating student-volunteers were less than enthused during a majority of the workshop and even failed to ask questions or seek information that would have assisted them in their placements. Also, the exposure to an expert in the field of early childhood education and child psychology lent no further motivations to share their Canadian experiences in the field with the facilitator. As explained in the discussion of Dewey's understanding of experiential learning in chapter 6 by Broom and Bai in this volume, the students' understanding of global citizenship education became somewhat removed while in the practice of service learning. Therefore, the student-volunteers missed out on the opportunity of having an authentic community learning experience that would have met authentic community needs.

In hindsight, it was recognized that in comparison to the service-learning trips to Jamaica, The Lock spent less time engaging in pre-departure activities with this partner institution. As a result, there may have been bigger gaps in understanding the purpose of the service-learning curriculum with the partnering institution and their student-volunteers. We advocate that reflective practice that goes beyond the scope of student-volunteers' programs is necessary. Engaging and reflecting on issues that are local to the host country opens student-volunteers to view issues beyond their own social context. The focus on reflective practice offered in this chapter is similar to the study presented in chapter 8 by Gisolo and Stanlick in this volume, where they concluded that "community-based service-learning experiences proved to be an effective educational tool," engaging student-volunteers' "hearts and minds, as well as to address very tangible needs in the target population." We therefore deconstruct the challenges to expressing our vision for service-learning programing with our partner institutions in the subsequent section of the discussion.

Disrupting the Expert

Thus far, we have explored how The Lock sought to dismantle the power and privilege of student-volunteers and volunteers in order to enrich the service-learning program experience. In many ways, several of the student-volunteers perceived themselves as having particular layers of expertise within the host community. In the following discussion, however, we consider the lessons learned not only from dismantling the perceived expertise of student-volunteers but also from deconstructing our own notions of being experts within the service-learning environment. In the end, we hope that these disruptions can inform future practice and understandings of global citizenship and service learning. According to The Lock, its journeys in providing service learning required constantly reshaping its practice based on the ever-changing service-learning and global citizenship environment. What could The Lock have done differently as an organization to not only ensure that some of the programs continued but also that the challenges faced were addressed?

Our first moment of disruption is the recognition that intercepting perceptions of power and privilege begins with pre-departure activities. Through building a prior relationship with the Canadian partner institution and their student-volunteers, community organizations – and in this case The Lock – could create and solidify a collective vision for service learning. Therefore, we contend that service learning goes beyond developing a cultural experience, and The Lock's service-learning brand is a part of a reflective practice framework that is cognizant of the implications of previous knowledge in understanding local everyday actions observed in the service-learning environment. In many ways, there is a clear distinction in Jamaicans' local everyday actions between those who participate in pre-departure service learning and those who do not. Once on the ground, student-volunteers who engaged critically in pre-departure service-learning activities demonstrated awareness of their own assumptions and expectations; as well, they were able to name their assumptions as being part of larger North American discourses, which frames the "other" as inferior, threatening, or dysfunctional.

For instance, during our evening de-briefs in Jamaica, student-volunteers raised questions around their previous views of Jamaican family structures. Before arrival in Jamaica, many had assumed that Jamaican families are primarily single-parented, and this was based on the high rates of dangerous activity present in Jamaican society. Through work in the service-learning projects student-volunteers saw that family structures, although non-traditional – single-parent homes, for instance – were still rooted in the community. Open dialogue that was fostered prior to being on the ground allowed student-volunteers and faculty the room to deconstruct their previously held assumptions and acknowledge how singular narratives of a group of people are manifested. These singular narratives are entrenched in the ways that Jamaican people are represented in Canadian media, marking them as violent, disruptive, and unlawful. Terry Roswell and Beverley Folkes (2007, 302) argue that popular Canadian discourses construct Jamaican culture as a threat that is "easily imported into Canada," and subliminal messages remain at the forefront of many Canadians' filtering their interactions with Jamaicans. They further argue that negative connotations represented in media are produced as biological, denoting "Jamaicans who are constitutionally disorderly. It's in their makeup and they are anti-authority" (Clare 1984, quoted in Roswell and Folkes 2007, 304; see also Fleras 2004). Negative perceptions are entrenched in public imaginations, as Roswell and Folkes argue, where Canadians identify Jamaicans as being linked as only disruptive. True transformable learning comes from the dismantlement of one's own view of the "other" and questioning the source of their beliefs.

Ziauddin Sardar (1999) argues that the real power of the West is located in defining the other. Therefore, some constructions of global citizenship are anchored in Western ideologies that may or may not be critical of the role of Eurocentrism and imperialism in international development work. We have seen, through our practice, that international placements and educational programs fall into the same discourse, where student-volunteers wanting to embark on a global exchange are immersed deeply in Western ideologies and discourses. Sardar (1999, 46) is critical of international education and how development is understood through a singular lens. He says that seeing the world as a "global village means shrinking distances, compressing space and time [and] shaping the world in the image of a singular culture and civilization." In other words, Eurocentrism becomes the political and social filter through which we think and conceptualize the world. It is also the way we organize knowledge (Sardar 1999; Hatton and Smith 1995). Thus, these programs are constructed and are reflective of the culture that they are developed within. We advocate that reflections (both collective and individual) encourage debates around one's privileges and pose questions for some deeper conversations about the various meanings of development and citizenship. More importantly, reflective practice invites a conversation around the interconnectedness between Canada and the Caribbean that is current and ongoing (and also includes colonial history, various migration policies, trade agreements, and so on). Understanding the interlocking issues of former and modern relations intentionally moves student-volunteers and faculty alike from observers of a culture to active learners. Samantha Dear and Erin Sharpe (2013, 55) argue that there is "significance to focusing on intercultural exchange and dialogue. It forms solidarity between both the student-volunteers from abroad and the community, helps to reduce distance and encourage student-volunteers to work together." International service-learning curriculum must lend room for discomfort and honestly reflect the impact student-volunteers have on the community but more importantly the impact the community has on them (Dear and Sharpe 2013).

The absence of a pre-departure relationship in some ways disrupted the process in which The Lock performed service learning. Based on our experiences, higher-learning institutions were sometimes resistant to or lacked an understanding of the organization's approach to global citizenship education and service learning. We believe this divided vision of global citizenship and service learning is partially due to the culture of international placements and organizational partnerships. Here, from the institution's perspective, the partnering organization – The Lock – is sometimes only seen as a means to safe accommodations, or a middle-man. Consequently, global citizenship and service-learning curricula are, in many ways, often viewed as a secondary piece to student-volunteers' international experiences. In hindsight, we observed that the resistance to The Lock's approach to global citizenship and service learning was due to the comfort level of both the facilitators and administrations, where the organization's curriculum needed to fit into the mandate of their institutions. As we explored these challenges, we resolved that we could have been more cautious about the nature of our partnerships with post-secondary institutions, or even made a greater effort to advocate for the importance of our service-learning curriculum in the entire international experience. As positioned by the introduction by Aboagye and Dlamini in this volume, it is important to question how the quality and content of global citizenship education affects the ability to produce globally minded student-volunteers.

For example, the student-volunteers in the programs in Grenada were taken to the famous Grenadian Fish Fridays, where local fishermen and restaurant owners come together to show off their various culinary skills. It is a family and community affair that is slowly diminishing for various reasons – it does not ideally fit the larger image of a conventional tourist activity, as it is a rustic local experience. As service providers and global citizenship educators, we wanted student-volunteers to understand some of the globalized influences that are impeding on family values and childhood education overall. Grenada is a small community that is impacted by foreign goods. If fish are being imported into the country for a cheaper cost than the local catch, what are the impacts to fishing families' livelihood? Similar to the introductory workshop, the student-volunteers were disconnected from the context and/or were unable to come to terms with why Fish Friday was integral to their practicum placements, or their experience in Grenada. We concluded that it was the lack of unravelling of these nuances in pre-departure sessions and preconceived information about the island, and/or discussing the complex social and economic environment that Grenada exists in, during pre-departure that left the student-volunteers with gaps of knowledge. Instead, student-volunteers were more interested and enthusiastic about engaging in the island tour or relaxing on the beach, more tourist-geared experiences, because both the organization – The Lock – and the post-secondary institution promoted these activities prior to their trip. We acknowledge that there were pieces of Grenada embedded into their course curriculum, but it remained at the theoretical level, leaving student-volunteers disconnected from existing issues on the ground. The experience became a way of adding international education to their list of credentials.

A second moment of disruption comes with our questioning of how the partner institutions and the organization define and then provide tangible returns to the community. Here are some reflective questions:

What kind of tangible returns are provided for the community? How does the program address the needs of the community? How is the program organized in a way such that it can continually meet this community need? One way that The Lock has attempted to meet community needs is by having constant dialogue with the host community about what can be accomplished within the project timeline. During infrastructural projects in Jamaica, for instance, school principals led the building and design process and were in constant negotiation with The Lock. On the other hand, in every service-learning trip, material donations were provided to the hosting and partner schools and organizations. However, are these annual material donations sufficient, and is it enough to solely build a classroom or playground or inject student-volunteers in a classroom for a few weeks?

Conclusion

Unfortunately, many international development projects are unsustainable, partly because the majority of programs are not designed with the community's needs at heart. The Lock and its partner post-secondary institutions are no exception to this shortcoming. At the end of our service-learning programs in Grenada, we objectively questioned our ability to provide tangible returns to the host community, even in the arena of sharing knowledge and expertise. In Jamaica, specifically, most of the organization's programs struggle with sustaining their yearly activities, even after running for over a few years. Although in Grenada we provided donations to the schools where the practicum placements took place, and the teachers were grateful for the opportunity to share a classroom space with their foreign counterparts, we question what this program really provides for the community. The program in Grenada has now ceased to exist, and all the groundwork which was begun, along with the community that was an integral part of the program, has been left in the wind. We therefore propose that The Lock market its service-learning program as possessing tangible community return. In this sense, our very packaged product of service learning should not only be geared towards the student-volunteers who participate, but should also be open to the community members who are engaged in the curriculum. Through our programs, we should create more open spaces for knowledge to be shared among the student-volunteers and the host community partners, and should use more of the feedback from the community to further develop the delivery of our service-learning programs. Local partners can also be trained to provide some of our programs in the host community so that if, for some reason, the organization cannot continue its international trips, the communities themselves can continue the projects. This, in our opinion, is one of the most significant ways that we as an organization can build capacity within the region, and is the true effect of global citizenship education.

Lastly, we learned that it is integral for every international service-learning program to be rooted in a social justice framework. The justification for this proposal is built upon the belief that global citizenship education and service learning is an exchange between student-volunteers and the host community. According to McKee (2016), civic engagement is a major goal of global citizenship education and service learning (5). So, in order to accomplish this goal, student-volunteers and staff involved in service-learning programs should develop awareness of social inequalities and injustices and work alongside communities to provide change. For instance, student-volunteers are working and living within a context that they should not only understand but also have awareness of the implications and consequences of their actions. In many ways, this awareness begins with being grounded in global citizenship education theories and having clear program outlines, where the expectations of the program for student-volunteers and the rigour of the program are concisely defined.

Prior to embarking on international service-learning experience, student-volunteers should be aware that their very ability to travel to another country to gain professional and personal experience is a sign of privilege and power. Therefore, understanding the position that one holds as a participant in relation to other individuals in the local context is necessary. We consider that this can be done with more comprehensive discussion and understandings of conceptions of global citizenship. When global citizenship education and service learning functions within a social justice framework, it endeavours to allow student-volunteers to ask: How does my presence in this community foster or perpetuate relationships of oppression and inequality? How has my understanding of the world, or even the context that I have chosen to be a part of, been shaped by my history, class, gender, and race? These questions, like the process of reflection that we have illustrated above, urges the participant to be in a constant state of critical reflection. McKee (2016, 6) asserts that the goal of service learning is to enable students to question preconceived notions about society, so that they can use the differences seen in their lives and the communities they service to critically reflect on why there may be differences and gaps. In all, our hope as practitioners of global citizenship and service learning is that other institutions and organizations continue the critical reflections needed to establish meaningful, accessible, and community-oriented programing. Without such efforts, the very idea of global citizenship, which endeavours to change the world, is inevitably lost.

NOTES

1 The reflection that opens this chapter was written by Karen Naidoo after facilitating a group of Canadian post-secondary students during their international placements in Grenada. Karen was forced to think through the intersecting notions of power and privilege while in her role as a project manager. This post-program reflection sparked deeper questions around students' expectations of exploring service-learning projects abroad and the meaning of global citizenship education on a whole.

2 The Lock is a pseudonym used to maintain the privacy of the non-profit organization used throughout this chapter.

3 Edward Said, in his work *Orientalism*, defined the construction of power through his comparison of the "other" as the "Orient" and the "Occident" (see Said 1994, 3). Said argues that the school of Orientalism is a human production of power between the Occident and the Orient, dating over 4,000 years. This construction of power defines historical and cultural relationships, the discipline of science, and ideological suppositions, which include "images and fantasies about a region of the world called the Orient" (Said 1985, 2). Said's work is used in post-colonial studies to explain the impacts of the colonial legacy on former colonial subjects. We use Said's work to specifically discuss the images and fantasies of the Caribbean that are historically rooted in the colonial project. Moreover, the colonial gaze is then the perpetuation of this view of colonized people as "other," which allows the beneficiaries of the colonizer to continue to observe and objectify the people they encounter.

4 Some post-secondary schools selected students of various groups to attend these service-learning trips. No particular program of study was favoured over another. As a result, this created a dynamic group of students and faculty members, each bringing their own area of expertise to how they interpret and engage with the service-learning program.

5 "Everything irie" is a Rastafari expression that was embodied by the tourist industry of Jamaica to advertise that everything is always good and pleasurable in Jamaica, while "Pure Grenada" is the 2018 campaign by the Board of Tourism in its efforts to re-brand Grenada as an "authentic" Caribbean destination.

REFERENCES

Arat-Koc, S. 2001. "The Politics of Family and Immigration in the Subordination of Domestic Workers in Canada." In *Family Patterns Gender Relations*, 2nd ed., edited by J.B. Fox. Oxford: Oxford University Press.

Arvast, A. 2006. "From Community to Commodity College: Globalization, Neoliberalism and the New Ontario College Curricula." *Canadian Journal of Educational Administration and Policy* 50: 1–21.

Benoit, L. 2014. "Glocal Tourism: Conflicts of Development in Grenada." PhD diss., Brandeis University.

Brigham, M. 2011. "Creating a Global Citizen and Assessing Outcomes."*Journal of Global Citizenship & Equity Education* 1, no. 1: 15–43.

Calliste, A. 2001. "Black Families in Canada: Exploring the Interconnections of Race, Class, and Gender." In *Family Patterns Gender Relations*, 2nd ed., edited by J.B. Fox. Oxford: Oxford University Press.

Chan, A.S. 2005. "Policy Discourses and Changing Practice: Diversity and the University-College." *Higher Education* 50, no. 1: 129–57. https://doi.org/10.1007/s10734-004-6351-3

Chang, J.M. 2002. "Preservation of Transformation: Where's the Real Educational Discourse on Diversity?" *The Review of Higher Education* 25, no. 2: 125–60. https://doi.org/10.1353/rhe.2002.0003

Chase, M.M., A.C. Dowd, L.B. Pazich, and E.M. Bensimon. 2014. "Transfer Equity for 'Minoritized' Students: A Critical Policy Analysis of Seven States." *Educational Policy* 28, no. 5: 669–717.

Dear, S., and E.K. Sharpe. 2013. "Points of Discomfort: Reflections on Power and Partnerships in International Service-Learning." *Michigan Journal of Community Service Learning* 19, no. 2: 49–57.

Fleras, A. 2004. "Racialising Culture Culturalising Race: Multicultural Racism in a Multicultural Canada." In *Racism Eh? A Critical Inter-Disciplinary Anthology of Race and Racism in Canada*, edited by C. Nelson and C. Nelson. Concord, ON: Captus Press.

Fook J., S. White, and F. Gardner. 2006. "Critical Reflection: A Review of Contemporary Literature and Understandings." In *Critical Reflection in Health and Social Care*, edited by J. Fook, S. White, and F. Gardner. Maidenhead, UK: Open University Press.

Ford-Smith, H. 1995. "Come to Jamaica and Feel Alright: Tourism, Colonial Discourse and Cultural Resistance." In *The Reordering of Culture: Latin America, The Caribbean and Canada in the Hood*, edited by A. Ruprecht and C. Taiana. Ottawa: Carleton University Press.

Goudge, P. 2003 *The Power of Whiteness: Racism in Third World Development and Aid*. London: Lawrence and Wishart.

Hatton, N., and D. Smith. 1995. "Reflection in Teacher Education: Towards Definition and Implementation." *Teaching and Teacher Education* 11, no.1: 33–49.

Henry, F. 1968. "The West Indian Domestic Scheme in Canada." *Social and Economic Studies* 17, no. 1: 83–91.

Hernandez-Ramdwar, C. 2016. *Introduction to the Caribbean: Diversity, Challenges, Resiliency*. Dubuque, IA: Kendall Hunt Publishing.

Jamaica Tourist Board. n.d. "Jamaica Tourist Board: Brief History." Accessed 28 April 2020. http://www.jtbonline.org/jtb/

Jorgenson, S., and L. Shultz. 2012. "Global Citizenship Education (GCE) in Post-Secondary Institutions: What Is Protected and What Is Hidden under the Umbrella of GCE?." *Journal of Global Citizenship & Equity Education* 2, no. 1: 1–22.

Kelleher, A., and L. Klein. 2006. *Global Perspectives: A Handbook for Understanding Global Issues*. 3rd ed. New York: Pearson.

Keshtiaray, N., M.H. Yarmohammadian, A. Yousefy, and S. Zahabioun. 2013. "Global Citizenship Education and its Implications for Curriculum Goals at the Age of Globalization." *Zahabioun* 6, no. 1: 20–45. https://doi.org/10.5539/ies.v6n1p195

Lawson, E. 2013. "The Gender Working Lives of Seven Jamaican Women in Canada: A Story about 'Here' and 'There' in a Transnational Economy." *Feminist Formations* 25, 1: 138–56. https://doi.org/10.1353/ff.2013.0002

Lewin, R. 2009. "The Quest for Global Citizenship through Study Abroad." In *The Handbook of Practice and Research in Study Abroad: Higher Education and the Quest for Global Citizenship*, edited by R. Lewin. New York: Routledge.

McKee, R.L. 2016. "International Service-Learning: Common Goals and Issues Among Programs Across Disciplines." *Journal of Service-Learning in Higher Education* 5, no. 1.

Momsen, J.D., and R.M. Torres. 2005. "Gringolandia: The Construction of a New Tourist Space in Mexico." *Annals of the Association of American Geographers* 95, no. 2: 314–35. https://doi.org/10.1111/j.1467-8306.2005.00462.x

Montero, G. 2011. "Multicultural Tourism, Demilitarization, and the Process of Peace Building in Panama." *The Journal of Latin American and Caribbean Anthropology* 19, no. 3: 418–40. https://doi.org/10.1111/jlca.12103

Nickols, S.Y., N.J. Rothenberg, L. Moshi, and M. Tetloff. 2013 "International Service-Learning: Students' Personal Challenges and Intercultural Competence." *Journal of Higher Education Outreach and Engagement* 17, no. 4: 97–124.

Oxfam Canada. n.d. "Qualities of the Global Citizen." Accessed 6 April 2011. http://www.edu.gov.mb.ca/k12/cur/socstud/foundation_gr9/blms/9-2-4d.pdf

Podur, J. 2012. *Haiti's New Dictatorship: The Coup, the Earthquake and the UN Occupation*. New York: Pluto Books.

Roswell, T., and B. Folkes. 2007. "Racializing Crime: Challenging Notions of A Black Canadian Identity." In *Multiple Lenses: Voice from the Diaspora*, edited by D. Divine. Newcastle, UK: Cambridge Scholars Publishing.

Said, E. 1985 "Orientalism Reconsidered." *Race & Class* 27, no. 2: 1–15. https://doi.org/10.1177/030639688502700201

– 1994. *Culture and Imperialism*. New York: Vintage Books.

Sardar, Z. 1999. "Development and the Locations of Eurocentrism." In *Critical Development Theory*, edited by R. Munch and D. O'Hearn. New York: Zed Books.

Sheller, M. 2003. *Consuming the Caribbean: From Arawaks to Zombies*. London: Routledge.

Unterhalter, E. 2009. "What Is Equity in Education? Reflections from the Capability Approach." *Studies in Philosophy and Education* 28: 415–24. https://doi.org/10.1007/s11217-009-9125-7

Van Eeden, J. 2004. "The Colonial Gaze: Imperialism, Myths, and South African Popular Culture." *Design Issues* 20, no. 2: 18–33. https://doi.org/10.1162/074793604871266

Zemach-Bersin, T. 2009. "Selling the World: Study Abroad Marketing and the Privatization of Global Citizenship." In *The Handbook of Practice and Research in Study Abroad: Higher Education and the Quest for Global Citizenship*, edited by R. Lewin. New York: Routledge.

8 Promoting Global Citizenship outside the Classroom: Undergraduate-Refugee Learning in Practice[1]

GISELLA GISOLO AND SARAH ELIZA STANLICK

As global service learning and nuanced approaches to global citizenship education continue to develop, we stand at a critical juncture in higher education to make learning experiences deep, critical, and ethical (Hartman et al. 2013; Hartman, Paris, and Blache-Cohen 2014). There are more opportunities than ever to engage in service learning in meaningful and uplifting ways for participants and stakeholders; however, these opportunities are dependent on collaborative decision-making processes between educators and community partners. This chapter is a case study of global service learning in a local US context, focused on community–university partnerships to support refugee settlement in Allentown, Pennsylvania. The purpose is to illustrate a high-quality global service-learning program that is still growing; additionally, this growth presents opportunities to refine for the future as well as to offer reflective lessons for other practitioners. What follows is a discussion and analysis of the design, implementation, and impact of a semester-long global service-learning project conducted in the fall/winter of 2010–11, through a partnership between the local refugee resettlement agency – the local chapter of Catholic Charities, a faith-based social services organization – and a private research university, Lehigh University, all located in Eastern Pennsylvania. Since 2016, Catholic Charities has been replaced by Bethany Christian Services, with which the university continues to partner. The project that is the basis of this chapter was part of "Introduction to Global Citizenship," a foundational writing-intensive course that constitutes a core requirement for first-year students pursuing the Global Citizenship certificate program at Lehigh University. The course instructors used feedback the course participants to develop best practices for service learning in order to inform future iterations of the service-learning component for students in subsequent cohorts, which continue to participate in service learning to this day. Upon completion of a literature review on global citizenship education (or GCE), and to help examine the effectiveness of course instruction and content, the following research questions were crafted:

1. How does service learning in a local context allow for students to practice and apply skills of global citizenship education?
2. Can service learning affect conceptual change in undergraduate first-year students in the way they see themselves as global citizens and in the way in which they perceive their civic self-efficacy?
3. How do undergraduate students exhibit change and growth through their reflective practice? And are such self-reported accounts accurate measures of such change?

The rationale for the study reported in this chapter is demonstrated through a brief survey of relevant literature related to service learning, the project's design and methodology, and the student development data elicited from the project.

Literature Review

Service learning is an activity within or outside of a course that educates students towards the goals to "(a) participate in mutually identified service activities that benefit the community, and (b) reflect on the service activity in such a way as to gain further understanding of course content, a broader appreciation of the discipline, and an enhanced sense of personal values and civic responsibility" (Bringle, Hatcher, and Clayton 2013, 105). Distinctions are made between service learning in different contexts, including international service learning, which involves crossing a geographic border, and global service learning, which has a global component but does not mandate leaving one's home country (Bringle, Hatcher, and Jones 2012; Hartman et al. 2013).[2] Service learning in an undergraduate context has been shown to be an effective tool for learners to gain curricular knowledge and develop character (Wade and Saxe 1996; Naidoo 2008; Jenkins and Sheehey 2019). Service learning can foster positive cognitive and emotional growth through experiential learning opportunities in a variety of settings and across developmental levels (Eyler 2000; Steinke and Buresh 2002). Learners grapple with issues of identity development, societal inequality, agency, and civic engagement that can then tie in with prior knowledge and personal experiences (Mitchell 2015; Hartman and Kiely 2014; Mbugua 2010).

Any high-quality learning experience is characterized by a reflection component that helps facilitate understanding (Wiggins and McTighe

2005). Service learning is no exception, and reflective practices are key to its success (Ash and Clayton 2009). Reflection as a tool promotes metacognition and emotional exploration as learners relate new knowledge and experiences to their own understandings and prior knowledge (King and Kitchener 2004; Blumenfeld 2010; Chick, Karis, and Kernahan 2009). Reflection has been shown throughout the literature to be the assessment of choice both for both measuring individual growth in service learning and for the success of the program (Blumenfeld 2010; Cord and Clements 2010; Novak, Markey, and Allen 2007). Through reflective processes from journaling to blogging to portfolio creation, learners can exhibit their understanding of global citizenship and changes in their conception of themselves as global citizens (Mautadin, Santally, and Boojhawon 2012). Such constructivist exercises have been shown to improve students' long-term retention of knowledge and experiences (Hmelo-Silver 2004; Levesque-Bristol and Stanek 2009).

Through reflection, students reveal how they understand the experiences and how they connect them to larger concepts learned in the curriculum. Sheckley and Keeton (1997) offer a framework to understand service learning and the ways in which students process those experiences. They theorize that learning happens in three ways for students: accordion, conduit, and cultural. Accordion learning experiences create cognitive dissonance and force the learner to grapple with knowledge that contradicts previously held beliefs. Conduit learning experiences give students information that works with prior schemas to make more concrete or to understand previously held concepts. Finally, cultural experiences offer new information that neither goes against or with prior knowledge but rather broadens one's worldview. This framework was chosen due to its ability to encompass the broad spectrum of experiences and information processed by the learner and as an adequate operational model of their understanding of that information, and other chapters in this volume also point to the importance of reflection in global service learning (see, for example, chapter 2 by Stanlick, and chapter 7 by Naidoo and Benjamin).

Program and Project Background

The Global Citizenship Program at Lehigh University is aimed at preparing students for civically engaged learning and living in a culturally diverse and rapidly globalizing world. The program emphasizes critical analysis, values reflection, and aims at structuring impactful educational experiences through which students can learn to negotiate cross-national and cross-cultural boundaries and develop a solid sense of personal and social responsibility to the global community. Envisioned as an interdisciplinary certificate program rather than a traditional major or minor, the program attracts students from all three of Lehigh University's undergraduate colleges (Arts and Sciences, Engineering, and Business and Economics), and offers an integration of curricular, co-curricular, service-learning, and study abroad experiences so as to address the personal and civic development of students. The program strives to achieve the following interrelated goals:

1. Structure learning opportunities for the students that can involve them not only intellectually (via more traditional, scholarship-based classroom learning), but also emotionally (via engaging forms of experiential learning and empathy-building experiences);
2. Provide students with knowledge and awareness of global inequalities, while also nourishing their ability to become agents of change and preparing them for transformational leadership in a global world;
3. Challenge the students to make meaningful connections between the local and the global, and to identify theoretically poignant analogies between their domestic environments and the foreign environments they are being exposed to through their two study-abroad experiences.

The service-learning experience presented in this chapter served particularly well in achieving these goals. From a program perspective it proved to be an effective tool through which to engage the hearts and minds of the student participants, as well as to address very tangible needs in the target refugee population.

As a prelude to this study, we experimented for several years with service-learning projects implemented in the local community. While the students admitted in the program are, for the most part, self-selected in that they show the highest degree of eagerness to travel abroad and explore unfamiliar cultures, they are sometimes less ready to observe and analyse the complexities and correlations that globalization brings about in their own local communities. As the researchers observed, the typical global citizenship student is often fascinated by far-away destinations and distant challenges, but less cognitively and emotionally equipped to reflect on how globalization has been changing our own familiar environments and local communities. For this reason, the Global Citizenship Program seeks to provide students with opportunities for civically engaged interactions with local neighbours that have a strong international and/or intercultural component.

The refugee service-learning project, which is the focus of this chapter, was designed to provide a meaningful civic experience for the students soon to head to Malaysia for their university-sponsored trip abroad. Through connection to local community leaders, an opportunity arose to partner with the local chapter of Catholic Charities that served a population of a few hundred refugees mostly coming from South-East Asia, Northern Africa, and the Middle East. Amongst them, the presence of a sub-group of Burmese refugees, who had spent some time as asylum seekers in a UN refugee camp near Kuala Lumpur while waiting for their final resettlement destination, offered the best service-learning community for our students. By reflecting upon these unexpected connections, and by drawing parallels between "here" and "there," the students had an opportunity to be exposed to the "human face" of globalization. This prompted a high degree of compassion amongst the students, while at the same time offering them a priceless learning opportunity to draw important global-to-local connections at the cognitive level as well.

Project Design

For this project, twenty-three first-year global citizenship students embarked on a semester-long service-learning project with twelve refugees. In order to design an experience that would be personally meaningful and academically solid, we had to make sure that the following design criteria were met: (1) identify and address specific needs for both the student and the refugee populations; (2) ground the experience in appropriate scholarly work; (3) provide the students with the tools to be able to become active co-planners of the experience, and not just passive executors; and (4) complement the experience with a variety of reflective assignments that would help the students tie the experience back to some scholarly discussion.

The first and second criteria were met by a careful preparatory stage that occupied the students for the first four weeks of the semester. At the beginning of the semester, the refugees were invited on campus to present their perspectives in the form of a panel. It was clear that the refugees were eager to share their stories and to overcome their shyness and linguistic barriers in order to show their appreciation to the country and the organization that had assisted them so heavily in their resettlement process. In order to prepare students for the exchange of personal feelings, as well as of life stories that would otherwise be hard to share, a preliminary class meeting with a refugee caseworker from Catholic Charities who was assisting the refugees on a daily basis laid the groundwork for an understanding of the complexity of the process that leads to final refugee resettlement. The high level of professional expertise and personal compassion displayed by the refugee caseworker provided the students with additional opportunities for reflection. As one student put it:

> After listening to the presentation on refugee resettlement and management I gained an overall view of how the process of resettling refugees works in the United States, the obstacles the refugees face when resettling in America, and what my fellow classmates and I should expect when we are working with the refugees. One fact I learnt that struck me the most was that about 15 million people on our planet are refugees, all trying to resettle to a safe place away from the terror, prosecution, oppression, danger, and fear that tore them away from their homes. This number is too big for me to even wrap my head around ... The presentation also gave me a better understanding of how much bureaucracy a refugee has to go through to obtain legal status as a refugee. People can be waiting for years to be relocated, sitting in camps or apartments waiting and waiting for an answer.

This is how one of the students reflected upon this panel presentation:

> I learned that being a refugee is much more mentally challenging than physically challenging. Also, I think refugees tend to value personal connection over physical aid, and I will make a conscious effort to provide a personal connection in my own interaction with the Lehigh Valley refugees. Moreover, yesterday's presentation reiterated the idea that a refugee basically must restart their life when they move to a new country. When one of the refugees said that she went from having everything to having nothing, I suddenly grasped the magnitude of the changes a refugee encounters.

Another student debriefed that first moving encounter thus:

> One of the refugee stories we heard was very moving and inspirational. This refugee was forced to spend two months in prison just because he questioned authority and asked about his rights. We live in the United States and we sometimes take for granted the rights we have, the rights that the government cannot take away. We have read about and idolized leaders such as Rosa Parks, Susan B. Anthony, and Nelson Mandela, who have taken their stand against injustices. The refugee who was imprisoned, to me, is a leader, similar to the leaders we read about in our history

textbooks; he spoke up for what was right, despite the significant dire consequences to himself and his family.

The information presented by the refugee caseworker was echoed in some of the scholarly readings assigned for the course. These included reports on refugee resettlement trends and demographics around the world and in the United States, as well as an article on the reactions spurred in the New Orleans populace, in the wake of Hurricane Katrina, by the improper use of the term "refugee" by the media to describe the victims of that catastrophe (Lim 2009; Somers et al. 2006). The class discussions that were elicited by comparing proper and inappropriate "labels," as well as stereotypes attached to such labels, were quite effective ways of bridging classroom learning and the real-life experiences that the students were beginning to be exposed to via the refugees' and caseworker's testimonials.

In line with the third criterion for a meaningful service-learning experience outlined above, we aimed at providing an opportunity for service that would develop the students' character and worldview, rather than a simple transfer of content and information. A series of preliminary meetings with the refugee caseworker had helped us narrow down some key areas to focus our efforts on, namely, English as a Second Language (ESL) instruction (with a special emphasis on workplace and medical terminology and etiquette) and computer literacy, introduction to US customs and culture, and arts and crafts sessions for the children of the refugees. Despite the availability of several ready-made instructional tools, we wanted to make sure that the students could contribute to designing their own instructional tools, tailoring them to the particular needs and characteristics of the population they were going to serve. For that reason, the students were provided a minimal framework, and some simple assignments aimed at helping them refine their own personal learning objectives and teaching strategies.

The first such assignment asked the students to reflect on how to "bring service and learning together." Table 8.1 presents co-generated learning objectives between students, instructors, and community partners.

Based on the identification of mutually relevant objectives, the first assignment then brought the students' planning one step forward by asking them what service-learning strategies would allow for both the educational needs of the Global Citizenship Program and the practical needs of the refugees to be fully met. Again, a sample of the students' own, self-generated responses is reported in table 8.2.

Table 8.1. Co-generated learning objectives

	Educational objectives for GC	Community agency needs/ objectives
Instructor objectives	Understand the importance of global change through local interaction.	Support refugees with basic orientation and "getting to know the Lehigh Valley" needs (ESL, computer literacy, arts and crafts).
	Reflect about what makes a person a legal citizen and/or an active citizen.	Model for the refugees the spirit of solidarity, servant leadership, and self-reliance that is touted as part of our American social fabric.
Student-generated objectives	Understand the relationship between helping/volunteering with refugees and becoming a better global citizen.	Meet refugees where they are in teaching or connecting to resources they ask to explore more or that are identified by the community partner.
	Learn to listen, practice cultural humility, and empower refugees' sense of place and belonging in the United States.	Expose the refugees (and especially their children) to positive, friendly, and welcoming neighbours to create a first contact community of positivity.
	Learn how life in the United States is different from life in the refugees' societies.	Provide resources and instructions for refugees to effectively communicate in a society that relies so heavily on technology.
	Reflect on how Americans treat people who do not "belong" and the social isolation of being a newcomer to the United States.	Educate and connect refugees to opportunities available for their education and personal enjoyment.
	Understand what kind of struggles refugees go through when transitioning from their homeland.	Celebrate and provide avenues for the refugees to incorporate aspects of their own culture in their new American experience.
	Understand cultural barriers and how to express and overcome them. Practice cultural humility.	Offer an open, safe space to encourage the refugees to share about their experiences and for our students to do the same.
	Understand the root causes of the problems the refugees face and what needs to change in order to address those causes.	Help the refugees become more competitive on the US job market.

Table 8.2. Student-generated service-learning strategies

Instructor prompt	Student-generated service-learning strategies
Given the objectives above, what would be the best service-learning strategy to meet those objectives?	GC students will create a supportive, empowering environment for the refugees to eagerly learn basic survival skills, and for them to be comfortable to share the real life political/social injustices and problems from their respective countries and in the United States.
	GC students will create a safe and supportive environment where they can listen to the refugees' questions, evaluate their previous knowledge about ESL and technology, and try to address their specific needs on a one-on-one basis.
	GC students will use their previous knowledge of learning a foreign language and talking to people whose first language is not English to better teach English and other skills to the refugees.
	GC students will use the information available to achieve clear goals with the help of carefully planned lesson plans.

A second assignment subsequently asked the students (who were by then divided into small teams of three to four students each) to reflect upon "best practices" to achieve the objectives identified through the first assignment. The students were presented with a list of resources (gathered from the internet upon doing research on a variety of programs – mostly offered by non-profit organizations – working with refugee resettlement issues) and were asked to compare and contrast resources and teaching techniques, and identify what tools could be best used given the specific logistical constraints and challenges (e.g., transportation issues, timing issues, conflicts with classes and after-class activities, uneven levels of English language proficiency).

A third preparatory assignment then asked the students' teams to further build on this knowledge by making specific, detail-oriented plans on how to structure the various sessions and by preparing engaging, self-contained, age-appropriate and impactful lesson plans. This last preparatory stage allowed for the students' teaching to be extremely effective and focused, and hence for the refugees to take best advantage of the face time. The student teams alternated for the rest of the semester offering computer literacy, ESL, and US culture classes and activities for children, offering a total of about thirty hours of service to the refugees, and using class time to debrief on each session with the rest of the class and the instructor and to reflect upon what they were teaching as much as what they were learning.

An important part of such learning was finding appropriate opportunities for the researchers to intersperse the students' activities with meta-level questions hinging on substantive ethical issues. Such issues include critical reflection on the ultimate goals of the service activities they were being involved in developing (e.g., "Are we attempting to help the refugees, or are we really helping ourselves understand refugee issues as they relate to our own personal aim of achieving a global citizenship education?"), or the potential hubris involved in the students' willingness to serve (e.g., "Are we attempting to change the world through our service, or are we just changing ourselves in the way we view refugee issues in the world?"). Questions were also raised by the researchers coordinating the activities concerning the limits of the students' involvement (e.g., "How do you think you should conduct yourselves if the refugees ask you to befriend them on Facebook and share personal moments in their lives with you?"), and the high sensitivity and vulnerability of the population the students were trying to serve (e.g., "If we elicit responses we were not expecting or that are not in line with our preconceived thoughts, or that we should not feel prepared to address, should we try to change those responses, or respect them for their diversity and complexity?"). The researchers were often positively impressed by the thoughtfulness of the students' responses to the above ethical meta-questions, especially considering the relatively young age of the group and the relatively short length of the project (some of these higher-level student reflections are deeply intertwined in the quotes reported in the findings section below). Likewise, it was important for the researchers to maintain a level of distance from the students while coordinating such a highly humanitarian project, in order to minimize bias in the assessment of each student's performance of the assigned tasks as part of their evaluation within the context of a credit-bearing academic experience.

In an effort to maintain the highest level of objectivity, as the students were eagerly working on the project throughout the semester, the authors made sure to assess the project's impact with the use of a mixed methodology. According to the fourth criterion for an impactful service-learning experience as outlined above, reflective assignments of various kinds accompanied the students through this journey. The next section describes in detail how the authors performed the study and the steps involved in our methodology.

Methodology and Data Analysis

As mentioned in the introductory statement, our purpose was to understand best practices for service learning, as well as the ability for reflective writing and practice to capture undergraduate global citizen identity development. The researchers used a qualitative research approach comprised of surveying, interviews, and document analysis to achieve their purpose. The methodology was informed by the work of Tashakkori and Teddlie (2010), who assert that deep qualitative research, with some quantitative insights, has developed in recent years into a scientifically sophisticated practice of gathering mixed-methods data. Utilizing this methodology, we aimed to understand the complex reality of identity development for these first-year students and their growth as global citizens through in-classroom curriculum and experiential service-learning opportunities.

As both the Oxfam (2006) and UNESCO (2014) curricula for global citizenship outline, students evolve in a number of domains: civic agency, orientation towards social justice, resiliency and flexibility, connected thinking, and empathy. Thus, we needed to choose appropriate tools to gather robust data and evaluate that development. In order to understand the ways in which students were developing their identities as global citizens, the assessments were designed to provide solid data. From a qualitative perspective, reflection was key both as processor of the experience and as the product of the students' learning. This reflection came in many formats: group reflection at the end of each session with the refugees, reflective writing assignments, and the student creation of an e-portfolio that displayed evidence of their global citizenship development. A survey was administered prior to the service-learning experience and again at the conclusion of the semester to capture perspectives on service and social justice, prior knowledge, and psychosocial factors.

Qualitative data analysis took place in phases and in capacities both individual and collaborative. First, we combed through the qualitative data individually to capture and understand patterns and thematic overtones. The second-level analysis then incorporated the framework of Sheckley and Keeton (1997) to assess the process of service learning by the students and their method of utilizing the knowledge that was presented to them in each session. Finally, the qualitative and quantitative data was triangulated to understand the connections between the students' perceptions of their own experience, the impact that interactions with the refugees had on them, and the way they responded to the challenges and successes of working in a community-based partnership towards a social justice aim. The next section presents in some detail our findings and the most meaningful highlights of learner experience and transformation.

Themes, Patterns, and Learning from the Data

Theme 1: Service Learning Supports Student Practice and Application Skills of Global Citizenship Education

Throughout the analysis of the documents and notes from sessions with the students, the theme of development of a global citizenship identity clearly emerged. Frequently, students said that they were unclear about what global citizenship technically was, or had a grasp of its theory but not of how it would be put into practice. As evidenced by their writings, the students grappled with the definition and worked out their own understanding of what it meant to be a global citizen. These characteristics included acting on a local level to affect change globally, respecting cultural differences, improving their cross-communication skills, and the importance of volunteerism. One student clearly articulated this through the metaphor of bread, likening her prior knowledge to raw dough that had been kneaded and crushed into a new framework. This is one example of a recurring theme through the work of students who had not previously seen the possibilities for local manifestations of global citizenship work. Student writings also indicate their acceptance of global citizenship as a process. In another student's words, "we came just that much closer to being global citizens."

Theme 2: Service Learning Can Affect Conceptual Change in Undergraduate First-Year Students to Identify as Global Citizens with Civic Self-Efficacy

We found that the depth of emotion and transformative experience through service learning was apparent. Empathy was a key indicator for this change in the students. While our sample of students was small, interesting patterns for growth emerged. Quantitatively, data was inconclusive for a pattern of change for our students in terms of empathy, as no trend or correlation appeared to explain the changes. This could be attributed to a number of reasons, ranging from quality of individual engagement with the experience to outside first-semester stressors that could have affected the students. However, key patterns that emerged in the reflective writing pointed to increased compassion and understanding for the refugees and their challenges in a new environment. Through reflective writing, participant observation, and conversations with other students, many students demonstrated that they could relate the refugees' experience to their own as first-year students in a new environment, trying to acclimate and understand a new culture. In the work of all of the students, words such as "moving," "inspirational," and "grateful" were used to explain their experience. More specifically, students articulated that "a true global citizenship should approach any service project focusing on commonalities rather than differences and without rigid expectations for their interaction with the people they will be working with."

Using constructivist models of education, students were involved in the planning and implementation of lesson plans for the refugees, as well as being self-reflective practitioners guiding their own education. Through student-generated program objectives and service-learning strategies, students were given the ability to play a vital role in the success of the project (see tables 8.1 and 8.2). Such responsibility was reflected in the quality of their created materials for the refugees as well as their reflective writings, which mentioned feeling the importance of their work for their own development as well as the benefit of the refugees. For instance, one student cited her work teaching ESL to the refugees, and theorized that such a small act could nevertheless encourage the perception of education as important for the refugees, thus impacting themselves and their children. The student's writing indicated pride and amazement at her own ability to make such an impact. It also gives the instructors insight into misconceptions that the students might hold (for instance, ethnocentric assumptions on quality education a student may hold that are harmful to the community partners). Such assumptions reinforce a colonial or saviour mentality that is not compatible with an ethical, empowered framework of global citizenship education.

Theme 3: Critical Reflection Provided Examples of Undergraduate Students' Change and Growth

Literature indicates that reflection is a necessary tool that promotes metacognition and processing of identity development. Using the framework of Sheckley and Keeton (1997), the reflective writings showed that students did process information in the forms of accordion (stretching held assumptions), conduit (reinforcing held assumptions), and cultural (introducing completely new information) learning. The majority of information processing came from the accordion effect, with students learning or transforming knowledge that was in opposition to previously held beliefs. Reflection allowed students to work through the complexities of global citizenship. As one student stated, global citizenship seemed a "broad, even confusing concept." Through service learning they found, rather, that it has a variable meaning but has concrete steps for application. This is a detail that would not have been captured in numbers, but was an obvious learning moment found in the qualitative work. As exhibited in the deep reflection conducted by students throughout the semester, reflection served as a tool for both processing and understanding conceptual change as it happened in the learners.

Data from student assignments supporting examples of accordion learning are most prevalent. Examples ranged from reconsidering one's own cultural traditions to a widened sense of the shared human experience. One student grappled with their pre-existing notion of citizenship and, through their experience with the refugees, reconsidered and widened their definition:

> The refugee project made me re-evaluate my stance on the concept of "citizenship." I am a born citizen of the United States, yet I don't fully understand the reasons behind American traditions. Although understanding American traditions is not a qualification of being an American citizen, shouldn't this be considered? Through the refugee project, [this course] has made me question why I qualify as a citizen in a social sense, rather than just in a legal sense.

Other students grappled with their own agency and the ability to be flexible and resilient in the face of challenges. One student reflected: "Throughout both projects, I needed to keep a positive mindset even when projects did not go well, think on my feet, and work with my peers to make a positive impact. My experience showed me that global citizenship does begin in one's own community."

The many different insights that the students shared with the instructors through their reflections indicated that they were in a process of expanding their global citizen identity through a variety of experiential and curricular insights. Through the act of applying global citizenship education in a service-learning context, they had the opportunity (as is explicated in their writing) to deepen their education in ways that would have been less likely in a classroom-only setting.

Implications for Educators and Administrators

The positive outcomes for student learning as well as the perceived benefit to the community partner leads to the conclusion that there is value in the addition of service learning to global citizenship curricula.

Community-based service learning indeed proved to be an effective educational tool through which to engage the hearts and minds of the student participants, as well as to address tangible needs in the target population. Our data analysis and evaluation showed that, by the end of the service-learning project they had embarked on, the students achieved a higher level of appreciation of the impact of local civic engagement to address issues that have a global reach. Student participants showed not only a higher degree of understanding of the global power dynamics pushing individuals to claim asylum-seeking status, but also a higher level of empathy for the struggles and tribulations of those who traumatically lost their citizenship status in their home country. Thus, as was the intent of the service-learning experience, they displayed a higher level of global citizenship learning and a heightened sense of personal and civic empowerment.

Future iterations of this program will continue to engage the students through an empowerment model allowing for student-generated lesson plans, assessment, and implementation. This methodology allowed for student growth, exploration of their connection with the community, and building self-efficacy, which was considered essential for their development as global citizens (albeit in early stages for many). With that in consideration, the team will also continue working closely with our community partner. The program has maintained the relationship with the local refugee service organization, and has continued to coordinate programing for our students and the community. We would look to expand our assessment beyond the students and engage refugees as well, to see what programing particularly helps their transition and what learning occurs through these sessions. This can allow for a meaningful experience for both the students *and* the refugees. This collaboration gave both the facilitators and the students the ability to be more connected with the community and their work's impact.

Finally, the use of both qualitative and quantitative approaches to evaluate service learning in the global citizenship context is a useful framework for future studies. Through the triangulation of data sources, it was apparent that the students grew and processed information about the experience meaningfully through the constructivist tasks of reflection, teaching, writing, and portfolio creation. If we had used only qualitative or only quantitative assessments, we could have missed out on the larger picture of the transformative experiences the students had. Our approach gave us ample data with which to work and to understand how to design future assessments and iterations for maximum student and refugee growth.

Lessons for Educators Developing GC Curricula

As educators, the experience yielded many lessons for planning a successful service-learning project in the area of global citizenship. The points below elaborate on those lessons and give guidance to educators who want to implement a similar experiential learning endeavour.

Lesson 1: Strive to Create a High-Quality Service-Learning Experience (HQSLE)

When designing the experience for our global citizenship learners, the markers of a high quality service-learning experience (HQSLE) were at the forefront of our minds. HQSLEs have the following characteristics: integrated learning, community service, collaborative development and management, civic engagement, contemplation, and evaluation and disclosure (Smith et al. 2011). Some of the following lessons will be breakouts of the larger framework of a HQSLE, but it is important to note as an instructor that this framework will help maximize student learning and students' ability to make meaning of the experience. Service learning must be an integrated, well-planned endeavour that speaks to multiple student learning styles and connects with the community more deeply and meaningfully. By following the hallmarks of an HQSLE, educators can better ensure a transformative, meaningful process by which the students grow, coupled with an ethical empowerment model with community partners.

Lesson 2: Connect Meaningfully and Systematically with the Content of the Curriculum

Beyond the quality of the experience itself, it is critical for service learning to have a strong connection to readings, curricula, and assignments. As an instructor, the goal is to both develop the students' social and emotional capacity to view critically their role in the world, and to increase their understanding of the historical, economic, and societal events that shape the current global landscape. In order to create that awareness, integrated learning that connects the experiential with content is necessary. Thus, the instructor should plan scaffolded exercises for the semester in which the service learning will take place to prepare and guide the students' learning process. The following framework for academic assignments was adopted for this service-learning experience:

- Readings assigned to the students in preparation for the interaction with the refugees;

- Step-by-step assignments through which students were encouraged to prepare lesson plans and teaching tools that would guarantee a high-impact interaction with the refugees and the most effective use of everyone's time;
- A series of presentations, lectures, and excursions that encouraged meaningful, reciprocal interaction with first-hand accounts from our community partners. We were intentional and planned such events in partnership, where those sharing their stories were already comfortable and enjoyed relaying history to the students. Two other particularly strong programs were a presentation by our main contact, a Catholic Charities caseworker who shared the daily challenges faced by both the refugees and the resettling organization, and a lecture by a senior officer of the UN High Commissioner for Refugees, which followed the completion of the project;
- Reflective essays and in-class discussions, whereby students had the opportunity, individually or as a team, to draw lessons from the experience and to elaborate the at times emotionally charged encounters and events.

The purpose of this approach is twofold: (1) bridging the theoretical with the experiential, and (2) bridging the local with the global. As the semester-long project unfolded, it became apparent from the reflective assignments and in-class discussions, as well as from informal conversations, that the students were starting to attach real names and faces to abstract or complex concepts such as global citizenship, human rights, the value of democracy and freedom, and so on. Students were able to grasp how borders are becoming more and more fluid in today's rapidly changing world, and how global citizenship can present itself right in one's own background in the humbling semblance of the refugees. The interaction with the everyday challenges faced by the refugees allowed our students to cultivate an inner desire to become their public voices within the campus and local community, as well as to advocate for the respect of their rights as citizens as well as, ultimately, as human beings.

Lesson 3: Integrate Critical Reflection for Students to Process Experiences

The role of reflection is critical to the development of learner behaviours and attitudes, students' ability to process the experience, and the ability to make meaning out of prior experiences as connected to the current context. For experiential learning in any format – internships, project-based learning, or service learning – the ability to process one's own experience and tie it to prior knowledge is essential for lasting knowledge creation. Further, critical reflection, as evidenced in both formative and summative formats before, during, and after the experience, can help to uncover opportunities to correct false assumptions, challenge pre-existing notions, and introduce materials that can confront historical inaccuracies that are rooted in students' misconceptions.

For the instructor, reflection serves as a measure of individual learner change and allows for qualitative assessment of the success of the program overall. Frequent reflection allows for mediation between the experiential and academic-content aspects of service learning. If students are reflecting frequently, they are relating to the instructor/facilitator's concerns, issues, or misunderstandings that can be remedied early for longer-term learning and higher student satisfaction. It also allows the instructor to change course or to emphasize certain lessons that might help make the experience more worthwhile. In addition, it allows for the educator or peers to provide critical pushback on assumptions, unconscious bias, and power/privilege.

Instructors can create reflective assignments in many formats, including peer de-briefs and discussions, online discussion forums, individual formal writing assignments, persuasive speeches, writing of op-ed pieces, and other constructivist writing tasks that ask students to reflect on their experience and create. In this instance, students had the opportunity to reflect through discussion at the end of each session and through written assignments completed for credit.

Lesson 4: Work Closely and Respectfully with Community Partners

The importance of working with an empowered, stable community partner cannot be overstated. From a logistical standpoint, a competent and engaged community partner can help manage the administration of the project, connect to a community in need, provide space or a meeting place for that community, and negotiate resources – both social and tangible – to make the project a success. Oftentimes, an asymmetry of resources exists, with one partner bringing more tangible resources to the table than the other. Recognizing this is essential, as you can discuss the fair balance of expectations and encourage collaboration to make the most of scarce resources.

In an academic sense, the importance of working with a community partner hinges on the development of shared goals and vision for how the program will be carried out. Those facilitating the experience – both the professor/teacher and community representative – must be invested in its success for community members and the students.

For the professor/teacher, they must commit to the goal of delivering appropriate service to the community and not infringing upon the good works that are already being done in the community. The community organizer needs to pledge to help the students to learn and grow, while recognizing the students' emotional and social maturity and capacity to make mistakes while learning.

The purpose of the service-learning program in this capacity is to provide a meaningful experiential component that will develop the characteristics of a cognizant global citizen. To that end, the service provided needs to be critically viewed by our students, constantly assessing if the program is of benefit to the community, and responding to their needs as opposed to dictating from the outside. It mirrors behaviour for the students in connecting with other communities and creates understanding and respect between participants. Thus, sustainability can be achieved when the two partners work together to communicate expectations and satisfaction with the experience. Sustainability is both the ability for students to have an ongoing learning experience and the community getting continual service and care beyond that one round of student learning. By continually assessing and discussing milestones and the positive/negative experiences created through service learning, there is an open dialogue for improving the program and recruiting future participants on both sides. Facilitators can build a lasting relationship that will allow expansion or innovation of service learning in future iterations.

Conclusion

The refugee service-learning component of the Global Citizenship Program's first-year experience has proven to be both a successful learning experience for the students and a valuable contribution to the community. For the purposes of this study, the focus was on individual change in the students and their ability to operationalize global citizenship. Service learning does have the potential to affect students' concepts of themselves as global citizens, as students practice theoretical concepts learned in the classroom. A deep, multifaceted qualitative design allowed for a look at the service-learning process that was holistic and grounded, and captured well a burgeoning understanding of oneself as a global citizen.

For the educator, service learning in a global citizenship capacity is a natural fit that provides a transformative, experiential learning environment for student growth. Students have the capacity to practice content knowledge and theoretical concepts hands-on, while reflecting on their own growth throughout the experience. It is with this in mind that educators must seriously consider adding a service-learning component to their curriculum. Likewise, institutions of higher education should include this type of academic coursework in their curriculum, if they seek to provide experiential opportunities to develop and test students' notions of global citizenship as it is applied in the local community. Few activities offer such opportunity to connect with international content knowledge and concepts while promoting the emotional-social growth necessary to develop global citizens.

NOTES

1 This chapter is a revised version of an article that appeared under the title "Promoting Global Citizenship outside the Classroom: Undergraduate-Refugee Learning in Practice," *Journal of Global Citizenship & Equity Education* 2, no. 2 (2012): 98–122.

2 It is important to note that there is ambiguity in the way that concepts are used in literature. The literature identifies Global SL as service learning that has a component of "the global" but can happen in your backyard (e.g., service learning with cultural centres or on refugee/migration issues), but international service learning implies that you have to cross borders. Some literature uses "global learning" to refer to both local service learning and international service learning.

REFERENCES

Ash, S.L., and P.H. Clayton. 2009. "Generating, Deepening, and Documenting Learning: The Power of Critical Reflection in Applied Learning." *Journal of Applied Learning in Higher Education* 1 (2009): 25–48.

Battistoni, R.M., N.V. Longo, and S.R. Jayanandhan. 2009. "Acting Locally in a Flat World: Global Citizenship and the Democratic Practice of Service-Learning." *Journal of Higher Education Outreach and Engagement* 13, no. 2: 89–108.

Blumenfeld, E.R. 2010. "Reflections on Student Journals and Teaching about Inequality." *Journal of Poetry Therapy* 23, no. 2: 101–6. https://doi.org/10.1080/08893675.2010.482812

Bringle, R.G., J.A. Hatcher, and P.H. Clayton, eds. 2013. *Research on Service-Learning: Conceptual Frameworks and Assessments*. Sterling, VA: Stylus Publishing.

Bringle, R.G., J.A. Hatcher, and S.G. Jones, eds. 2012. *International Service Learning: Conceptual Frameworks and Research*. Sterling, VA: Stylus Publishing.

Chick, N.L., T. Karis, and C.L. Kernahan. 2009. "Learning from Their Own Learning: How Metacognitive and Meta-Affective Reflections Enhance Learning in Race-Related Courses." *International Journal for the Scholarship of Teaching and Learning* 3, no. 1: 16. https://doi.org/10.20429/ijsotl.2009.030116

Cord, B., and M. Clements. 2010. "Reward through Collective Reflection: An Autoethnography." *E-journal of Business Education and Scholarship of Teaching* 4, no. 1: 11–18.

Eyler, J.S. 2000. "What Do We Most Need To Know about the Impact of Service-Learning on Student Learning?" *Michigan Journal of Community Service Learning*, Special Issue no. 1: 11–17.

Hartman, E., and R. Kiely. 2014. "Pushing Boundaries: Introduction to the Global Service-Learning Special Section." *Michigan Journal of Community Service Learning* 21, no. 1: 55–63.

Hartman, E., R. Kiely, J. Friedrichs, and J. Boettcher. 2013. *Building a Better World: The Pedagogy and Practice of Ethical Global Service-Learning*. Sterling, VA: Stylus Publishing.

Hartman, E., C.M. Paris, and B. Blache-Cohen. 2014. "Fair Trade Learning: Ethical Standards for Community-Engaged International Volunteer Tourism." *Tourism and Hospitality Research* 14, nos. 1–2: 108–16.

Hmelo-Silver, C.E. 2004. "Problem-Based Learning: What and How Do Students Learn?" *Educational Psychology Review* 16, no. 3: 235–66. https://doi.org/10.1023/b:edpr.0000034022.16470.f3

Jenkins, A., and P. Sheehey. 2019. "A Checklist for Implementing Service-Learning in Higher Education." *Journal of Community Engagement and Scholarship* 4, no. 2: 6.

King, P.M., and K.S. Kitchener. 2004. "Reflective Judgment: Theory and Research on the Development of Epistemic Assumptions through Adulthood." *Educational Psychologist* 39, no. 1: 5–18. https://doi.org/10.1207/s15326985ep3901_2

Levesque-Bristol, C., and L.R. Stanek. 2009. "Examining Self-Determination in a Service Learning Course." *Teaching of Psychology* 36, no. 4: 262–6. https://doi.org/10.1080/00986280903175707

Lim, S-L. 2009. "'Loss of Connections Is Death': Transnational Family Ties Among Sudanese Refugee Families Resettling in the United States." *Journal of Cross-Cultural Psychology* 40, no. 6: 1028–40. https://doi.org/10.1177/0022022109346955

Mautadin, G., M.I. Santally, and R. Boojhawon. 2012. "Conceptual Proposal: Integrating E-Portfolios in Innovative Pedagogical Scenarios for Enhancement of Students' Online Learning Experiences. Learning Design Specification for an Innovative E-Portfolio Module for the University of Mauritius." *International Journal of Learning* 18, no. 5: 7–22. https://doi.org/10.18848/1447-9494/cgp/v18i05/47521

Mbugua, T. 2010. "Fostering Culturally Relevant/Responsive Pedagogy and Global Awareness through the Integration of International Service-Learning in Courses." *Journal of Pedagogy/Pedagogický Casopis* 1, no. 2: 87–98. https://doi.org/10.2478/v10159-010-0011-8

Mitchell, T.D. 2015. "Using a Critical Service-Learning Approach to Facilitate Civic Identity Development." *Theory Into Practice* 54, no. 1: 20–8.

Naidoo, L. 2008. "Crossing Borders: Academic Service Learning as a Pedagogy for Transnational Learning." *International Journal of Learning* 15, no. 3: 139–46. https://doi.org/10.18848/1447-9494/cgp/v15i03/45676

Novak, J.M., V. Markey, and M. Allen. 2007. "Evaluating Cognitive Outcomes of Service Learning in Higher Education: A Meta-Analysis." *Communication Research Reports* 24, no. 2: 149–57. https://doi.org/10.1080/08824090701304881

Oxfam Development Education Programme. 2006. *Education for Global Citizenship: A Guide for Schools*. London: Oxfam GB.

Sheckley, B.G., and M.T. Keeton. 1997. "Service Learning: A Theoretical Model." In *Service Learning: Ninety-Sixth Yearbook of the National Society for the Study of Education*, edited by J. Schine. Chicago: University of Chicago Press.

Smith, B.H., J. Gahagan, S. McQuillin, B. Haywood, C.P. Cole, C. Bolton, and M.K. Wampler. 2011. "The Development of a Service-Learning Program for First-Year Students Based on the Hallmarks of High Quality Service-Learning and Rigorous Program Evaluation." *Innovative Higher Education* 36, no. 5: 317–29. https://doi.org/10.1007/s10755-011-9177-9

Sommers, S.R., E.P. Apfelbaum, K.N. Dukes, N. Toosi, and E.J. Wang. 2006. "Race and Media Coverage of Hurricane Katrina: Analysis, Implications, and Future Research Questions." *Analyses of Social Issues and Public Policy* 6, no. 1: 39–55. https://doi.org/10.1111/j.1530-2415.2006.00103.x

Steinke, P., and S. Buresh. 2002. "Cognitive Outcomes of Service-Learning: Reviewing the Past and Glimpsing the Future." *Michigan Journal of Community Service Learning* 8, no. 2: 5.

Tashakkori, A., and C. Teddlie, eds. 2010. *Sage Handbook of Mixed Methods in Social and Behavioral Research*. Thousand Oaks, CA: Sage.

United Nations Educational, Scientific, and Cultural Organization (UNESCO). 2014. *Global Citizenship Education: Preparing Learners for the Challenges of the Twenty-First Century*. Paris: UNESCO.

Wade, R.C., and D.W. Saxe. 1996. "Community Service-Learning in the Social Studies: Historical Roots, Empirical Evidence, Critical Issues." *Theory & Research in Social Education* 24, no. 4: 331–59. https://doi.org/10.1080/00933104.1996.10505783

Wiggins, G.P., and J. McTighe. 2005, *Understanding by Design*. Alexandria, VA: Association for Supervision and Curriculum Development.

9 Social Justice and Global Citizenship Education in Social Work Context: A Case of *Caveat Emptor*

PAUL BANAHENE ADJEI

Caveat emptor is Latin for "Let the buyer beware," implying that buyers assume the risk in transactions. In this case, should buyers later discover defects in the goods bought, they cannot reclaim damages from the seller. Therefore, it devolves upon buyers to ensure that goods bought are in perfect condition before completing transactions.

I employ the phrase "caveat emptor" as a general caution to social work educators that the task of preparing social work students as global citizens in contemporary social work education comes with certain challenges. These challenges are in many ways fueled by the shifting political, economic, and social conditions in today's world, as well as the historical tensions between caseworkers and social reformers that started in the early days of the social work profession and have solidified over the last two centuries (Fehr 2013, 24). Thus, social work educators who teach social justice education should be prepared for a messy, challenging, and discomforting learning environment. The core ideas in this chapter are drawn from two sources: (1) scholarly publications on the teaching of social justice in educational context, and (2) the author's personal experiences teaching social justice at the Bachelor of Social Work (BSW) and Master of Social Work (MSW) levels in a social work program where the majority of the students appear to be White. I use the socially constructed term "White" to mean individuals who link their ethnic ancestry to Europe. This chapter is driven by the questions: What kind of discursive practices do social work educators need to offer as counter-reading to the liberal notion of social justice that re-inscribes dominant ideologies while claiming to support social transformation? What pedagogical strategies do social work educators need in order to address what Gayatri Spivak calls "sanctioned ignorance" – meaning the way in which *"know-nothingism"* (Spivak 1999, x) about social justice and global citizenship education is justified and even rewarded in social work context? In what ways do social work educators situate their teaching philosophy and classroom deliveries beyond self-interest and an empty sense of obligation as they prepare students to become global citizens? What are the negative undercurrents – tensions, contestations, fear, shame, and anxiety – that come with teaching social justice and global citizenship education in social work classrooms? The rest of the chapter is devoted to engaging these questions.

Social Justice and Global Citizenship Education in Social Work Context

Social justice and respect for human rights at the local, national, and international levels is one of the important six core values of the social work profession. In fact, the Code of Ethics of the Canadian Association of Social Workers (CASWE 2005) states that social workers

> believe in the obligation of people, individually and collectively, to provide resources, services and opportunities for the overall benefit of humanity and to afford them protection from harm. Social workers promote social fairness and the equitable distribution of resources, and act to reduce barriers and expand choice for all persons, with special regard for those who are marginalized, disadvantaged, vulnerable, and/or have exceptional needs. Social workers oppose prejudice and discrimination against any person or group of persons, on any grounds, and specifically challenge views and actions that stereotype particular persons or groups. (5)

The Code of Ethics expects social work practitioners to "advocate for equal treatment and protection under the law and challenge injustices, especially injustices that affect the vulnerable and disadvantaged" at both local and global level.

Although the Code of Ethics identifies the pursuit of social justice as a core value to the social work profession, its view of social justice is limited because the focus has been about distributing or redistributing society's resources, and in the process has ignored systemic and structural inequities that sustain unequal distribution of resources in the first place (Mullaly 2007). Further, the Code of Ethics does not provide adequate and clear understanding of what constitutes "social justice" (Banerjee 2011; Galambos 2008; Hollingsworth 2003; Larkin 2004; Reisch 2002). Not surprisingly, there appears to be disagreement about the most effective approach to pursuing social justice in social work (Adjei 2013; Hardina 2000, 2004). For social work educators, this definitional ambiguity of social justice presents a challenging task for preparing social work students adequately for practice at the local and global levels (McLaughlin 2006; Reisch 2002). Therefore, definitional clarity is needed if social work educators are to integrate social justice education in the social work curricula. The remaining part of this section critically examines some definitions of social justice in context of social work education.

Scanlon (1988) contends that social justice is often used to satisfy the utilitarian principle, which states that what constitutes "good" must be separated from what constitutes "right." Whatever is considered good for the greater number of people is good, even if it is not right (Von Mises 1953; Friedman 1973; Hayek 1976). The utilitarian's subscription of social justice implies that institutional arrangements must always favour the greater number of people, even if it means some people (the minority) will be neglected and suffer in the process (Adjei 2013). The limitation of this approach, as Solas (2008) has pointed out, is that "it does not matter, except indirectly, how the sum of satisfactions (i.e., the greatest good or happiness) is distributed among individuals over time. The aim is simply to maximize the allocation of the means of satisfaction, that is, rights and duties, opportunities and privileges, and various forms of wealth. However, when the principle of utility is satisfied there is no assurance that everyone benefits" (815).

I wrote in Adjei (2013) that in the environment of utilitarianism, equity and fairness are illusive (81). The utilitarian's approach to the pursuit of social justice is disturbing and can render social workers' commitment to a fair and just society passé. According to Nussbaum (2006), "utilitarianism's commitment to aggregation creates problems for thinking well about marginalized or deprived people, for whom some of the opportunities that utilitarianism puts at risk may have an especially urgent importance" (73). In his decision on *Eaton v. Brant County Board of Education,* the Supreme Court judge, Justice John Sopinka writes: "The blind person cannot see and the person in a wheelchair needs a ramp. It is the failure to make reasonable accommodation, to fine tune society so that its structures and assumptions do not result in the relegation and banishment of disabled (people) from participation, which results in discrimination against them" (*Eaton v. Brant County Board of Education* 1997, 3). Justice Sopinka's ruling reminds us that in the absence of the needed resources that allow marginalized groups to function to their fullest potential, social inequality is created.

Robert Barker (1999) defines social justice as "an ideal condition in which all members of a given society have the same basic rights, protections, opportunities, obligations and social benefits" (451). Although Barker's definition improves on the utilitarian's approach to social justice, it still has loopholes because it focuses more on "equality of treatments" than "equality of outcomes" (Adjei 2013). An equality-based social justice approach assumes that the whole society and its institutions function in neutral, fair, and objective ways. Therefore, everyone is equally positioned to succeed. The assumption of the fairness and neutrality of society ignores the reality that social arrangements benefit some people more than others and do not include everybody equally. Thus, to lump all people together to compete for the same resources ignores the glaring fact that the playing field is not level for everybody. The late US President Lyndon Johnson (1965), in his 4 June 1965 speech at Howard University, raises moral and ethical questions about equality-based approach to social justice: "You do not take a person who, for years, has been hobbled by chains and liberate him [or her], bring him [or her] up to the starting line of a race and then say, 'You are free to compete with all the others,' and still justly believe that you have been completely fair. Thus it is not enough just to open the gates of opportunity. All our citizens must have the ability to walk through those gates."

The principle of fairness, at least as stipulated in President Johnson's speech, requires that the playing field be levelled first before one can talk about competition. In the environment of equal treatments, it is almost impossible to attain social justice for the marginalized and the disadvantaged. The pursuit of social justice in social work contexts must speak to differences in a politicized way to open discussions about unfair and unjust distribution of power and resources in society.

John Rawls (1971), in one of the problematic seminal works in the field of social work, uses the phrase "undeserved inequalities"[1] in his conception of social justice to refer to individuals and groups who have been disadvantaged by social conditions such as poverty, racism, sexism, ableism, citizenship, Islamophobia, and homophobia. The disadvantage occurs through systemic arrangements that reward and punish people based on skin colour, sexuality, ability, social status, gender location, religion, and nationality. Rawls, therefore, calls for a redistributive model of social justice where basic goods and services are made available to those citizens who are in need of them. In Rawls's model of social justice, additional attention and resources are given to people who are victims of inequities. In this model of social justice, giving more resources to the underprivileged is a moral obligation (see Van Soest 1995, 1811). Not surprisingly, Rawls's conception of social justice is heavily celebrated in the social work profession. In the article "Am I My Brother's Keeper?" Zygmunt Bauman (2000, 9), who appears to have drawn from Rawls's redistributive model of social justice, argues, "One can measure the carrying capacity of a bridge by the strength of its weakest pillars. The human quality of a society ought to be measured by the quality of life of its weakest members. And since the essence of all morality is the responsibility which people take for humanity of the others, this is also the measure of a society's ethical standard."

However, not all social work educators agree with Rawls's egalitarian approach to social justice. Iris Marion Young (1990), the feminist educator, has pointed out that Rawls's egalitarian-liberal approach to social justice "tends to ignore the social structure and institutional context" (5). Issahaku (2018) also notes that Rawls's model of social justice does not create transformative action; additionally, it reduces equitable distribution to matters of individual opinions. Rawls's model of social justice therefore maintains the status quo and leaves the marginalized, the disadvantaged, and the most vulnerable unaffected by structural changes. Young (1990) therefore recommends that Rawls's egalitarian-liberal approach to social justice must combine with effort to equally recognize and challenge cultural imperialism.

In this chapter, I adopt the definition of social justice from the works of Fraser (2005, 2008), who identifies it as something predicated on the dismantling of institutions and structures of domination that disadvantage certain people from exercising their full rights as members of a society. Accordingly, Fraser (2005) argues that "the most general meaning of justice is parity of participation. According to this radical-democratic interpretation of the principle of equal moral worth, justice requires social arrangements that permit all to participate as peers in social life. Overcoming injustice means dismantling institutionalized obstacles that prevent some people from participating on a par with others, as full partners in social interaction" (73). Three key concepts are consistent with how Fraser talks about social justice: distribution, recognition, and representation. Fraser (2005) notes that people's full participation as members of a given society can be impeded if they are denied the resources needed to interact and relate to others as peers. Such impediments create distributive injustice or maldistribution which further prevent people "from interacting on terms of parity by institutionalized hierarchies of cultural value that deny them the requisite standing; in that case they suffer from status inequality or misrecognition" (74). Representation, according to Fraser, concerns the political dimension of justice, where inclusionary and exclusionary practices deny others the rights and space to make justice claims on matters relevant to their well-being.

From Fraser's definition, social justice is about ensuring a fair and equitable application of administrative policies, laws, and procedures to impact positively on all service participants in the field of social work. In this sense, social justice is about paying attention to how social policies and administrative practices can affect racialized, classed, gendered, sexualized, disabled, and Aboriginal people differently, and the need for advocacy to be done on their behalf. An administration of social policies and laws within the lens of social justice calls for different empathetic relations and understanding of service users' needs and issues.

It is therefore imperative that social justice education (SJE) prepares Social Work practitioners to be aware of how institutional and systemic arrangements affect people negatively. Such education must challenge learners' hegemonic assumptions and judgments about socially disadvantaged people. Chapter 5 by Mikhaela Gray-Beerman in this volume describes such education as global citizenship education (GCE), which is understood to be an approach to developing learners' awareness of universal human rights and freedoms as well as to empowering learners for informed, active, productive and responsible decisions and actions that can help solve the world's difficult problems. GCE, according to the Maastricht Global Education Declaration (Europe-Wide Global Education Congress 2002), "is education that opens people's eyes and minds to the realities of the world, and awakens them to bring about a world of greater justice, equity and human rights for all" (2). Drawing further on the importance of GCE in gender-sensitivity learning, Gray-Beerman suggests that such "education provides a pathway for reconstructing societal views that degrade, disrespect, and exclude women." Global citizenship education helps students realize that "no local loyalty can ever justify forgetting that each human being has responsibilities to every other" (Appiah 2006, xvi).

Myers (2006) suggests "three curricular topics that need to be considered for a global-oriented citizenship education: (1) international human rights as the foundation of global citizenship, (2) the reconciliation of the universal and the local, and (3) political action beyond the nation state" (10). Such education, like social justice education, must help learners reimagine and support a just and civil society. GCE and SJE, no matter how they are defined, cannot be left only in the hands of not-for-profit organizations or civil society groups. Social work education can play a vital role in helping to create and strengthen learners' capacities and capabilities to defend human rights. The follow-up discussion focuses on the challenges of SJE and GCE in current social work education.

Social Justice Education and Global Citizenship Education at the Crossroads in Social Work

Social work since its inception has had two fundamental ideological stances that have informed and shaped the place of social justice and human rights in the profession. The first ideological stance is rooted in a perspective of moral certainty, which suggests that individuals' problems are the result of their failed personal responsibility. Those who embraced the ideas of liberalism with emphasis on individual responsibilities and actions aligned with the work of Mary Richmond and her Charity Organization Society (COS). The COS firmly believes that poverty can be cured in society not by distributing relief but by the personal rehabilitation of the poor (Franklin 1986). In her paper "The Settlement and Friendly Visiting," Richmond wrote: "If I could choose a friend for a family fallen into misfortune and asking for relief … I would rather choose for them one who had this practical resourcefulness than one who had a perfect equipment of advanced social theories . . . The former would find the most natural and effective way out … the other would say that the whole social order was wrong and must pay a ransom for its wrongness by generous material help to its victim" (Colcord and Mann 1930, 122).

The second approach is rooted on pragmatism, which suggests that social problems exist not because people are morally reprehensible but because the macro-systems treat people differently, and in so doing put some people at an advantage and others at a disadvantage. Those who embrace a pragmatic approach to social work align with the works of Jane Addams and the Settlement House Movement (SHM; see Franklin 1986, 507). Addams's SHM engaged in activities that aimed to improve society while challenging institutional policies and practices that affected people negatively.

In many ways, the operations of Mary Richmond's COS and Jane Addams's SHM provided conceptual frameworks that directed social justice education within social work education (Franklin 1986). According to Lundblad (1995), the desire to pursue social justice among other things inspired Jane Addams to seek social work education that helps practitioners develop meaningful interpersonal relationships and a sense of humanity, instead of an education system that produces elitist practitioners. Jane Addams's approach to social issues served as the foundation that revived social justice education in social work (Lundy 2004; Hick 2006).

In Canada, the economic crises of the 1980s presented a new change to social workers who aspire to Jane Addams's social justice–oriented approach to practice. In the 1980s, Canada changed from a country exporting primary products to one exporting manufactured goods. At this same time, Canada mechanized its manufacturing industry, leaving fewer people in employment. These two changes led to mass unemployment, high interest rates, inflation and high government spending, and indebtedness. In response to the economic crises, the Canadian government introduced pro-market programs that included privatizing social service programs and reducing funds going into social welfare programs (Fehr 2013). The ascendancy of corporate culture into social service delivery, also known as neo-liberalism, led to a social system that provides inadequate safety nets for the poor and most marginalized members of society, in spite of constitutional guarantees. With emphasis more on protecting dollars than on serving the interest of diverse and marginalized communities, access to state resources in times of need became an unconscionable luxury available to the very select few (Giroux 2011). In this corporate culture of social service delivery, social workers were asked to make a choice between ensuring efficient utilization of limited resources on the one hand, and protecting and upholding the value of human life on the other. With job insecurity, the choice for the latter – protecting and upholding the value of human life – became an afterthought for many social workers (Issahaku 2018; Margolin 1997; Olson 2007; Slavin 2002).

Within social work education, there are fading academic supports and growing intolerance for social justice and human rights pedagogies in social work programs. Some social work educators who aligned themselves with dominant conservative ideology engaged in academic programing and curricula content management that undercut social justice and global citizenship education (Fehr 2013; Hair 2015; Issahaku 2018; Reisch 2002). Issahaku (2018), for example, notes that the meritocratic criteria and requirements in admission and enrollment procedures, as well as hiring decisions in many social work schools in Canada, are unjustly situated and disadvantage racialized and Aboriginal people, as well as non-European international students. Even where social justice and global citizenship education is encouraged, there is still resistance to certain types of course contents. For example, contents such as anti-Black racism, Whiteness and White privileges, the history of Canada's colonialism and genocidal practices on Indigenous peoples, and the complicit roles of social workers in Canada's residential schools are frowned upon in social justice and global citizenship education (Issahaku 2018).

In effect, there is a lack of accountability within social work schools in Canada to ensure that programs are routinized within radical social justice education and GCE. Not surprisingly, students go through their social work education sometimes learning little to nothing about the world and the interrelatedness of global problems. Even in cases where students receive social justice and global citizenship education, the content is spurious and sometimes "reduced to simplistic stereotypes or vague generalizations" (Hawkins 2009, 117). Banks (2004, 291) wrote a while ago that the greatest threat to the world is not illiteracy but unwillingness among the people in the world to move pass their differences – cultures, races, religions, and nations – to work together "to solve the world's intractable problems such as global warming, the HIV/AIDS epidemic, poverty, racism, sexism, and war." The fear is that unless something radical is done about this growing trend, social justice and global citizenship education will continue to receive little attention in social work classrooms.

In the era of Trump's presidency, there is a mainstreamed politicization of racist, xenophobic, Islamophobic, and anti-Semitic thoughts and practices. There is also the rise of White nationalism in the United States, Canada, the United Kingdom, and Europe. Social work education has a decision to make in this era: whether to produce learners who remain silent and neutral in the face of politics of exclusion and bigotry, or learners who refuse and resist. However, as Elie Wiesel, the Nobel Peace Prize winner and Holocaust survivor reminded us, "There may be times when we are powerless to prevent injustice, but there must never be a time when we fail to protest" (Wiesel 1986, para. 29). The discussion that follows outlines some pedagogical strategies that can help the teaching of social justice and global citizenship education in social work classrooms.

Pedagogical Strategies of Teaching Social Justice and Global Citizenship Education in Social Work Classrooms

Given the challenges as well as the opportunities of social justice and global citizenship education in social work, it is important that educators' pedagogical strategies aid students' learning needs and styles. It is important for Social Work educators to recast the popular "teaching and learning" into "learning and teaching." The order is important, because teaching something does not necessary guarantee learning. In fact, the third principle guiding the accreditation of Canadian social work education programs emphasizes students' *learning objectives* rather than educators' *teaching objectives*.[2] In view of that, the present chapter outlines four important strategies that can aid students' learning in social justice and global citizenship education in social work classrooms. These strategies are informed by scholarly publications as well as the experiential knowledge of the author, who has taught social justice and global citizenship education for the last five years at both BSW and MSW levels. These suggested strategies are not mutually exclusive to other strategies in use by other social justice educators in social work education.

Valuing Students' Prior Knowledge

One of the critical parts of teaching social justice is to begin lessons from what students already know. In *How People Learn: Bridging Research and Practice*, Suzanne Donovan, John Bransford, and James Pellegrino (1999) noted that "students come to the classroom with preconceptions about how the world works. If their initial understanding is not engaged, they may fail to grasp new concepts and information presented in the classroom, or they may learn them for purposes of a test but revert to their preconceptions outside the classroom" (2). Audrey Sewell (2002) also notes that students do not enter into classrooms with empty heads to be filled with knowledge. In fact, students already carry with them pre-existing knowledge, beliefs, and worldviews; therefore, if new information provided by teachers does not fit with what they already know, students may choose to reject new information outright or, as Dovovan, Brandsford, and Pelligrino (1999) suggest, learn them for purposes of passing the course but revert to their pre-existing knowledge outside the classroom. Sewell (2002) suggests four ways learners respond to learning in any classroom context: (1) Learners delete existing wrong beliefs and knowledge; (2) Learners modify preexisting knowledge so that it "fits" the new information; (3) Learners modify the new information so that it "fits" what is already known; (4) Learners reject the new information altogether.

These observations are important in teaching social justice and global citizenship education in a social work context. The dominant knowledge about racism, sexism, classism, ableism, Islamophobia, anti-Semitism, ageism, sanism, and homophobia is taught through everyday socialization processes (Peters 2002; Stevenson and Arrington 2009). Social work students' pre-existing understandings of race, gender, socio-economic status, disability, sexuality, religion, age, and immigration status are the foundation upon which they participate in any class discussion. It is therefore important that social work educators structure their pedagogical practices to draw out students' pre-existing knowledge, which Carey and Gelman (1982) argue can be accurate or inaccurate, in order to begin new learning. This means that in social justice and global citizenship education classroom, lessons can either confirm or challenge students' pre-existing knowledge. It also means that learning in social justice and global citizenship education can take place in the form of unlearning pre-existing knowledge. From my experiences as a social work educator, the difficult part of teaching social justice and global citizenship education is not when you ask students to learn new things about social inequities, but when you call on students to unlearn what they already know and even privilege as "normal" and normative (Britzman 1998; Kumashiro 2000). This is the more reason why social justice and global citizenship education must help students to unmask or make visible the privilege of certain identities, and the invisibility of this privilege even to its beneficiaries (Giroux 2011).

What this means is that social work educators cannot take neutral a position in social justice and global citizenship education classrooms. The teaching of social justice and global citizenship education is a political act. As Abramovitz (1993) aptly notes:

> All social work is already political, because it deals either with consciousness or the allocation of resources. Because it is impossible to avoid politics in this respect, it is far better to address these issues explicitly than to pretend that they do not exist. The political character of all social work and the adverse effects of the market economy on personal well-being suggest that teaching students how to foster individual and social change may be a more ethical option than endorsing apolitical social work. The latter, after all, typically blames the victim and deflects attention from the more systemic causes of many personal and social problems. (6)

In view of that, while social work educators may allow room for students' freedom of expression and willingness to critique knowledge content in social justice and global citizenship education classrooms, they must play active roles in the classroom interactions. They must ensure that discussions do not recreate marginalization for already oppressed students such as Muslim, racialized, gay, lesbian, bisexual, queer, and trans students, women, and poor working-class students. Ultimately, students ought to feel secure and confident before sharing information and engaging in spaces of learning. If social justice and global citizenship educators do not invest in the social dynamics of the classroom, the process of learning becomes disrupted, which can lead to social dysfunction and alienation. Several scholars (Boler 2004; Boler and Zembylas 2003; Ellsworth 1989; Leonardo 2009), however, have warned that creating safe classroom spaces where students can engage one another respectfully and critically is illusory, because of embodied historical difference.

Jakubowski and Visano (2002) note that emotions and discomfort may arise whenever social justice and global citizenship issues are tabled for discussion, but what is of importance is that marginalized groups should not be silenced or denied voice based on how the discussion is managed. Allowing voices of the marginalized brings about complex questions, such as: What should be the responsibility of social justice and global citizenship educators when dominant students make comments that are homophobic, Islamophobic, racist, sexist, xenophobic, or even hegemonic? Do social justice and global citizenship educators keep quiet and assume that all students are entitled to their opinions? Alternatively, should social justice and global citizenship educators intervene in correcting the students with dominant views? I am in agreement with Frantz Fanon (1963, 1967) and Albert Memmi (1965) that the oppressor needs the oppressed if they are to understand oppression and privileges. This means that dominant students cannot have deep intellectual insights into their oppressive and colonizing acts and relations without the inputs of oppressed students. In this context, no dominant thinking should be "inoculated" from critical interrogations in social justice and global citizenship education classrooms. Davis and Steyn (2012) have suggested that "safe space" should be constructed "as a way of thinking, feeling, and acting that fosters students' critical rigor" (Zembylas 2015, 166).

Antonio Gramsci (1971) astutely observed that the "starting-point of critical elaboration is the consciousness of what one really is, and is 'knowing thyself' as a product of the historical process to date, which has deposited in you an infinity of traces, without leaving an inventory" (324). Gramsci's observation is noteworthy in social justice classrooms where BSW and MSW students come to know themselves, their histories, and how certain values they hold dear came to be normalized in society. In my chapter, "Resistance to Amputation: Discomfort Truth about Colonial Education in Ghana" (Adjei 2010), I wrote about my personal shame, guilt, disappointment, and anger when I was confronted with information about Christianity. A religion I hold dear and have devoted myself to since childhood was complicit in the enslavement, genocide, and colonization of my people and many other groups in the world. I saw first-hand how hard it was to be confronted with something one is not ready to know.

The observations made in Adjei (2010) are particularly true for BSW and MSW students who arrive in social justice and global citizenship education classrooms with a self-belief that they are going to make the world a better place. Most times, these students have never been asked to self-reflect on their privileges as members of dominant groups. In fact, some have been taught not to see their privileges or to see their privileges as normal (Hackman 2005). The breaking point for some students is when they are called upon to confront their own privileges as they relate to racism, sexism, classism, ableism, Islamophobia, and homophobia in society. Some cannot comprehend the fact that despite their passion to transform the world, they are complicit to systemic and institutional racism, sexism, classism, Islamophobia, homophobia, and ableism. While others get ashamed and feel guilty of their history and privileges that link them to the oppression of others, some also get defensive by quickly drawing attention to their own victimhood with regard to other forms of social oppression.

bell hooks (1994) and Beverly Daniel Tatum (1992) both observe that any effort to transform the educational institution to response to the needs of diverse populations must pay particular attention to students' fears, shame, guilt, anger, denial, and anxieties. Tangney (1996, 741) argues that shame and guilt are internal affective states that are difficult, if not impossible, to assess directly. For Helen Block Lewis (1971), shame is a general negative feeling towards oneself in response to some misdeed or shortcoming, whereas guilt is a negative feeling about a specific event, rather than about the self. Fellows and Razack (1998) also describe the behaviour where students assume victimhood with regard to their other identity while claiming innocence to the oppression of others as "the race to innocence." An example could be when a White female student draws attention to sexism in society to demonstrate that although she may be privileged by race, she is equally oppressed by her gendered location.

The real concerns of guilt, shame, fear, anxiety, and denial in social justice and global citizenship education classrooms is that they not only produce entrenching positions that stifle any meaningful and fruitful discussion on social injustice principles but they are also the means for avoiding personal and social responsibility and accountability with regard to one's privileges. In social justice and global citizenship education, social work educators must help students to develop empathetic understanding for themselves as a first and necessary step in understanding the pervasive nature of oppression (Garcia and Van Soest 1997, 120). The second step, according to both Edwards-Orr (1988) and Van Soest (1995), is to help students to confront and undo distortions introduced by their privileges, which have led to an overestimation of themselves – if their group identity has been positively stereotyped – or an underestimation of themselves, if their group identity has been negatively stereotyped. Megan Boler (1999, 177) argues that emotions are connected to power relations that discipline what we observe and dismiss through observation. There is therefore the need for constant reflection of self, through a pedagogy of discomfort one can begin to think of self-differently through personal inquiry. bell hooks (1994) once remarked that part of doing critical work is to start with oneself. Sometimes, the hardest part of social justice and global citizenship education is the ability to courageously examine and critique oneself or to graciously accept criticisms that are targeted at one's own unearned privileges and power. The personal is always rebellious and unwilling to change. bell hooks (1989) talks about her own upbringing and the difficult hurdles she had to climb as a black woman growing up in the South – a location where black bodies, especially black women, were supposed to be "tongueless" unless they had been asked to talk. For hooks, her activism needed to start from within – within her community where suppression of women's voices was normalized. Hence, the emergence of "bell hooks – a sharp tongued woman, a woman who spoke her mind, a woman who was not afraid to talk back" (hooks 1989, 210). There is a need for self-implication, self-criticism, and self-reflexivity in social justice and global citizenship education classrooms, and the role of social work educators is to help students to engage in self-reflexivity.

Teaching the Place of Critical Thinking in Social Justice Education

Throughout the years that I have been involved in social justice and global citizenship education, I have noted that hegemonic knowledge functions as a taken-for-granted knowledge, what Gramsci (1971) refers to as "commonsense knowledge." In fact, neo-liberal ideas about social justice and GCE can be seductive and very appealing to the uncritical mind. According to Neuman and Blundo (2000), students must be encouraged to recognize and consider that the way in which "they view the world has significant consequences for their work and those with whom they will be working" (27). Gibbons and Gray (2004) conceptualize critical thinking as "a social constructionist understanding of the world whereby knowledge is a social construction; where the limits of knowledge are recognized; and where knowledge is seen as ever changing, even shifting and unstable. This is regarded as a very different process from learning to apply knowledge that one accepts uncritically as true, reliable and correct" (19). Kurfiss (1989) defines critical thinking as "the process of figuring out what to believe or not about a situation, phenomenon, problem or controversy for which no single definitive answer or solution exists. The term implies a diligent, open-minded search for understanding, rather than for discovery of a necessary conclusion" (42).

Kurfiss's definition is important in social justice and global citizenship education. Teaching social work students about social inequities and structures of oppression is the first step to a larger process. Students must also learn and know how to use the acquired knowledge to formulate effective plans of action. Ellsworth (1992) describes the assumptions underlying critical pedagogy as "the teaching of analytic and critical skills for judging the truth and merit of propositions, and the interrogation and selective appropriation of potentially transformative moments in the dominant culture" (96). Knight (1992) also offers a list of skills necessary for critical thinking that includes the development of cogent arguments, clear definitions, problem-solving strategies, information organization, and creativity (also see Mumm and Kersting 1997, 76). Without critical thinking skills, Social Work students will be limited to challenge oppression (Freire 2007; hooks 1994; Kumashiro 2000, 37).

In teaching critical thinking to help push a social justice and global citizenship education agenda, social work educators must first acknowledge the limits and incompleteness of their knowledge about certain social justice issues and learn with humility to seek authentic sources to expand their knowledge of the subject area(s), rather than relying on their own interpretations. Social work educators cannot expect social work students to act on the knowledge of social justice and global citizenship if the information provided to students is not critical and thorough enough to take social actions. Hackman (2005) speaks about the importance of content mastery in the social justice and global citizenship education classroom: "Content mastery is the first component of effective social justice education because information acquisition is an essential basis for learning. Without complex sources of information, students cannot possibly participate in positive, proactive social change" (104). Searching for authentic sources also implies that Social Work educators become mindful of what students are reading in the course. In *Lies My Teacher Told Me: Everything Your American History Textbook Got Wrong*, Loewen (1996) writes about the empowering effects of historically biased history books on students' learning. This is all the more reason why social work educators should ensure that the reading sources used in social justice and global citizenship education classrooms are not books and articles written from dominant perspectives. The teaching of social justice and global citizenship is not an intellectual stimulation exercise for the learning pleasures of students. The goal is to help students use the information gained in class to critique systems of power and inequities in society, as well as to identify social structures that keep those inequities alive (Hackman 2005). Hackman (2005) further warns that "thinking about an issue" should not be confused with "critical thinking" (106). Information sources in social justice and global citizenship education should emerge from multiple but non-dominant perspectives, and those non-dominant perspectives should be seen as independently valid and not as an add-on or competing discourse to the dominant hegemonic views.

Centring Race, Racism, and Whiteness in Social Justice and GCE Classrooms

Howard Winant (1994, 267) noted that the "world today is a racial battlefield." Winant's observation can be extended to the social work profession, where Whiteness has taken total control of the profession (Sakamoto 2007). Although race-based statistics on social workers in Canada does not exist, many scholars have argued that the majority of social workers in Canada are Whites (Baines 2004, 2011; Gosine and Pon 2011; Jeffrey 2005; Mullings 2012; Pon, Gosine, and Philip 2011; Yee, Wong, and Janczur 2006). Likewise, despite the absence of race-based statistics on enrolment populations across social work programs in Canada, a visit to many social work programs will reveal that White students dominate the enrolment population (Lum 2004). Not surprisingly, Whiteness continues to be the normative standard in social work practice (Jeyasingham 2011; Walter, Taylor, and Habibis 2011; Young 2004). Within social work education, Whiteness is the underlying currency that shapes the nature of teaching curricula as well as the ideologies that guide pedagogical practices. As Armstrong and Wildman (2008) note in the context of law school in the United States, "In this racialized world, race enters the law school classroom even when faculty do not name or discuss it" (652). Similarly, social work education culture tends to "whitewash" the social work profession, often ignoring the significant roles of Whiteness and White privileges in the construction of the profession.

I borrow from Thompson's (2011) "Summary of Whiteness Theory" to treat Whiteness not as a biological category but as a social construction. Critical race theorist George Lipsitz (1995) describes Whiteness as a form of property. As a property – whether the property is conceived of as legal or cultural – Whiteness has been used historically in contradictory ways to assign power and privilege to people who identify as White, pass as White, and are honorarily accepted as White (Thompson 2011). For instance, during the Apartheid regime of South Africa, the Japanese in South Africa, although they were not White, were allowed to tap into the privilege and power reserved for Whites. Similarly, in the United States and Canada, Jews, Irish, and Italians, although they possess White identity, were previously denied access to privileges and power assigned to Anglo-Saxon Whites. Thompson (2011) argues that Whiteness operates in a mechanism that is sometimes polemical and paradoxical. On one hand, Whiteness is normalized, taken for granted, and therefore invisible. On the other hand, Whiteness is the preferable condition in almost every aspect of society that carries power and privileges. In *Playing in the Dark: Whiteness and the Literary Imagination*, the African American literary writer Toni Morrison (1993, 17) used a fishbowl that contains fish and water as a metaphor to describe the invisibility of Whiteness. Whiteness is invisible because, like the fishbowl containing water and fish, observers normally cast their gazes on what is inside the fishbowl – the water and the fish – rather than the fishbowl itself.

What this means for social justice and global citizenship education is that race, racism, and Whiteness should be the central underpinning for understanding, unpacking, and examining social inequities in Canada. It is critical for social justice and global citizenship educators to cast their gaze on the system of domination that continues to maintain White supremacist ideologies, values, knowledge, and practices in the social work profession in Canada. To ignore this reality is to contribute to the colonial and racist history that has sustained such ideology and culture.

However, there are fundamental challenges teaching race, racism, and Whiteness in Social Work education. First, as noted in (Adjei and Gill 2013), race, racism, and Whiteness are hot-button topics in Canadian society (134). Evoking race, racism, and Whiteness in any discussion in Canada and the United States is likely to bring unpleasant tensions, passions, anger, fear, and anxiety. As a result, we fail to either speak or acknowledge race, racism, and Whiteness, even when legitimate concerns involving inequity, injustice, and differential power issues are tabled for discussion. Second, as Kincheloe et al. (2000) and Picower (2009) note, Whiteness operates in varied ways, so that sometimes the beneficiaries of Whiteness show up in social justice and global citizenship education classrooms unaware of their racial identity and how it has contributed to their successes in society. Applebaum (2005) also notes:

> The discourse of meritocracy functions to marginalize certain groups of people by allowing whites to direct attention away from their own privilege and to ignore larger patterns of racial injustice. The assumption that people get ahead as a result of individual effort or merit conceals how

> social, economic and cultural privileges facilitate the success of some groups of people but not others. Moreover, it allows the privileged to see themselves as innocent bystanders rather than participants in a system that creates, maintains and reproduces social injustice. (286)

Third, even those White students who are aware of their racial identity and the unearned privileges that come with it still believe themselves to be good and moral citizens who cannot perpetuate racial inequality or social injustice (Applebaum 2005, 278). Banks (2004) notes that "the increasing ethnic, cultural, language, and religious diversity in nation-states throughout the world has raised new questions and possibilities about educating students for effective citizenship" (289). In social justice and global citizenship education, students must be made aware that "goodness" and "racism" can coexist within us. Therefore, there is a limit to engaging in defensiveness and a pedagogy of guilt when charged as "racists."

Fourth, social work educators of colour often face students' hostility and students' backlash when they talk about race, racism, and Whiteness in the social work profession. Students' anonymous course and online evaluations can target professors of colour who make race, racism, and Whiteness important topics in their social justice and global citizenship education classroom. One of my senior colleagues was described in course evaluations as anti-White because she makes race, racism, and Whiteness central to her social justice and global citizenship education class. Elsewhere, Ahmed (2012) also writes about the predicament of women of colour whose scholarship critically engages race, racism, and Whiteness:

> The woman of color isn't a real scholar; she is motivated by ideology: The woman of color is angry. She occupies the moral high ground. The woman of color declares war by pointing to the complicity of white feminists in imperialism. The woman of color is racist (and we hurt, too). The woman of color should be grateful, as she lives in our democracy. We have given her the right and the freedom to speak. The woman of color is the origin of terror, and she fails to recognize violence other than the violence of white against black. The exercising of this figure does more than make her work: *it is a defense against hearing her work.* (162, emphasis in original)

In the United States, Robert Chang (1993) also reports an anonymous student evaluation that he received after his first year of teaching law: "Leave the racist comments out. Go visit Korea if you don't like it here.

We need to unite as a country not drive wedges between us" (88). In my own classes, on several occasions, I have had to make myself the centre of racial analysis when I have to respond to students' inquiries about my experiences of racism in Canada. Although I acknowledge my students' genuine intent to learn, I have to recount my painful experiences of racism so that my White students can learn from it. Moments like this create a certain level of vulnerability for professors of colour and discourage many from engaging race, racism, and Whiteness in social work education. Dutta et al. (2016), however, note that moving outside of our comfort zone as social justice and global citizenship educators meant "embracing vulnerabilities in teaching and learning" (351). So how does one teach race, racism, and Whiteness in the midst of these challenges?

Social work educators should use what Megan Boler (1999) theorizes as a *pedagogy of discomfort*. It is a teaching practice that "begins by inviting educators and students to engage in critical inquiry regarding values and cherished beliefs, and to examine constructed self-images in relation to how one has learned to perceive others" (Boler 1999, 177). A pedagogy of discomfort encourages students to move outside their "comfort zones" and question their "cherished beliefs and assumptions" (Boler 1999, 176). The assumption here is that through discomforting feelings students are forced to confront their dominant beliefs, social habits, and normative practices that sustain social inequities (Zembylas 2015, 163). Berlak (2004) have argued that if social justice and global citizenship education stand a chance of unsettling cherished beliefs about the world, then some level of learners' discomfort is not only unavoidable but also may be necessary. Felman (1992) also concludes: "If teaching does not hit upon some sort of crisis, if it does not encounter either the vulnerability or the explosiveness of a (explicit or implicit) critical and unpredictable dimension, it has perhaps not truly taught ... I therefore think that my job as a teacher, paradoxical as it may sound, was that of creating in the class the highest state of crisis that it could withstand, without 'driving the students crazy,' without compromising the students' bounds" (53). Kumashiro (2000) reiterates Felman's points by insisting that it is both pedagogically and ethically appropriate to evoke discomforting feelings in students as long as "the harm" done in students is dealt with appropriately (79; see also Zembylas 2015, 165).

One way of using the pedagogy of discomfort in social justice and global citizenship education is to include assignments that will allow students to talk about race, racism, and Whiteness. In two such assignments, students were made to form a group of four students. They were then given a set of questions directly related to race, racism, and Whiteness to discuss. The discussion was supposed to be video recorded. In the second part of the assignment, students were asked to write a reflection paper about their experience doing this particular assignment. The purpose of this course assignment was to compel students to critically reflect on course readings on race, racism, and Whiteness, as well as to "push" students into those spaces of discomfort where they have to do soul-searching and speak openly about the privileges that come with their social locations. It was also to make the unfamiliar familiar as well as to force students to work with difficult knowledge. The advantage of assigning good course marks to such assignments is that it compels students to not easily gross over the readings on race, racism, and Whiteness but to seriously engage them if they want to earn good marks in the course.

Teaching Intersectionality in the Social Justice and Global Citizenship Education Classroom

It is because of the tendency for race, racism, and Whiteness to disappear in social justice and global citizenship education clasroom that this chapter insists on centering race, racism, and Whiteness in social justice and global citizenship education. This does not suggest that social justice and global citizenship education should be limited to race, racism, and Whiteness. Social justice and global citizenship education cannot focus only on one oppression and leave others intact. Teaching intersectionality in social justice and global citizenship education helps students to understand multiple and complex ways in which identity markers of race, class, gender, sexuality, disability, age, citizenship, religion, language, ethnicity, and others interact to shape multiple dimensions of one's identity (Crenshaw 1991). Further, it helps students to understand how different forms of marginality and structures of dominance – ableism, sexism, heterosexism, classism, racism, sanism, ageism, ethnocentrism, colonialism, Islamophobia, and anti-Semitism – intersect, shift, and influence changes in social conditions. It helps students to see that people can assume the role of "oppressor" and "oppressed" in different situations. This means that we cannot deal with the questions of complicity, accountability, and responsibility as if, somehow, oppression is perpetuated by someone else and not ourselves. An active role in fighting social injustices and human rights violations does not inoculate one from being complicit in the oppression of others.

Humour as a Pedagogical Tool for Teaching Social Justice

In teaching social justice and global citizenship education in a social work context, educators can rely on humour as a mechanism to help students grapple with the content of the course material. Berk (1996, 1998), Glenn (2002), and Pollio and Humphreys (1996) note that the use of humour in teaching has both psychological and physiological effects on learners. Although Garner (2003) previously cautioned against the use of humour in teaching, as humour has potential of causing as much harm as good, he also noted in that when used appropriately, humour carries sufficient power to have positive effects on students learning and retention (Garner 2006). Some educators may argue that issues of social justice and global citizenship education are too serious to use humour to teach, as such an approach has the potential of trivializing and disrupting learning (Ascham 1969; Cantor and Venus 1980; Gutek 1970; Terry and Woods 1975). This position, however, can be contested, because many studies have shown that "humour facilitates attention and motivation, improves teacher-student rapport, and makes taboo subjects more acceptable" (Bryant, Comisky, and Zillmann 1979, 111). In my own social justice and global citizenship education classroom, I have drawn on humour as a pedagogical tool to facilitate the discussion of topics that students may found uncomfortable. The effectiveness of humour as a pedagogical strategy is noted by students through feedback from course evaluations. In one course evaluation questionnaire independently administered online by Memorial University of Newfoundland, one student wrote under the question "If you had to select the best aspects of this course, what would they be?": "Paul is hilarious, always held our attention and made class fun." Another student wrote "Excellent prof. Loved his classes, they were always fun." Of course, citing these students' comments is not self-serving but to illustrate that humour can be an important pedagogical tool for critical learning in social justice and global citizenship education.

Conclusion

We have arrived at the threshold where social work education should count for something. The world around us is filled with examples of authoritarian populist leaders in recent times, who claim to speak for "the people" but build their popularity and followers by demonizing racialized immigrants, Muslims, refugees, the poor, and other disadvantaged communities. In the United States, President Donald Trump built his whole political campaign and electoral success on racist,

Islamophobic, xenophobic, and sexist rhetoric (see, Adjei 2018). In the United Kingdom, the Brexit campaign could not have been successful without Boris Johnson's and Nigel Farage's racist, xenophobic, and Islamophobia promises to restore White national and cultural identity in the UK. In France, Marine Le Pen's racist, xenophobic, and Islamophobic rhetoric received national approval when her Front National party swung from 4 per cent in 2007 to placing second in the first round behind Emmanuel Macron in the French 2017 general election. In Sweden, the national support for the nationalist, anti-immigrant Swedish Democrats has grown to a party that won forty-nine seats in the 2014 elections, and is now the second-most popular political party in Sweden (Sennero 2017). The story is not different in Brazil, as well as in Denmark, Greece, Poland, Hungary, Austria, Italy, the Netherlands, and other European countries. In some parts of Africa, some African leaders have used lesbians, gays, bisexuals, and transgender minorities to create a moral panic among their conservative backers to divert attention from their leadership failures, as seen in Egypt, Zimbabwe, and Tanzania (Roth 2018). On the environmental front, we continue to see a strong link between human rights violations and environmental abuses at the global level (Human Rights Watch 1992). In China, several thousand children have suffered permanent mental and physical disabilities as a result of lead poisoning (Human Rights Watch 2011). In Nigeria more than 400 children have been killed by lead poisoning (Human Rights Watch 2012). In the Philippines, many children are at risk of death or permanent physical disabilities, as there is a widespread mercury pollution created by artisanal gold mines (Human Rights Watch 2015).

The fear is that this trend has no way of stopping, as more people continue to feel threatened by "economic dislocation and inequality caused by globalization, automation, technological change; feared cultural shifts as the ease of transportation and communication fuels migration from war, repression, poverty, and climate change; [and] societal divisions between cosmopolitan elites who welcome and benefit from many of these changes and those who feel their lives have become more precarious" (Roth 2018, para. 7).

However, these examples should not induce despair but rather determination and action to "push back against those who would reverse hard-fought progress" made on global human rights and social justice (Roth 2018, para. 64). Social work educators need to reexamine their mandate and consider what they can do to prepare students to protect human rights and social justice from populist assaults. Given that social justice and global citizenship education is the place where one can disrupt dominant discourses and ideologies while inspiring new learning, social work education can use social justice and global citizenship education to inspire students to challenge and resist global human rights violations and social injustices.

In the present chapter, I have outlined some pedagogical strategies that can help the teaching of social justice and global citizenship education in a social work context. These strategies, as I have already mentioned, do not replace those already in use by other social work educators, but just add to them. I end this chapter with a profound quote from a source known more from the culture of rap music than for academic writing, the late African American hip-pop cultural icon Tupac Shakur: "I'm gonna change the world, but I guarantee you that I will spark the brain that will change the world. And that's our job. It's to spark somebody else watching us" (quoted in Nastasi 2014, para 5).[3] This should be the rallying cry of social work educators to change the minds and thoughts of social work students to make them better global citizens.

NOTES

1 I argue that this concept is problematic because it celebrates the notion of individual resilience and an uncontextualized notion of resource distribution. It also fails to account for the socio-cultural backgrounds of and structural barriers to the marginalized.

2 "Core learning objectives for students link student learning objectives to the promotion of excellence in social work education, scholarship, and practice with a social justice focus and guide both curriculum design and the delivery of field education" (CASWE 2014, 3).

3 Though not readily acknowledged by academics, Tupac Shakur is also well known for coining the concept, "a rose that grew in concrete." For other adaptation and uses of this concept, see for example, Duncan-Andrade (2009); Dlamini (2015).

REFERENCES

Abramovitz, M. 1993. "Should All Social Work Students Be Educated for Social Change?" *Journal of Social Work Education* 29, no. 1: 6–12. https://doi.org/10.1080/10437797.1993.10778794

Adjei, P.B. 2010. "Resistance to Amputation: Discomfort Truth About Colonial Education in Ghana." In *Fanon and Education: Thinking through Pedagogical Possibilities*, edited by G. Dei and M. Simmons. New York: Peter Lang.

– 2013. "The Non-Violent Philosophy of Mahatma Gandhi and Martin Luther King Jr. in the 21st Century: Implications for the Pursuit of Social Justice in a Global Context." *Journal of Global Citizenship & Equity Education* 3, no. 1: 80–101.

– 2018. "Race to the Bottom: Obama's Presidency, Trump's Election Victory, and the Perceived Insidious Greed of Whiteness." *Race, Gender & Class* 25, nos. 3–4: 43–67.

Adjei, P.B., and J.K. Gill. 2013. "What Has Barack Obama's Election Victory Got to Do with Race? A Closer Look at Post-Racial Rhetoric and Its Implication for Antiracism Education." *Race Ethnicity and Education* 16, no. 1: 134–53. https://doi.org/10.1080/13613324.2011.645576

Ahmed, S. 2012. *On Being Included: Racism and Diversity in Institutional Life.* Durham, NC: Duke University Press.

Appiah, K.A. 2006. *Cosmopolitanism: Ethnics in a World of Strangers.* New York: W.W. Norton.

Applebaum, B. 2005. "In the Name of Morality: Moral Responsibility, Whiteness and Social Justice Education." *Journal of Moral Education* 34, no. 3: 277–90. https://doi.org/10.1080/03057240500206089

Armstrong, M.J., and S.M. Wildman. 2008. "Teaching Race/Teaching Whiteness: Transforming Colorblindness to Color Insight." *NCL Review* 86: 635. https://doi.org/10.2139/ssrn.1108471

Ascham, R. 1969. "The Scholemaster." In *The Educating of Americans: A Documentary History*, edited by D. Calhoun. Boston: Houghton Mifflin.

Baines, D. 2004. "Caring for Nothing: Work Organization and Unwaged Labour in Social Services." *Work, Employment & Society* 18, no. 2: 267–95. https://doi.org/10.1177/09500172004042770

–, ed. 2011. *Doing Anti-Oppressive Practice: Social Justice Social Work.* 2nd ed. Halifax: Fernwood Publishing.

Banerjee, M.M. 2011. "Social Work Scholars' Representation of Rawls: A Critique. Journal of Social Work Education." *Journal of Social Work Education* 47, no. 2: 189–211. https://doi.org/10.5175/jswe.2011.200900063

Banks, J.A. 2004. "Teaching for Social Justice, Diversity, and Citizenship in a Global World." *The Educational Forum* 68, no. 4: 296–305.

Barker, C. 1999. *Television, Globalization and Cultural Identities.* Buckingham, UK: Open University Press.

Bauman, Z. 2000. "Special Essay. Am I My Brother's Keeper?" *European Journal of Social Work* 3, no. 1: 5–11. https://doi.org/10.1080/714052807

Berk, R. 1996. "Student Ratings Often Strategies for Using Humor in College Teaching." *Journal on Excellence in College Teaching* 1, no. 3: 71–92.

– 1998. *Professors Are from Mars, Students Are from Snickers.* Madison, WI: Mendota.

Berlak, A. 2004. "Confrontation and Pedagogy: Cultural Secrets and Emotion in Antioppressive Pedagogies." In *Democratic Dialogue in Education: Troubling Speech, Disturbing Silence*, edited by M. Boler. New York: Peter Lang, 2004.

Boler, M. 1999. *Feeling Power: Emotions and Education* New York: Routledge.

– 2004. "All Speech Is Not Free: The Ethics of 'Affirmative Action Pedagogy.'" In *Democratic Dialogue in Education: Troubling Speech, Disturbing Silence*, edited by M. Boler. New York: Peter Lang.

Boler, M., and M. Zembylas. 2003. "Discomforting Truths: The Emotional Terrain of Understanding Difference." In *Pedagogies of Difference: Rethinking Education for Social Change*, edited by P.P. Trifonas. New York: Routledge Falmer.

Britzman, D.P. 1998. *Lost Subjects, Contested Objects: Toward a Psychoanalytic Inquiry of Learning*. Albany, NY: SUNY Press.

Bryant, J., P. Comisky, and D. Zillmann. 1979. "Teachers' Humor in the College Classroom." *Communication Education* 28, no. 2: 110–18. https://doi.org/10.1080/03634527909378339

Canadian Association of Social Workers (CASWE). 2005. *Code of Ethics 2005*. Ottawa: Canadian Association of Social Workers.

– 2014. "CASWE-ACFTS Standards for Accreditation." Revised and approved August 2014. https://caswe-acfts.ca/wp-content/uploads/2013/03/CASWE-ACFTS.Standards-11-2014-1.pdf

Cantor, J., and P. Venus. 1980. "The Effect of Humor on Recall of a Radio Advertisement." *Journal of Broadcasting & Electronic Media* 24, no. 1: 13–22. https://doi.org/10.1080/08838158009363961

Carey, S., and R. Gelman. 1982. "Student Preconceptions of Introductory Mechanics." *American Journal of Physics* 50: 66–71. https://doi.org/10.1119/1.12989

Chang, R.S. 1993. "Toward an Asian American Legal Scholarship: Critical Race Theory, Post-Structuralism, and Narrative Space." *California Law Review* 81: 1241–323. https://doi.org/10.2307/3480919

Colcord, J., and R.Z.S. Mann. 1930. *The Long View: Papers and Addresses by Mary E. Richmond*. New York: Russell Sage Foundation.

Crenshaw, K. 1991. "Mapping the Margins: Intersectionality, Identity Politics, and Violence against Women of Color." *Stanford Law Review* 43 (6): 1241–99. https://doi.org/10.2307/1229039

Davis, D., and M. Steyn. 2012. "Teaching Social Justice: Reframing Some Common Pedagogical Assumptions." *Perspectives in Education* 30, no. 4: 29–38.

Dlamini, S.N. 2015. "Youth Challenging Community: Between Hope and Stigmatization." *Educação e Pesquisa* 41: 1229–52.

Donovan, M.S., J.D. Bransford, and J.W. Pellegrino, eds. 1999. *How People Learn: Bridging Research and Practice*. Washington, DC: National Academy of Sciences.

Duncan-Andrade, J.M.R. 2009. "Note to Educators: Hope Required When Growing Roses in Concrete." *Harvard Educational Review* 79, no. 2: 231–43.

Dutta, U., T. Shroll, J. Engelsen, S. Prickett, L. Hajjar, and J. Green. 2016. "The 'Messiness' of Teaching/Learning Social (in) Justice: Performing a Pedagogy of Discomfort." *Qualitative Inquiry* 22, no. 5: 345–52. https://doi.org/10.1177/1077800416637623

Eaton v. Brant County Board of Education, [1997] 1 S.C.R. 241.

Edwards-Orr, M.T. 1988. "Helping White Students Confront White Racism." In *Annual Program Meeting of the Council on Social Work Education*. Atlanta, GA: Council on Social Work Education.

Ellsworth, E. 1989. "Why Doesn't This Feel Empowering? Working through the Repressive Myths of Critical Pedagogy." *Harvard Educational Review* 59: 297–324. https://doi.org/10.17763/haer.59.3.058342114k266250

– 1992. "Why Doesn't This Feel Empowering? Working through the Repressive Myths of Critical Pedagogy." In *Feminisms and Critical Pedagogies*, edited by C. Luke and J. Gore. New York: Routledge.

Europe-Wide Global Education Congress. 2002. "Maastricht Global Education Declaration." https://rm.coe.int/CoERMPublicCommonSearchServices/DisplayDCTMContent?documentId=090000168070e540

Fanon, F. 1963. *The Wretched of the Earth*. Harmondsworth, UK: Penguin.

– 1967. *Black Skin, White Masks*. New York: Grove Press.

Fehr, L. 2013. "The Meaning of Social Justice to Social Work Students." PhD diss., Memorial University of Newfoundland.

Fellows, M.L., and Razack, S. 1998. "The Race to Innocence: Confronting Hierarchical Relations among Women." *The Journal of Gender, Race & Justice* 1, no. 2: 335–52.

Felman, S. 1992. "Education and Crisis, or, Vicissitudes of Listening." In *Testimony: Crises of Witnessing in Literature, Psychoanalysis, and History*, edited by S. Felman and D. Laub. London: Routledge.

Franklin, D.L. 1986. "Mary Richmond and Jane Addams: From Moral Certainty to Rational Inquiry in Social Work Practice." *Social Service Review* 60, no. 4: 504–25. https://doi.org/10.1086/644396

Fraser, N. 2005. *Reframing Justice*. Amsterdam: Uitgeverij Van Gorcum.

– 2008. "Abnormal Justice." *Critical Inquiry*, 34, no 3: 393–422.

Freire, P. 2007. *Pedagogy of the Oppressed*. New York: Continuum.

Friedman, M.1973. *The Machinery of Freedom*. Chicago: University of Chicago Press.

Galambos, C. 2008. "A Dialogue on Social Justice [Editorial]." *Journal of Social Work Education* 44: 1–5.

Garcia, B., and D. Van Soest. 1997. "Changing Perceptions of Diversity and Oppression: MSW Students Discuss the Effects of a Required Course." *Journal of Social Work Education* 33, no. 1: 119–29. https://doi.org/10.1080/10437797.1997.10778857

Garner, R.L. 2006. "Humor in Pedagogy: How Ha-Ha Can Lead to Aha!" *College Teaching* 54, no. 1: 177–80. https://doi.org/10.3200/ctch.54.1.177-180

Garner, R. 2003. "Which Came First, the Chicken or the Egg? A Foul Metaphor for Teaching." *Radical Pedagogy* 5, no. 2: 205–12. https://doi.org/10.2139/ssrn.2562098

Gibbons J., and M. Gray. 2004. "Critical Thinking as Integral to Social Work Practice." *Journal of Teaching in Social Work* 24, nos. 1–2: 19–38. https://doi.org/10.1300/j067v24n01_02

Giroux, H. 2011. "Neoliberalism as a Form of Public Pedagogy: Making the Political More Pedagogical." https://www.academia.edu/12795711/Neoliberalism_as_public_pedagogy

Glenn, R. 2002. "Brain Research: Practical Applications for the Classroom." *Teaching for Excellence* 21, no. 6: 1–2.

Gosine, K., and G. Pon. 2011. "On the Front Lines: The Voices and Experiences of Racialized Child Welfare Workers in Toronto, Canada." *Journal of Progressive Human Services* 22, no. 2: 135–59.

Gramsci, A. 1971. *Selections from the Prison Notebooks*. London: Lawrence and Wishart.

Gutek, G.L. 1970. *An Historical Introduction to American Education*. New York: Thomas Y. Cromwell.

Hackman, H.W. 2005. "Five Essential Components for Social Justice Education." *Equity & Excellence in Education* 38, no. 2: 103–9. https://doi.org/10.1080/10665680590935034

Hair, H.J. 2015. "Supervision Conversations about Social Justice and Social Work Practice." *Journal of Social Work* 15, no. 4: 349–70. https://doi.org/10.1177/1468017314539082

Hardina, D. 2000. "Models and Tactics Taught in Community Organization Courses: Findings from a Survey of Practice Instructors." *Journal of Community Practice* 7, no. 1: 5–15. https://doi.org/10.1300/j125v07n01_02

– 2004. "Guidelines for Ethical Practice in Community Organization." *Social Work* 49, no. 4: 595–604. https://doi.org/10.1093/sw/49.4.595

Hawkins, C.A. 2009. "Global Citizenship: A Model for Teaching Universal Human Rights in Social Work Education." *Social Work* 10, no. 1: 116–31.

Hayek, F.A. 1976. *Law, Legislation and Liberty*, Vol. 2, *The Mirage of Social Justice*. London: Routledge and Kegan Paul.

Hick, S. 2006. *Social Work in Canada: An Introduction*. 2nd ed. Toronto: Thompson Books.

Hollingsworth, L.D. 2003. "International Adoption among Families in the United States: Considerations of Social Justice." *Social Work* 48: 209–17. https://doi.org/10.1093/sw/48.2.209

hooks, b. 1989. *Talking Back: Thinking Feminist. Thinking Back*. Boston, MA: South End Press.

– 1994. *Teaching to Transgress*. New York: Routledge.

Human Rights Watch. 1992. *Defending the Earth: Abuses of Human Rights and the Environment*. New York: Human Rights Watch and Natural Resources Defense Council.

– 2011. "China: Children Poisoned by Lead and Denied Treatment." 15 June. https://www.hrw.org/news/2011/06/15/china-children-poisoned-lead-and-denied-treatment

– 2012. "Nigeria: Child Lead Poisoning Crisis." 7 February. https://www.hrw.org/news/2012/02/07/nigeria-child-lead-poisoning-crisis

– 2015. "Philippines: Children Risk Death to Dig and Dive for Gold." 29 September. https://www.hrw.org/news/2015/09/29/philippines-children-risk-death-dig-and-dive-gold

Issahaku, P. 2018. "The Rhetorical Versus the Practicality of Social Justice in Canadian Social Work: Implications for Social Work Practice in Post Truth and Reconciliation Commission Report." Paper presented at the Canadian Association of Social Workers Congress, University of Regina, Regina, AB, 28–31 May.

Jakubowski L., and L. Visano. 2002. *Teaching Controversy*. Halifax: Fernwood Publishing.

Jeffery, D. 2005. "'What Good Is Anti Racist Social Work If You Can't Master It'? Exploring a Paradox in Anti Racist Social Work Education." *Race Ethnicity and Education* 8, no. 4: 409–25. https://doi.org/10.1080/13613320500324011

Jeyasingham, D. 2011. "White Noise: A Critical Evaluation of Social Work Education's Engagement with Whiteness Studies." *British Journal of Social Work* 42, no. 4: 669–86. https://doi.org/10.1093/bjsw/bcr110

Johnson, L.B. 1965. "Equal Opportunity Is Not Enough." Address presented at Howard University, 4 June. https://www.nytimes.com/2003/07/03/opinion/l-lbj-on-race-equality-362220. html

Kincheloe, J.L., S.R. Steinberg, N.M. Rodriguez, and R.E. Chennault. 2000. *White Reign: Deploying Whiteness in America*. London: Palgrave Macmillan.

Knight, C. 1992. "Teaching Critical Thinking in the Social Sciences." *New Directions for Community Colleges* 77: 63–73. https://doi.org/10.1002/cc.36819927707

Kumashiro, K.K. 2000. "Towards a Theory of Anti-Oppressive Education." *Review of Education Research* 70, no. 1: 25–53. https://doi.org/10.3102/00346543070001025

Kurfiss, J.G. 1989. "Helping Faculty Foster Students' Critical Thinking in the Disciplines." In *New Directions for Teaching and Learning*, edited by A.F. Lucas. San Francisco: Jossey-Bass.

Larkin, H. 2004. "Justice Implications of a Proposed Medicare Prescription Drug Policy." *Social Work* 49: 406–14. https://doi.org/10.1093/sw/49.3.406

Leonardo, Z. 2009. *Race, Whiteness and Education*. New York: Routledge.

Lewis, H.B. 1971. *Shame and Guilt in Neurosis*. New York: International Universities Press.

Lipsitz, G. 1995. "The Possessive Investment in Whiteness: Racialized Social Democracy and the 'White' Problem in America." *American Quarterly* 47, no. 3: 369–87. https://doi.org/10.2307/2713291

Loewen, J.W. 1996. *Lies My Teacher Told Me: Everything Your American History Textbook Got Wrong*. New York: Simon & Schuster.

Lum, D. 2004. *Social Work Practice and People of Color: A Process-Stage Approach*. Pacific Grove, CA: Brooks/Cole Publishing Company.

Lundblad, K.S. 1995. "Jane Addams and Social Reform: A Role Model for the 1990s." *Social Work* 40, no. 5: 661–9. https://doi.org/10.1093/sw/40.5.661

Lundy, C. 2004. *Social Work and Social Justice: A Structural Approach to Practice*. Peterborough, ON: Broadview Press.

Margolin, L. 1997. *Under the Cover of Kindness: The Invention of Social Work*. Charlottesville: University of Virginia Press.

McLaughlin, A. 2006. "Clinical Social Work and Social Justice." *Dissertation Abstracts International* 67, no. 11: 4337.

Memmi, A. 1965. *The Colonizer and the Colonized*. Boston: Beacon Press.

Morrison, T. 1993. *Playing in the Dark: Whiteness and the Literary Imagination*. New York: Vintage Books.

Mullaly, B. 2007. *The New Structural Social Work*. Oxford: Oxford University Press.

Mullings, D.V. 2012. "The Racial Institutionalization of Whiteness in Contemporary Canadian Public Policy." In *Critical Issues / Series 'Ethos' – on Whiteness*, edited by N. Falkof and O. Cashman-Brown. Oxford: Inter-Disciplinary Press.

Mumm, A.M., and R.C. Kersting. 1997. "Teaching Critical Thinking in Social Work Practice Courses." *Journal of Social Work Education* 33, no. 1: 75–84. https://doi.org/10.1080/10437797.1997.10778854

Myers, J.P. 2006. "Rethinking the Social Studies Curriculum in the Context of Globalization: Education for Global Citizenship in the Us." *Theory & Research in Social Education* 34, no. 3: 370–94. https://doi.org/10.1080/00933104.2006.10473313

Nastasi, A. 2014. "25 Thought-Provoking Tupac Quotes About Life and Art." Flavorwire, 4 September. http://flavorwire.com/475968/25-thought-provoking-tupac-quotes-about-life-and-art/

Neuman, K., and R. Blundo. 2000. "Curricular Philosophy and Social Work Education: A Constructivist Perspective." *Journal of Teaching in Social Work* 20, nos. 1–2: 19–38. https://doi.org/10.1300/j067v20n01_03

Nussbaum, M. 2006. *Frontiers of Justice*. Cambridge, MA: Harvard University Press.

Olson, J.J. 2007. "Social Work's Professional and Social Justice Projects: Discourses in Conflict." *Journal of Progessive Human Services* 18, no. 1: 45–69. https://doi.org/10.1300/j059v18n01_04

Peters, M.F. 2002. "Racial Socialization of Young Black Children." In *Black Children: Social Educational and Parental Environments*, edited by H.P. McAdoo. Thousand Oaks, CA: Sage.

Picower, B. 2009. "The Unexamined Whiteness of Teaching: How White Teachers Maintain and Enact Dominant Racial Ideologies." *Race Ethnicity and Education* 12, no. 2: 197–215. https://doi.org/10.1080/13613320902995475

Pollio, H., and W. Humphreys. 1996. "What Award-Wining Lecturers Say About Their Teaching: It's All About Connection." *College Teaching* 44, no. 3: 101–6. https://doi.org/10.1080/87567555.1996.9925562

Pon, G., K. Gosine, and D. Phillips. 2011. "Immediate Response: Addressing Anti-Native and Anti-Black Racism in Child Welfare." *International Journal of Child, Youth and Family* Studies 2, nos. 3–4: 385–409.

Rawls, J. 1971. *A Theory of Justice*. Cambridge, MA: Belknap Press.

Reisch, M. 2002. "Defining Social Justice in a Socially Unjust World." *Families in Society* 83: 343–54. https://doi.org/10.1606/1044-3894.17

Roth, K. 2018. *The Pushback against the Populist Challenge*. New York: Human Rights Watch. https://www.hrw.org/world-report/2018/pushback-against-the-populist-challenge

Sakamoto, I. 2007. "An Anti-Oppressive Approach to Cultural Competence." *Canadian Social Work Review/Revue Canadienne de Service Social* 24, no. 1: 105–14.

Scanlon, T. 1988. "Contractualism and Utilitarianism." In *Utilitarianism and Beyond*, edited by A. Sen and B. Williams. Cambridge: Cambridge University Press.

Sennero, J. 2017. "Anti-Immigrant Sweden Democrats Move into Second Place in Polls." Reuters, 23 March. https://www.reuters.com/article/us-sweden-politics/anti-immigrant-sweden-democrats-move-into-second-place-in-polls-idUSKBN16U1NS

Sewell, A. 2002. "Constructivism and Student Misconceptions: Why Every Teacher Needs to Know About Them." *Australian Science Teachers Journal* 48, no. 4: 24.

Slavin, P. 2002. "Profession Strained in Canada." *NASW News*, 15 March.

Solas, J. 2008. "What Kind of Social Justice Does Social Work Seek?" *International Social Work* 51, no. 6: 813–22. https://doi.org/10.1177/0020872808095252

Spivak, G.C. 1999. *A Critique of Postcolonial Reason: Toward a History of the Vanishing Present*. Cambridge, MA: Harvard University Press.

Stevenson, H.C., and E.G. Arrington. 2009. "Racial/Ethnic Socialization Mediates Perceived Racism and the Racial Identity of African American Adolescents." *Cultural Diversity and Ethnic Minority Psychology*15, no. 2: 125. https://doi.org/10.1037/a0015500

Tangney, J.P. 1996. "Conceptual and Methodological Issues in the Assessment of Shame and Guilt." *Behavior Research Therapy* 34, no. 9: 741–54. https://doi.org/10.1016/0005-7967(96)00034-4

Tatum, B.D. 1992. "African-American Identity Development, Academic Achievement, and Missing History." *Social Education* 56, no. 6: 331–4.

Terry, R.L., and M.E. Woods. 1975. "Effects of Humor on the Test Performance of Elementary School Children." *Psychology in the Schools* 12, no. 2: 182–5. https://doi.org/10.1002/1520-6807(197504)12:2%3C182::aid-pits2310120210%3E3.0.co;2-3

Thompson, Audrey. 2011. "Summary of Whiteness Theory." http://www.kooriweb.org/foley/resources/whiteness/summary_of_whiteness_theory.pdf

Van Soest, D. 1995. "Peace and Social Justice." In *The Encyclopedia of Social Work*, edited by R.L. Edwards and J.G. Hopps. Washington, DC: NASW Press.

Von Mises, L. 1953. *The Theory of Money and Credit*. New Haven, CT: Yale University Press.

Walter, M., S. Taylor, and D. Habibis. 2011. "How White Is Social Work in Australia?" *Australian Social Work* 64, no. 1: 6–19. https://doi.org/10.1080/0312407x.2010.510892

Wiesel, E. 1986. "Hope, Despair and Memory." Paper presented at the Nobel Lecture, Oslo, Norway, 11 December. https://www.nobelprize.org/prizes/peace/1986/wiesel/lecture/

Winant, H. 1994. "Racial Formation and Hegemony: Global and Local Developments." In *Racism, Modernity and Identity: On the Western Front*, edited by A. Rattansi and S. Westwood. London: Polity Press.

Yee, J., H. Wong, and A. Janczur. 2006. *Examining Systemic and Individual Barriers of Ethnoracial Minority Social Workers in Mainstream Social Service Agencies: A Community Project*. Toronto, ON: Canadian Heritage and Ryerson University, Faculty of Community Services.

Young, I. 1990. *Justice and the Politics of Difference*. New York: Princeton University Press.

Young, S. 2004. "Social Work Theory and Practice: The Invisibility of Whiteness." In *Whitening Race: Essays in Social and Cultural Criticism*, edited by A. Morton-Robinson. Canberra, Australia: Aboriginal Studies Press.

Zembylas, M. 2015. "'Pedagogy of Discomfort' and Its Ethical Implications: The Tensions of Ethical Violence in Social Justice Education." *Ethics and Education* 10, no. 2: 163–74. https://doi.org/10.1080/17449642.2015.1039274

10 Global Citizenship Education: Institutional Journeys to Socially Engaged Students in Canada

EVA ABOAGYE

One of the purposes of post-secondary institutions has been to develop civic knowledge in students. The commitment to civic engagement at institutions has been particularly important in recent times, in a more interconnected and globalized world. Technology has provided instant access and images of whatever is happening in other parts of the world; consequently, campuses of post-secondary institutions have been locations of local, national, and international activism on a number of issues. Global citizenship education (GCE), or education for producing a more globally aware and engaged graduate, is now commonly used to introduce initiatives aimed at educating students to be responsible members of the interconnected and ever-smaller world. Each post-secondary institution that makes GCE a focus has its own way of approaching it, with some institutions approaching it in a more centralized and administrative way and others approaching it with a more decentralized style, with individual schools and faculties leading it.

Writing on global citizenship education, Shultz (2007) discusses various approaches and goals that have been used in global citizenship education in post-secondary institutions. She looked first at the neo-liberal approach that was linked to economic participation and focused on enabling students to acquire the necessary skills for transnational mobility. Study-abroad programs and internationalization of the curriculum were some of the key parts of the neo-liberal approach. The second is what she calls the radical approach, in which students take a more active role in international issues, with a strong opposition to global and multinational institutions, which are seen as creating and perpetuating global inequality. Schultz's third approach is the transformational approach, which looks at factors that cause exclusion and disparity at the local, national, and global levels. It looks at educating students to be more engaged and to understand the causes of inequality and, more importantly, to equip them to make a difference in the world. It is important to recognize that institutions may engage in one or more of Schultz's approaches, and that a number of these approaches can be found at the same time at any given time in the history of post-secondary institutions.

Using Schultz's framing, this chapter presents the approaches of two institutions that have made educating global citizens an institutional goal: Centennial College (Centennial) in Toronto, which started a GCE program in 2004, and the University of British Columbia (UBC) in Vancouver, which started a GCE in 1997. These institutions have been chosen for examination because they represent the dynamic approaches to GCE that are used by post-secondary institutions in Canada. As well, between 2002 and 2014 the author was an employee of Centennial and therefore had an in-depth experience of the institutional GCE processes. For data, this chapter analyses publicly available documents on the institutions; additionally, the author relies on personal observations made at the time that she was an employee at Centennial.

This chapter's definition of global citizenship education follows that offered in chapter 6 by Broom and Bai in this volume. In their chapter, Broom and Bai explore contemporary definitions of the term "global citizenship education." First is the cosmopolitan notion of global citizenship education, which is about nation building; also, there is the notion of global citizenship that is about diversity, social justice, cultural awareness, and human rights. Centennial and UBC both followed the definition of GCE that is about diversity, social justice, cultural awareness, and human rights. Both definitions, however, have something in common, which is a discussion about strategies towards producing citizens who can make an impact in the local and global world. The fact that there are many definitions of global citizenship education also means institutions are able to approach it from many different angles, which are all part of the discussion in this chapter.

Centennial, a large community college located in a suburb of Toronto, has a diverse student population, a strong commitment to social justice, and a history of involvement in the community in which it is located. The college's board of governors developed a diversity statement to clearly declare the institution's commitment to diversity and equity. Part of the statement reads:

> We believe individual and systemic biases contribute to the marginalization of designated groups. These biases include race, sex, gender, sexual

> orientation, age, disability, ancestry, nationality, place of origin, colour, ethnicity, culture, linguistic origin, citizenship, creed (religion, faith), marital status, socio-economic class, family status, receipt of public assistance or record of offence. We acknowledge that resolving First Nations sovereignty issues is fundamental to pursuing equity and social justice within Canada. (Centennial College n.d.b)

In 2004, a new president, Ms. Ann Buller, assumed the leadership of Centennial, who was equally committed to social justice and had a passion for making a difference in the community. Part of Buller's role was to put the above-quoted commitment to social justice and equity into action; thus, she embarked on a process to harness the college's strength in diversity and social justice by creating structures for a learning-centred institution that was focused on global citizenship education. In this way, at Centennial, GCE initiatives and activities came from and were led by the leadership of the institution.

The University of British Columbia also articulated a commitment to preparing students to be global citizens. With a diverse student population, UBC views diversity as a strength and has a focus on global citizenship education. In 1998 UBC created a strategic plan called TREK 2000, which, among other things, called for an intentional commitment to transcultural and intercultural approaches to learning (UBC n.d.a, 3). In 2005, while developing a new strategic plan, there was renewed commitment towards training students to be global citizens. This was affirmed in TREK 2020, which included a statement to "prepare students to become global citizens, promote the values of a civil and sustainable society." Unlike Centennial, where leadership created GCE programs, at UBC leadership used the strategic plan to encourage faculty to develop and implement GCE initiatives, thus making its approach comparatively grassroots.

The Post-Secondary Context and Definition of Global Citizenship Education

This section explains how Centennial and UBC defined global citizenship education; as well, it presents how intergovernmental organizations like UNESCO and the United Nations define global citizenship education.

According to UBC (n.d.a), global citizens are "individuals who have developed an understanding of the interconnected world and who deeply appreciate and value ecological sustainability and social justice" (7). Also, UBC identifies elements for developing global citizenship to include knowledge and understanding; cognitive, social, and practical skills; and dispositions (values and attitudes). UBC's TREK 2020 vision statement states, "The University of British Columbia aspiring to be one of the world's best universities, will prepare students to become exceptional global citizens, promote the values of a civil and sustainable society, and conduct outstanding research to serve the people of British Columbia, Canada and the World."

Centennial (n.d.a) defines global citizenship as "an increasing awareness that our lives are connected to the lives of people across the world, that we are members of a global community with rights and responsibilities to do our part to ensure sustainability of resources, social justice and equity for all are achieved locally and globally." UNESCO (2015) defines Global Citizenship Education as education that "aims to equip learners of all ages with those values, knowledge and skills that are based on and instill respect for human rights, social justice, diversity, gender equality and environmental sustainability and that empower learners to be responsible global citizens" (1). Also, the UN has identified global citizenship education as one of the targets for sustainable development. In the Sustainable Development Goals, Target 4.7 calls for a commitment to ensure that by 2030, "all learners acquire the knowledge and skills needed to promote sustainable development, including among others, through education for sustainable development and sustainable lifestyles, human rights, gender equality, promotion of a culture of peace and non-violence, global citizenship and appreciation of cultural diversity and of culture's contribution to sustainable development." In all these definitions, the common thread is on educating students to take care of themselves, others, and the world's resources.

This chapter presents a case study on global citizenship education initiatives in post-secondary institutions. Heale and Twycross (2018) describe a case study as "an intensive, systematic investigation of a single individual, group, community or some other unit in which the researcher examines in-depth data relating to several variables" (7). In the context of this chapter, Centennial and UBC are studied in depth, providing an opportunity to compare cross-institution approaches to GCE. As stated above, this chapter analyses public documents and reflections of the author, who was employed at Centennial at the time when the college introduced GCE as a signature learning experience for students. The institutions' practices were examined through "text mining" their publicly available documents. That is, in each policy document, the study was interested in examining the use of phrases and words that aligned with global citizenship education as defined by the UN and other organizations. In the end, the document analysis examined how words and phrases such as signature learning experience, equity, diversity, GCE curriculum, international service-learning experiences, global citizenship, human rights, inclusion, and cultural and intercultural competencies, were connected to a "global learning outlook" within institutional mandates.

An Environment for Change: The Student Population

The student population at Centennial was 11,026 (full time equivalents) in the 2017–18 academic year (Colleges Ontario 2019) and about 18 per cent were international students. At the time of the transition under President Buller's administration, Centennial had close to equal numbers of males and females at the school, with females making up a slightly higher proportion. More than a third of the students came from backgrounds with a first language that was neither English nor French. About a quarter of the student population described themselves as Canadian, while a fifth described themselves as South Asian Canadian and a similar proportion as Chinese Canadian. A tenth of the population described themselves as Caribbean Canadian (Aboagye 2009).

The student population at the University of British Columbia is also diverse. In 2015–16, there were a total of 64,798 students at UBC, and out of that number, 17,225 were international students from more than 160 countries, representing about 21 per cent of the student population (UBC 2017). Although both institutions are diverse, the source of their diversity is different. In the 2018–19 academic year, the highest proportions of international students at UBC were from China, followed by United States, India, the Republic of Korea, and Japan (UBC 2019). Earlier, Coutts (2012) had stated that the diversity at UBC was not only from international students; in fact, 45 per cent of all domestic students are of Chinese, Japanese, or Korean background and only 51 per cent of domestic students' first language is English. Providing further detail of the international student population, Coutts explained that 44 per cent of international students are Chinese, Japanese, or Korean; 37 per cent speak English as a first language; and 19 per cent are from the United States. At Centennial, however, the diversity of the student population could not be pointed to one geographic region; rather, when compared to UBC, students arrived from dispersed national and international regions.

New Leadership and Commitment to Change

Changes in institutional leadership often force institutions to revisit their values, goals, mandates, and practices. At Centennial and UBC, new leadership served as a catalyst to enhance and focus on institutional commitment to diversity and global citizenship education.

At Centennial, President Buller had been a past employee of the institution; she returned with a renewed commitment to diversity and equity and had been given a mandate by the board of governors to leverage diversity as a strength of the institution. Buller created a leadership team and gave it the mandate to create an action plan towards a social justice and inclusive learning environment. Buller's team created a set of action and program documents that would guide decisions at the college. These included reaffirming the institution's mission and revising the college's vision statement, and the creation of new policies, curriculum, and initiatives to support the community around the college. One of those initiatives, Helping Youth Pursue Education (HYPE), took Centennial's commitment to equity and social justice and directly linked it to its immediate community. HYPE was a summer program for out-of-school youth aged thirteen to twenty-nine that helped them transition back to the education system.

At UBC, the focus of their journey was also the result of new leadership and a commitment to leverage students' diversity and create graduates who are passionate about serving their communities. Under President Martha Piper, and in the strategic plans from TREK 2000 to TREK 2020, UBC expressed a commitment to global citizenship education with the goal of "integrating global knowledge, skills and perspectives in the curriculum" (UBC n.d.b, 3). Piper indicated in 2000 that "the graduates of UBC will value diversity, work with and for their communities, and be agents for positive change. They will acknowledge their obligations as global citizens, and strive to secure a sustainable and equitable future for all." As with any organization, making profound institutional changes requires putting in place structures to support that change; plus, it requires mobilizing knowledge so that those involved can understand the changes and the principles underpinning those changes.

The Structures and Guiding Principles for Change

Centennial and UBC took different approaches for their GCE journeys. These approaches could also be attributed to differing institutional cultures: typically, in Canada, faculty in the university sector are granted much more curriculum freedom than their college counterparts. Thus, and not surprisingly, while Centennial College took a more centralized approach, the process at the UBC was more diffused and implemented from the faculty level. An advantage of using a more centralized approach is that the commitment gets implemented in all areas of the institution, as against when it is championed from the faculty level, where not all faculties may have the same level of commitment to the initiative. Limits of this centralized approach are that administration could implement change in more autocratic ways than desired.

One of the main commitments at Centennial College was a plan to make the college into a learning-centred institution. Buller began a college-wide discussion about making the college "a truly learning-centered college; one that competes effectively in the new post-secondary education environment by putting students first in everything we do … we could do this by drawing on our long-standing strengths, and by building new capabilities that would make us a leader in Canada and the world" (Centennial College 2005). Consequently, in 2005, a taskforce was created to work on specific parts of the learning-centred institution.

The concept of the learning-centred college was developed by Terry O'Banion (1997), who identified some key foundational principles for a learning centered college. According to him, the learning centered college (1) creates substantive change in individual learners; (2) engages learners as full partners in the learning process, with learners assuming primary responsibility for their own choices; (3) creates and offers as many options for learning as possible; (4) assists learners to form and participate in collaborative learning activities; (5) defines the roles of learning facilitators by the needs of the learners; and (6) its facilitators succeed only when improved and expanded learning can be documented for its learners (47).

For Centennial College, the process of becoming a learning-centred institution involved adopting O'Banion's principles as well as principles that were unique to the college. Principles unique to Centennial included: to create change in individual learners; to assist learners in collaborative learning activities; to use learners' needs to define the role of leaders and learning facilitators; to document improved and expanded learning; to create accountability for learning throughout the organization; and to entrench diversity and human rights principles and competencies. The process of becoming a learning-centred institution started with the revision of the college's academic framework and the reaffirmation of Centennial's commitment to student success, access, excellence, inclusion, technology, promoting communities of learning, and encouraging partnerships.

The transition into this learning-centred institution led to the creation of new roles and positions, which included the position of Chief Learning Officer and Vice President, Academic, as well as the Centre for Organizational Learning and Teaching, which provided professional development opportunities for faculty and staff. There were also institutional changes, such as the change of the Human Rights Office into the Office of Equity, which later evolved into the Institute for Global Citizenship and Equity.

President Buller created a taskforce with three sub-groups: Learning for All, Performance Indicators, and Signature Learning Experience (SLE), which were to lead the changes. Among other activities, the SLE taskforce developed curriculum for a course that later became the Global Citizenship and Equity course. An international service-learning component was later added to the course, and the Philosopher's Café, a forum to discuss issues of global citizenship and equity; a journal of global citizenship and equity; and a magazine, Global Citizen Digest, were added to share ideas and practices on global citizenship and equity. Altogether, the work of these three sub-groups formed the backbone for a learning-centred college.

At UBC, it was more individual schools and departments that developed initiatives to move the global citizenship agenda forward. Global citizenship activities and programs included a global citizenship project by the Faculty of Arts and Science; a joint program by the Faculty of Education with the Centre for Intercultural Communications; and the establishment of a global service-learning endowment. There were also specific activities for students that included a forum for discussing global citizenship issues, initiated by the Vice President of Student Affairs. Also, there were specific student-initiated activities, and an outreach program to the external community. Finally, there was the development of a toolbook with resources to support faculty implementing global citizenship principles in their curriculum.

Centennial College: The Signature Learning Experience

At Centennial, the development of SLE for students was assigned to the above-mentioned sub-group of the President's Taskforce, which was tasked with working out the details of what the experience would look like and how to link it to the college's commitment to human rights and diversity. Signature learning experiences are normally developed by institutions to provide students with additional learning outside their core program areas. Shulman (2005), who studied signature pedagogies in professional education, documents the characteristics of signature pedagogies. According to him, these are pedagogies of uncertainty, pedagogies of engagement, and pedagogies of formation. They are pedagogies of uncertainty because the process relies on the response of students to each other and to the instructor, and neither the instructor nor the students know exactly what is going to happen. They are pedagogies of engagement because they work best when the students are actively participating in the learning, and they are pedagogies of formation because they teach students habits of mind and of heart. They can build identity and character, dispositions and values.

In general, institutions have approached SLEs in different ways. Kentucky Wesleyan College, for example, has a number of SLEs embedded in their programs. Faculties of the college and a number of departments have created "Signature Learning Experiences that allow students to explore the world around them outside the classroom," which are "designed to help students think critically, appreciate diversity and live successfully in a complex rapidly changing world" (Aboagye 2011, 177). Northeastern University has developed signature co-op placements and experiential learning opportunities all around the world for its students. At Philadelphia University, the approach was to "create a Centre for Signature Learning that will promote, facilitate, and document the development of curriculum that is active, collaborative, real world and infused with liberal arts … The Center will serve as a nexus for continuous faculty development, pedagogical experimentation, and research in the area of active integrative learning. The Center will facilitate the development, refinement, and dissemination of a distinguishing pedagogy for the University" (151).

The focus at Philadelphia was to create what they termed "engaged learning" – that is, learning that is built on doing things and other experiences that allow the student to apply their learning to real-world problems, collaborating with others and developing lifelong learning skills. The goals also included the following:

- All academic programs will include and document components of experiential learning, which may include studio, labs, research, study abroad, fieldwork, short courses, internships, preceptorships and clinical rotations, and co-curricular programs with Student Life.
- Globalize the campus and curriculum through enhanced use of study abroad, short courses, study tours, inter-session experiences, faculty exchange, international/intercultural campus events, global course content and recruitment of international students. (Aboagye 2011, 177)

At Spelman College, the approach is to transform the student and faculty experience by developing an integrated learning plan that connects curricular and co-curricular experiences. The program called My Integrated Learning Experience or Spelman MILE aims to deliver "a more holistic education by integrating a rigorous curriculum with both applied and service learning, teamwork and leadership development, and diversity and global learning" (Spelman College n.d.). The Spelman MILE, according to Spelman College, "will be a distinct signature program, characterized by an integrated learning experience for every student". Spelman hopes to provide the following to their students (taken from their 2011 Strategic Plan):

- Global engagement, including at least one meaningful international travel experience;
- Opportunities for undergraduate research and career related internships;
- Alumnae connections to strengthen our sisterly bonds early on;
- Leadership development focused on individual potential and best practices;
- Service learning that pairs hands-on community engagement and coursework.

In order to proceed with the implementation of the SLE, and in line with the movement towards a learning-centred college at Centennial, it was important for faculty and staff to embrace the concepts that were put forward by the sub-group. The college hired two consultants to facilitate discussion on the SLE. Following the work of the consultants, a faculty member was assigned the responsibility to research the kinds of competencies that faculty and staff would need for the college to begin to embark on a signature learning experience based on diversity. His research looked at different organizational models for achieving equity. The models included:

- The status quo organizations that implement only a limited number of equity initiatives, mostly in response to legislation. (As he put it, the question for these organizations was: Is this necessary?)
- The valuing-diversity organization, where differences are acknowledged and attempts are made to initiate equity initiatives. (The question for these organizations is whether it is "important for the bottom line.")
- The transformative organizations, which recognize that all political/philosophical approaches must be considered in the context of a

> human rights framework. (These organizations embrace equity and inclusion for all social groups). (Singh 2005, 9)

The recommendation from the document was to follow the transformative model. Describing the model in her report, the president stated that: "The transformative model described in the document goes beyond valuing differences to seeking to actively eliminate injustice and inequity in the whole organization and developing new competencies to reflect our diversity" (Centennial College 2005). This was the direction that Centennial College decided to embark on in this project.

The research made recommendations for principles and practices to be used for the transformation of the curriculum. Some of the key areas of learning recommended for students were critical historical context of Canada's peoples; analysis of the structures that perpetuate and maintain inequality; theories of difference; developing social responsibility; and professional preparation. The research also looked at competencies for faculty and staff. In her final report on the work of the President's Taskforce on Learning, the president summed it up by writing: "We want to create a distinctive and inclusive learning environment that will enable students to integrate and apply knowledge, skills and attitudes to value diversity, promote social justice and become socially responsible in both local and global communities" (Centennial College 2006).

University of British Columbia: Global Citizenship Activities

At UBC, with its decentralized approach, various parts of the university community created activities to enhance global citizenship education. At the faculty level, there was the Terry Project, created by the Faculty of Arts and Sciences, which was an interdisciplinary project to educate undergraduate students about pressing global issues like climate change, poverty, conflict, and disease. The project had many parts, including a speaker's series, TEDx student conference, an interdisciplinary academic course, and an online community. The course was called the Arts and Science Integrated Course – Global Issues (ASIC 200), where students could learn about selected global issues from all perspectives.

Other faculties also developed global citizenship projects and incorporated global citizenship issues and ideas in their core and elective courses. The Faculty of Education, for example, worked with the Centre for Intercultural Communication and developed a course about global citizenship that brought students in three countries together in an online environment. This allowed students to work and learn together, enriching their learning environment. The faculty also developed the Global Students Speakers' Bureau, which supported international and domestic students in developing their global citizenship narratives. A global service-learning endowment was established to support students as global citizens responding to those in need around the world.

There were student-initiated projects, such as the Global Outreach Students Association, the Youth millennium project, and the Community Health Initiative by University Students. The university also created a learning exchange to offer educational opportunities to people in Vancouver's Eastside, as well as engage UBC students, faculty, and staff in a process of service and reflection. In order to consolidate the changes and to provide resources for faculty, staff, and students, a toolbook was created.

Curriculum Change and Renewal

The work at Centennial on the diversity framework set the context for the transformation of the college curriculum. The college was set on a path of providing students with an education that would be transformative and would also be based on social justice and equity principles. Thus, Centennial embarked on a journey that involved a complete overhaul of existing pedagogical approaches and put the issue of diversity and inclusion in the classroom and in the curriculum, and at the centre of teaching and learning. Hackman (2005) discusses five essential learning components for social justice education, and indicates that they should provide the student with the specific tools they need in their learning journey. First is content mastery, which consists of the student getting factual information, contextualization, and analysis at both the macro and micro level. The other elements include critical thinking and the analysis of oppression, tools for action and social change, personal reflection, and awareness of multicultural group dynamics. The changes that took place in the curriculum at Centennial College allowed programs to incorporate some of these elements.

In her article, "Leadership for Social Justice and Equity," Kathleen Brown (2004) looks at a process for developing academic leaders who are "committed to social justice and equity" (77). She identifies three pedagogical strategies that can be used to educate people in social justice and equity: critical reflection, rational discourse, and policy praxis. She writes, "A critical stance frames this discussion by outlining clearly the need for professors to retool their teaching and courses to address issues of power and privilege" (78). She proposes a model that "promotes awareness through critical reflection, acknowledgement through rational discourse, and action through policy praxis." In all these theories, critical thinking, some reflection, and a call to action are an anchor for global citizenship education.

The question of how students are educated continues to be of interest to academics, and how we prepare students for the world should be of concern to all academics; Centennial College was actively engaged in this dialogue. Merryfield et al. (2008) look at the whole idea of developing world-mindedness in students, and ask the following questions, which are central to the debate on how students should be educated: "Are today's students being prepared to understand and become engaged as world-minded citizens? Will they take off the blinders of ethnocentricism or ignorance and see the entire world? Will they learn from other cultures and care about the rest of the planet?" (7). These seem to be the driving questions for both institutions; and from the journeys they undertook, the answer seems to be that as institutions, we are going to make it possible for that to happen.

The Process for Curriculum Innovation

The SLE taskforce at Centennial made recommendations to the college to adopt a signature learning experience for students that would be unique to the college. After the work of the task force was done and their recommendations submitted to the president, a working group was struck to work out the details for a course on global citizenship and equity. The working group was made up of faculty representatives from each of the eight schools. The group "engaged in their own learning activity to understand social justice and diversity issues up-close" as part of the process. The group also created a textbook to go with the course. This was groundbreaking work. As Gaudelli (2009) points out in his article, "A variety of factors may explain why global citizenship curriculum making remains largely untouched in the space of schools and in the hands of teachers and students, namely due to a lack of consistency, lack of curriculum history, and lack of epistemological clarity" (77). The working group at Centennial worked on creating a curriculum for global citizenship, which would be a compulsory general education course for all students at the college.

At the University of British Columbia, the creation of the educators' toolbook on global citizenship helped bring together stories of best practices that could be shared among faculty, and also provided resources they could use. The toolbook provided key elements for faculty in developing courses that would embed global citizenship competencies. The areas of competency covered by the toolbook are presented in the appendix of this chapter. They covered four broad areas: Knowledge and Understanding, Dispositions, Social, and Cognitive Skills, and under each of these broad areas were a number of technical and soft skill areas to cover. The toolbook goes on to provide specific topics to be covered in those four areas and provides examples of how other faculty have incorporated these skills in their curriculum. Identifying the four areas and some details ensured that even though each faculty independently decided on how to incorporate GCE in their curriculum, there was some consistency on the areas that were covered.

Global Citizenship Courses as an Integral Part of Developing Students Who Are Global Citizens

Centennial College: The Signature Learning Experience (SLE) Course for Students

The main component of the SLE is the course that was developed. The course itself provided a framework for exploring five core concepts: Personal Identity and Values; Inequality and Equity; Social Analysis; Social Action; and Reflective Practice. Through the course, the understanding of historical and theoretical concepts is developed, as well as critical thinking and analytical skills. A program advisory committee made up of internal and external members was also created to provide advice and input on the new course. The working group created a course on global citizenship and equity with learning outcomes and expectations. The signature learning experience general education course was introduced in 2006 as General Education 500: Signature Learning Experience. It was described as follows: "This course provides the opportunity to develop the skills required to work and live in a diverse world. It represents a foundational, unique and critical look at the roots and impact of inequality and discrimination related to issues of social justice, the environment, technology and energy. Learners explore personal and social responsibility in their communities, personal lives and in global and local work environments. Critical analysis of ideas and the examination of values and identities will assist learners to develop communication, advocacy and conflict resolution skills" (Centennial College 2010).

The SLE Working Group developed a textbook called *Global Citizenship from Social Analysis to Social Action*. The course was piloted in Fall 2006, Winter 2007, and Summer 2007. Professional development activities were organized for faculty who were assigned to teach the course. In addition to the general education course, there was also portfolio learning, involving the use of portfolios by students to document their learning development as global citizens throughout their program of study. As well, there was professional development and learning for all college staff, through specific learning activities and also through making the compulsory course available to staff. The final portion was the embedding of equity and global citizenship competencies across the college by encouraging people to value diversity and difference, and to embrace and promote equity and inclusion.

University of British Columbia: Global Issues in an Arts and Sciences Course

At UBC, an interdisciplinary course was created for both science and arts students with the knowledge and the practical skills required to become engaged citizens in the local, national, and international civil community. The course, ASIC 200: Global Issues in the Arts and Sciences, allowed students drawn from both the Faculty of Science and the Faculty of Arts to think about global issues and the responsibilities and obligations of global citizenship in a critical manner.

The learning objectives of ASIC 200 were:

- Acquire a range of analytical perspectives used in the physical and life sciences and the social sciences and humanities to investigate global issues.
- Build an appreciation for the importance of interdisciplinary knowledge, education, and dialogue in meeting global challenges.
- Actively participate in group exercises to develop team work and leadership abilities.
- Develop the skills necessary for active engagement in global issues in local, national, and international civil society, which will include future studies, role-play scenario design, educational writing, final report composition, and creative expression and presentation of ideas.[1]

A number of programs also incorporated global citizenship in their curriculum at UBC. For example, in media studies, the global citizen stream considers questions such as:

- What does it mean to be a citizen?
- How have forces of globalization changed the meanings and practices of citizenship?
- How are we shaped by and identified with our local, ethnic, and national communities?
- What are our responsibilities and obligations as citizens, on both a local and global scale, in thinking about representing others and ourselves?

- Which stories and memories are heard in particular places and times, and which others are silenced?

There is also a general global citizenship course, Perspectives on Global Citizenship. The course is designed to complement students' specialized areas of learning, and to challenge students to consider what responsibility they have – within their political, social, cultural, and professional contexts – to participate as active global citizens. Themes in the course include:

- Ethics of global citizenship;
- What is global citizenship;
- The challenges of global divisions: race, ethnicity, nation, state;
- Challenging old conceptions of citizenship: diversity and multiculturalism;
- The challenge of being informed: media, communications and critical thinking;
- Poverty;
- Requirements for a healthy society;
- Consumerism and consumer choices;
- Human impact on the environment;
- Sustainability;
- Global citizenship in action.

These are all opportunities that were available to students at UBC, but unlike at Centennial, they were not compulsory courses, so students who were interested could choose to explore developing their skills as global citizens.

Building Reflective and Critical Thinkers

For both UBC and Centennial, reflective practice was an important part of the curriculum. Through the courses, students gained an understanding of historical and theoretical concepts, learned to reflect on those thoughts as well as developing critical and analytical skills. Reflection is seen as an important part of the development of the student. In her article on defining reflective thinking, Rodgers (2002) examines the theory of reflective thinking as developed by John Dewey. Rodgers identifies four main criteria for reflection:

1. Reflection is a meaning-making process that moves a learner from one experience into the next with deeper understanding of its

relationships with and connections to other experiences and ideas. It is the thread that makes continuity of learning possible, and ensures the progress of the individual and, ultimately society. It is a means to essentially moral ends.
2. Reflection is a systematic, rigorous, disciplined way of thinking, with its roots in scientific inquiry.
3. Reflection needs to happen in community, in interaction with others.
4. Reflection requires attitudes that value the personal and intellectual growth of oneself and of others. (845)

Student Reflection on the Global Citizen Course

On the website of the University of British Columbia, reflection posts from some of the students (UBC Global Citizens n.d.) speak to both what the students wanted out of the course, what they gained from it, and how it transformed them for the future (UBC n.d.b). This reflection by Lauren Shykora, a student in Global Citizens 2015–16 with an intended major of international relations, speaks both to the pedagogy and instruction and also to its impact on her future career:

> I chose the CAP Global Citizens Stream because it immersed me in a small yet diverse student group to collaborate and discuss a wide range of contemporary topics of global citizenship, while linking ideas between different discourses. The joint lectures with all CAP professors were particularly memorable and highlighted the interactive and collaborative nature of the CAP program. My year in CAP consolidated my decision to major in international relations, and I hope to later find a career in international humanitarian work.

Nicolo Jimenez, on the other hand, from the same year and with an intended major in human geography, articulates his desire to be part of a community both in and out of the classroom and to the specific content that he got out of the course:

> I chose to enrol in CAP was because I longed to be part of a community that strove for excellence not only in the classroom, but as active global citizens. Through the Global Citizens stream, I was exposed to a wide array of courses that challenged us to examine our world in their specific contexts and to make connections across multiple academic discourses. CAP made the daunting transition from high school to university almost seamless and enabled me to develop great relationships with my peers, but also with my professors over the school year.

The reflective piece in the course at Centennial was meant to allow students to think about the things they had learnt and experienced in life. After the pilot project, some of the students were able to present some of their work at various college events. The presentations documented some of the transformative learning that was taking place in the classroom. Anita Bouchard, a student from 2008, commented on her learning experience: "The class opened me up to a lot of concepts, some of which I keep in mind even now, and probably will for the rest of my life. By the end of the class, I was sorry to see it end – it was such an amazing experience and I will never forget it" (Centennial College 2008). Imran Hasan, a student from 2007, commented: "After being exposed to the range of topics that GNED 500 offers, my thirst for knowledge has substantially increased. The SLE has helped me to tie in politics, history, social justice and debate at a level I can appreciate and understand" (Centennial College 2008).

Institutional Initiatives to Embed GCE

At UBC, the Office of Regional and International Community Engagement was created, which is committed to working to overcoming complex social and ecological challenges, while Centennial created the Institute for Global Citizenship and Equity.

Other initiatives at Centennial included a number of publications, conferences, and workshops, and a discussion forum and a social action fund to support social action projects. The publications included a magazine, *Global Citizen Digest*, which was mainly for internal community members and allowed faculty, staff, and students to explore ideas on global citizenship and equity and share some of their thoughts and practices. There was also an academic journal, *Journal of Global Citizenship and Equity Education*, which allowed people to publish academic articles on global citizenship and equity education and was more focused on the external community. A discussion forum called The Philosopher's Café was also introduced.

Conclusion and Key Lessons for Implementing GCE

This chapter has discussed how two institutions approached the development of GCE curriculum differently. While Centennial took a more centralized approach, at UBC, individual departments and faculties decided if they wanted to implement GCE in their programs. There are advantages and disadvantages to each approach. With the centralized approach, there was more commitment from the college leadership, with resulting resources being made available for the initiative. Relatively speaking, GCE was uniformly implemented through a compulsory general education course for all students. The disadvantages were that it took some time to get faculty to "buy into" the changes and to take full responsibility of the initiative; also, this approach did not allow for departments to be innovative and creative in their implementation.

At UBC, once the idea was approved for the institution, individual departments and faculties were encouraged to implement it and to develop their own initiatives. There was faculty ownership of the GCE initiative; as well, the decentralized approach allowed room for creativity and innovation. Comparatively, the disadvantage was that it did not achieve the cross-university implementation that Centennial achieved, because not all faculties implemented GCE in their programs.

Critical thinking has always been a part of the process and expected outcomes of post-secondary education. What is unique with GCE is that with critical thinking comes the expectation and facilitation of students' action. Both Centennial and UBC encouraged students to critically reflect on their own lives and experiences, and also on global issues. Having a reflective portion to GCE allows students to solidify the learning and also helps them articulate the learning. Centennial took this a step further by creating electronic portfolios as a requirement for GCE. These enabled students to showcase their professional growth and learning in GCE and also to make this accessible to potential employers.

At both institutions, community partnerships were developed at the departmental or faculty level. Most initiatives were mainly with community organizations with which faculty were already working or had existing projects and partnerships. These projects involved both local and international partnerships. As noted in chapter 7 by Naidoo and Benjamin and chapter 6 by Broom and Bai, both in this volume, questions and concerns exist about the long-term impact of these short-term international service-learning experiences and how much students are able to learn during those trips. Yet it has also been shown that service learning can help to reinforce the learning in the classroom (see chapter 8 by Gisolo and Stanlick in this volume).

The idea of providing students with a transformative education and inculcating in them shared values and action in making a difference in the world is one of the United Nation's targets in the Sustainable Development Goals (SDGs) developed in 2015. In Target 4.7 of the SDGs there is a call for education to do more than provide technical skills to students; it calls for education to create a global citizen for a more sustainable world. For post-secondary institutions, the SDGs provide further momentum for GCE. Centennial and UBC took different modes to create institutions that are committed to global citizenship and also to educating students to be more aware and caring of their world. For Centennial, approaching GCE from a centralized perspective allowed it to be implemented across all programs. It also had the advantage of a uniform curriculum content.

At UBC, many faculties adopted their own approaches to GCE and introduced different initiatives within programs aimed at educating students to be global citizens. This approach allows for more creativity and innovation at the department level, but does not allow for a uniform curriculum or for it to be implemented across the institution.

Our world currently faces a number of challenges, poverty, inequity, terrorist threats, and environmental degradation, for which we seek answers. As we move into a new global era where the world is looking at the 2015 SDGs and hoping that we give the next generation the skills and values they need for the world today, focusing on educating post-secondary students to be global citizens will take a more central focus in discussions. Institutions will be looking at how best to approach this in their institutions, and these two examples provide options for institutions as they define their own journeys to graduate students who are true global citizens.

Appendix. University of British Columbia's Toolbook Competencies

Element	Component Parts
Knowledge and Understanding	Social justice and equity Diversity Globalization and interdependence Sustainability Environment and resources Peace and conflict
Dispositions (Values and Attitudes)	Individual self-esteem Empathy and respect Commitment to social justice and equity Valuing and respecting diversity Concern for the environment Commitment to action
Social Skills	Communication Education and public information skills Participation Leadership
Cognitive Skills	Critical thinking Analytical thinking Reflective thinking Strategic thinking

Source: UBC (n.d.a).

NOTE

1 From the course outline, at https://www.terry.ubc.ca/2011/01/06/asic-200-course-outline-2011/, accessed 25 June 2020.

REFERENCES

Aboagye, E. 2009. "Diversity at Centennial." *Global Citizen Digest*, Centennial College, inaugural issue: 42–5. https://p.widencdn.net/hpz79i/IGCE_GCDigest-2009fall

– 2011. "Developing Signature Learning Experiences: A Case Study of an Institution's Transformative Journey towards Global Citizenship and Equity." *Journal of Global Citizenship and Equity Education*, no. 1: 148–63.

Brown, K.M. 2004. "Leadership for Social Justice and Equity: Weaving a Transformative Framework and Pedagogy." *Educational Administration Quarterly* 40, no. 1: 77–108. https://doi.org/10.1177/0013161x03259147

Centennial College. 2005. "Becoming the Learning-Centered College: An Update on the President's Task Force on Learning." https://p.widencdn.net/hpz79i/IGCE_GCDigest-2009fall

– 2006. "Becoming the Learning-Centered College: Final Report on the President's Task Force on Learning." Toronto: Centennial College.

– 2008. "Signature Learning Experience: Global Citizenship, Social Justice and Diversity." Internal document available from the Centre for Organizational Learning and Teaching.

– 2010. "Global Citizenship: Social Analysis to Social Action." Course outline.

– 2011. "Developing Signature Learning Experiences: A Case Study of an Institution's Transformative Journey towards Global Citizenship and Equity." *Journal of Global Citizenship and Equity Education*, no. 1: 148–63.

– n.d.a. "Global Citizenship and Equity Integration." https://www.centennialcollege.ca/centres-institutes/centre-for-global-citizenship-education-and-inclusion/global-citizenship-education/global-citizenship-and-equity-integration/

– n.d.b "Statement of Diversity." https://www.centennialcollege.ca/about-centennial/college-overview/statement-of-diversity/

Colleges Ontario. 2019. "Environmental Scan Student and Graduate Profiles 2019." https://www.collegesontario.org/en/resources/2019ES-student-graduate-profiles

Coutts, L. 2012. "Who Are Our Students? Implications for Teaching and Learning." UBC, Centre for Teaching, Learning and Technology, 15 August. https://ctlt.ubc.ca/2012/08/15/who-are-our-students-implications-for-teaching-and-learning/

Gaudelli, W. 2009. "Heuristics of Global Citizenship Discourses towards Curriculum Enhancement." *Journal of Curriculum Theorizing* 25, no. 1: 68–85.

Hackman, H.W. 2005. "Five Essential Components for Social Justice Education." *Equity and Excellence in Education* 38: 103–9. https://doi.org/10.1080/10665680590935034

Heale, H., and A. Twycross. 2018. "What Is a Case Study?" *Evidence Based Nursing* 21, no. 1: 7–8. https://doi.org/10.1136/eb-2017-102845

Merryfield, M., J. Tin-Yau Lo, S. Cho Po, and M. Kasai. 2008. "Worldmindedness: Taking Off the Blinders." *Journal of Curriculum and Instruction* 2, no. 1: 6–20. https://doi.org/10.3776/joci.2008.v2n1p6-20

O'Banion, T. 1997. *A Learning College for the 21st Century*. Lanham, MD: Rowman and Littleman.

Philadelphia University. n.d. "Strategic Plan 2010–2013." http://www.philau.edu/strategicinitiatives/signaturelearninggoals.htm. Accessed 4 May 2020.

Rodgers, C. 2002. "Defining Reflection: Another Look at John Dewey and Reflective Thinking." *Teachers College Record* 104, no. 4: 842–66. https://doi.org/10.1111/1467-9620.00181

Shulman, S. 2005. "Signature Pedagogies in the Professions." *Daedalus* 134, no. 3: 52–9.

Shultz, L. 2007. "Educating for Global Citizenship: Conflicting Agendas and Understandings." *Alberta Journal of Educational Research* 53, no. 3: 248–58.

Singh, C. 2005. "Curriculum Diversity Framework Document." Internal document available from the Centre for Organizational Learning and Teaching, Centennial College.

UNESCO. 2015. "Global Citizenship Education: UNESCO's Approach." 21 January. http://www.unesco.org/new/fileadmin/MULTIMEDIA/HQ/ED/pdf/questions-answers-21jan-EN.pdf

United Nations. 2015. "Transforming our World: The 2030 Agenda for Sustainable Development." UN Resolution A/RES/70/1. Adopted 25 September.

University of British Columbia (UBC). 2019. "2018/19 Annual Report on Enrollment." https://academic.ubc.ca/sites/vpa.ubc.ca/files/documents/2018-19%20Enrolment%20Report.pdf

– 2017. *2016/17 Annual Report on Enrolment*. Vancouver: UBC.

– n.d.a. *Road to Global Citizenship: An Educator's Toolbook*. Edited by Y. Harlap. Vancouver: UBC.

– n.d.b. "Global Citizens." Coordinated Arts Program." Accessed 4 May 2020. http://cap.arts.ubc.ca/testimonials/global-citizens/

11 They Want to Be Global Citizens: Now What? Implications of the NGO Career Arc for Students, Faculty Mentors, and Global Citizenship Educators[1]

ANDREW M. ROBINSON

This chapter addresses the impact that global citizenship education (GCE) may have on students and provides insights that can expand GCE beyond the traditional academic sphere into a promising terrain of extracurricular experiences and career preparation.

Many faculty members work hard to deliver GCE that inspires students to want to do something about "human rights, gender equality, [the] promotion of a culture of peace and non-violence, global citizenship and appreciation of cultural diversity" (United Nations n.d.; see also the discussion of GCE and gender inclusion in chapter 5 by Gray-Beerman in this volume). When students respond to a call to human rights action by asking for advice about career options that will allow them to put what they have learned into practice, many faculty have difficulty responding. Reasons for this difficulty vary: either most of faculty members' professional work experience is limited to academia; or, if they have worked outside academia, it is often not in fields in which our students may be interested. Also, when faculty look to the academic literature for assistance, related resources can be limited. This chapter addresses this career-counselling gap with respect to students who seek to apply their GCE in careers in nongovernmental organizations (NGOs). I teach in a human rights program; others may teach in international studies, political science, sociology, international development, global studies, peace and conflict studies, women's studies, geography, or any other programs that open doors to conversations about global citizenship. While students who want to make global citizenship their work may focus in many sectors (government, law, healthcare, certain aspects of private sector, for-profit organizations), many Canadian students who we inspire, like 23 per cent of American liberal arts students (Koc 2010), are interested in working in the nonprofit sector. This chapter aims to assist faculty and students by sharing results of a survey that helps map out key features of the NGO "career arc," and by so doing, reveals traits associated with an individual who is suitable for this sector and associated strategies to use to successfully begin a career in the sector.

Two definitions of the word "arc" make it an apt metaphor for the career. One, the arc as "a continuous progression or line of development" (*Merriam-Webster's New Collegiate Dictionary*, 11th ed.), presents the career as having a beginning and extending out to adult working life. Another definition from the same dictionary, the arc as "something arched or curved," reminds us that, much like standing on an arc, at any point along the career path it can be impossible to see what lies ahead over the "horizon." This inability to see over the horizon can make it difficult for students to assess whether a career started immediately out of college will still be attractive to them in ten or twenty years. It also makes it difficult for students and NGO staff in the early years of their careers to know how best to prepare to get the most out of their careers. When students approach professors, career counselors, and other mentors for guidance, many, especially those who have not worked in this sector, can find it challenging to provide informed advice.

At present, there is little literature that adopts the perspective of students and faculty mentors in the context of global citizenship education. In the non-profit leadership and management literature, scholars have adopted theoretical perspectives to create typologies of career patterns, assess executive director competencies, and evaluate the quality and sustainability of employment in this sector (Ahmed 2005; Almond and Kendall 2000; Amar 2017; Carter 2016; Driver 1980; Harrow and Mole 2005; Norris-Tirrell, Rinella, and Pham 2018; Suarez 2010). Scholars have also embraced managerial perspectives to better understand how to motivate, manage, and retain employees (Akingbola 2006; Ban, Drahnak-Faller, and Towers 2003; Coleman Selden, and Sowa 2015; Jaskyte 2016; Kim and Lee 2007; Kunreuther 2003; Lee and Wilkins 2011; Onyx and Maclean 1996; Turner and Maher 2009). Scholars in other disciplines have adopted a primarily curriculum-development perspective to assess the career relevance of, and to suggest improvements to, their degree programs (Breuning, Parker, and Ishiyama 2001; Collins, Knotts, and Schiff 2012; Dolan 2002; Fletcher 2005; Haas and Robinson 1998; Herman and Renz 2007; Kuh 1995; McKinney, Saxe, and Cobb 1998; Peters and Beeson 2010; Robinson 2013; Sagen, Dallam, and Laverty 2000; Wilson and Larson 2002). Scholars rarely explicitly draw out the implications of their research and related courses for students or early career employees; further, those who do often offer brief, indirect comments in passing (Haas and Robinson 1998, 360; Koc 2010).

This chapter advances our thinking about how to help prepare students for global citizenship–inspired careers by discussing four key topics. First, it offers a partial snapshot of the NGO career arc based upon the results of an exploratory survey conducted in 2010 of staff working in the Canadian province of Ontario. Second, beginning with pre-career experiences, the chapter discusses the importance of diverse forms of participation in extracurricular activities, including involvement in campus clubs, volunteering, and international internships. Third, the chapter addresses the question of whether a BA is sufficient as a credential for entering and advancing within the NGO sector. This third discussion leads to a presentation of typical career patterns of those who work in the NGO sector as well as the positions people hold and the related skills necessary to perform effectively. Fourth, and finally, the chapter discusses the role of gender in the NGO sector.

Presenting the study's findings in this manner is intended to offer "a view over the horizon of the career arc" that students and their mentors can use to make informed decisions about the suitability of GCE in the NGO sector. Further, since this view is informed by the responses of people who work in this sector, it will help students and non-profit staff determine how to best prepare for the next stages in their careers. As such, it is hoped that the chapter finds its way into syllabi of undergraduate career preparation courses.

As discussed by Shultz (2007) and Cameron (2014), this chapter acknowledges that the very meaning of global citizenship and related education is highly contested. Nevertheless, similar to other authors in this volume, the chapter situates itself with respect to a three-part definition of GCE: (1) GCE equips students with knowledge to understand and make sense of major issues and processes that are shaping the world; (2) it encourages students to adopt a sense of responsibility to address world problems; and (3) it provides students with skills and competencies that will enable them to act to address those problems. Given the very broad nature of this tripartite definition of GCE, it should be clear, and this chapter affirms, that GCE is an interdisciplinary project that, when well executed, will require students to explore diverse corners of post-secondary educational institutions.

The three elements of the GCE definition point us towards distinct disciplinary strengths. The first element primarily concerns knowledge about the way the (human) world works; this is primarily the domain of the social sciences (e.g., political science, sociology, economics, history). The second element is much more affective in nature, since it presumes students have a particular orientation towards knowledge: they desire to apply it to address world issues and problems. While this can also be the domain of traditional disciplinary social sciences (depending on the orientation of particular departments), it is especially the domain of specialized interdisciplinary social science programs, like international development, peace and conflict studies, and human rights, that incorporate/apply this element. Finally, the third element, as this chapter emphasizes, concerns practical skills that are not typically the domain of social science programs; rather, they tend to be the domain of programs with a more professional orientation (e.g., leadership, business, social work, public policy) and extracurricular activities and commitments.

Given the involvement of multiple disciplines in realizing the GCE project, we can also note that there are multiple points of entry for students seeking to realize GCE in full. Some students will develop their knowledge of world issues and sense of responsibility to do something about them by majoring in traditional disciplinary or specialized interdisciplinary social science programs, and then develop relevant skills and competencies by taking skills courses from applied and professional programs offered at their post-secondary institutions or by pursuing postgraduate credentials from university professional programs (e.g., social work, MBA, public policy, law) or community college post-graduate certificates (e.g., human resources management, project management, social media marketing). Other students, conversely, will develop practical skills in more professional programs and develop their GCE knowledge and orientation through social science courses taken as electives and/or through post-graduate study.

An important upshot of these observations about how and where students access the various elements of GCE is that if we, as educators, desire to promote GCE, we do not have to leave the possibility that students will put the three parts of global citizenship education together for themselves by happenstance. There are a number of creative ways we can actively assist students to make these connections. Two examples come readily to mind. One is to create specializations within program curricula to point program majors towards the elements of GCE they are missing (e.g., including a global citizenship specialization, made up of relevant social science courses, within a business or social work program, or including a global citizenship skills and competencies specialization, made up of relevant courses from professional and applied programs, within a social science program). The second example is to create, and promote to social science majors, articulation agreements with local community colleges that will enable them to develop practical skills and competencies on an accelerated basis.

The discussion in this chapter adopts the perspective of those teaching in traditional disciplinary or specialized interdisciplinary social science programs and focuses on key aspects of the third part of the definition of GCE: identifying the skills and competencies students will need to live out their global citizenship commitments through their careers and identifying opportunities that will help students develop them. The next section begins by describing the survey method that is the basis of this chapter. The chapter then discusses the survey findings through five sections that address (1) pre-career experiences; (2) career patterns; (3) types of occupations; (4) how executive directors differ from other workers in this sector in terms of their motivations, roles, and skills required to be successful; and (5) the role of gender in career advancement. The discussion of these five survey results sections uses scholarly literature where it is available.

Survey Method

This chapter draws upon selected results from an online survey conducted using Survey Monkey in 2010. The purposes of the survey were: to inform curriculum development in an interdisciplinary undergraduate human rights program; to assess the workplace relevance of social science/liberal arts BAs (Robinson 2013); and to inform the provision of credible advice to students considering careers in the NGO sector. The last purpose is the focus of this chapter. The survey was addressed to staff at Ontario-based NGOs that advance human rights. The survey was reviewed and approved by Wilfrid Laurier University's Research Ethics Board, and was supported with a small grant funding from Laurier's Educational Development Office.

The questionnaire included sixty-five questions.[2] This chapter draws upon responses to questions that addressed respondents' personal and educational backgrounds, the nature of their current positions, the skills they believe are required to be successful in their positions, and, among those respondents who had experience hiring entry-level employees, what they valued when hiring entry-level employees.

The survey was conducted using a two-step non-probabilistic snowball type sampling method. First, the researcher identified over 1,000 organizations, which were reduced to 126 after reviewing organization websites for fit with the study's parameters: the NGO must have staff physically located in Ontario and the NGO must "advance human rights." For this study, an organization was considered to "advance human rights" if one of the following applied to it: (1) it says that advancing human rights (or rights found in the Canadian Charter of Rights and Freedoms) is its core purpose or is part of its core purposes; (2) it says it uses human rights to advance its core purposes;

(3) it justifies its core purposes, at least in part, in terms of human rights; or (4) it includes itself in the directory at Charityvillage.com (a leading Canadian non-profit website) under the heading "Human Rights and Civil Liberties." In the second step, staff members were invited to participate either directly or, where contact information was not available online, by asking executive directors to forward invitations to staff. Whether contacted by email or through regular mail, respondents were provided with a unique identification code to ensure that only appropriate respondents completed the survey. Overall, 220 individuals, including 34 executive directors, responded, and 201 surveys were completed in full.[3] SPSS was used to collate the responses and, where appropriate, to analyse them using chi-square tests of cross-tabulated categories, analysis of variance, and the Mann-Whitney U test; findings that were statistically significant are noted as such in the text.

The study's objectives and its exploratory nature necessitated that it be limited to Ontario-based NGOs that advance human rights. Thus, caution should be exercised in generalizing the nature of the NGO career arc beyond the geographical Ontario context and the subset of NGOs that advance human rights. While such caution is indeed warranted, there are good reasons to believe that the findings discussed here offer insight into NGO careers more broadly. This is because, considering the geographic context, it is quite common in the literature to report on studies limited to federal states or provinces or even subregions within these (see, for example, Haas and Robinson 1998; Kim and Lee 2007; Onyx and Maclean 1996; Suarez 2010). The jurisdiction in this study, the Canadian province of Ontario, is Canada's largest province, has over 13 million inhabitants, and is home to Canada's capital, Ottawa, and its largest city, Toronto. As such, it has much in common with other English-speaking industrialized democracies.

The study's focus on NGOs that advance human rights is broadly encompassing; it reflects the documented trend of NGOs adopting the normative language of human rights (Chong 2009; Hopgood 2009; Kindornay, Ron, and Carpenter 2012; Nelson and Dorsey 2008; Olawoore 2017). For instance, when asked to name the central focus of their current employer, survey respondents identified a broad range of fields, including international development (23 per cent), human rights and civil liberties (18 per cent), poverty and/or social justice (13 per cent), education (9 per cent), health (7 per cent), research and policy development (6 per cent), children, youth, and families (5 per cent), disabilities (3 per cent), and women (3 per cent). The scope of their employers' focus also varied, ranging from those that were purely local to those focused on provincial, national, and international levels. Finally, the organizations also varied in size; about one-third of respondents indicated they worked in organizations with 1–10 employees, one-third in organizations with 11–50 employees, and one-third in organizations with 51+ employees. While the survey respondents represented a broad range of organizations, caution should be exercised when considering these results in the context of NGOs that do not share these characteristics, especially those that rely more heavily on staff with professional credentials (e.g., lawyers, doctors).

Findings and Discussion

Pre-career Experiences

This section explores what the survey responses suggest about the relationship between key pre-career experiences and academic credentials and participation in the non-profit sector after graduation. The observations should be of particular interest to students considering career options and faculty and other mentors offering advice.

IT IS NEVER TOO LATE TO TAKE AN INTEREST IN THE NGO SECTOR

Some undergraduates, when encountering other students who "have wanted to work for an NGO for as long as they can remember," may be intimidated into thinking that it is just too late for them to even try. While one might think that the earlier a person took an interest in the sector, the more likely he/she would be to find employment and be successful in it, the results suggest that this is not necessarily the case.

There is no strong relationship between the time when a person took an interest in the sector and their subsequent employment. Table 11.1 indicates that respondents ($N = 220$) are about evenly divided between early interest-takers, defined as those who started seriously considering working for an organization like their present employer during high school or prior to completing their first post-secondary program (23 per cent + 25 per cent = 48 per cent), and late interest-takers (12 per cent + 36 per cent = 48 per cent), who started later. In fact, 36 per cent of respondents did not seriously consider the sector until after entering the workforce.

The fact that late interest-takers work in the sector does not necessarily mean that the sector is a good fit for them. One way this might be expressed is by their leaving the sector quickly after entering. To test this possibility, respondents were divided between those who have worked in the sector for five years or less ($n = 85$) and those who have

Table 11.1. Time respondent first took an interest in working for an organization like his or her present employer

When respondent first seriously considered working for an NGO	%
In high school or earlier	23
During first degree or diploma	25
During post-graduate study	12
After entering the workforce	36
Don't remember/other	4

worked longer (presumably sufficient time to determine whether the sector is a good fit; n = 132); this revealed no statistically significant difference between early and later interest-takers. Finally, comparison using another proxy for fit – becoming an executive director – also fails to reveal a statistically significant difference between early and late interest-takers.

These observations affirm the relevance of GCE within the post-secondary sector. Despite the exposure to world issues, social justice, and volunteering opportunities that many students receive in high school, these findings suggest that many students who are suited to practice global citizenship through careers in the NGO sector may not even be considering the possibility. These findings suggest that faculty who encounter students who take an interest in the NGO sector as a way to express newfound commitments to global citizenship should feel confident when encouraging late interest-takers to explore this career option.

PARTICIPATION IN CAMPUS CLUBS AND VOLUNTEERING IS CORRELATED WITH CAREERS IN NGOS

Rosch and Collins (2017) suggest that participation in student organizations is associated with career success. This claim finds support from a number of survey questions. For instance, when asked to rate a number of pieces of advice for obtaining a good entry-level job in an organization like the one for which they work, 46 per cent of respondents rated "Volunteer with any NGO" as "vital."

A relationship between participation in campus clubs and volunteering (which was specified as campus-based clubs, associations, campus chapters of non-profits/NGOs, student government, etc.) and NGO careers is also suggested in table 11.2, which shows that 63 per cent of survey respondents indicated they had participated in campus clubs

Table 11.2. Relationship between types of participation in student clubs and volunteering and perception that participation helped respondent obtain first job

Participation in student clubs and volunteering	% expressing belief that participation helped in obtaining first post-education employment
Served in an executive role	63
Never served in an executive role	27
Belonged to one organization	27
Belonged to two to three organizations	51
Belonged to four or more organizations	73

and volunteering.[4] This rate is similar to the percentages of nonprofit staff found to engage in volunteering in Australia (70 per cent; Onyx and Maclean 1996, 339–40) and the United States (73 per cent; Lee and Wilkins 2011, 51). The strength of the connection between volunteering and working in the nonprofit sector is also supported by Lee and Wilkins's (2011) comparative study of public and non-profit managers, in which they found that "people who volunteered were 10 percent more likely to work in the non-profit [than in the public] sector" (53).

Finally, this relationship finds support in respondents' subjective perceptions of its value. When asked if they thought their experience in campus clubs and volunteering helped them obtain their first post-graduation job, 44 per cent said they thought it had impressed the organization that hired them; an additional 6 per cent indicated that their first job was with an organization to which they had belonged as a student.

BUT "JUST" BELONGING DOES NOT APPEAR TO HELP MUCH

The importance of active participation stands out when attention is limited to the 63 per cent of respondents who participated in student clubs and volunteering. For instance, while 63 per cent of those who had held executive positions believed their involvement helped them get their first job, this was only true of 27 per cent of those who never served as an executive ($p < 0.01$). Even more striking, seven of the eight respondents who obtained their first job with an organization to which they had belonged as a student had served in an executive role. A similar pattern emerges when the number of organizations to which respondents reported belonging is considered: while only 27 per cent of those who belonged to just one organization thought their participation helped them obtain their first job, this was true of 51 per cent who belonged to two or three and 73 per cent of those who belonged to four or more ($p < .01$). Students are often told that the real value of joining clubs and volunteering requires active and engaged participation; this advice can now be backed up with empirical evidence based on the experience of people who work in the sector.

A further implication of this finding is that if GCE aims to provide students with the skills and competencies that will enable them to act on their sense of responsibility to address global problems, then such "extracurricular" activities should be considered as part of the overall design of the GCE curriculum. (For a detailed discussion of the implications of this survey's findings for liberal education, please see Robinson [2013]). Of course, another way to build such experiences into curricula is community service learning.

COMMUNITY SERVICE-LEARNING COURSES MAY HELP LATE INTEREST-TAKERS TO FIND REWARDING CAREERS

Responses to questions concerning participation in campus clubs and volunteering were also analysed by dividing respondents between those who were early interest-takers in a career in the NGO sector (i.e., those who said they first seriously considered working for an NGO while they were in high school or while studying for their first degree or diploma) and late interest-takers (i.e., those who first took an interest after completing their first degree or diploma). The results raise serious concerns about the possibility that there may be many students who could become late interest-takers and find rewarding careers in the NGO sector, but do not because they are never exposed to the sector (see, e.g., Nemenoff 2013). While the survey, by its very nature, did not gather data on those who never took an interest in the sector, comparison of late interest-takers to early interest-takers indicates that the later someone takes an interest in the sector, the less likely he/she is to engage in behaviours that correlate to subsequent employment in the NGO sector: early interest-takers are more likely to participate in campus clubs and volunteering (74 per cent versus 51 per cent for late interest-takers, $p < .01$); to have belonged to more than one organization (84 per cent versus 70 per cent, $p < .05$); and to have served in an executive position (71 per cent versus 55 per cent, $p < .05$). These findings lead to the following question: How many more late interest-takers might find rewarding careers in the NGO sector if they had been exposed to community service learning as undergraduates? This question points to the value of placing community service-learning courses (which require students to work a prescribed number of hours with NGOs and, usually, to write reflection papers based on their experience) in post-secondary programs.

Besides providing late interest-takers opportunities to explore global citizenship-friendly career options, which they may never have discovered on their own, service learning can also help prepare them to be successful in such careers. Survey respondents strongly endorsed service learning as general preparation for working in their organizations. Amongst a range of forms of assignments, "Service learning/internship in an NGO" ranked second only to "Individual oral presentation," with 56 per cent of respondents saying it constituted "extremely useful" preparation.

INTERNATIONAL INTERNSHIPS AND EXPERIENCE DO PROVIDE VALUABLE CAREER PREPARATION

While some have questioned the value of international internships and experience (see, e.g., Cameron 2014, 36–7; and Shultz's 2007 description of the neoliberal global citizen as "traveler"), survey respondents suggest that such experiences do hold the potential to provide valuable preparation for successful careers advancing the goals of their organizations. This is suggested by the 47 per cent of respondents who described "International education/volunteering/internships" as an extremely useful form of assignment to prepare for work in their organizations.

Thus, while there are very good reasons to be concerned about how service learning and international experiences as part of the GCE curriculum may construct harmful conceptions of the student as global citizen (see, for instance, chapter 7 by Naidoo and Benjamin in this volume), we should not lose sight of the very practical benefits these experiences can have. Besides providing an opportunity for students of GCE to "do good" in the present (Cameron 2014, 36), such placements, if properly conceived and executed, can help students develop skills, competencies, and relationships that will help them advance global justice throughout their careers.

THE BA IS SUFFICIENT TO SECURE ENTRY-LEVEL POSITIONS

Anecdotal information suggests that students are often told that they need an MA to pursue a career in this sector. This study does not support this advice, at least not for recent graduates seeking entry-level positions. This conclusion finds support in responses to a number of questions. For instance, when asked directly, only 16 per cent of respondents rated a master's degree as "vital" for securing a good entry-level job. Similarly, when those who had experience hiring entry-level employees ($N = 155$) were asked about the desirability of various credentials for entry-level positions, more rated the BA as "highly desired" (46 per cent) than the MA (31 per cent). The employability of the BA is reinforced by examining the highest educational credentials held by respondents in their twenties, those most likely to hold entry-level positions: BA (53 per cent), BA plus post-graduate college diploma[5] (14 per cent), MA (24 per cent), and college diploma (2 per cent). Thus, students who want to gain practical experience after earning a BA, or who just want to take a break from their education, do not appear to be harming their chances to start a career in this sector.

A POST-BA CREDENTIAL APPEARS INCREASINGLY NECESSARY TO PROGRESS IN THE SECTOR

This claim is supported by a number of findings. First, when comparing the highest credential held by respondents aged thirty and over, most of whom should be beyond entry-level positions, the MA is more widely held (39 per cent) than the BA (25 per cent, $p < 0.01$). In fact, 64 per cent of those aged thirty and over hold a post-BA credential (e.g., post-grad college diploma, MA, LLB, PhD). This is similar to the 70 per cent Haas and Robinson (1998, 357) found in Santa Clara County, California, and higher than the 53.1 per cent Lee and Wilkins (2011) found among American non-profit managers (51).

Further analysis suggests that the perceived need to obtain additional credentials is increasing. For instance, when respondents are divided by age in decades, the average number of years between when they earned their two most recent credentials is declining: thirties: 5.5 years; forties: 5.6 years; fifties: 10.5 years; sixties and over: 13.8 years. The increasing pressure to earn a post-BA credential is also suggested by the generally increasing percentage of people who had earned their post-BA degree while they were in their thirties: 39 per cent; forties: 21 per cent; fifties: 18 per cent; sixties: 33 per cent.[6]

While the BA appears to be sufficient for obtaining entry-level positions, students need to be advised that if they intend to pursue careers and advance in this sector, they will likely need to earn a post-BA credential. This also means that undergraduates who are hoping to enter this sector need to be reminded of the importance of maintaining grades that will gain them admission to desirable MA, law, or other relevant programs. As for when best to pursue a postgraduate credential – immediately upon completing the BA or after obtaining some work experience – the survey offers no insight. As for which credential to pursue, students might begin by consulting works by Ahmed (2005), Dolan (2002), and Haas and Robinson (1998).

Finally, this pattern of young workers who are professionally engaged in advancing the project of global citizenship returning to school for further education appears to provide an important additional opportunity to advance the project of GCE. Unlike undergraduates, most of whom have very limited life experience, graduate programs in "applied global citizenship" could provide an opportunity for practitioners to reflect upon deeper issues raised by theorists of GCE (e.g., "thick global citizenship" in Cameron 2014; "postcolonial GCE" in Pashby 2012) in light of their lived experiences. This could also provide an opportunity for faculty to inform their own scholarship by testing their ideas against the experience of such professional graduate students.

Career Patterns

Drawing upon respondents' patterns of movement between organizations and across sectors, their reasons for being attracted to their present positions, and the skills they use in them, this section discusses general features of most careers in the sector, including typical career patterns and differences between recent entrants and those more established in the sector.

THE SPIRAL CAREER IS THE TYPICAL CAREER PATTERN

While NGO and public sector careers are both likely to appeal to those who find intrinsic rewards in serving their community, each sector tends to support distinct career patterns that some individuals will find appealing and others unattractive. As Michael J. Driver (1980) has argued, "organizations and groups can ... develop prevailing career concepts [which include] specific assumptions about reward systems, career paths, the role of development and training, and basic attitudes towards human beings" (12). Driver described four career concepts of which the linear concept is typically associated with the public sector and the spiral concept is typically associated with the non-profit sector (see also Ban, Drahnak-Faller, and Towers 2003; Harrow and Mole 2005; Kim and Lee 2007). This study affirms the association between the NGO sector and spiral careers. The distinctions Driver draws between spiral and linear career concepts provide an excellent comparative framework for students and their mentors to evaluate the potential fit with temperaments and other aspirations.

Onyx and Maclean (1996), following Driver, suggest that career concepts can be distinguished by three key features: "extent and direction of job change, pattern of work values, and preferred organizational processes" (332). Regarding the extent and direction of job change, the linear career "embodies the notion that a career is a series of upward moves within a field. There may be changes in organization to avoid blocking but the key ingredient is steady upward movement" (Driver

1980, 10). The spiral career, by contrast, "is seen as a cyclic process in which one changes field or major direction in cycles about five to ten years. There may be upward movement within a cycle, but the shift between cycles is often lateral." Regarding values, Onyx and Maclean (1996) say that linear careers appeal to "those who value prestige, management skills, high income, power and achievement" (332), while spiral careers appeal to those who cherish work they consider "*both* socially worthwhile and personally rewarding" (341, emphasis in original), and that provides "opportunities for self-development," involves new challenges, requires creativity and multiskilling, and permits them to exercise of autonomy (332). Finally, regarding organizational settings, linear careers are usually pursued within large, hierarchical structures, spiral careers within "open system[s] with low structure" (341).

Consistent with the cyclic nature of the spiral career, survey respondents reported patterns of fairly frequent changes in positions within and across organizations and sectors. Those respondents who had worked ten years or more in the NGO sector since completing their most recent education ($N = 104$) reported holding an average of 2.5 positions (with the same or a different organization) per decade, about 4 years per position. This compares with Onyx and Maclean's (1996) finding of an average of 3.6 positions over the last ten years, or 2.8 years per position (336). While respondents' careers appeared to become more settled as they aged – the average time they reported spending in their most recent position increased steadily with age (twenties: 2.3 years; thirties: 3.9 years; forties: 4.5 years; fifties: 5.9 years; sixties and older: 6.0 years) – the average was still consistent with Driver's five to ten year cycles. Respondents also reported much movement between organizations: 68 per cent reported having worked for more than one organization and, of those, 38 per cent reported having worked for two organizations, 43 per cent for three to five, and 10 per cent for more than six. They also reported much movement between sectors: 30 per cent had worked in one other sector, 6 per cent in two, and 2 per cent in three; among these 20 per cent had experience working in government, 20 per cent in the for-profit sector, and 8 per cent for a union. Even the direction of movements between organizations resisted the linear pattern: only 15 per cent reported having moved exclusively between organizations like their present employer; only 35 per cent worked exclusively with organizations like their present employer since entering the subsector; and fully 51 per cent reported having moved back-and-forth between organizations like their present employer and organizations with a different focus.

Respondents' motivations and values were also consistent with the spiral career pattern. When asked why they chose to work in the

Table 11.3. Percentage selecting reasons for choosing to work in the non-profit/NGO sector

Reason	%
Commitment to social change	82
Philosophical or political commitment	53
Volunteer experience	30
Personal life experience (e.g., former user)	23
By chance/through networking	23
Religious commitment	12
Influence of family (e.g., parents)	11
Other	10
Hours/location convenient for family commitment/lifestyle	9
Study placement	8
Only job available	5

non-profit/NGO sector (table 11.3) the top reasons they cited reflected the desire for work that is socially worthwhile: commitment to social change (82 per cent), and philosophical or political commitment (53 per cent). No other reasons were chosen by more than a third of respondents. Similarly, when asked to rate each of fourteen possible reasons for finding their present position attractive, the top reasons respondents rated as either "Attractive" or "Very attractive" (appendix 1 to this chapter) were consistent with spiral career motivations: work that is socially worthwhile – contribute to social change (97 per cent), organizational philosophy (83 per cent), work on human rights issues (86 per cent); challenges and opportunities for self-development – interesting/challenging work (96 per cent), extend personal skills (86 per cent), career opportunities (68 per cent), change of pace (60 per cent); and autonomy – access to decision-making (74 per cent), influence policy development (72 per cent), work independently (65 per cent). Conversely, values associated with the linear career ranked consistently low: increased salary (42 per cent), greater prestige (40 per cent), and more budget responsibility (32 per cent). Finally, while one might suspect that insecurity of employment is the real reason for the cyclic pattern of respondents' careers, this is not supported by the reasons they gave for entering the sector (the option "only job available" ranked last at 5 per cent), or for finding their current position attractive: previous job ended (29 per cent), job security (37 per cent).

The results also provide indications that respondents work in organizational settings with features typically associated with the spiral career pattern: relatively small, flat/non-hierarchical, emphasizing multiskilling more than specialization, and facilitating "interpersonal closeness" (Driver 1980, 14) or what Onyx and Maclean (1996) call a "social dimension" (338). As for size, the majority of respondents (69 per cent) report working in organizations of less than fifty people: one to ten employees (33 per cent); eleven to fifty (36 per cent); fifty-one or more (31 per cent). Low levels of specialization and an emphasis on multiskilling are suggested by the fact that, when asked to indicate the percentage of a typical week they devote to each of eleven significant functions (e.g., budgeting and financial management, project management, providing service to clientele), respondents reported performing an average of 7.5 functions in an average week. That such multiskilling is a characteristic of the sector and not just of small organizations is suggested by the fact that the average number of tasks performed is almost identical for staff working for organizations with fifty or fewer employees (7.5) and those with more than fifty (7.4). Finally, the relevance of interpersonal closeness/a social dimension is suggested by the fact that 87 per cent of respondents selected "good group of people to work with" as one of their reasons for finding their present position attractive (appendix 1 to this chapter).

One lesson of this section is fairly clear: students considering careers in the NGO sector should be encouraged to seriously consider whether they would be happier pursuing a linear- or a spiral-patterned career. For example, are they more interested in status and promotions or in doing work that is socially worthwhile while exercising a fair degree of control over the nature of their job? Finally, while it is never good practice to accept and to leave jobs lightly, students should be aware that relatively high rates of turnover are rooted in the nature of the sector (junior employees often return to school; spiral careerists tend to leave their positions to seek new challenges), so they can take this into consideration when considering pursuing new opportunities in the future.

MORE ESTABLISHED STAFF MEMBERS TEND TO WORK IN SMALLER ORGANIZATIONS AND PLACE GREATER EMPHASIS ON MANAGEMENT AND FINANCIAL SKILLS

The survey facilitated comparisons between "recent entrants" (treated as those in their twenties) and more established staff (those aged thirty and above), which identified patterns that should be of interest to students, new staff, and their mentors.[7]

Comparison of employment data between recent entrants and more established staff suggests a general pattern whereby staff often begin their careers in larger organizations but tend to move to smaller organizations as they gain experience. This is suggested by the fact that recent entrants are disproportionately employed in larger organizations – they constitute 46 per cent of respondents who reported working in organizations with fifty-one or more employees, but only 19 per cent of those in smaller organizations ($p < .001$) – and that the average age of staff in smaller organizations (forty-three) is significantly higher than in larger organizations (thirty-eight, $p < .01$). Sadly, but not surprisingly, recent entrants' connection to the workplace also appears to be more tenuous: while they hold a proportionate share of full-time jobs, they are over-represented among those holding contract positions: they hold 42 per cent of contractual positions, but only 23 per cent of ongoing positions ($p < .01$). The positions of recent entrants also appear to be slightly, but significantly, more specialized as measured by the average number of types of tasks they perform in a typical week (7.1 versus 7.9 for those thirty or older, $p < .05$). Thus, recent entrants working in larger organizations would be well advised to network with more senior colleagues in smaller organizations to learn why they work in these organizations and, if the reasons prove desirable, how to prepare to obtain such positions.

Other comparisons suggest that people's priorities may change as they become more established in this sector. For instance, when asked why they found their current position attractive, recent entrants placed greater emphasis than established staff on characteristics related to becoming established in the workforce – training opportunities ($p <. 05$), career opportunities ($p < .001$), job security ($p < .05$); gaining status and broadening experience – greater prestige ($p < .01$), more staff responsibility ($p < .05$), work with new client group ($p < .05$); as well as change of pace ($p < .05$) and good people to work with ($p < .001$). When asked about the importance of various skills and competencies to success in their positions, more established staff placed greater emphasis than recent entrants on skills and competencies related to management and finance – ability to hold effective meetings ($p < .05$), negotiation skills ($p < .001$), accounting, budgeting, financial management ($p < .05$), grant writing ($p < .001$), understanding the government context ($p < .001$), and understanding of non-profit law/legal issues ($p < .05$). This comparison provides an excellent example of the value of looking over the horizon of the career arc. As Ban, Drahnak-Faller, and Towers (2005) observe, it is often the case that "people in nonprofits have backgrounds in social work, theology or humanities that do not provide them with adequate management skills" (149). With knowledge of the priorities of more established staff, students and recent entrants may accelerate their careers by taking courses or seeking experiences to help develop them earlier.

Types of Occupations

This section explores an important consideration for those contemplating careers in any sector of the economy: the types of occupations it supports and the key skills and tasks that these occupations tend to require. Differences are noted between three distinct categories of occupation: core staff, support staff, and executive directors.

THE SECTOR MAINTAINS A VARIETY OF TYPES OF POSITION

The survey asked respondents for job titles (actual or descriptive) that indicate what they do in their present positions. These responses informed the creation of a typology of nine types of occupations in the sector (see appendix 2 to this chapter). Given the small numbers in some of the occupational groups, the percentages should only be treated as general indicators of the relative size of the categories in the sector. If a distinction is made between core staff – whose occupations are closely related to the organization's defining mission – and support staff – who perform functions that are vital to the life of the organization as an organization, but involve skills that are not closely related to its defining mission (e.g., internal operations and administrator/executive assistant) – then a first observation is that core staff positions make up the overwhelming majority of occupations in the sector. Within core staff, program management, at 42 per cent, is by far the largest type of occupation. This includes job titles related to creating, managing, delivering, and promoting the organizations' programs. The next largest category is executive director (16 per cent). While this proportion may seem large, it is less surprising once it is recalled that one third of respondents work for organizations with one to ten employees. The executive director category was followed by advocacy (11 per cent) and a number of other core staff occupations clustered around 5 to 6 per cent: managing youth, volunteers, campus chapters, and/or membership; fundraising; public relations/communications; and research.

To gain a general sense of the mix of functions associated with each occupation, answers to the question concerning the percentage of a typical week respondents devote to each of eleven functions were compared to produce appendix 2 to this chapter, which shows the top three functions associated with each position category. While the functions, and especially their ranking, represented in appendix 2 should be treated as illustrative rather than definitive, the takeaway point for students and their mentors should be that there is no such thing as a "job in an NGO." Rather, there are a wide range of specific occupations, each with its own mix of responsibilities and, thus, each suited to people with different temperaments, abilities, and skill sets. Students would be well advised to learn about these different positions and to avail themselves of low-risk opportunities to give them a trial run through student clubs, volunteering, and internships. Students also need to know that specialized courses and training programs exist to prepare them for many of these occupations, such as fundraising and development, event management, and volunteer management.

Besides providing a very general basis for comparing NGO sector occupations, two other lessons can be drawn from appendix 2. First, those considering careers in this sector would do well to seek opportunities to gain skills and experience in project management, as this is the only function that is listed for all types of core staff. Second, students who presently lack skills related to management functions should not consider this an insurmountable barrier to entering the sector, as these functions do not rank highly amongst the work performed by core staff. But, as noted in the comparison of recent entrants to more established staff, students should be advised to seek opportunities to develop such skills as soon as possible.

EXECUTIVE DIRECTORS ARE DIFFERENT

Students and recent entrants who hope to become executive directors will likely be interested to know what this survey indicates about executive directors. While NGO executive directors who responded to this survey ($N = 34$) do not differ significantly from their colleagues with respect to the reasons they entered the sector, key differences do appear with respect to why they found their present position attractive and the functions their positions require them to perform.

With respect to why they found their present positions attractive, the executive directors' responses differed from their colleagues' by placing significantly greater emphasis on "influence policy development" ($p < .01$), "access to decision making" ($p < .05$), and the more linear-career oriented characteristic, "more budget responsibility" ($p < .05$). Their colleagues, conversely, placed more emphasis on factors Driver (1980) associates with the spiral career pattern: growth – training opportunities ($p < .05$), and career opportunities ($p < .05$) – and nurturance – good people to work with ($p < .05$), good management structure ($p < .05$) – as well as job security ($p < .01$). To clarify, the point is not that these motivations ranked especially highly for executive directors or their colleagues, but they did differ and the differences were statistically significant.

Regarding the work their positions require them to perform, executive directors' responses suggest, unsurprisingly, that they spend more time performing management functions than their colleagues. In particular, executive directors indicated they spent statistically significantly more time performing the following functions: budgeting and financial management ($p < .001$), managing employees ($p < .001$), public relations, public speaking, and public advocacy ($p < .05$), and, not so clearly related to management, fundraising (other than grants; $p < .001$). The emphasis on management is also reinforced by the one function executive directors indicated they spent statistically significantly less time performing than their colleagues: providing services to clientele ($p < .01$). The emphasis on management is also reflected in the skills that executive directors placed significantly greater emphasis on than their colleagues. These related to management – entrepreneurship ($p < .001$), ability to manage human resources ($p < .01$), accounting, budgeting, financial management ($p < .001$) understanding non-profit legal issues ($p < .001$); representing the organization – public relations ($p < .05$), networking (public-private-non-profit; $p < .05$); and fundraising – grant writing ($p < .001$), fundraising (other than grants; $p < .001$). This finding is consistent with the literature. Amar (2017) found that financial and communications skills were among the key skills executive directors need, and Dolan (2002, 281) found that fundraising and grant writing were the top two training needs identified by non-profit executive directors he surveyed.

While it is not likely to come as a surprise that executive directors spend more time than their colleagues performing management functions and that they place greater emphasis on management skills, what may be surprising is how strikingly this sets them apart from their colleagues and the spiral career pattern. The differences between the nature and requirements of executive directors' work and that of most other positions in the NGO sector raise two questions. First, why would someone who was attracted to a sector dominated by the spiral career pattern want to take on such a position? The survey has nothing to offer in answer to this question, but it seems reasonable to advise students and staff contemplating becoming executive directors to consider these differences carefully in light of their own interests and inclinations. Second, how can prospective executive directors develop the skills the position requires when these skills do not appear to be required to perform successfully in other positions within these organizations? While the survey did not address this second question directly, it allows consideration of how present executive directors may have prepared.

Suarez (2010) found that only 56 per cent of the non-profit leaders in his sample "had any management experience before assuming their current position" (701). On reflection, this is not surprising, given the few opportunities to develop management experience that are likely to be found in a sector characterized by generally flat, non-hierarchical organizations. How then do many of them develop the skills required of executive directors? One possibility, education, is supported by the fact executive directors in this study's sample tended to be more highly educated than their colleagues: 74 per cent of the executive directors held a post-BA credential compared to 53 per cent of their colleagues ($p < 0.05$). The breakdown by highest credentials held was: PhD – 12 per cent; MA – 35 per cent; MBA – 9 per cent; other MA-level management degree – 6 per cent; and post-grad diploma – 12 per cent. The percentages for advanced university credentials were similar to what Suarez (2010) and Norris-Tirrell, Rinella, and Pham (2018) found. It is also worth noting that, while it has been suggested that business credentials are becoming more valued in the nonprofit sector (Murray 2008), the results of this survey support Suarez's (2010) observation "that management credentials generally have not been necessary for attaining a leadership position in the nonprofit sector" (701; see also Haas and Robinson 1998, 356).

Another possibility is that executive directors may have developed skills through prior experiences. This seems to be borne out by the fact that executive directors tend to have been employed in the sector longer than other staff (an average of seventeen versus eleven years, $p < .001$). They may also have developed useful skills through experience they gained working in other sectors. Since completing their most recent degree or diploma, 47 per cent of the executive directors reported having worked in another sector: 32 per cent in the for-profit sector, 32 per cent in government, and 6 per cent in unions. It seems likely that had they been asked this question with regard to their entire careers, the percentages would have been even higher.

Those contemplating becoming executive directors in the NGO sector should realize that this will require developing many skills that are not otherwise highly valued in the sector and that they will likely have to look elsewhere – returning to school or working for a time in another sector – to develop these skills. (For further discussion of executive directors' prior experiences, see Norris-Tirrell, Rinella, and Pham [2018].)

The Role of Gender in Career Advancement

This final section discusses three gender patterns that emerge from the data that should be of interest to students considering working in this sector: an apparent increase of feminization; a disproportionate number of male executive directors; and a relative openness to women seeking leadership positions.

THE WORKFORCE APPEARS TO BE BECOMING INCREASINGLY FEMINIZED

It is well known that workers in this sector are predominantly female: 71 per cent of respondents to this survey were women; Almond and Kendall (2000) report a figure of 67 per cent for the United Kingdom (216); Onyx and Maclean (1996) cite a 70 to 80 per cent figure for the United States and report 79 per cent for their Australian sample (336). What may be surprising is that analysis of this study's data suggests that the proportion of women may be increasing: while 65 per cent of those aged thirty and older were women (a ratio of almost two to one), this is true of 86 per cent of those in their twenties (a ratio of more than four to one, $p < .01$). This finding suggests a need for more research, both to determine if the pattern suggested here holds up more broadly and, if it does, to determine why it is occurring, since it is consistent with both the possibility that fewer young men are entering the sector than in the past and that women are leaving the sector at disproportionately higher rates than men as they age.

WOMEN ARE PROPORTIONATELY UNDERREPRESENTED AMONG EXECUTIVE DIRECTORS

For a sector whose workers are 70 to 80 per cent female, women represent a surprisingly small percentage of those holding top executive positions: this study found they held 50 per cent of the positions; Norris-Tirrell, Rinella, and Pham (2018) observed 54 per cent amongst a sample of people holding executive positions in large American nonprofits; Suarez (2010) reported figures of 66 per cent for the United States nationally and 54 per cent for his sample from the San Francisco Bay Area (700); and a recent report from the United Kingdom suggests that women hold only 25 per cent of senior executive officers at the largest charitable organizations (Jarboe 2012).[8] Not only does the present study find that one in four male respondents were executive directors, compared to only one in ten female respondents ($p < 0.01$), but analysis of the data also suggests that this situation does not appear to be improving: when executive directors aged fifty and over are compared to those under fifty, males turn out to be more overrepresented among executive directors in the younger cohort (16 per cent of males are executive directors compared to 5 per cent of females) than amongst those aged fifty or more (38 per cent versus 22 per cent). The word *appear* is used advisedly above, since while this finding may reflect an increase in male overrepresentation, it is also consistent with what could be a static pattern of women moving into leadership roles later in their career than men. Further, this finding is not supported by Norris-Tirrell, Rinella, and Pham's (2018) observation that the percentage of female executives was higher amongst younger cohorts.

While this finding requires further research, analysis of the present data suggests some avenues for further study. The overrepresentation of males among executive directors does not appear to be explained by differences in educational backgrounds: the survey revealed no statistically significant difference between males and females regarding post-BA credentials. Nor does the survey provide support for the possibility that men are treated preferentially: there are no statistically significant differences between rates at which men and women are employed full- versus part-time or between those employed on an ongoing versus contractual basis. Differences between men's and women's prior experience in other sectors appears more promising, but the difference found in this survey (44 per cent of men had such experience compared to 34 per cent of women) was not statistically significant.

Another possibility is that, on average, the men and women who are attracted to work in the sector differ in their motivations and their attitudes to the functions required by their work in ways that lead disproportionately more men to seek and retain executive director positions. This finds some support in Damman, Heyse, and Mills's (2014) finding that rates of promotion to management in one particular international NGO was more highly correlated with working in a male- or female-dominated profession than with being male or female. Since the present study was not designed to explore this question, the meaning of the gender differences it reveals with respect to attitudinal questions is not obvious: while men placed greater emphasis than women on the opportunity to influence policy development as a reason for finding their present position attractive ($p < .05$) and on entrepreneurship as a skill they considered important to success in their position ($p < .05$), women placed greater emphasis than men on ability to work with a team ($p < .05$), interpersonal skills ($p < .05$), and ability to work with the unknown ($p < .05$) as important to success in their positions. Of course, these findings only raise deeper questions. Even if it is the case that women's underrepresentation among NGO executive directors is partly explained by general differences in women's earlier career choices and their attitudes towards different aspects of their jobs, we can still ask why these differences exist. As suggested in the study on human trafficking and gender equality in chapter 5 by Mikhaela Gray-Beerman in this volume, part of the reason for these underlying differences in career choices and attitudes may be found in sexist understandings of gender roles in the Canadian context, including the "belief that women are subordinate to men." Clearly there is much more here that needs to be researched.

NEVERTHELESS, THE NGO SECTOR IS A PROMISING DESTINATION FOR WOMEN SEEKING LEADERSHIP OPPORTUNITIES

While the 50 per cent representation of women among executive directors appears low when compared to their 71 per cent representation among respondents, it actually compares favourably with other sectors. For instance, in Canada, in 2012 the non-profit organization Catalyst reported that women held only 18 per cent of senior officer positions among the *Financial Post* 500 leading for-profit companies and only 27 per cent of such positions in Crown (i.e., government-owned) corporations (Catalyst 2013, 1). Recent statistics for the United Kingdom suggest a similar comparison between large charitable and large for-profit organizations (25 per cent versus 4 per cent; Jarboe 2012). Thus, while the news is not all good, the study does suggest that for young women seeking opportunities to attain top leadership positions in their chosen careers, the non-profit sector offers relatively better opportunities than the for-profit sector.

Conclusion

This chapter began by noting a problem faced by many faculty involved in various forms of GCE. Once we have inspired students to care about global justice and to desire to act upon it, students often come to us seeking advice about career choices in sectors in which we have little or no personal experience. By discussing findings from a survey of staff working in one of the sectors many of our students are likely to work in – the non-profit/NGO sector – we have gone some distance towards addressing this problem and, one hopes, demonstrating the value of research that adopts the perspective of students and their mentors with the aim of helping them gain a view over the horizon of prospective career arcs. In so doing, we have identified an area for expanding GCE curriculum that can prove invaluable to our students.

As an attempt to respond to a perceived need, the snapshot of the NGO sector career arc that has been developed here should help facilitate better advice and more informed decision-making about career choices and career preparation. In answering its four research questions, this chapter has provided much for those contemplating careers in the sector to consider: the value of active participation in student clubs, volunteering and service-learning courses; examples of what the spiral career pattern means in practice and why people enjoy it; evidence of the openness of the sector to late interest-takers, to those whose highest credential is a BA, to those presently lacking management skills, and to women seeking leadership opportunities, but also evidence of the need to obtain further educational credentials and to develop management and financial skills over time, especially if one hopes to become an executive director; examples of the various types of positions the sector offers and encouragement to gain knowledge of them early and to identify specific educational and other opportunities to prepare for them. In addition to this, for those who find themselves mentoring students, the chapter has provided evidence to back up their advice based on the experience of those who work in the sector.

This chapter has also drawn attention to an area for expanding GCE curriculum: the relationship between key applied experiences, such as the role of extracurricular activities, service learning, and international internships and experiences, and the preparation of students to put their global citizenship orientations into practice throughout their careers. It is hoped that by framing the role of such activities in this way, the discussion of the place of such activities in GCE might be expanded. While it is important that we consider such questions as how these experiences construct the identity of the international intern/volunteer, we also need to ask how global citizenship educators can prepare students to engage in these activities in ways that will enhance students' ability to advance global justice throughout their careers. By considering how GCE can prepare students for, and make connections with, careers advancing the goals of GCE, we not only do right by our students, we will also advance the goals of global justice itself.

As social science research, this study has both affirmed much that has been noted in the existing literature and added to it incrementally in several ways: by asking staff and executive directors about their pre-career experiences; directly soliciting opinions about the value of various educational credentials and extracurricular experiences; providing a rudimentary typology of positions in the NGO workplace; and identifying key differences between executive directors and other staff. The study also raises questions, the answers to which would further enhance our ability to mentor students and staff. Some were noted above, concerning trends related to gender. Focusing as it did on people currently employed in the sector, the survey also left unanswered other questions about the career arc, the answers to which would be of great interest to students and their mentors: Why do people leave the sector? What are the typical ages and stages at which they leave? And where do they go?

If part of what we do as professors and teachers is to motivate students to want to be good global citizens, then we also take on an obligation to provide them with good answers when they ask us what to do next. A career in the NGO sector is one of the most obvious choices for students seeking to put their concern for global justice and sense of responsibility into practice. This chapter, it is hoped, has gone some way towards helping the reader prepare to answer student questions. It has also shown that there is much more to be discovered, documented, and shared, especially concerning where executive directors develop their management skills, how and why people leave the sector, and the role of gender in shaping employment patterns.

Appendix 1 Percentage Selecting Reasons for Finding Present Positions "Attractive" or "Very Attractive"

Reason for finding present position attractive	%
Contribute to social change	97
Interesting/challenging work	96
Good people to work with	87
Extend personal skills	86
Work on human rights Issues	86
Organizational philosophy	83
Network with other agencies	75
Access to decision-making	74
Influence policy development	72
Career opportunities	68
Work independently	65
Change of pace	60
More staff responsibility	56
Good management structure	52
Convenient location	51
Work with new client group	51
Training opportunities	49
Create a new service	46
Increased salary	42
More flexible hours	41
Greater prestige	40
Job security	37
More budget responsibility	32
Previous job ended	29
Less management responsibility	10

Appendix 2 Top Three Functions Performed by Position Types

Type of position	Percentage of respondents	1st	2nd	3rd
Program management/ coordinating	42	Project management	Providing services to clientele	Networking/ liaising with other NGOs
Executive director	16	Public relations, public speaking, public advocacy	Project management	Managing employees
Advocacy/ outreach/public engagement/ education	11	Public relations, public speaking, public advocacy	Networking/ liaising with other NGOs	Project management
Management of youth, volunteers, campus chapters, or membership	6	Project management	Providing services to clients	Managing volunteers/ student or local chapters
Communications/ media/public relations	6	Public relations, public speaking, public advocacy	Project management	Managing volunteers/ student or local chapters
Fundraising/ development	6	Project management	Fundraising (other than grants)	Networking/ liaising with other NGOs
Research	5	Providing services to clients	Monitoring human rights violations: information gathering, research, and documentation	Project management
Internal operations	4	Budgeting and financial management	Providing services to clients	Grant-writing and follow-up
Administrator/ executive assistant	4	Providing services to clients	Budgeting and financial management	Fundraising (other than grants)

NOTES

1 This chapter is a revised version of an article that appeared under the title, "They Want to Be Global Citizens – Now What? Implications of the NGO Career Arc for Students and Faculty Mentors," *Journal of Global Citizenship & Equity Education* 3, no. 1 (2013): 13–33.
2 The length of the survey makes it difficult to appendix in this chapter; however, it is available to readers upon request.
3 This sample size compares well with that of other published studies on the NGO sector; for instance, Onyx and Maclean (1996) had 162 usable responses, Haas and Robinson (1998) had 208, and Kim and Lee (2007) had 198.
4 Even more students may have been involved in volunteering in general (i.e., off campus), but the survey did not ask about that.
5 This is a condensed version of a community college program that is offered to students who already possess a university degree or college diploma.
6 Those holding PhDs were excluded from this calculation, as their educational trajectory tends to differ markedly from those pursuing terminal MAs.
7 Age was used as a proxy for being established staff, rather than position in the organization, because the generally flat structure of these organizations makes it very difficult to determine a person's status from their job title.
8 The report's focus on the largest organizations likely underrepresents the percentage of women executive directors for the sector as a whole, since Harrow and Mole (2005) found that the proportion of male executive directors increases as organization size increases (86).

REFERENCES

Ahmed, S. 2005. "Desired Competencies and Job Duties of Non-Profit CEOs in Relation to the Current Challenges: Through the Lens of CEOs' Job Advertisements." *Journal of Management Development* 24, no. 20: 913–18. https://doi.org/10.1108/02621710510627055

Akingbola, K. 2006. "Strategy and HRM in Nonprofit Organizations: Evidence from Canada." *International Journal of Human Resource Management* 17, no. 10: 1707–25. https://doi.org/10.1080/09585190600964350

Almond, S., and J. Kendall. 2000. "Taking the Employee's Perspective Seriously: An Initial United Kingdom Cross-Sectoral Comparison." *Nonprofit and Voluntary Sector Quarterly* 29, no. 2: 205–31. https://doi.org/10.1177/0899764000292001

Amar, P. 2017. "Leadership and Management Competencies for Future Nonprofit Executives: A Modified Delpid Study." PhD diss., University of the Rockies.

Ban, C., A. Drahnak-Faller, and M. Towers. 2003. "Human Resource Challenges in Human Service and Community Development Organizations: Recruitment and Retention of Professional Staff." *Review of Public Personnel Administration* 23, no. 2: 133–53. https://doi.org/10.1177/0734371x03023002004

Breuning, M., P. Parker, and J.T. Ishiyama. 2001. "The Last Laugh: Skill Building through a Liberal Arts Political Science Curriculum." *PS: Political Science and Politics* 34, no. 3: 657–61. https://doi.org/10.1017/s1049096501001056

Cameron, J.D. 2014. "Grounding Experiential Learning in "Thick" Conceptions of Global Citizenship." In *Globetrotting or Global Citizenship: Perils and Potential of International Experiential Learning*, edited by R. Tiessen and R. Huish. Toronto: University of Toronto Press.

Carter, D.A. 2016. "What Skills and Competencies Do Executives of Nonprofits Need to Succeed: An Interpretive Multiple Case Study." EdD diss., University of St. Thomas.

Catalyst. 2013. "2012 Catalyst Census: Financial Post 500 Women Senior Officers and Top Earners." Catalyst: Workplaces that Work for Women, 19 February. http://www.catalyst.org/knowledge/2012-catalyst-census-financial-post-500-women-senior-officers-and-top-earners

Chong, D. 2009. "Economic Rights and Extreme Poverty: Moving Toward Subsistence." In *The International Struggle for New Human Rights*, edited by C. Bob. Philadelphia: University of Pennsylvania Press.

Coleman Selden, S., and J.E. Sowa. 2015. "Voluntary Turnover in Nonprofit Human Service Organizations: The Impact of High Performance Work Practices." *Human Service Organizations: Management, Leadership & Governance* 39, no. 3: 182–207. https://doi.org/10.1080/23303131.2015.1031416

Collins, T.A., H. Gibbs Knotts, and J. Schiff. 2012. "Career Preparation and the Political Science Major: Evidence from Departments." *PS: Political Science and Politics* 45, no. 1: 87–92. https://doi.org/10.1017/s1049096511001764

Damman, M. L. Heyse, and M. Mills. 2014. "Gender, Occupation, and Promotion to Management in the Nonprofit Sector: The Critical Case of Médecins Sans Frontières Holland." *Nonprofit Management & Leadership* 25, no. 2: 97–111. https://doi.org/10.1002/nml.21114

Dolan, D.A. 2002. "Training Needs of Administrators in the Nonprofit Sector: What Are They and How Should We Address Them?" *Nonprofit Management & Leadership* 12, no. 3: 277–92. https://doi.org/10.1002/nml.12305

Driver, M.J. 1980. "Career Concepts and Organizational Change." In *Work, Family, and the Career: New Frontiers in Theory and Research*, edited by C. Brooklyn Derr. New York: Wiley.

Fletcher, K.M. 2005. "The Impact of Receiving a Master's Degree in Nonprofit Management on Graduate's Professional Lives." *Nonprofit and Voluntary Sector Quarterly* 34, no. 4: 433–47. https://doi.org/10.1177/0899764005279762

Haas, P.J., and M.G. Robinson. 1998. "The Views of Nonprofit Executives on Educating Nonprofit Managers." *Nonprofit Management & Leadership* 8, no. 4: 349–62. https://doi.org/10.1002/nml.8404

Harrow, J., and V. Mole. 2005. "'I Want to Move Once I Have Got Things Straight': Voluntary Sector Chief Executives' Career Accounts." *Nonprofit Management & Leadership* 16, no. 1: 79–100. https://doi.org/10.1002/nml.91

Herman, R.D., and D.O. Renz. 2007. "Nonprofit Management Alumni Knowledge, Skills, and Career Satisfaction in Relation to Nonprofit Academic Centers Council Curricular Guidelines: The Case of One University's Master's of Public Administration Alumni." *Nonprofit and Voluntary Sector Quarterly* 36, no. 4: 98S-109S. https://doi.org/10.1177/0899764007305049

Hopgood, Stephen. 2009. "Dignity and Ennui: Amnesty International, Amnesty International Report 2009: The State of the World's Human Rights, London: Amnesty International Publications." *Journal of Human Rights Practice* 2, no. 1: 151–65. https://doi.org/10.1093/jhuman/hup025

Jarboe, N. 2012. "Advancing Women's Leadership in the Charitable Sector." Institute of Chartered Accountants in England and Wales. http://www.icaew.com/en/technical/charity-and-voluntary-sector/volunteering/charity-trustee/charity-trustee-role-and-responsibilities-new/advancing-womens-leadership-in-the-charitable-sector (no longer available)

Jaskyte, K. 2016. "Work Values of Public, Nonprofit, and Business Employees: A Cross-Cultural Evidence" *International Journal of Public Administration* 39, no. 3: 184–93. https://doi.org/10.1080/01900692.2014.1003386

Kim, S.E., and J.W. Lee. 2007. "Is Mission Attachment an Effective Management Tool for Employee Retention? An empirical Analysis of a Nonprofit Human Services Agency." *Review of Public Personnel Administration* 27, no. 3: 227–48. https://doi.org/10.1177/0734371x06295791

Kindornay, S., J. Ron, and C. Carpenter. 2012. "Rights-Based Approaches to Development: Implications for NGOs." *Human Rights Quarterly* 34, no. 2: 472–506. https://doi.org/10.1353/hrq.2012.0036

Koc, E.W. 2010. "NACE Research: The Liberal Arts Graduate and the College Hiring Market." *NACE Journal*. November. http://www.naceweb.org/Publications/Journal/2010november/NACE_Research__The_Liberal_Arts_Graduate_and_the_College_Hiring_Market.aspx

Kuh, G.D. 1995. "The Other Curriculum: Out-of-Class Experiences Associated with Student Learning and Personal Development." *The Journal of Higher Education* 66, no. 2: 123–55. https://doi.org/10.1080/00221546.1995.11774770

Kunreuther, F. 2003. "The Changing of the Guard: What Generational Differences Tell Us about Social-Change Organizations." *Nonprofit and Voluntary Sector Quarterly* 32, no. 3: 450–7. https://doi.org/10.1177/0899764003254975

Lee, Y.-J., and V.M. Wilkins. 2011. "More Similarities or More Differences? Comparing Public and Nonprofit Managers' ob Motivations." *Public Administration Review* 71, no. 1: 45–56. https://doi.org/10.1111/j.1540-6210.2010.02305.x

McKinney, K., D. Saxe, and L. Cobb. 1998. "Are We Really Doing All We Can for Our Undergraduates? Professional Socialization via Out-of-Class Experiences." *Teaching Sociology* 26, no. 1: 1–13. https://doi.org/10.2307/1318675

Murray, S. 2008. "MBA Route Boosts Non-Profit Sector: Organisations in the Social Sector Are Now Looking to Recruit Employees with Private Sector Skills." *Financial Times* (London), 28 July: 10.

Nelson, P.J., and E. Dorsey. 2008. *New Rights Advocacy*. Washington, DC: Georgetown University Press.

Nemenoff, E.K. 2013. "You Mean I Can Get Paid to Work Here? The Impact of Happenstance, Socialization, Volunteering and Service-Learning on Nonprofit Career Awareness." PhD diss., University of Missouri-Kansas City.

Norris-Tirrell, D., J. Rinella, and X. Pham. 2018. "Examining the Career Trajectories of Nonprofit Executive Leaders." *Nonprofit and Voluntary Sector Quarterly* 47, no. 1: 146–64. https://doi.org/10.1177/0899764017722023

Olawoore. B. 2017. "The Implications of the Rights-Based Approach on NGOs' Funding." *Development in Practice* 27, no. 4: 515–27. https://doi.org/10.1080/09614524.2017.1307943

Onyx, J., and M. Maclean. 1996. "Careers in the Third Sector." *Nonprofit Management & Leadership* 6, no. 4: 331–45. https://doi.org/10.1002/nml.4130060404

Pashby, K. 2012. "Questions for Global Citizenship Education in the Context of the 'New Imperialism': For Whom, by Whom?" In *Postcolonial Perspectives on Global Citizenship Education*, edited by V. de Oliveira Andreotti and L.M.T.M. de Sousa. New York: Routledge.

Peters, R., and M. Beeson. 2010. "Reducing the Gap between Skills Sought by Employers and Developed by Education." *PS: Political Science and Politics* 43, no. 4: 773–7. https://doi.org/10.1017/s104909651000123x

Robinson, A.M. 2013. "The Workplace Relevance of the Liberal Arts Political Science BA and How It Might Be Enhanced: Reflections on an Exploratory Survey of the NGO Sector." *PS: Political Science & Politics* 46, no. 1: 147–53. https://doi.org/10.1017/s1049096512001308

Rosch, D.M. and J.D. Collins. 2017. "The Significance of Student Organizations to Leadership Development." *New Directions for Student Leadership* 155: 9–19. https://doi.org/10.1002/yd.20246

Sagen, H.B., J.W. Dallam, and J.R. Laverty. 2000. "Effects of Career Preparation Experiences on the Initial Employment Success of College Graduates." *Research in Higher Education* 41, no. 6: 733–67.

Shultz, L. 2007. "Educating for Global Citizenship: Conflicting Agendas and Understandings." *The Alberta Journal of Educational Research* 53, no. 3: 248–58.

Suarez, D.F. 2010. "Street Credentials and Management Backgrounds: Careers of Nonprofit Executives in an Evolving Sector." *Nonprofit and Voluntary Sector Quarterly* 39, no. 4: 696–716. https://doi.org/10.1177/0899764009350370

Turner, F., and C. Maher. 2009. "Managing Career Development in the Not for Profit Sector." *Business Leadership Review* 6, no. 4. http://www.mbaworld.com/blr-archive/issues-64/6/index.pdf

United Nations. n.d. "Sustainable Development Goals." https://sustainabledevelopment.un.org/sdgs

Wilson, M.J., and R.S. Larson. 2002. "Nonprofit Management Students: Who They Are and Why They Enroll." *Nonprofit and Voluntary Sector Quarterly* 31, no. 2: 259–70.

Conclusion: Global Citizenship Education – The Present and the Future

EVA ABOAGYE AND S. NOMBUSO DLAMINI

The world has changed in the last two decades. There has been extraordinary innovation in areas such as technology, medicine, and food security, and yet there is still so much disparity among nations and peoples. Technology has made these disparities more evident and news from all parts of the world is available within minutes everywhere. There is evidence of increasing recognition that we are all responsible for working towards alleviating existing global socio-economic inequities. From the Millennium Development Goals of the past to the Sustainable Development Goals of today, the nations of the world are moving towards awareness and commitment to sustainable and equitable development. There is a growing recognition that our futures are linked and that no nation is an island, and yet there is so much more left to do. However, as these changes are happening, there is also a growing rise in nationalism, a growing indifference to the suffering of others, a rise in ultranationalist groups, and an increase in the acquisition of destructive military arsenal. Leaders have been elected into power on an ideology that is inward looking and hostile to outsiders.

International agencies like the United Nations and UNESCO have issued a call for education to be a part of preparing the next generation to understand their role in developing a sustainable world and how global inequality is located in past histories of colonialism, hegemony, and power across nations. Nations are now more visibly interconnected; however, practices of domination and oppression continue to permeate the very fiber of this connectivity. The role of global citizenship education (GCE) in institutions of higher learning is to bring a focus on information and opportunities that allow students to criticize and participate in actions that challenge existing structures of domination worldwide. Some institutions and academics have answered that call and have started programs, courses, and activities on GCE.

In this context, the OECD/Asia Society (2018) in its publication *Educating for Global Competence in a Rapidly Changing World* asks an important question: Why teach for global competence? Included in its reasons for us to educate students to be global citizens is the fact that global competence is necessary for economic, cultural, and technological reasons and to help the world achieve the UN Sustainable Development Goals. These are important reasons and this book examines some persistent and entrenched issues of this age and how some institutions and academics approach GCE. In our world today, we find desperate levels of poverty in the midst of extraordinary wealth; the unequal access to basic resources like healthcare, education, clean water, and other basic necessities. Part of what we should achieve with GCE is to educate students on the importance of taking care of the vulnerable in our world today. We have to educate students to the fact that it is not okay to simply acquire wealth while others are living in poverty; live in freedom and peace while other parts of the world are experiencing oppression and wars; and have access to excellent education and healthcare while other parts of the world lack basic amenities. There should be a commitment to make the world a better place for all.

We live in a world challenged by threats to human safety and security, such as wars in the Middle East and parts of Africa, dangerous access to nuclear and other military arsenal, despotic and corrupt governments, and terrorist organizations that show a complete disregard for human life. There is also a crisis in the movement of displaced people and world leaders who look on unconcerned. Human safety and security are constantly under threat in different parts of our world today. There is a constant threat to the environment and to future generations. All these issues point to an urgent need for all of us to begin to see the world as one place and to see our lives as interconnected so that we can indeed achieve the goal of making the world a better place for everyone.

What better place to achieve this goal than in the education system where people learn their place as responsible members of their societies. Different parts of the education system from primary to secondary are beginning to address these issues and some post-secondary institutions are leading the way as well. Our objective in compiling the chapters in this book is to add to the literature on defining GCE, explore how we can achieve a commitment to create global citizens, and provide case studies and strategies for faculty on how others have tackled that commitment.

The chapters in this book have explored issues in GCE from its definition, to where to include it in curriculum, to examples of how others have included it in their programs. Themes that run through all the different definitions of GCE are the importance of students being able to be critically aware of the issues of the world today, to be open to appreciate differences, to be good stewards of the environment, and to act in ways that will sustain our world and its people. In the post-secondary sector, the questions we asked were where this could be done, what could be taught, and how this could be done to achieve this end.

Where

Post-secondary institutions have an important role to play in this goal and in deciding where in the curriculum to place GCE content. Leaders of institutions have to lead with a commitment to GCE and look at ways of implementing it in their institutions. One of the first questions an institution will have to grapple with is whether this goal can be achieved by leaving it to come from faculty and departments or whether it can best be achieved by leading from the top. In chapter 10, Aboagye explores how Centennial College in Toronto and the University of British Columbia took different approaches to implementing GCE in their curriculums. The college sector provides relatively more flexibility for the leadership of the institution to lead the charge and this has advantages in terms of being able to provide a common curriculum across the institution and being able to directly allocate resources to it. The university sector provides relatively more flexibility for faculty members to lead the charge in terms of implementing GCE in their curriculum. In this book, we have examples of how some faculty have incorporated GCE into their programing that includes international and local service-learning programs.

Compulsory general education courses are one option available to institutions as was done at Centennial. These courses can be used as part of student programs. Faculty have an opportunity in these courses to educate students on the issues that face the world today and to teach them how to critically think about their role in the world. For example, knowing and understanding the issues identified in the Sustainable Development Goals should be an expectation of any graduate from any post-secondary institution. Ultimately, institutions and academics will have to choose the best options on where in the curriculum they can incorporate GCE based on their institutional cultures.

What

Once institutions, departments, or faculties have decided to include GCE in their curriculum, the next question is what should that curriculum include? The chapters in this book have explored both curricular and co-curricular approaches to including GCE in the curriculum. There have been a wide range of options for curriculum that have been suggested and used by different institutions. Curriculum for GCE should include learning what global citizenship means in the current world context. Students should come out being aware of the acute need for the present and future generations to understand the dynamics of our current world and the need for them to play their part as responsible global citizens. They should understand the historical context of today's society, its social development, and the role of globalization. The global systems (political, geographic, economic, and social) are all a result of history and global power dynamics, and students should know and understand how these systems have operated in the past and how they continue to operate now. Students should also learn about their identity and learn how to appreciate diversity. The world is very diverse in many different ways and we are all interconnected. An opportunity to appreciate the differences would make the world a better place for all. Developing a critical democratic perspective on global issues is so crucial in our world today when truth is sometimes sacrificed in our reliance on quick and easily accessible information or misinformation. Developing skills to take action to address global issues or learning to be an activist should be the end goal of each GCE course. The end result of learning about current global issues, power dynamics, and inequalities, and evaluating all of these with a critical perspective should lead to a commitment to making the world a more sustainable place for everyone.

On co-curricular activities, there is service learning at both the local and global levels. Service learning with the right combination of activities and experiences has the power to introduce students to a lot of the issues they explore in GCE. In order for these activities to achieve the goals of GCE, authors in this book have pointed out the importance of preparing students before, during, and after these experiences. They also point to the need to encourage students to practice open mindedness and reflection.

Progress has been made in GCE; however, there are still a few areas that need further exploration. One of these areas is a clear and unified articulation of GCE learning outcomes, learning processes, and how to assess outcomes. Authors in this volume elucidate that GCE goes beyond the content of what is being taught; as such, it includes approaches to students' character development. Students not only learn about political, social, and economic interconnectedness of the world but also develop a sense of individual and collective relationship to and for the world. In this volume, the chapters that discuss local and international experiential learning show how such projects can nurture a sense of students' connection and care for others. Nevertheless, regardless of goals and its character-building components, GCE and its proponents are yet to measure the long- and short-term impacts or the longevity of the overall learning outcomes in students. OECD (2018) has developed a framework for assessing outcomes for students in the secondary level, which was implemented in 2018. Post-secondary institutions can use this to develop a framework that can work in post-secondary institutions as well.

How

Another aspect looked at is the relationship between applied aspects of the GCE curriculum such as extra-curricular activities, service learning, international internships and experiences, and the preparation of students to put their GCE orientations into practice throughout their careers. GCE goes beyond mere learning to a commitment to action and actual involvement in global citizenship activities; as such, service learning and the application of theoretical concepts to everyday practice are important for any project of educating students. We also learn that there are a wide variety of subject themes covered under global citizenship education and that most institutions will have a course that offers some form of internal and/or external experiential learning activities for students; while others will not have experiential learning components – they will focus more on a mix of core global citizenship courses (courses on sustainability and the environment; and courses on ethnic and cultural issues). We also learn that global citizenship education transcends the boundaries of content knowledge into the area of character development and that service learning has the potential to affect students' concepts of themselves as global citizens.

This is an important time in our world today politically, economically, and socially. Individuals, groups, and even governments continue to challenge the movement towards globalism and the call for a more connected and interdependent world. Events in Europe, including decisions by the British to move away from the European Union, the rise of ultra-nationalist groups in both Europe and America, and the resentment to reaching out and helping displaced people are evidence of this challenge. There is also an awareness of how disproportionately the world's resources are distributed and how wealth is held in only a few hands while a majority of people live in poverty. Our environment is under a lot of stress and scientists continue to warn us every day about being aware and living sustainably, but there are also people who challenge these facts and continue to deny the precarity of our existence. These issues are important and can no longer be left to a few leaders to resolve. We therefore need students, the future leaders of this world, to know, understand, and be able to respond to these issues.

The United Nations has provided the vision and framework in the Sustainable Development Goals of how we can change our world. But ultimately, we need people who are committed and passionate and able to make a difference in the world. Through the United Nations mandate, the world has committed to sustainable development goals that,

> by 2030, ensure that all learners acquire the knowledge and skills needed to promote sustainable development, including, among others, through education for sustainable development and sustainable lifestyles, human rights, gender equality, promotion of a culture of peace and non-violence, global citizenship and appreciation of cultural diversity and of culture's contribution to sustainable development. (UN SDG – Target 4.7)[1]

Ultimately, we need people who are committed and passionate and able to make a difference in the world and that is why GCE is so important in our post-secondary institutions As educators in post-secondary institutions, we have a part to play in developing the next generation not only to understand the issues of social and economic inequality, political and civil unrest facing us but also to understand the action-oriented difference they can make both locally and in the wider world. We have provided examples of what is currently happening through GCE initiatives and we hope that these will act as examples for others. We also hope the chapters in this book will provide material for additional discussions on the role of educators in developing global citizens for the world.

NOTE

1 Available at https://sustainabledevelopment.un.org/sdg4

REFERENCE

OECD/Asia Society. 2018. *Educating for Global Competence in a Rapidly Changing World*. Paris: OECD. http://doi.org/10.1787/9789264289024-en

Contributors

Eva Aboagye is Program Manager, Research and Innovation, George Brown College, Ontario, Canada. Aboagye's career has encompassed research on global citizenship and equity, institutional planning, research and teaching. As Program Manager, Eva provides guidance and management of research methods and budgets to researchers applying to or currently awarded funds from the Social Sciences and Humanities Research Council (SSHRC). Before joining George Brown, Aboagye served as Senior Researcher for the Institute for Global Citizenship, Equity, and as Director of Policy at Centennial College. Aboagye has a PhD and MEd in Higher Education from the University of Toronto, and a BA (Hons.) in Sociology and English and a Graduate Diploma in Population Studies from the University of Ghana.

Heesoon Bai is Professor in the Faculty of Education at Simon Fraser University, British Columbia, Canada. Bai's research interests cluster around examining and deconstructing ontological and epistemological assumptions that underlie our cultural practices, especially our ethics and aesthetics. Her work calls for reanimation of ourselves within all spheres of humanity in the service of living ethically with all beings and in beauty. More recently, she has been focusing on contemplative pedagogy as a way to counteract the destructive and hurtful values and beliefs embedded in capitalist industrial civilization and to offer a vision of deep democracy that includes "more-than-human" beings.

Paul Banahene Adjei is Associate Professor and Interim Associate Dean, Graduate Program and Research in the School of Social Work at Memorial University of Newfoundland, Newfoundland, Canada. He has cumulatively taught social justice and global citizenship education for twelve years at the University of Toronto and at Memorial

University of Newfoundland. Adjei's teaching and research interests are in the areas of adaptation and integration processes of new and old immigrants of the African-Canadian communities in Canada. He has published over twenty refereed essays in scholarly journals and as book chapters, co-edited one book with Professor George Dei, and read over thirty refereed papers at international conferences.

Clinton Beckford is Professor and Associate Dean of Teacher Education in the Faculty of Education at the University of Windsor, Ontario, Canada. Dr. Beckford's area of expertise is geography, where his substantive research focuses on issues of environment and sustainability in the context of food, agriculture, and food security. As a social scientist and social studies teacher, the issue of active and participatory citizenship is one of his key research interests. A major plank of his current research interest is the role of community service praxis in the development of pre-service teachers in the context of global education and citizenship. He currently leads international community service-learning projects for teacher candidates and graduate students in Jamaica and Tanzania. Beckford is also a well-published scholar and experienced researcher. He has developed and taught undergraduate and graduate courses in environmental education and implemented sustainability projects in Jamaica with teacher candidates.

Marie Benjamin is an educator in Toronto, Ontario, and in Grenada, West Indies. Through a combination of her cross-country teaching experiences, she has developed a perception of education as a field that extends beyond the classroom. Benjamin is currently exploring the interconnection between instructional design and e-learning; as such, she has worked as a learning mentor with the Teaching and Learning Commons at Yukon College, Canada, and as a course development assistant with the University of the West Indies, Open Campus. She also works with innovative community and educational programs for youth and adults in the Caribbean and in Canada. Some of these experiences include creating international service-learning curricula and coordinating and hosting international service-learning projects for Canadian students travelling to Jamaica and Grenada. Benjamin holds a BA (Hons) in International Development and a Master of Education from York University.

Catherine A. Broom is Associate Professor at the Okanagan School of Education, University of British Columbia, Okanagan, British Columbia, Canada. Broom's teaching and research interests include social studies methods, history and philosophies, history of education and curriculum, ecological education, culture and education, and alternative and holistic educational practices.

S. Nombuso Dlamini is Associate Professor in the Faculty of Education at York University. Known for her studies examining youth negotiations of identity in new urban environments, Dlamini was the inaugural Jean Augustine Chair in Education in the New Urban Environment. She is the author of *Youth and Identity Politics* (2005) and the editor of *New Directions in African Education* (2008); her youth-focused research asks questions about how global youths' sojourner lives generate valuable social capital that reconfigures the local urban spaces while also resulting in new complexities of educating unfamiliar "others." Dlamini is involved in multi-year research projects conducted in international settings (Tanzania, Nigeria, and South Africa). Her scholarly interests include critical pedagogy, postcolonial theory and de-colonizing research methodologies, studies in youth social identities, socio-cultural studies in education, literacy and critical sociolinguistics, migration and diaspora studies, and gender matters.

Gisella Gisolo is Director of Study Abroad at Princeton University in Princeton, New Jersey, USA. Gisolo studied philosophy and cultural anthropology at the University of Pavia, Italy, and received her PhD in philosophy from the University of Florence. Prior to joining Princeton University, she served as the Director of International and Off-campus Education at Lafayette College in Easton, Pennsylvania, and as the Director of the Global Citizenship Program, a four-year interdisciplinary certificate program at Lehigh University in Bethlehem, Pennsylvania. She has been a visiting professor at Grand Valley State University in Grand Rapids, Michigan, where she taught courses in ethics and philosophy. At Princeton, she serves as advisor to students who want to study abroad, oversees the development of new study-abroad opportunities, and assesses the outcomes of those opportunities. Her research interests include the ethical implications of global citizenship education and the use of service-learning experiences to enhance undergraduate students' sense of civic engagement.

Mikhaela Gray-Beerman is Director of Education and Research for Fight4Freedom, an organization dedicated to ending sex trafficking and sexual exploitation in Canada and in the world. The work she does is informed by the many resilient and inspiring women and girls who have entrusted their stories to her. During her graduate studies at York University she pursued scholarship in the area of human trafficking and education. GCE intersects with her research as she explores how to better equip the next generation to join the fight against human rights violations like human trafficking. Gray-Beerman is the host of a RogersTV television program on human trafficking called "Freedom Fighters: Code Gray" and she is the chair of Untied Freedom, an anti-human trafficking committee. In 2018, she spoke as a witness to the House of Commons Standing Committee of Justice and Human Rights in relation to the national consultation launched on human trafficking in Canada.

Kevin Kester is Assistant Professor of Comparative International Education and Peace/Development Studies at Seoul National University. He researches educational responses to peace, conflict, and development in local and global contexts. His most recent book is *The United Nations and Higher Education: Peacebuilding, Social Justice and Global Cooperation for the 21st Century* (2020). Kester completed his PhD and post-doctoral research at the University of Cambridge. Prior to moving to Seoul National University, Kester was Assistant Professor of International Education and Global Affairs at Keimyung University and Director of Education at Queen's College.

Karen Naidoo is a researcher and educator in Toronto, Ontario, Canada. Naidoo's research interest investigates how young Canadian-Caribbean people living in Toronto understand and respond to mental health issues. Her research significantly interrogates how state institutions use race and culture to determine the ways in which health resources are distributed. She is involved in international research projects (Barbados, Grenada, and Jamaica) that examine transnational youth voices, and mental health education. Naidoo's professional experiences include facilitating global citizenship education initiatives at Centennial College and she is now an instructor with the Caribbean studies diploma program at Ryerson University. Her work on international service learning draws from her own experiences as a global citizenship educator and coordinator within the context of the Caribbean and Canada. Naidoo holds a PhD in Education, an MA in Environmental Studies, and a BA (Hons.) in Sociology.

Andrew M. Robinson is Associate Professor and Program Coordinator for Human Rights and Human Diversity and Law and Society at Wilfrid

Laurier University, Ontario, Canada. His research is on the moral and practical capacity of liberal-democratic states to accommodate deep cultural diversity. As such, he has interests in Canadian politics and contemporary political theory in general, and in judicial politics, federalism, and human rights in particular. He is especially interested in the Canadian case as an example of how human rights law and values in the international community make their way inside the sovereign state where individuals can enjoy them.

Sarah Eliza Stanlick is a faculty member in the Global School at Worcester Polytechnic Institute. She was the founding director of Lehigh University's Center for Community Engagement and faculty member in Sociology and Anthropology. She previously taught at Centenary College of New Jersey and was a researcher at Harvard's Kennedy School, assisting the US Ambassador to the United Nations, Samantha Power. She belongs to organizations like the Society for the Study of Social Problems (SSSP) and the International Association for Research on Service Learning and Community Engagement (IARSLCE), as well as co-chairing the Imagining America Assessing the Practices of Public Scholarship (APPS) research team. She has published in journals such as the *Michigan Journal of Community Service Learning*, *Social Studies*, and the *Journal of Global Citizenship and Equity Education*. Her current interests include global citizenship, health and human rights, transformative learning, and the internet's impact on empowerment and capacity to build community.

Index

www.ingramcontent.com/pod-product-compliance
Lightning Source LLC
LaVergne TN
LVHW040152080826
844660LV00014B/930/J

9781487506377